SCULPTURE OF COMPASSION:

THE PIETÀ AND THE BEGUINES IN THE SOUTHERN LOW COUNTRIES

c. 1300 - c. 1600

BY

Joanna E. ZIEGLER

Bruxelles - Brussel - Rome
1992

PREFACE AND ACKNOWLEDGMENTS

This study began in 1985 when Peter Timms, Director of the Fitchburg Art Museum, offered me the opportunity of putting together an exhibition concerning some aspect of late medieval religious art. The proposal was appealing, not in the least because I had just recently completed a doctoral dissertation on Gothic architecture in the southern Low Countries and was pleased at the prospect of setting my research sights elsewhere — at least for the moment. That moment lasted, as the present book attests, rather longer than I had expected it to. And although the Fitchburg Art Museum ultimately was not the recipient of the show, it was they who precipitated my desire to explore an area of scholarship quite distinct from the one I encountered during dissertation research. My friends encouraged the excitement of the Fitchburg project to prevail over my concerns about entering into quite alien scholarly territory. And for that I remain extremely grateful.

In 1985 my exhibition, *The Word Becomes Flesh: Radical Physicality in Religious Sculpture of the Later Middle Ages,* was mounted at the Cantor Art Gallery, Holy Cross College, Worcester, Massachusetts. For the exhibition I assembled thirteen late medieval sculptures from American collections in the northeast, each of which treated the *Pietà* theme. In the accompanying catalogue I explored (albeit quite prematurely) a select audience for the sculptures in the southern Low Country Beguines — lay holy women living in community without vows in extensive housing settlements.

In retrospect my focusing on the Beguines in the southern Low Countries (present-day Belgium) was predictable. One course with Bryce D. Lyon (Professor Emeritus, Brown University) was enough to arouse a passion for Belgian history that has proven as durable as it is ardent. And in 1985, having just acquired a sense of Belgium's medieval building history, I was lured by the chance to discover something about its sculptural past as well — a past about which the art history texts I read at that time had only the most abbreviated things to say. And pressured by friends in Belgium to learn something (anything) about their beloved Beguines, I heeded the call to learn more about the history of women's piety there. But, then again, I was already intrigued by having seen many a Belgian woman piously rapt in prayer with sculpture, rather than marveling at the moulding profiles of the architecture that enclosed her!

The combination of pressures proved challenging and time-consuming, for it asked me to learn about many things from many kinds of sources and a variety of disciplines. As I hang up these many research hats now, I see that however cumbersome it has been to wear them, they facilitated a view onto the situation in a remarkably unclouded way. The Beguines and the sculpted *Pietàs* of the southern Low Countries played a momentous part in the transformation of religious art that took place on the cusp of the modern era. That transformation has to do with the emergence of an art of little sculpted statuettes that anyone could own, and that everyone could pray to. The implications of the rise of this kind of statuary, privately owned and used, are considerable for the history of art. They suggest that the medium of sculpture, and the genre of free-standing groups (particularly the *Pietà*), may help us understand the difference between ''art'' and ''material culture' — a difference that from my experience of western art history I am still profoundly interested in grappling with. The *Pietà* was a kind of halfway point between the poles of art and material culture, or of aesthetic and vernacular quality. In this book I have tried to illuminate the phenomena — the medium of sculpture, pious women, and ordinary people as owners and viewers — that begin to show the rupture between material culture and aesthetic achievements.

I first wish to acknowledge Mieke Leroy, who provided expert assistance with archival research, and Véronique Lambert, who not only helped locate bibliographic and museum catalogue citations but watched over the text in the phase immediately before publication. I am indebted to Roze-Marijn Quintijn for her generosity in permitting me to quote from her unpublished master's thesis on the rules of beguinages in the southern Low Countries.

Several people in Belgium and the Netherlands also lent valuable assistance to the project: P.H.M. Boselie (Gemeente Archief Sittard), Else Gyselen-Van Houtte, Annemie Hansen, Jos and Marie Hougaerts, Aloïs Jans, Godelieve Jans, A. Lemeunier (Musée d'Art religieux et d'Art mosan, Liège), Leon Smets (Provinciaal Museum voor Religieuze Kunst, Sint-Truiden), C. Van de Wiel (Archief Aartsbisdom Mechelen-Brussel), and Karel Verhelst (Documentatiecentrum, Sint-Truiden).

In the course of taking on not only one new field of study but several, many colleagues helped by reading, commenting, criticizing, correcting and pointing out facts, and sharing publications: Svetlana Alpers, Lorraine Attreed, Arnoud-Jan Bijsterveld, Deborah Boedeker, Brenda Bolton, Caroline Walker Bynum, Catherine Schulze Carrigan, Marjorie B. Cohn, Hermona Dayag, Antoine De Schryver, Dennis Devlin, Colin Eisler, J. Lizabeth Fackelman, Katherine Gill, Oleg Grabar, Jeffrey Hamburger, John ("Hamster") Hamilton, Sun Hee Hess, Richard Kieckhefer, Margot King, Ellen Kittell, Valerie Lagorio, Thomas Lyman, David Nicholas, Judith H. Oliver, James F. Powers, Lionel Rothkrug, Corine Schleif, Anne Markham Schulze, John Steyaert, Paul Trio, Paul Vandenbroeck, John van Engen, Renée E. Watkins, Ulrike Wiethaus, and Helen Zakin. For help with translations, thanks are due to Susanne Vivian Cloeren and Tony Reekmans.

I was especially fortunate to have been asked to lecture on this material many times over the years. Comments and criticism from the various audiences helped me frame the material more precisely than would have been possible had I stayed isolated by the quiet confines of my study. For extending invitations, I thank: Barbara Anton of the Pembroke Center for Women's Studies of Brown University, Barbara Apelian-Beal for the University of Massachusetts at Amherst, Ludo Milis of the University of Ghent, Kathleen Okruhlick and the Centre for Women's Studies and Feminist Research (University of Western Ontario), Bonnie Perry for the Union Theological Seminary, Peter Wells for inviting me to present a paper to the American Archaeological Association, and Helen Zakin of the State University of New York at Oswego. I wish to thank especially Hilde de Ridder-Symoens for her support. She gave me two opportunities to present my ideas to Dutch and Belgian scholars, once for the Medieval Study Group of the Free University of Amsterdam, and again for a group of historians she gathered at her home in Ghent. These scholars gave me much in the way of historical refinement. John Giles Milhaven also deserves special thanks here. From the outset, he has supported my work by inviting me many times to lecture in his seminars, where he encouraged me to think broadly and deeply. Throughout, he has commented, bolstered, guided, and inspired me; finally, his views and writings stand palpably behind the investigation undertaken by this study.

Art historians Craig Harbison and Virginia Chieffo Raguin have very generously supported my work, often by forcing me to clarify my arguments (by doubting them, always when it was appropriate). Colleague and anthropologist Susan Rodgers is also owed special thanks for spending many hours with me, sharing ideas and bibliography on the anthropology of religions, reviewing what must have been for her very elementary anthropological problems; she helped give me access to and deep enthusiasm for symbolic and cultural anthropology. Over the years, I have discussed the problems involved in doing this kind of study of medieval sculpture with Kathryn Brush (Mellon Fellow, Harvard University), whose work on historiography and Gothic sculpture I very much admire. The hypotheses and attitudes of this study are, of course, wholly my own.

For supporting trips related to this book and numerous stays in Belgium between 1985 and 1991 I am deeply grateful to my colleagues at Holy Cross, especially the faculty who sat on the Committee for Research and Publication; and to the Dean of the College and Vice President for Academic Affairs, Frank Vellaccio, for funding my trips to conferences. Others at Holy Cross to be thanked are Alexa Mayo (Dinand Library), Ken Scott (Data Processing), Kathy Vairo (Visual Arts Department); Mark A. Abdoo, class of 1991, and Samantha Russo, class of 1992. Eleanor Binnall (Slide Curator, Visual Arts Department) deserves special mention for her patience and help throughout.

To Elisabeth Dunn (The Art Institute of Chicago) I extend long overdue thanks and praise. She was my research assistant and companion during the exhibition preparation in 1985 and now, as though full-circle, she text-edited this book, caring for the details and understanding the issues surrounding the *Pietà* with truly unusual sensitivity. Judith Tolnick, who helped coordinate text, bibliography, and photographs, also taught me many things about art objects as well as committed friendship. Without her, I seriously doubt whether any of this would have come about at all.

Walter Simons's help in many ways permitted me to write this book. Over the past years, Walter has read many drafts of many papers and lectures, given me references, visited churches and archives with me. Walter Simons's role, like the one formerly occupied for many years by Bryce D. Lyon, has been as a strenuous trainer in historical materials, encouraging the ideas to take the shape I wanted, pointing my way in and out of the most appropriate and illuminating historical and archival sources. It is Ludo Milis, however, who first stimulated and controlled this project. He put prickles in my head and thorns in my side — cajoling, needling, challenging, indeed teaching me how to think about most of the problems with which this study is concerned. He taught me how to argue, and gave me the confidence and skills to do so. This was a priceless thing to have gotten from the master and maker of stirring visions of medieval history.

8

Finally, although his taste for Belgian beer remains highly underdeveloped, Kermit Champa's companionship made me happy, and his aesthetic conscience kept me honest.

July 1991
Providence,
Rhode Island

ABBREVIATIONS

A.R.A. = Brussels, Algemeen Rijksarchief / Archives générales du Royaume

B.A.O.C.M.W. = Brussels, Archief van het Openbaar Centrum voor Maatschappelijk Welzijn / Archives du Centre public d'aide social

NOTE: References originally published more than one decade ago are noted on the second mention in the footnotes by the original date of publication, followed by the date of the edition consulted, thus: Pater (1877; 1910).

ABBREVIATIONS OF THE RULES FOR BEGUINES

Antwerp (1323) = Statutes of the Beguinage in Antwerp, 1323, ed. Philippen, *De Begijnhoven,* pp. 336-38.

Bruges (circa 1290) = Rule of the Beguinage of the Vineyard in Bruges, ca. 1290, ed. Hoornaert, "La plus ancienne Règle," pp. 17-79.

Ghent Memorandum (1328) = Memorandum presented to the delegates of the bishop of Tournai in favor of the Beguinage of Saint Elisabeth in Ghent, 1328, ed. Béthune, *Cartulaire,* pp. 73-76.

Ghent Rule (before 1354) = Rule of the Beguinage of Saint Elisabeth in Ghent, included in the Statutes of 1354 (but probably older), ed. Gysseling, "De oudste statuten van het Groot Begijnhof," pp. 5-13.

Leuven (Small Beguinage) = Ordinance of 1369 and Statutes of 1416, ed. Smeyers and Van Buyten, "De oudste statuten," pp. 22-26.

Liège (circa 1246) = Statutes of the Beguine communities in the diocese of Liège, c. 1246, ed. Philippen, *De Begijnhoven,* pp. 303-09.

Lier (1401) = Statutes of the Beguinage of Lier, 1401, ed. Philippen, *De Begijnhoven,* pp. 339-43.

Sint-Truiden (fourteenth century?) = Statutes of the Beguinage in Sint-Truiden, possibly dating from the fourteenth century, ed. Philippen, *De Begijnhoven,* pp. 309-14.

To My Mother

It is strange that the tactile sense, which is so infinitely less precious to man than sight, becomes at critical moments our main, if not only, handle to reality.

Nabokov, *Lolita*

PART I

ART HISTORICAL PROBLEMS

INTRODUCTION

This book explores the exchange between ordinary beholders and the *Pietà*, that great Christian image where Mary holds on her lap the body of her dead Son. My study attempts to show that the relationship between common Christian believers and the *Pietà* is primarily a private and sensory one, that those who visit the image do so in order to experience feelings of a most personal, inner sort. Wherever located — in domestic niches or on official altars, in roadside chapels or in urban parish churches — the sculpted *Pietà* becomes the setting for a private enactment of basic human feelings.

To pursue the exchange between the material (object) and the immaterial (feeling), and to explore the construction of emotions through art, this inquiry charts many territories. Readers familiar with the period of the fourteenth and fifteenth centuries will immediately sense my emphasis on the history and theory of devotional art and mysticism. Greatly expanded in the past two decades, scholarship in these fields has brought to light a formidable body of evidence about religious practice, including the use of art objects in worship. Scholars have based much of their research on evidence from devotional handbooks, the lives of mystics (the *vitae*), passion tracts, and theological treatises on meditation from many European countries. Art historians have recently begun using such documentary evidence in their investigations of religious images to demonstrate that during the later Middle Ages devotional art was inextricably bound to a local, social, and cultural matrix of religious practice and piety. My impetus to isolate a single devotional object in this study springs from a desire to apply those same scholarly procedures to untested waters, and to question whether the *Pietà*, like other devotional objects, emerged as a response to the requirements of devotional practice and spiritual priorities. Recent art historical scholarship has prompted me to explore the social setting in which the demand for the *Pietà* as an object of devotion crystallized as a means to explain the initial appearance of this image type.

This investigative approach, focused on the history of the local environment, does not explain, however, why the *Pietà* outlasted the later Middle Ages, becoming a standard fixture of the modern Catholic church and a highly valued object of daily prayer. [1] This question has interested me greatly. The repertory of Christian religious art was sensationally boosted in the fourteenth century by the invention of many new themes and subjects, and the *Pietà* was but one among them. In fact, it is no exaggeration to say that during the later Middle Ages religious art of the Christian West reached its apogee, when its corpus of images was as diverse, inventive, complex, and rich as it ever had been or would be. Yet of the marvelous, strange, and tender themes to emerge during and just after the turn of the fourteenth century — John Sleeping on the Bosom of the Lord, for example, or Mary in Childbed — only the *Pietà* has retained a compelling, persistent appeal to viewers down to the present day. Of the countless fourteenth- and fifteenth-century iconographic themes (so many that scholars to this day have not unearthed them all [2]) only the *Crucifixion*, the Virgin and Child [3] and the *Pietà* survived those centuries to be housed in church, chapel, cathedral and home throughout the post-Reformation Catholic world, and in lands far away from northern Europe, its native birthplace.

In light of the myriad of religious art themes to emerge in that pivotal period, the *Pietà* is exceptional for its longevity; and that longevity is due, I believe, to its nearly universal Catholic appeal. As a general object of private prayer, the *Pietà* draws beholders from centuries as discontinuous as the fourteenth and nineteenth and brings them to religious settings as dissimilar as a Flemish rural roadside chapel and a Neoclassical Parisian parish church. [4] Over the centuries, succeeding generations of believers from any number of given locales developed customs for personalizing and affirming devotion to single *Pietàs* and have continued to commission and produce new *Pietà* figures for devotional use. [5] The image persisted — as an iconographic type and in individual examples — across several epochs and through more than five centuries to become popular in cultures quite distinct from the one in which it first appeared.

The *Pietà's* longevity is indeed remarkable, and it suggests that the distinctive priorities of any given, single culture are probably not the decisive factor in the image's appeal. Why, to cite one of the underlying questions of this book, has the *Pietà* been so widely used in Catholic countries as an instrument of private prayer? And why has the *Pietà* persisted in that religious role for so long? To make sense of this question means acknowledging that the *Pietà* might offer the onlooker the opportunity for elemental forms of human experience, experiences not bound to a given culture or specified by a specific historical period. The Christians who have beseeched *Pietàs* cannot be neatly circum-

16

scribed by specific geographical or temporal boundaries. On the contrary, the *Pietà* exercises an effect somewhat independent of time or place. What are the qualities of this image that enable it to transcend the restrictions of a specific time or place and achieve a universal Catholic appeal?

The *Pietà's* longevity and its Catholic universality demand that certain strategies and types of evidence be marshalled over others in this study. Historical and sociological interpretation explain a great deal about the fourteenth century, about the social basis of religious belief, and about the cultural institutions behind it; these perspectives also illuminate the particular devotional and ritual functions that initially gave rise to the *Pietà*. But historical and sociological interpretations fall short of exposing the psychic ground, if you will, of the image — where things such as private, inner feeling between beholder and object occur.

In the following pages I attempt to uncover the realm of affective appeal to private feeling engendered by the *Pietà*. Two scholars from separate disciplines encourage me to do so, although neither of them specifically addresses the problem of the *Pietà*. I refer first to the philosopher William James, who in 1902 published a series of lectures in what was to become a major treatise on mysticism, *The Varieties of Religious Experience*. I refer secondly to the British anthropologist Rodney Needham, who in 1967 advanced in a small but challenging article a theoretical view of percussion and its role in inducing states of transition. [6]

With his *The Varieties of Religious Experience*, William James (1842-1910) produced a fundamental study of the psychology and philosophy of religion. First delivered as the Gifford Lectures at Edinburgh in the Spring of 1902, *The Varieties* remains one of the most widely used analyses of conversion, saintliness, and other forms of the religious impulse. For our purposes, the book's chief significance lay in James's claim that the central religious experience is the mystical state. James saw this state as an altered state of consciousness. In his critique of James, Yale professor John E. Smith explained it this way:

> Unlike many other treatments of the subject, James's emphasis falls neither on religion as doctrine or precisely articulated belief, nor again on religion as cult or liturgical community, but rather on religion as a peculiar force in the *living experience* (author's italics) of individuals. [7]

17

James proposed a language, and hence a system, for extracting from the evidence of the mystical experience of individuals its nature as "sensation" or "inner feeling." No study of mysticism in medieval religion has, as far I know, attempted to discover the subjectively emotional, non-discursive content of mysticism. Because of James's emphasis on the mental state associated with the religious experience, and his opinion that it is *sui generis, The Varieties* receives special attention in the theories investigated in this book.

Needham worked within the larger anthropological research tradition treating shamanism and trance, forms of ritual contact with the supernatural. Needham's article proposes a provocative hypothesis about the connection between percussion and transition rituals. He argues that percussive sounds are "resorted to in order to communicate with the other world."[8] It is not the specifics here that interest us as much as their broader implications for the study of cultural history. Needham sees something at work which he calls the "universal psychic appeal" of a certain kind of phenomenon, in this case, percussive noise. His hypothesis states that there are certain phenomena that affect people outside the sphere of rational discourse, affect them in similar ways, but that are organized by different societies according to each culture's particular social formats — for example, that percussive noise can be generated either by drums or bells. Such phenomena Needham calls universal.

James and Needham both address, in the form of psycho-analytic hypotheses, the force of "living experience" in individuals as they confront the sacred. James calls it "immediate feeling"; Needham, simply "feeling." And, interestingly, they arrived at those terms while attempting to understand altered states of consciousness during religious experience — James while working on mysticism and Needham on percussion and states of transition in trances in non-Western village cultures. Both scholars dwell on the power of feeling, that singular experience which they claim is so basic to human nature as to be nearly impossible to define — that is, universal. This is a valuable idea for studying the *Pietà*. Feeling, following James and Needham, does not occur in the mind; it is not an analytical concept. In that sense, feeling's principle arena lies outside the sphere of the conscious (where language-based ideas take place). Hence the difficulty of communicating it in words. By its very nature, feeling cannot be understood the way other experiences can, as a function of rational intelligence or thoughtful action. Feeling is intuitive and emotional; it is a sensation, a state of being, not a thought. The definition of feeling as sensation acknowledges that the five senses, as both authors claim, are the only vehicle

18

for producing and fostering inner feelings. The senses, not intelligible ideas, are feeling's point of entry, its record, and its effect. The senses and the sensory are the *content* of feeling.

For scientific reasons, academic inquiry has avoided pursuing research into the wordless vagaries of such a realm. How can something as immaterial as feeling be demonstrated? Where lies its proof? Yet despite the demands of scientific scholarship for incontrovertible facts and hard proof, I believe that in trying to understand the continuous appeal of the *Pietà* across the centuries, we cannot avoid at least testing the hypothesis that immediate feeling, grounded in the senses, is indispensable to a full understanding of this form of sacred art. The *Pietàs* themselves have persistently prompted me to explore this hypothesis. A word of explanation is in order, which will serve at the same time to illuminate the limits of this study. I investigate here a corpus of *Pietàs* venerated in the southern Low Countries from the beginning of the fourteenth century until approximately the second half of the sixteenth, the era of the Protestant Reformation. Those dates bracket, on the one side, the first-ever appearance of the *Pietà* in the southern Low Countries and, on the other, the violent destruction of images and the rupture to practices of image devotion by the Iconoclasts. The destroyers, or image-breakers, vented their fury against idolatry especially on the sculpture, particularly in the territories under investigation here. [9]

The end point of my investigation in some ways is more arbitrary than the beginning. For while the Iconoclasts' fury deprived many a devout of their much-loved objects, it scarcely touched their need for such images. When the dust of image-breaking settled, devotional objects reappeared in Low Country church and home in numbers so profuse that many a modern-day visitor will judge them, even by standards of the most ardent, enthusiastic Catholics, as altogether excessive. With the post-Reformation period, those religious objects, old as well as new, increasingly became social as well as spiritual centers. [10] The seventeenth century witnessed the reappearance and revitalization of religious confraternities (with strongly local, medieval antecedents) whose meetings were structured principally around ritual relations with specific sacred objects. [11] At roughly the same time, local devouts in the Low Countries developed and turned into public ritual such practices as washing and dressing sacred objects and holding processions in their honor.

I have argued elsewhere that in the southern Low Countries devotion to religious objects metamorphosed continuously from the fourteenth century onwards. [12] The evidence of the central role of sacred objects in that society is

[margin handwriting: immediate feeling helps to explain the sacred art]

19

striking, especially considering that obstructions to the belief in the power of devotional sculpture arose frequently and often violently. There had been several major religious and secular wars — for example, multiple occupations by foreign countries, and two attempts, one in the sixteenth and another in the late eighteenth century, to abolish local customs of practicing the Catholic faith. What this means is that in the southern Low Countries the Reformation interrupted people's relations with their objects without, as happened elsewhere in northern Europe, terminating those relations altogether. [13] The events of the sixteenth century are thus used in this book merely as a convenient point to pause and gather up threads, there to be picked up later in another study finalizing the history of devotion to the *Pietà* in the modern period.

The decision to concentrate on the *Pietàs* of the southern Low Countries rests on several other factors. To start with, I know of no catalogue or comprehensive study of *Pietàs* as a group from the region of the southern Low Countries in any language. At first this was appealing as a scholarly gap waiting to be filled. But intimacy with Low Country *Pietàs* opened up issues whose implications far outweighed the gains of simply filling in a research blank. When I first began this research in 1985, there was only a handful of local articles and not a single book dedicated to the topic of Low Country *Pietàs*. The reasons are explored below in chapter 1. I briefly call attention here, however, to the one opinion accepted by our specialists without exception: that the *Pietà* was invented in, produced by, and exported from the Rhineland. To put this in anachronistic but not, I think, irrelevant terms, the *Pietà* is a German thing. *Pietàs* are viewed as inheritors and propagators of an essentially Germanic character; whether that character is defined as style or devotional practice makes very little difference. Thus to isolate the Low Countries as a vital constituent of the history of the *Pietà* has proven to be anything but a simple scholarly matter.

The principle of inherent Germanness in our study of *Pietàs* is compounded by the fact that Low Country *Pietàs* are made as sculpture in-the-round. Not until after the Reformation did painters take up themes of the *Pietà* — and then they did so vigorously. There were exceptions, of course, and the fifteenth-century Flemish painter Rogier van der Weyden comes immediately to mind. [14] But generally speaking, during the period we are considering, the *Pietà* developed as and remained in the Low Countries a sculptured type. Scholars have not been interested in this three-dimensional character of the *Pietà*; nor have they been much concerned with its geographical setting in the

20

southern Low Countries. There are two factors at work. First, the study of medieval sculpture, as Kathryn Brush recently pointed out, has been principally guided by French and German scholars investigating French and German sculpture.[15] Brush views that tradition as driven by a desire to advance geographical primacy in matters of sculpture achievement — in modern terms, to celebrate nationalism in the arena of sculpture history. England, Spain, and Italy, where medieval sculpture developed largely autonomously, have been isolated (for political reasons) from those discussions as a matter of course. But the Low Countries, whose territories were often closely aligned with what was happening nearby, were either drawn inexorably into the Franco-German scholarly orbit or shut out from it altogether. The result is that the few scholars who have treated religious sculpture in the Low Countries at all have done so with an eye for calibrating the degree to which it was influenced by its two commanding neighbors.[16] The history of medieval sculpture in the Low Countries as an independent medium whose style and role are generated by internal (local) rather than external (Franco-German) pressures remains to be written.

Second, study of the *Pietà*, because of the theme's place and date of origin, has also been determined by the concerns of post-medieval, Netherlandish scholarship. I am referring particularly to the primacy of attention to two-dimensional media, painting, drawing, and the graphic arts, such as prints and the printed book. So scarce are studies of the sculpture of the fourteenth through sixteenth centuries from the Low Countries[17] that the organization dedicated to studying the field, The Historians of Netherlandish Art, fully acknowledged the situation by devoting two special sessions to the problem in its conference of 1989. The call for papers describing the conference's objectives lays bare the condition with admirable accuracy when it cites ''the predominance of certain media, such as painting and prints, and the neglect of others, such as architecture and sculpture, in the art historical literature.''[18] This primacy, recognized by the specialists, reveals what my research has long seen to be the case: that the *Pietà* has not profited from either the tradition of or the recent advances in the study of Netherlandish art.[19]

My procedures for this inquiry, especially the questions I have asked, have arisen as much from looking at the objects as they have from reading about them. There was hardly any choice when no focused scholarly discussion preceded me, where no specified, established ideas were there to embrace or reject, when no local theory existed to refine or refute, and no conversations, as

21

it were, among luminaries were there to listen in on. So I took to visiting village churches, stopping at roadside chapels and abandoned shrines, to peering up at street corners and detecting niches tucked into walls and over doors. In short, wherever the pious took to their prayers, I sought out. Even (or in some cases especially) shrines that were abused or in the most humble settings provided a wealth of information about the devout who pray to *Pietàs*. Thus fieldwork, as much as library and archival study, prompted me to undertake the particular goal stated at the beginning of this book, that of exploring the realm of private feeling experienced by ordinary viewers of the *Pietà*.

I saw many old *Pietàs* still in use. The two figures, Mary and the grown Christ, were there as a kind of living presence for their onlookers. Those people, knelt in prayer, obliviously wrapped inside their petitions to the sculpture, praying, murmuring, softly speaking to, or maybe with, the image. It was the full-bodied, three-dimensional essence of the images, their sculpture-in-the-roundness, that struck me repeatedly. Believers came to pray to quasi-lifelike figures. What is more, most of the worshippers I saw were women. The still "living use" of the *Pietà*, its presence as rounded three-dimensional sculpture, and the women devout engaging in what to this scholarly unbeliever was an intensely felt, passionate dialogue — those are the things that guided my questions and ultimately gave this research its particular pulse and character.

[1] For an analysis of more than 6,000 active pilgrimage shrines in modern European Roman Catholicism, including those to the "suffering Mary," see Mary Lee Nolan and Sidney Nolan, *Christian Pilgrimage in Modern Western Europe* (Chapel Hill: University of North Carolina Press, 1989). For the *Pietà*, see especially p. 198: "At least 185 active shrines are primarily focused on a cult image depicting Mary with the dead Christ. Although examples are found in most parts of continental Europe, 70 percent are concentrated in culturally Germanic areas including France's Alsace region and Italy's Trentino-Alto Adige region."

[2] The bearded female saint, Wilgefortis (also known by other names, such as Oncummer, Ontcumber, Livrade) has received no attention by art historians. Walter Simons (The Institute for Advanced Study) and I are jointly preparing a study of Wilgefortis.

[3] The *Virgin and Child* here exemplifies the iconographic type of the standing figure, a type that includes the equally popular standing figures of saints.

[4] See, for example, Germain Pilon, *Pietà* (sixteenth century), in Saint-Sulpice, Paris; and Nicolas Coustou, *Pietà* (1723), in Notre-Dame, Paris.

22

⁵ The *Pietà* of Bree (Inv. no. 15, plate 17), dating from circa 1400, has been used as a devotional object continuously over the centuries. Its ritual longevity is discussed in J.E. Ziegler, "The Medieval Virgin as Object: Art or Anthropology?," *Historical Reflections / Réflexions Historiques* 16 / 2-3 (1989): 251-64.

⁶ William James, *The Varieties of Religious Experience: A Study in Human Nature* (1901-02; New York: NAL Penguin, 1958); Rodney Needham, "Percussion and Transition" (1967), in William A. Lessa and Evon Z. Vogt, eds., *Reader in Comparative Religion: An Anthropological Approach,* 4th ed. (New York: Harper & Row, 1979): 311-17. Needham's article first appeared in *Man* 2 (1967): 606-14. I refer throughout to the reprinted version in Lessa and Vogt.

⁷ John E. Smith, "William James's Account of Mysticism; A Critical Appraisal," in *Mysticism and Religious Traditions*, ed. Steven T. Katz (Oxford: Oxford University Press, 1983): 247-79, esp. p. 247.

⁸ Needham (1967) in Lessa / Vogt (1979), p. 315.

⁹ The fact that many sacred objects survived the Iconoclasts suggests that the original quantity of sculpture must have been immense.

¹⁰ Many people in the Low Countries are still very active in their veneration of sacred objects. Good numbers today still make the pilgrimage walk to Scherpenheuvel; there is a periodical devoted to articles on cult objects, entitled *Devotionalia: Periodiek voor verzamelaars van devotionalia* (Eindhoven), which always includes the dates and places of the markets for exchanging religious articles, as well as a "personals" column which indexes a wealth of modern devotional interests.

¹¹ Ziegler, "The Medieval Virgin" (1989); Louis Chatellier, *The Europe of the Devout: The Catholic Reformation and the Formation of a New Society,* trans. Jean Birrell, (1987; Cambridge: Cambridge University Press, 1989).

¹² Ziegler, "The Medieval Virgin" (1989).

¹³ For a discussion of the repercussion in painting, and on Protestant painters, see David Freedberg, "The Problem of Images in Northern Europe and Its Repercussions in the Netherlands," *Hafnia: Copenhagen Papers in the History of Art* (1976): 25-45. The best discussion of iconoclasm in English remains David Freedberg's "Art and Iconoclasm, 1525-1580: The Case of the Northern Netherlands," in *Kunst voor de Beeldenstorm: Noordnederlandse Kunst, 1525-1580*, ed. J.P. Filedt Kok, W. Halsema Kubes, and W.T. Kloek (Amsterdam: Rijksmuseum, 1986): 39-84; and idem, *Iconoclasm and Painting in the Revolt of the Netherlands, 1566-1609* (New York: Garland Press, 1987). For a bibliography on iconoclasm, consult D. Freedberg, *Iconoclasts and Their Motives* (Maarssen: Gary Schwartz, 1985); and Linda and Peter Parshall, *Art and the Reformation. An Annotated Bibliography* (Boston: G.K. Hall, 1986).

¹⁴ For a discussion, with citation of scholarly sources, of the *Pietà's* relation to painting, and to Rogier van der Weyden especially, see below, chapter 1, n. 57.

¹⁵ Kathryn Brush, "The Naumburg Master: A Chapter in the Development of Medieval Art History," *Gazette des Beaux-Arts* (in press); and idem, "The Renaissance Paradigm: Founding Perspectives on the Study of Gothic Sculpture," (Paper delivered at the Annual Conference of the Renaissance Society of America, Duke University, Durham, North Carolina, 12-14 April 1991).

[16] See below, chapter 1, especially my discussion of de Borchgrave d'Altena. One should review precisely the impact and importance of Paul Clemen's survey of Belgian monuments, begun in 1917, to "make a collection of the dispersion and partial loss of art historical material during the last war years" (p. v), published in his edition, *Belgische Kunstdenkmäler*, 2 vols. (Munich: Bruckmann, 1923). Each province was organized through a department head; among those responsible were numerous well-known art historians — among others, Baum and Hamann, with counsel from Köhler, Goldschmitt, Graul, Dvořák, and von Bode. One also needs to keep in mind the Mosan style problem. Traditionally, the style of the Mosan region has been treated as the forward-moving pulse of sculpture in the region of the western Low Countries. This view continues to characterize the study of medieval sculpture there. For that point, see *Rhin-Meuse: Art et Civilisation 800-1400*, exh. cat., (Cologne and Brussels: Kunsthalle and Musées Royaux d'Art et d'Histoire à Bruxelles, 1972); and *Die Parler und der Schöne Stil 1350-1400: Europäische Kunst unter den Luxemburgen*, exh. cat., 3 vols. (Cologne: Museen der Stadt Köln, 1978).

[17] Just before this study went to press, an exhibition of late medieval sculpture from the Limburg region was mounted at the Provinciaal Museum voor Religieuze Kunst, Begijnhof Sint-Truiden, Belgium; see *Laat-gotische beeldsnijkunst uit Limburg en Grensland* (Sint-Truiden: Provincie Limburg Culturele Aangelegenheden, 1990).

[18] ,,Call for Papers'' announcement for the conference, *In Search of the Netherlandish Tradition,* held on 26-28 October, 1989, in Cleveland, Ohio.

[19] Retables are the only genre of sculpture to have received continuous, serious scholarly attention. See especially the writings of Robert Didier in this area. I address the situation of the free-standing sculpture genre in chapter 1, in terms of its link to and derivation from the problems of painting (i.e., narrative and market issues).

CHAPTER 1

THE PIETA: SCULPTURE OR PAINTING?

Sculpture is the art *par excellence* of savages who carve fetishes very adroitly long before they undertake painting, which is an art of profound reasoning and requires for its enjoyment special initiation.

Charles Baudelaire (*Salon* of 1846)

In 1927 Erwin Panofsky published his seminal study of the "Imago Pietatis" (known in English as the "Man of Sorrows").[1] The impact of this essay on the general study of devotional art can hardly be overestimated. It spawned a highly specialized bibliography that promptly assumed monumental proportions. For the future of the *Pietà*, the image in which Mary holds the body of the dead Christ in her lap, Panofsky's article proved just as momentous. It altered the definition of the *Pietà* radically from what it had been before by putting an end to the view that this image type had emerged as one of a small group of iconographical innovations exclusive to German sculpture of the fourteenth century.[2] Panofsky's article therefore fixes a point of closure in the scholarship of *Pietàs*.

Before 1927 sculpture was viewed as the most important medium for objects of religious contemplation and private lay devotion during the later Middle Ages.[3] With his "Imago Pietatis" essay, Panofsky divested sculpture of its singular hold on the devotional market, shifting scholars' attention to painting. In his investigation of panel paintings of Christ as Man of Sorrows ("Imago Pietatis" images), Panofsky employed and defined the concept of the *Andachtsbild*, or "devotional image," a class of art objects used as instruments for religious contemplation by individuals.[4] Panofsky defined the *Andachtsbild* in essentially negative terms. In his explanation, the *Andachtsbild* was neither a scenic narrative image nor a cultic, hieratic, "representational" image. The distinguishing element of the *Andachtsbild*, that which delimited it from both the narrative and the iconic images, was its capacity to allow for the contemplative absorption of the viewer. Panofsky understood the *Andachtsbild* as an image that eliminated the distance between viewer and object that was unavoidable with the scenic narrative or hieratic image.

If one endorses, as I do here, the theory that the affective impact of the *Pietà* is uniquely attributable to its medium as sculpture, then the consequences of Panofsky's ideas are tremendous. Panofsky's entire edifice rests on classifications deduced from the analysis of painting. [5] Later scholars have consistently ignored this essay and its bias toward painting, as they have been preoccupied with the headier task of charting the constellation of intellectual luminaries around which Panofsky's ideas revolve. [6] In fact, neither Michael Podro nor Michael Ann Holly, Panofsky's recent historiographers, makes a single reference to that scholar's immensely seminal ''Imago Pietatis'' text. [7] Yet when seen from within the field of medieval art that essay is progenerative. It parented a distinct family of scholarship in the discourse on devotional imagery in general; and that scholarship has proven the most important factor in determining what we know (or do not know) about the *Pietà* today. [8] To understand specialized writing about the *Pietà* at all, we must account for the development of the literature of devotional art, an account that in many ways Panofsky initiated.

Some sense of the distinctive character of Panofsky's article will help to explain the course of scholarship it charted. So complex was the scaffolding of criteria Panofsky erected for defining the concept of devotional art that scholars became preoccupied largely with the problem of how to decipher his criteria. Even today, in attempting to penetrate the bibliography of devotional art, many will promptly be struck by the intricate interdependency of the discourse it contains; they will find the footnote references repetitive, working with and always citing the same body of articles and books. [9] Few areas of art historical research challenge their readers with an edifice like this one, a veritable maze of inward-looking ideas and references, all adding onto the central core of Panofsky's criteria in almost inconceivably infinite variations.

I do not presume even now to grasp fully all of what these authors say, nor do I have any desire to add to what is already a rather fine-spun, fragile, hermeneutical enterprise. What interests me about these discussions is that in the overwhelming space given over to reconstructing or, in some cases, deconstructing Panofsky's definitions, comparatively basic issues like the unique aesthetic qualities of individual media — sculpture especially — were set aside. [10] Gradually but inevitably the theory of the sculptural primacy of the *Pietà* lost its clarity and interest. This situation, its why and wherefore, is the bibliographic keystone of my study of the *Pietà*.

Around 1920, things were different. Sculpture was then considered the prime medium of medieval devotional art. Wilhelm Pinder devoted several studies to that problem, as did his prolific contemporary, the German art and architectural historian, Georg Dehio. [11] It was the concept of the *Andachtsbild* that interested them, as it would Panofsky later. Fundamental differences between their approaches and his obtain, however. Pinder and Dehio were far more precise than Panofsky about the definition of an *Andachtsbild*. They restricted it to a limited group of iconographical inventions in fourteenth-century German sculpture — the Man of Sorrows, the *Christus-Johannes Gruppe* (the image of the sleeping John leaning against Christ, excerpted from images of the Last Supper), the *Schutzenmantelmadonna*, Mary in Childbed, and the *Pietà*. For Pinder and Dehio those iconographical inventions found their most brilliant manifestations in the "plastic" arts, or sculpture. [12] Unlike Panofsky, who had begun by specifying what the *Andachtsbild* was *not*, they built their definition of the *Andachtsbild* in positive terms, by examining the early, sculpted devotional objects in which these iconographic themes appeared, and identifying the unique characteristics that gave these images their potency. Working from sculpture and seeking to define its visually inherent content, Pinder and Dehio proposed a concept of late medieval sculpture as an "isolating" art, a concept that strongly affected their interpretation of the *Pietà*.

By "isolating," they meant that sculpture, by its very nature as three-dimensional form, does not easily lend itself to depicting action in sequence, the cumulative effect of things unfolding across time. In this respect sculpture is unlike painting, whose flat surface gives artists the latitude to lay out multi-figural groups interacting and to depict their actions as sequences happening in time. Sculpture is better suited to treat individual figures, to draw them out of narration and away from the context of sequential events. In Dehio's and Pinder's terms, sculpture is better suited to "isolate" figures. It was this aspect, sculpture's non-narrative essence, that Pinder and Dehio saw to be creatively activated in fourteenth-century German devotional sculpture, most notably in the *Pietà*.

To convey the sculptural content of the *Pietà*, Pinder and Dehio turned to comparisons with poetry. [13] Poetry is like sculpture, they claimed, because it too is an isolating art. [14] Drama can tell of 'the many' (of the chorus) but poetry is the individual's art (of the monologue). [15] Drama and painting by

27

their forms are more appropriate to convey narratives, because they can easily handle groups, deeds, actions across time, the telling of stories and their interlocking into meaningfully related (interdependent) sequences. Poetry, by contrast, they viewed as resembling sculpture because it was more compact, less like epic narration than like song in stemming from a single voice, an individual's plea, a personal sorrow, a lament.

The subject of the *Pietà* can be found nowhere in that greatest of Christian narratives, the Bible. No gospel describes the scene; no evangelist wrote that after the Crucifixion Mary took her dead Son onto her lap. [16] Thus Pinder and Dehio looked beyond the biblical accounts and became receptive to sources other than narrative ones. What they discovered to account for the sudden appearance of the ''isolating'' content in German sculpture was highly appropriate, given their concern with religious devotion. The source they found, fourteenth-century German lyric poetry describing the sorrows of the Virgin, was close in both content and function to the objects they sought to understand. In 1920 Pinder published his article on the ''poetic roots'' of the *Pietà*, tracing them back as far as fourth-century Greek drama and forward to the *planctus*, or twelfth-century Latin sequences of the Lamentation of Mary beneath the cross (the *Planctus ante nescia*, for example, or the *Tractatus de Planctu*), and finally into fourteenth-century German mystical writings of Ludolf of Saxony and Henry Suso, among others. [17] A number of scholars have expanded this repertory of sources greatly and many have critiqued the approach. [18] Yet none has noted, let alone been stimulated by, the peculiar shape that those philological observations assumed. In them a number of important aesthetic paradigms began to emerge most saliently.

Pinder and Dehio phrased the interaction between poetry and imagery as one of longing, as a kind of wish-fulfillment. [19] They said that the lyrical poetry of the Virgin was a lament, a longing; that the Virgin's wish to hold became concretely fulfilled in the sculptures of the *Pietà*:

> The sculpted Pieta possesses, in its very nature, a poetic root. What it calls into reality is the tragic, self-deceiving wish of those left behind: to veil, through the last chance for an embrace, the impossibility of future embrace, to replace the real loss through the apparent possession, to replace one who is irrevocably lost through his transitory image. [20] (Pinder)

> It [the *Pietà*] is the creation of poets, not church dramatists. . . . Already the sorrows of Mary were song in the text: She stands beneath the cross, longs to hold

28

and kiss Him. . . . What in those texts was wish becomes in the sculpture of the Pietà reality. [21] (Dehio)

This stimulus from poetry, whence the theme migrated into sculpture, is what scholars since have largely discredited, especially because of Pinder's and Dehio's faulty chronology. [22] Working from improved scientific methods and from evidence drawn from a more accurate philological understanding of the literary data, subsequent scholars produced a totally different reconstruction of the chronology of the corpus of relevant texts. But the "corrected" result is not a triumph of the science of philology alone, for it called into question not merely the textual sources and their chronological participation in devotional sculpture, but also the comprehensive philosophical and aesthetic program that accompanied Pinder's and Dehio's discussions. That program ran a much deeper course than the apparently empirical corrections to its chronology would at first glance belie.

Pinder's and Dehio's ideas of lyrical feeling, wish, and dream, and the manifestation of these experiences in sculpture, are markedly like those of the German philosopher, Frederich Nietzsche, who in 1870-71 explored the essence and meaning of the arts of epic, sculpture, poetry, and music in his mighty text, *The Birth of Tragedy*. [23] Although it is well beyond the scope of the present book to explore the full consequence of his theories, Nietzsche's ideas stand visibly behind those of Pinder and Dehio. [24] Those ideas constitute a philosophy of the meaning of art which philological science rejected when it called into question (and ultimately discarded) the direct path from lyrical feeling to the plastic reality of the *Pietà*.

> The plastic artist, like the epic poet who is related to him, is absorbed in the pure contemplation of images. . . . The lyric genius is conscious of a world of images and symbols. . . . This world has a coloring, a causality, and a velocity quite different from those of the world of the plastic artist and the epic poet. [25] (Nietzsche)

> The German poetry in praise of Mary shows how the poet, feeling more and more distinctly, saw more and more clearly until . . . the inner picture achieved inner clarity. . . . The lyricist and the epic poet were followed by in the sculptor. [26] (Pinder)

29

In *The Birth of Tragedy* Nietzsche attempted to disclose the "Dionysian" content of music — its inchoate, intangible, primordial, in his terms, "orgiastic essence." For him lyric poetry "is dependent on the spirit of music . . . the poems of the lyrist can express nothing that did not already lie hidden in that vast universality and absoluteness in the music that compelled him to figurative speech."[27] He is writing here essentially about the aesthetic force of music, that great Dionysian experience of willing, longing, sorrowing, and rejoicing, with its "primordial contradiction and primordial pain in the heart of primal unity." Nietzsche will wrest that experience from language: ". . . all phenomena, compared with it [music], are merely symbols: hence *language*, as the organ and symbol of phenomena, can never by any means disclose the innermost heart of music."[28] The lyricist depends on the medium of music: music is all passion, desiring, and longing. Nietzsche's understanding of lyric poetry comes, then, from his views of the unique experiential and aesthetic power of the medium of music to be Dionysian, to move us as in a dream outside the clarity of Apollinian thought and language. When Pinder and Dehio mark the plastic arts (the sculpture of the *Pietà*) as the true vessel of the individual's feelings of lyric poetry, they are speaking about the power of the medium of sculpture to be like music, to be the locus of those overwhelming, Dionysian aesthetic passions.

We see this Nietzschian view manifested most clearly in the importance Pinder and Dehio place on dreams as a source of fourteenth-century sculptural vision. Nietzsche wrote that, "It was in dreams . . . that the glorious divine figures first appeared to the souls of men."[29] Pinder and Dehio claim that the *Pietà* is the concrete fulfillment of a wish or longing of the Virgin to hold, to rock, to cradle her dead Son. This view comes quite close to Nietzsche's idea that the illusions the artist apprehends belong merely to the realm of appearance, that they are not true evocations of reality. This connection illuminates others, especially around the shared use of the concept of *Versenkung*, or absorption, which led Pinder to explore, and eventually assert, that Germany with its creation of the *Pietà*, was a kind of second equal to ancient Greece and its sculptural creations.[30] He said, "Only the West, this time under German leadership, raised up the poetic dream (reverie, or vision) to the clarity of plastic vision. The fervent visualization of the Passion and the absorption in Mary had to intersect to produce it [the poetic dream]."[31] This resonates unmistakably with Nietzsche's passage, in which he says that "the beautiful illusion of the dream worlds . . . is the prerequisite of all plastic art, and of an important part of poetry also.''[32]

This intriguing kinship between philosopher and art historian is understandable, since the young Pinder had been a loyal follower of Nietzsche. Nietzsche's sister recalls that with ''two sixteen-year-old boys by the names of Wilhelm Pinder (not our Wilhelm Pinder) and Gustav Krug, [Nietzsche] founded a little society and christened it with the high-sounding name of ''Germania,'' despite the fact that it consisted of only three members. . . . In the winter of 1862, after the purchase of the piano arrangement of Richard Wagner's *Tristan and Isolde* . . . the three members found themselves embroiled in a discussion provoked by a paper written by Wilhelm Pinder on the theme: ''Music, the Daughter of Poetry.''[33]

Nietzsche was working out a larger programme for understanding the ''deepest significance''[34] of the related arts of poetry and music, prompted by his friendship with the German music-dramatist, Richard Wagner.[35] Regarding our present concern with the theory of sculptural primacy for the *Pietà*, it seems that Pinder's views of the particular ''isolating'' and subjective character of its sculptural content may largely have been introduced by Nietzsche. This alone, the proximity of these ideas to that peculiar philosopher, may have placed these ideas too far within the orbit of that controversial giant of intellectual and aesthetic culture, Wagner, for the burgeoning generation of scientifically-minded art historians to be very comfortable with.

When Panofsky extended the concept of the *Andachtsbild* to include painting, I suspect he did so at least partly to challenge an aesthetic paradigm, Wagnerian and Nietzschian, that had dominated German thought for well over half a century by that time. Recent intellectual biographies, ferreting out Panofsky's scientific method and especially its Hegelian roots, have not considered whether Panofsky's project to put history into art history did not in some fundamental way (whether consciously or not is quite beside the point) arise as a reaction to Wagnerian aesthetic ideology. That ideology was well in command, we must grant, of more territories of the production, analysis, and reception of the arts than the ideology of any art historian or intellectual during the first decade of the twentieth century ever has been.[36] If nothing else it is a matter of record that after 1927 Wilhelm Pinder would no longer engage in public discussion with Panofsky over the status and destiny of the discipline.[37]

Pinder and Dehio, however pressured their ideas were by contemporaneous categories of aesthetic theory, did not neglect historical and documentary explanations. In exploring lyric poetry as the *Pietà's* source, and seeking for an appropriately isolated spectator, the "quiet contemplator" in Pinder's words, they placed mystical poetry of fourteenth-century Germany directly in the context of the nuns of the Rhenish convents, a connection which even after numerous decades of sound historical research has yet to be comprehensively documented. Pinder and Dehio believed that the *Pietà* theme arose to serve individuals during non-liturgical moments of meditation and prayer, especially during Vespers, the time traditionally reserved for meditating on the Crucifixion. [38] This audience of individual worshippers was made up primarily of women mystics; hence, women's mysticism, in Pinder's and Dehio's view, was the "ground" upon which the *Pietà* first appeared. [39]

Panofsky also challenged this point directly when he challenged the convent as the setting by expanding the audience for devotional imagery to include *any* individual observers, not simply (or even predominantly) women. In 1981, the German art historian, Hans Belting, still found this remarkable:

> It was Erwin Panofsky who liberated the concept of the devotional image from its confinement to the nunneries of southwest Germany. In 1927 he argued that, by virtue of its form and content, the devotional image qualified as an instrument for religious contemplation by an individual. [40]

How striking Belting's rhetoric is, and how deftly it points to Panofsky's act as something of a salvific one. It had rescued devotional art from a single (and feminine, no less) gender and specific type of community and produced, as Belting reveals, something akin to relief among certain art historians. In Panofsky's own day, and increasingly in ours, many art historians are ready and anxious to observe devotional images at work in genuinely public spheres, where a maximum of social factors are at work. The convent, with its palpable religious overtones, is ambiguously public and collective, and much more restricted in the number and nature of its social issues than broad-based urban patronage is.

In addition to expanding the audience, Panofsky moved the discussion of devotional images into the two-dimensional (painting) arena. He focused his study of *Andachtsbilder* on panel painting. This proved important, too, for with it Panofsky enabled Italian painting, ever the fascinating phenomenon, to become part of the new and exciting discourse on the *Andachtsbild*. Suddenly the full force of Italian painting was pushed back from the Renaissance

32

to the eleventh and twelfth centuries as an essential catalyst in the emergence of "personal viewing," a phenomenon that had a tremendous impact on ideas about the purpose of art, with wide-ranging social and aesthetic implications. [41]

The introduction of a private setting encouraged scholars to move beyond the conservative and generally held view that religious art functioned as a form of instruction for the illiterate. [42] The Italian factor licensed scholars to pursue a wide range of sources and contexts of devotion in Byzantine pictorial and literary precedents, in changing liturgical practice and doctrinal emphases, in the increasing specification of practices of meditation and contemplation and, as seen most recently in Belting's work, in the social and psychological conditions of audience participation. With Panofsky, "devotional" became an entirely new, general category of late medieval art from which scholars were able to apply a nearly open-ended range of social, spiritual, practical, liturgical, doctrinal, and pictorial evidence — evidence grounded firmly in the documentary sources. No wonder, then, that when Panofsky wrested devotional art from the strictures of the categories of both sculpture and convents, he effected something of a revolution in the procedures and objectives of art historical research in that field.

However inclusive his view, it was Panofsky's contemporary, the French art historian and iconographer, Emile Mâle, who came closer to realizing the full implications of the devotional issue for the history of painting. Mâle's concerns arose as an attempt to chart the sources for the development of what he called "new sentiments" in French religious painting of the fourteenth through sixteenth centuries — sentiments of the touching, the picturesque, and the pathetic. He observed this development as happening in the decline of cathedral sculpture and in the rise of painted historiated scenes of the Passion. The latter, the scenes of Christ's suffering and death, were for Mâle among the most original of the fifteenth-century's creations. [43] Thus it was the appearance, first in texts and then in images, and the increasing quantity of Passion imagery that alerted Mâle to a change in religious sentiment from being intellectually centered to having a more emotional taste for suffering and contact with the humanity of Christ.

Mâle located the sources for this change in sensibility in three places: mystery plays, [44] the impact of the Franciscans, and the importations to the French court from Italy of pictorial innovations for depicting the Passion scenes. Mystery plays exerted a kind of re-fertilization of Franciscan spirituality, which had broadly disseminated to the laity the model of living in imitation of Christ's humanity. Mystery plays and Franciscan ideology, as Mâle argued it, seeded the taste in the viewing public for *imitatio Christi* — be like, act like, live and feel like the human Christ — a taste to which French artists responded particularly agreeably. They were helped toward finding their pictorial way in painting Passion scenes by Italian precedents. And, as Mâle pointed out, they even had the opportunity at the Papal court in Avignon during the latter half of the fourteenth century for direct exchange of views with their Italian counterparts.

For Mâle the pictorial results were as astonishing as the taste that drove them. Out of this sensibility, operating within the loosely defined framework of *imitatio Christi*, painters invented novel approaches to the Passion scenes, ones thoroughly narrative, full of anecdotes and specific details, and bristling with particulars of the stories. In his words, the handling was "touching and picturesque."[45] The new audience, with its taste for a distinctly anecdotal narrative approach to the Passion, and the new pictorial emphases are phenomena that for Mâle were the signs of the birth of "realism" in art.

Mâle did discuss the *Pietà*, but only briefly. He showed that the theme first appeared in French manuscripts around 1380[46] and became more frequent toward the end of the fifteenth and beginning of the sixteenth century, when the Feasts of the Seven Sorrows of the Virgin had become widely celebrated by the confraternities.[47] The *Pietà* was not, however, his chief concern. Yet Mâle had so profoundly modified the view of Passion iconography — that is, of those subjects that surrounded the *Pietà* theme — that treatments of the *Pietà* were henceforth affected by it.

It was Mâle's broadly speculative views on the anecdotal character of the new narrative painting that proved most consequential, although his evidence, especially his use of mystery plays as a source of Passion iconography and his chronology of Franciscan spirituality, has been criticized severely — much of his data was faulty. Nonetheless, the ramifications of his theory of narrative (in his terms, its "realism") on the research of devotional art have been tremendous.[48] In 1979 James Marrow set out, for example, to specify how the "descriptive and anecdotal material entered the Passion plays,"[49] that is, to specify what he called the "nebulous concepts" of "late medieval realism" and the "spirit of the times."[50] Examining more than three hundred largely unpublished Passion tracts written in "Netherlandic" between 1450 and 1550, Marrow's *Passion Iconography in Northern European Art of the Late Middle*

Ages and Early Renaissance breathed a kind of second life into the research on devotional painting, renewing its primacy in the scholarship of devotional art. Marrow's book gives Mâle's great theory of the birth of "realism" the contextual and philological specificity it deserves and that art historians today have come to expect. But in tightening up the context philologically, Marrow ultimately points out the true importance of devotional art as being not simply an issue of painting but of painting's life within the ambience of a literate elite. This premise bears strongly on our current understanding of the *Pietà*.

Marrow charts the evolution of Passion tracts, from tenth-century Latin into Franciscan circles (pseudo-Bonaventure and Ludolf of Saxony), to fourteenth-century Middle German Dominican texts, and into the Netherlands *via* the *Devotio Moderna* around 1400. Marrow proposes that we view the Passion scenes present in these tracts, all of them including the *Pietà*, in the context of private devotional practices. These practices, Marrow suggests, shift their center in the thirteenth century from the Dominican convents of the Rhineland to the Netherlands, where under the aegis of the Devotionalists (Marrow's term for the people belonging to the *Devotio Moderna* convents) they became formalized and systematized. To meditate on Christ's Passion, Marrow contends, was "the most typical expression of piety after the thirteenth century" and the Passion tracts, which start to appear at that same time and soon in rapidly increasing numbers, were expressly produced to service that piety.

Marrow's study, however innovative in determining the context, encompasses only a small segment of the population. The Passion tracts he analyzes address (in fact they assume) a literate audience, an audience as yet ill-defined by contemporary scholars. Marrow claims that the "*Passieboeken* [the passion tracts] flooded the new religious communities of the Netherlands, becoming one of the most typical organs of piety of the time, particularly in the convents."[51] Additionally, he says that "lay branches (third orders) . . . and their counterparts in extra-religious spiritual movements such as the Beguines and Beghards . . . imitated aspects of the piety of the regular religious orders."[52] These claims must be approached cautiously. First, we simply do not have the evidence to permit us to substantiate such claims of literacy, and certainly not for the Beguines, whose piety should hardly be described, moreover, as imitating that of the regular Orders. To assert that texts, and not cult statues, are the primary instrument of devotion is to characterize the consumers essentially as reading, or at least semi-literate, practitioners of their faith, something which is, as yet, impossible to confirm with regard to many a lay religious woman.

35

Scholars know very little about the nature of the devotional practices among the ordinary, often illiterate, populace in the period. [53] So Marrow's perspective completely passes over private devotion by those individuals who, like the Beguines, practiced and also hungered to see the human Christ but did so without routine exposure to literate or even semi-literate discourse. [54]

Although it was primarily Mâle who sought out the issue of narrative elaboration and the consequences of an anecdotal approach to the Passion themes, Marrow's study reveals the genesis of scholarship thereafter accurately. The *Pietà* ultimately came to be embedded as but one of the Passion stories in the larger program of narrative painting. That program has to do with painting's capacity for storytelling; and, as Marrow has shown, fourteenth- and fifteenth-century devotion ultimately put imagery into its service as text-dependent, "readable" narration.

Scholars of various methodologies did steadily lose sight of one issue — the *Pietà's* sculptural origins and nature. Panofsky's method of starting with criteria for defining devotional objects did ultimately prove to be one of the dominant approaches to specialized research on the *Pietà*. Panofsky defined the *Andachtsbild* as a vehicle of empathic feeling, showing it to be a specific type of object with a specific function. The subject matter of the *Andachtsbild*, its depictions and representations, were not part of large-scale narrative; it did not illustrate scenic history, nor was it a static cult image or hieratic icon. Rather the depiction of Christ existed in a realm somewhere in between the living (narration) and the dead (icon). The figure of Christ was removed from the multi-figural scenes of the Bible and isolated from the stories when he was represented in the *Andachtsbild* — for example, as the *Man of Sorrows*.

The view that the *Andachtsbild* isolated the figure from its narrative context was something Panofsky shared with Dehio, who had written about it some years before. However, Dehio observed that same feature as operating not in painted images, as Panofsky did, but in fourteenth-century devotional sculpture. Was the younger scholar of the "Imago Pietatis" essay perhaps reacting to Dehio's (and Pinder's) notion of the isolated, non-narrative moment of the *Andachtsbild* when he tested its application to the medium he was by far the more expert in? Notwithstanding this possibility, it is one of the curious twists of historiography that Panofsky's approach outlasted Dehio's, eventually assuming the commanding voice of authority on the subject to which all scholars as a matter of principle seem more or less obliged to respond. As for

Dehio's and Pinder's works, when they are cited, if at all, it happens in the dubious guise of the obligatory footnote.

With more space we could certainly account for this bibliographical condition by exploring Panofsky's apparently more scientific method, which encountered a community of art historians who were themselves similarly turning away from psycho-philosophical and formal issues of aesthetic emotion and media-specific address. [55] While those sorts of shifts in hermeneutical priorities are interesting to know about and in this case may even account for Panofsky's method and its success, more to the point is the factual result: the theory of devotional art arising in sculpture totally vanished in the wake of painting's primacy.

Not every scholar of devotional art chose to classify and define the subject as Panofsky proposed. Some specialists preferred to investigate the textual sources of devotional art rather than its form and content. Yet however different the emphases are from Panofsky's, their effect on our understanding of the *Pietà* has been much the same. The theme was drawn into the orbit of literature rather than investigated to find out how it asserted and communicated its separateness from the text once it appeared as sculpture. Pinder viewed the sources in contemporaneous lyric, epic, and mystical writings of the Lamentation of Mary on Calvary. Art historians Otto Von Simson (1953) and Tadeusz Dobrzeniecki (1967) worked similarly but from more strictly theological textual sources, especially those concerning the doctrine of *compassio* and *coredemptio*. [56] Those texts address whether Mary actively participates, which is to say cooperates, in the Redemption by offering her Son. Von Simson and Dobrzeniecki illuminated precedents for this cardinal doctrine of medieval Mariology in the theological treatises from the eleventh and twelfth centuries, on the one hand, and in the Old Testament prefigurations of the dead Son, on the other. Marrow also investigated texts, but he was less interested in them as a source disembodied, as it were, from the image. He was therefore less predisposed to view the text as a point of departure for the migration of the theme from word to image the way Von Simson and Dobrzeniecki are. Image is not separable in Marrow's view from text, nor is it simply an "illustration." The image *is* the text. The Passion tract *is* its images. As such, the whole arrangement of images, how they are sequenced and exactly what they depict, becomes the vehicle of private devotion. Thus in Marrow's scheme the text, to return to the theme of the *Pietà*, is not a distinctive source of imagery but an all-encompassing formula of viewing, a formula that remains inseparable from the pictorial conventions of story telling.

Marrow's views about Passion imagery, including the *Pietà*, presume a medium that operates from literary premises: inseparable from the text, functioning according to scenographic conventions, it is an art primarily of narration. This idea comes from Mâle, but its implications go beyond him. Marrow introduced the element of audience response when he linked the rise of methodical and systematized devotion to the sequential manner of organizing the imagery. This view claims that the manner of depiction specifies and conditions devotional habits. Narrative content — and this is the implication for the study of the *Pietà* that should be emphasized — therefore becomes the property and expectation of a special audience, one with privileged access to the imagery *via* books.

While the *Pietà* may frequently have been the subject of painted illustrations of Passion imagery, most ordinary individuals lacked access to those texts and therefore had precious little experience with the subtleties of the literary conventions accompanying them. Devotional texts are accessories of devotion for literate and semi-literate audiences only; the habits of viewing their pictorial narration, indeed the kind of special "training in looking" they presume and the systematization of devotion that results, should be cautiously reserved for a comparatively small and elite section of the general populace, at least until it can be demonstrated as having been otherwise.

The *Pietà's* relation to painting is therefore a most complicated one. [57] Panofsky invited scholars to view the theme as part of the new function of *Andachtsbilder*, a function that he viewed as being largely delimited by Byzantine panel painting and full-blown narrative painting. This approach, although methodologically not identical to Marrow's, is similarly grounded in the premise of narration. Panofsky defined an *Andachtsbild*, after all, as neither narrative nor hieratic. And whether interpreted as a criterion of classification (Panofsky) or as a formula for pictorializing and beholding storytelling (Mâle and Marrow), narrative is by far the interpretative model that we associate with the analysis of the medium of painting. When it tells stories, painting emulates the literary media and offers itself as something of a text, if not to be read, then there at least to be narratively deciphered. This, narrative, is the critical category where the *Andachtsbild*, and by association the *Pietà,* eventually ended up. The most important ideological presumption since 1927 has been that the *Pietà* is a thematic, functional, and phenomenological part of painting. [58]

One other complementary path of scholarship needs to be investigated, that having to do with the genesis of the *Pietà*. Pinder and Dehio attempted to establish as the source of the *Pietà* the mystical literature of fourteenth-century Germany, especially the writing for or about the Dominican nuns of Germany. This genre of writing, sometimes called visionary literature, has been closely associated with the convents of the Rhineland and with their production of the radical form of spirituality that arose in the thirteenth century, known as mysticism. [59] The convent chronicles and lives of holy women (*vitae*) in the Rhineland contain copious references to women's visions of Christ in a multitude of his human and sacramental manifestations, in childbed, on the cross, in the Host, to name but a few. These texts describe interactions among women and the sacred persons that are so similar to sculptural and painted imagery that scholars have hypothesized nearly causal links, in both directions, vision to image as well as the other way around. [60] One example will serve to illustrate this point. The fourteenth-century German nun and mystic, Mechtild of Hackeborn, wrote:

> At Vespers, one saw the Lord taken down from the cross. One also saw the Virgin Mary hold him in her lap and the prayerful Mother spoke to him: Come hither and kiss me my holy wonder, my beloved Son, whom I love so much. [61]

Mechtild's expression is typical of the visionary literature produced in the Rhenish convents during the thirteenth and fourteenth centuries. [62] It startles the modern reader, so rich, full, ''real' — so anecdotally comprehensive, art historically speaking — are these descriptions and depictions of human interaction with the divine. First tapped by Pinder and Dehio, the feminine literary audience is one of the most vital, and today most popular, frames in which to situate the genesis and context of devotional images. [63] Scholars have generally agreed for some time that there was a reciprocity between women's visions and artistic images. [64] Visionary literature opened up fertile fields of research, but it is by today's scholars especially that carefully localized, documentary evidence of individual women and specific settings is being comprehensively analyzed.

Scholars have raised similar questions about the practical use of the devotional imagery by individuals. How did such imagery help to induce a state of contemplation and meditation, if at all? The visions of great holy women were the supreme result — the gift of grace indeed — of ''imageless meditation'' and thus scholars have attempted to use concrete imagery as a means of sharpening their understanding of the true contemplative and visionary woman, who needs no such stimuli. This understanding has been extended to the ordinary individual, who could not "envision" without concrete assistance, and to explain how she might have used devotional images. [65] The writings by and about holy women (as well as the content of their visions) belong, however, to a very special group of devouts, truly a mystical elite. And like the issue of narration, written visions, either because of the male clerics who produced them or because the women were spiritually sophisticated enough to have had and communicated them, are a text-based phenomenon, which by their very nature are (and ought to remain) linked to the culture of the spiritual and clerical elite.

The publication in 1981 of Hans Belting's *Das Bild und sein Publikum* (1990; *The Image and Its Public*) marks the latest approach to the study of Passion themes, among them the *Pietà*. [66] It has to do with how an audience receives devotional images, the meanings it reads into them and what factors, on a practical and psychological level, determine that reading. Belting is not interested in the visions of women or the eccentric happenings within the convent walls; rather his attention is focused on the public sphere, where the "language of the image" [67] of devotion developed and became collectively recognized. Pictorial rhetoric is what Belting believes devotional art to be about, a rhetoric changing across time, like the changes in spoken language that happen because of evolving, conventional usage. This semantic function, or in scholarly terms, its synchronic condition, Belting seeks to reveal in the public's knowledge and practices of official cultic ritual, practices which are as diverse as the dialects of language itself.

> The devotional image did not originate in the seclusion of the individual's own room, but rather presupposes a collective experience of reality: in its subject matter it presupposes the objective reality of what the cult was about, and in its forms it presupposes the subjective experience available in the staging of the cult. In the songs of lamentation and the cultic plays of Holy Week, frontiers of psychological realism were explored in a way hardly possible in other areas of medieval culture. And in the devotional images, a pictorial rhetoric was developed that served this psychological realism and prepared the way for a new role and use of images as such. Texts and images complemented and corroborated each other in articulating the experience of a new and personally accessible reality. [68]

Belting speaks here at the end of his discussion of the *Pietà*, and claims that the "reciprocal relation between the reception of the cult and the reception of the cult's image . . . yields a new approach to understanding the Mother-and-Son Group that in Italy was called the *Pietà*, a name also used for the "Imago Pietatis."" [69]

Belting relates the *Pietà* theme to the monstrance, the eucharistic vessel for exhibiting the Host, the sacramental body of Christ in the consecrated bread. The cult of the sacrament of the Eucharist and the cultic rites of its exposition are that "reality to which the image refers." The rhetoric, Belting informs us, is centering on "a figure bearing and a figure being borne." The rhetoric also contains "formulae of presentation," from gestures based on fourteenth-century Italian dramatizations of Mary's lamentations. A combination of various aspects of the cultic rite (elevation of the Host, receiving communion, and the nature of eucharistic repositories), the gestures of actors, and audiences of cult plays thus suggest to Belting new ways to interpret the "origination of the devotional image." [70]

What Belting suggests is that private devotion is less important to the devotional image than "a collective experience of reality" which comes from the participation of the laity in "functions of public life in the cult practices of the church." The audience is conditioned by the changing patterns of the ecclesiastical rite, by its presentation or "staging" of the liturgy in official vessels and dramatic plays, in sum by social interaction to see, to believe, to observe particular meanings in the form. This collective social experience is the lens through which devotional images are seen. Collective experience is the direct experience of the laity, a kind of context that conditions how the image, and other aspects of reality, is understood and made understandable. In current discourse, the meaning of images is seen and argued as a function of a locally and culturally conditioned social reality. With particular gestures, and particular combinations of figures, audiences understood each according to their own collective psychology, a psychology that changed with the particular audience and was conditioned by the totality of visible and relevant socio-spiritual public events.

Certainly Belting massively broadens the field for investigating devotional imagery by showing how the meaning of images directly results from what a given audience brings to it. Reception theory, in art history as elsewhere, says that one hears (or sees) only what a given language of the ears (or eyes), conditioned by customary experience, permits it to; the meaning of an image is endowed by the collective culture that receives it.

Belting's work introduces to the study of devotional art a rigorous way to get hold of truly contemporaneous meanings, meanings tightly lodged in the local experience of large groups of viewers. [71] It embeds the object firmly in a setting of beholders, whose habits of seeing can be fixed according to the collective experiences of socio-spiritual reality routinely set before them. It draws our gaze away from the typology of source, form and function of devotional objects — away from our own, twentieth-century presumptions and pre-established conceptual categories — and focuses it on the receiving and viewing audience that initiates, maintains, transforms, and understands those objects. Belting indeed represents an innovative approach to Passion imagery. Yet it is an approach lodged so firmly in local settings, socio-historically defined, that it renews the call to document the visible and visualizable with as much written data as possible.

My approach shares much with Belting's, especially the conviction that the viewer's (and scholar's) truest and deepest pathway to an image's meaning is through the "psychological." Our means of accessing that reality is, however, ultimately quite dissimilar. I, too, am convinced that users endow images with their own meanings, and that meaning does therefore change with time. [72] I do not "read" in a *Pietà*, for example, what mothers who lost sons in World War II would have read. Differences in meaning of that sort happen in direct proportion to the distance between centuries which separate them. Indeed society and culture shape the beholder's inner viewpoint; they give people a range of experiential codes, based in shared political, social, cultural, and religious experiences. Society frames its members from above, and from below they fill that frame with the routine, with the day-to-day stuff. Shared experience is bound to a particular time and place, the sound of the first steam engine, for example, or the putrid smells of cities lacking proper hygiene, or occupation by a foreign country. Thus does shared experience greatly vary over time.

This sort of experience, as Belting demonstrates, is tied in the thirteenth century to particular social and institutional structures. The church, for instance, with its sacramental rites, religious feast days, and the like, constitutes the nucleus of the concept of pictorial rhetoric. The church is where people undergo collective experience; the church is how the image and the terms that make it comprehensible to us becomes visible.

42

What is crucial to realize, however, is that those terms, such as "exhibition of the Host," are translatable into language and everyday concepts. This aspect — the conceptual, the knowable, the translatable — I fully embrace as always present in the viewer's reading of an image. And although it forms the conscious social basis from which we interpret images, the "knowable," conceptual reality does not explain a host of other experiences that interest me here.

Some experiences, like aesthetic emotion or feeling, exist outside the social spheres of language and premeditated action. And, therefore, if we hope to explore the realm of aesthetic feeling, we must proceed by recognizing that meanings exist that are conditioned not solely by social institutions and collective experiences. There are meanings above and beyond what is bound to a particular time and place. Thus we must be willing to grant that there may be feelings not documented by the written sources concerning the local experiences of a given society, especially during the fourteenth and fifteenth centuries, when personal feeling was not yet a matter for written record.

The feeling of which I speak here I do not claim by any means as offering understanding or insight into the totality of possible meanings which spring from the well of one's particular culture. But I do believe that there are meanings — I should better state them as sensations or as feelings — that are not bound to given times or limited to single cultures. Those "feelings" the *Pietà* evoked when it struck the senses, especially that of touch, and passed through the veil of realism of the times. [73] As it did it penetrated into more obscure recesses, those not open to the light of day where the full impact of social interaction takes place, those darkly inhabited by a person's heart and soul.

[1] Erwin Panofsky, "'Imago Pietatis.' Ein Beitrag zur Typengeschichte des 'Schmerzensmanns' und der 'Maria Mediatrix'," in *Festschrift für Max J. Friedländer zum 60. Geburtstag* (Leipzig: E.A. Seemann, 1927): 261-308.

[2] See Sixten Ringbom, *Icon to Narrative: The Rise of the Dramatic Close-up in Fifteenth Century Devotional Painting* (1965; 2nd rev. ed., Doornspijk: Davaco, 1984): 53. A great deal of medieval European sculpture has traditionally been referred to in scholarship as "German." This usage of the term "German" is highly problematic, given the diverse cultural areas it has been used to designate. I use the term reluctantly here. My discussion of the historiography of this field requires me to recognize this term as common usage.

³ This view has not disappeared. For example, see Colin Eisler, "Review of Sixten Ringbom's *Icon to Narrative*," *The Art Bulletin* 51/2 (1969): 186-88, where he laments that Ringbom did not concentrate more on sculpture.

⁴ For an especially informative summary of various definitions of the devotional image, review the dialogue between Hans Belting and Sixten Ringbom on this issue, starting with Ringbom (1984), p. 56ff. Belting's response appears in *The Image and its Public in the Middle Ages: Form and Function of Early Paintings of the Passion*, trans. Mark Bartusis and Raymond Meyer (New Rochelle: Aristide D. Caratzas, 1990): 45, 49-50; this was originally published as *Das Bild und sein Publikum: Form und Funktion früher Bildtafeln der Passion* (Berlin: Gebr. Mann Verlag, 1981). See also Ringbom's review of Belting's *Das Bild und sein Publikum* in *The Art Bulletin* 65/2 (1983): 339-40. Comprehensive citation of the literature is found therein.

⁵ Panofsky's rejection of the designation of *Andachtsbilder* as inherently plastic was consistent with his rejection of linguistically formulated, phenomenological classification of artistic types. See Erwin Panofsky, "Der Begriff des Kunstwollens" (1920); for the English translation of this essay, see K.J. Northcott and J. Snyder, "The Concept of Artistic Volition: Erwin Panofsky," *Critical Inquiry* 8 (autumn 1981): 17-33. Panofsky challenged Wölfflin's use of "plastic" and "painterly" for Riegl's "haptic" and "optic," as he challenged the application of *a priori* theoretical categories then active in the psychological and "artistic volitional" (*Kunstwollen*) methods of art history. A philosophically grounded discussion of Panofsky's ideas takes place in Guido Neri, "The Artistic Theory of Erwin Panofsky," *Architectural Design* 51/6-7 (1981): 30-34. One might add to this discussion Jan Bialostocki, "Erwin Panofsky (1892-1968): Thinker, Historian, Human Being," *Simiolus* 4 (1970): 68-89; William S. Heckscher, "Erwin Panofsky, A Curriculum Vitae," in *Art and Literature, Studies in Relationship*, ed. Egon Verheyen (Durham, North Carolina: Duke University Press; and Baden-Baden: Valentin Koerner, 1985): 339-62.

⁶ Historiographers of Panofsky's thought have concentrated on intellectual history, especially on the impact of Hegel, and not on actual material evidence. For this reason, Panofsky's rejection of sculpture and embrace of painting has been less interesting to them phenomenologically.

⁷ Michael Podro, *The Critical Historians of Art* (New Haven: Yale University Press, 1982); Michael Ann Holly, *Panofsky and the Foundations of Art History* (New York: Cornell University Press, 1984).

⁸ Consult especially the works of Joseph de Borchgrave d'Altena. De Borchgrave d'Altena's name has been well-known in Belgium as well as abroad from nearly three decades of recording his interests in the *Pietà* and other art themes associated with it. In fact, his name has been nearly synonymous with that field of art historical research in Belgium. De Borchgrave d'Altena introduces four general points about the history and the nature of the *Pietà*: (1) The *Pietà*, a narrative theme comparable to the *Virgin in Majesty*, is found in all media (painting, engraving, sculpture, embroidery and tapestry, metalwork, and glass) and represents the Virgin mourning Jesus, alone or accompanied by diverse persons, such as John, the Magdalen, the Holy Women, Joseph of Arimathea, and Nicodemus (de Borchgrave d'Altena, "Vierges de Pitié," offprint [Virton: Michel Frères, 1965], p. 1). De Borchgrave d'Altena's notion that the *Pietà* is a theme equally at home in all media has its roots in the appearance of Panofsky's "Imago Pietatis" in 1927. Refer to the bibliography of this book for a partial list of de Borchgrave d'Altena's publications on iconography. A more comprehensive list is provided by *Publications*

du Comte J. de Borchgrave d'Altena 1924-1949 (N.p, n.d. [1950]). (2) The medieval origins of the *Pietà* date back to the fourteenth century and by all indications the image's first appearance in western Europe was in Germany, specifically in the Mosan region. The ultimate origins of the *Pietà* are in the Christian Orient (Byzantium), in the Lamentation theme, where Mary poignantly weeps over her divine Son. From there it spread as a pictorial formula to Italy. (3) In the fifteenth century, sculpture of the *Pietà* reflects the innovative emphases of Low Country painters of the theme, Rogier van der Weyden particularly, resulting in what de Borchgrave d'Altena terms a "revitalization" of the *Pietà* in both media. (4) Sculpted retables complete the development course of the *Pietà*.

9 See, for example, the bibliographies of Ringbom (1984) and Belting (1990).

10 An exception to this is Rudolf Paul Berliner, student of Max Dvořák and former Chief Conservator at the Bavarian National Museum in Munich. See his Die *Weihnachtskrippe* (Munich: Prestel Verlag, 1955), esp. p. 13. For a stimulating discussion of Berliner's method and hypotheses, see Susanne Vivian Cloeren, "Art Historical Research and the Infant Jesus Statuette: An Exegesis of Two Texts," (unpub. essay, College of the Holy Cross, Worcester, Massachusetts, 1990).

11 Wilhelm Pinder, "Marienklage," *Genius* 1 (1919): 200-08; idem, "Die dichterische Wurzel der Pietà," *Repertorium für Kunstwissenschaft* 42 (1920): 145-63; idem, *Die Pietà* (Leipzig: A. Seemann, 1922); idem, *Die deutsche Plastik von ausgehenden Mittelalter bis zum Ende der Renaissance* (Potsdam: Akademische Verlagsgesellschaft Athenaion, 1924): 91-101, 171-77; and Georg Dehio, "Andachtsbilder," in *Geschichte des deutschen Kunst*, vol. 2, rev. ed. (Leipzig: De Gruyter & Co., 1923): 117-23.

12 Dagmar Editha Lies, "Plastik als Gestaltung: Wilhelm Pinders Aussagen zur deutschen Plastik in den Jahren 1914-1930," (Inaugural dissertation, Rheinischen Friedrich-Wilhelms-Universität Bonn, 1980).

13 The distinctions between poetry and the representational arts were established in 1766 by Gotthold Ephraim Lessing in his *Laocoön: An Essay on the Limits of Painting and Poetry*, trans. Edward Allen McCormick (1766; Baltimore: Johns Hopkins University Press, 1984). Lessing tried to define the aesthetic laws governing the verbal art of poetry (time) and the visual art of painting (space). In his preface to the 1984 translation of Lessing's essay, Michael Fried characterized the essay as "Lessing's invention of the modern concept of an artistic medium." (p. viii)

14 This was the topos of Franz Hemsterhuis (1721-90), "Lettres sur la sculpture" (1765), in *Oeuvres philosophiques*, ed. Louis Susan Podro Meyboom (Leeuwarden: W. Eekhoff, 1846-50). Hemsterhuis deserves further study by art historians. Paul Frankl, in a chapter entitled "Stylistic Polarities" of his *The Gothic: Literary Sources and Interpretations through Eight Centuries* (Princeton: Princeton University Press, 1960), said: "The tendency to create pairs of antithetical concepts had appeared in Hemsterhuis merely as a clever mode of expression. It was adopted by Schiller, however, as well as by the brothers Schlegel, and has continued to flourish down to the present." (p. 772)

15 I use these terms to speak to a modern reader. Lessing, for example, would have applied the term "epic poetry" instead of "drama."

16 For a clear, concise exposition of the Old Testament prefigurations of the *Pietà*, see Tadeusz Dobrzeniecki, "Mediaeval Sources of the Pietà," *Bulletin du Musée National de Varsovie* 8 (1967): 5-24.

[17] Pinder (1920), pp. 150-57. See Sandro Sticca, *The 'Planctus Mariae' in the Dramatic Tradition of the Middle Ages*, trans. Joseph R. Berrigan (Georgia: The University of Georgia Press, 1988), for a formal study of the motif of the Laments of the Virgin.

[18] For criticism of Pinder's thesis, see W. Lipphardt, "Studien zu den Marienklagen," *Beiträge zur Geschichte der deutschen Sprache und Literatur* 58 (1934): 390-444; Hans Swarzenski, "Quellen zum deutschen Andachtsbild," *Zeitschrift für Kunstgeschichte* 4 (1935): 141-44; and R. Berliner, "Bemerkungen zu einigen Darstellungen des Erlösers als Schmerzensmanns," *Das Münster* 9 (1956): 96-117, esp. p. 112. Lipphardt (1934), contesting Pinder, proposed that the sources of the *Pietà* were in profane literature, German epic drama, and courtly epic. This approach was recently developed further by Ute Schwabe, "Sigune Kriemhilt, Maria und der geliebte Tode," in *Zwei Frauen vor dem Tode*, Verhandelingen van de Koninklijke Academie voor Wetenschappen, Letteren en Schone Kunsten van België, Klasse der Letteren 132 (Brussels: Paleis der Academiën, 1989): 77-143, with illustrations. E. Reiners-Ernst, *Das freudvolle Vesperbild und die Anfänge der Pieta-Vorstellung*, Abhandlung der Bayerischen Benediktiner-Akademie, vol. 2 (Munich: Neuer Filser Verlag, 1939) identified the *Pietàs* of the Middle Ages with the Germanic concept of fidelity: *triuwe*. See Lech Kalinowski, *Geneza Piety Średniowiecznej* (Cracow: Krakowska Drukarnia Naukowa, 1953): 108.

[19] The notion of longing and medieval sculpture calls to mind, indeed urges us to reconsider, parallels with Johann Joachim Winckelmann's views of antique sculpture. See Gert Schiff, "Introduction," in *German Essays on Art History* (New York: Continuum, 1988), esp. pp. xv-xvi.

[20] Pinder (1920), pp. 148-49. A stimulating and perceptive treatment of this same issue, which I have frequently consulted, is offered by Elisabeth Dunn entitled, "The non-narrative content of the northern European Pieta Figure: Experiential," (unpub. essay, College of the Holy Cross, Worcester, Massachusetts, 1985).

[21] Dehio (1923), p. 120.

[22] One is reminded here of Charles Rufus Morey, whose magnificent interpretation of medieval art has been brushed aside in much the same way. The inaccuracies of dates in Pinder's work outweigh, for many scholars, the brilliance of his theoretical interpretation. Stimulus from poetry to painting also forms part of a major debate predating Lessing (see n. 13 above). Interest in the parallels survived in the movement entitled *Strukturforschung*, which believed that poets and painters are joint bearers of a central pattern of sensibility. This movement was guided by Guido Kaschnitz von Weinberg and Friedrich Matz and is discussed by George Kubler, *The Shape of Time* (New Haven: Yale University Press, 1962): 27; and Sheldon Nodelman, "Structural Analysis in Art and Anthropology," in *Structuralism*, ed. Jacques Ehrmann (Garden City: Doubleday, 1970): 79-93.

[23] Friedrich Nietzsche, "The Birth of Tragedy out of the Spirit of Music" (1872), in *The Birth of Tragedy and the Case of Wagner*, trans. Walter Kaufmann (New York: Random House, 1967): 50.

[24] It is curious that Panofsky's framing of the *Andachtsbild* problem is similar to Pinder's and Dehio's, when he says that it is as different from both narrative and hieratic representation as "lyric is from epic or drama, on one side, or from liturgical poetry on the other" (Panofsky [1927], p. 264). Intellectual biographers of Pinder would rather interpret his interest in sculpture as the result of his belief in sculpture's essential German spirit. See Marlite Halbertsma, *Wilhelm Pinder en de Duitse Kunstgeschiedenis* (Groningen: Forsten, 1985).

[25] Nietzsche (1872; 1967), p. 50. According to Kaufmann the first edition of *The Birth of Tragedy* appeared in 1872, and it was published again with "slight textual changes" in 1874 and 1878; in 1886, Nietzsche gave it a new title page. I wish to recognize the fine essay, which I have consulted while preparing this section of the book, by Susan A. Nowicki entitled, "The Spirit Behind the Form: Wilhelm Pinder's *Die Pietà* and Friedrich Nietzsche's *Birth of Tragedy*," (unpub. essay, College of the Holy Cross, Worcester, Massachusetts, 1989) written in a tutorial jointly directed by myself and Irena Makarushka (Bowdoin College).

[26] Pinder (1922), p. 4.

[27] Nietzsche (1872; 1967), p. 55.

[28] Ibid.

[29] Ibid., p. 33.

[30] The German art historians' interest in comparing "German" medieval sculpture with Greek is presently under detailed investigation by Kathryn Brush (Mellon Fellow, Harvard University). See her essay on "The Renaissance Paradigm: Founding Perspectives on the Study of Gothic Sculpture" (Paper delivered at the International Congress of Mediaeval Studies, Kalamazoo, Michigan, May 1990).

[31] Pinder (1922), p. 4.

[32] Nietzsche (1872; 1967), p. 34.

[33] Elizabeth Foerster-Nietzsche, ed., *The Nietzsche-Wagner Correspondence* (New York: Liveright, 1949): 1-2.

[34] Nietzsche (1872; 1967), p. 56.

[35] Richard Wagner, "The Origins of Modern Opera, Drama, and Music," in *Wagner on Music and Drama: A Compendium of Richard Wagner's Prose Works*, ed. A. Goldman and E. Sprinchorn, trans. H. Ashton Ellis (1846-1879; New York: Da Capo Press, 1964): 95-178, esp. section 7, "Essence of the Romance," pp. 136-38. 'This dying, with the yearning after it, is the sole true content of the art which issued from the Christian myth. . . . The conscious stripping off the physical body, achieved with the whole force of will, the purposed demolition of actual being, was the object of all Christian art; which therefore could only be limned, described, but never represented, and least of all in drama. . . . The Passion plays of the Middle Ages represented the sufferings of Jesus in the form of a series of living pictures: the chief and most affecting of these pictures showed Jesus hanging on the cross; hymns and psalms were sung during the performance. The legend, that Christian form of the romance, could alone give charm to a portrayal of the Christian stuff, because it appealed only to the fantasy — as alone was possible with this stuff — and not to physical vision. To music alone was it reserved to represent this stuff to the senses also, namely, by an outwardly perceptible motion.''

[36] For an introduction to this situation and the overwhelming force (among painters, musicians, and intellectuals) of the aesthetic paradigm of "Wagnerism," see Kermit S. Champa, *The Rise of Landscape Painting in France: From Corot to Monet*, exh. cat., The Currier Gallery of Art, Manchester, New Hampshire (New York: Abrams, 1991): 23-63.

[37] See Heinrich Dilly, "Review of Marlite Halbertsma's *Wilhelm Pinder en de Duitse Kunstgeschiedenis*," in *Kunstchronik* 40 (September 1987): 444-50, esp. p. 450. The Jewish problem was already immanent by 1927. See David Carrier, "Circa 1640," *New Literary History* 21 (1989-90): 649-70.

[38] On the origin of the *Vesperbild*, see Wolfgang Krönig, "Rheinische Vesperbilder aus Leder und ihr Umkreis," *Westdeutsches Jahrbuch für Kunstgeschichte* 24 (1962): 97-191.

[39] That the *Pietà* may be art specifically intended for women has been suggested by numerous scholars; their work awaits a solid historiographical analysis. Some of the authors who hold this position are: Julius Baum, *Gotische Bildwerke Schwabens* (Augsburg and Stuttgart: Benno Filser, 1921); Walter Passarge, *Das deutsche Vesperbild im Mittelalter* (Cologne: F.J. Marcan, 1924); *Rhin-Meuse* (1972), pp. 30-31; Leonhard Küppers, "Marienklage," in *Die Gottesmutter. Marienbild in Rheinland und in Westfalen*, exh. cat., vol. 1 (Recklinghausen: Aurel Bongers, 1974): 277-90; W. Blank, "Umsetzung der Mystik in den Frauenklöstern," in *Mystik am Oberrhein und in benachbarten Gebieten*, exh. cat., Augustinermuseum Freiburg im Breisgau (Freiburg im Breisgau, 1978): 25-36; Johannes Werner, "Frauenfrömmigkeit: zur Entstehung der mittelalterlichen Andachtsbilder," *Münster* 35 / 1 (1982): 21-26; and Jeffrey Hamburger, "The Visual and the Visionary: The Image in Late Medieval Monastic Devotions," *Viator* 20 (1989): 161-82, esp. pp. 163-64. H. Van Os in his review of *Das Bild und sein Publikum* criticized Belting for downplaying "claustral devotion" in the west (*Simiolus* 14 / 3-4 [1984]: 226). Lionel Rothkrug speculated on the female devotional origins of the *Pietà* in healing shrines of the southern territories in Germany in his "Popular Religion and Holy Shrines: Their Influence on the Origins of the German Reformation and Their Role in German Cultural Development," in *Religion and the People, 800-1700*, ed. James Obelkevich (Durham: University of North Carolina Press, 1979): 20-86.

[40] Belting (1990), p. 41.

[41] Michael Baxandall, for example, developed a theory of artistic invention vis-à-vis the notion of interior vision or "private visualization" in quattrocento Italian painting. See Michael Baxandall, *Painting and Experience in Fifteenth-Century Italy: A Primer in the Social History of Pictorial Style* (London: Oxford University Press, 1972), esp. p. 47.

[42] A fascinating look at the use of images, Gregorian and other, appeared while I was in the course of finishing this book: David Freedberg's *The Power of Images: Studies in the History and Theory of Response* (Chicago and London: University of Chicago Press, 1989). Especially pertinent is the chapter entitled "*Invisibilia per visibilia*: Meditation and the Uses of Theory," pp. 161-91. The best critique (and so eloquently articulated) of art historians' unfailing and uncritical application to medieval art of the so-called Gregorian dictum of "art as texts for the illiterate" is by Lawrence G. Duggan, "Was art really the 'book of the illiterate'?" *Word & Image* 5 / 3 (1989): 227-51. The classic study of popular devotion in the medieval Low Countries is Jacques Toussaert, *Le sentiment religieux en Flandre à la fin du moyen âge* (Paris: Librairie Plon, 1963).

[43] Emile Mâle, *L'Art religieux de la fin du moyen âge*, 5th ed. (Paris: Armand Colin, 1949): 95.

[44] E. Mâle, "Le renouvellement de l'art par les mystères à la fin du moyen âge," *Gazette des Beaux-Arts* 46.1 / 31 (1904): 89-106, 215-30, 283-301, 379-94.

[45] Mâle (1949), p. 4. An important word to be understood historiographically, "picturesque" needs to be examined in the context of the eighteenth-century debate over the polarity of the arts, especially around Hemsterhuis. See above, n. 14.

[46] Ibid., p. 126.

[47] Ibid., p. 125. Confraternities were being founded in great numbers at that time, many specifically to venerate the Virgin of Sorrows [Fr. *Vierge de Pitié*]. For the Feast of the Seven Sorrows, see *Analecta Bollandiana* 12 (1893): 333ff. In 1423 the Synod of Cologne added to the feasts of the Virgin / the feasts of her anguish and sorrows. See J.D. Mansi, *Sacrorum Con-*

ciliorium, vol. 28 (Venice, 1785), col. 1057. For the Virgin of the Seven Sorrows in Belgium, see H. De Vis, "De Mariavoorstellingen in Vlaamsch Brabant," *Eigen Schoon & De Brabander*, n.s. 9, 17 / 3-4 (1934): 107-10; and Ed Speelman, *Belgium Marianum. Histoire du culte de Marie en Belgique* (Paris and Tournai: Casterman, 1859); for Germany, see *Stabat Mater. Maria unter dem Kreuz in der Kunst um 1400*, exh. cat. (Salzburg: Salzburg Cathedral, 1970): 31, 34ff., with a review of the literature.

[48] For criticism of Mâle's thesis of mystery plays as the source, see Belting (1990); Jacques Mesnil, *L'Art au nord et au sud des Alpes à l'époque de la renaissance; études comparatives* (Brussels: Van Oest, 1911); and K. Künstle, *Ikonographie der christliche Kunst*, vol. 1 (Freiburg im Breisgau: Herder, 1926-28).

[49] James H. Marrow, *Passion Iconography in Northern European Art of the Later Middle Ages and Early Renaissance: A Study of the Transformation of Sacred Metaphor into Descriptive Narrative* (Courtrai: Van Ghemmert, 1979): 3.

[50] Ibid., p. 2.

[51] Ibid., p. 21.

[52] Ibid., p. 26.

[53] See n. 42 above.

[54] Michael Camille, "Seeing and Reading: Some Visual Implications of Medieval Literacy and Illiteracy," *Art History* 8 / 1 (1985): 26-49. Camille makes some points in the direction of ordinary spectators, but a more comprehensive investigation of precisely how much "illiterate" people knew of "textual" things is still needed.

[55] See Panofsky's (1927) views on the necessity for more scientific methods in art history. See also J.E. Ziegler, "Wilhelm Worringer's Theory of Transcendental Space in Gothic Architecture: A Medievalist's Perspective" (Paper delivered at Hofstra University, April 1991; in preparation for publication with the conference papers).

[56] Otto G. Von Simson, "*Compassio* and *Co-Redemptio* in Roger van der Weyden's *Descent from the Cross*," *The Art Bulletin* 35 (1953): 9-16; and Dobrzeniecki (1967).

[57] See Mâle (1949), 16ff. The relation to painting is also a problem of sources. For example, the influence of Rogier van der Weyden (Rogier's *Deposition*, 1435) on sculptures of the *Pietà* has been treated many times. See John Steyaert, "Some Observations Concerning the Pietà from O.-L.-V.-van-Ginderbuiten in Leuven," in *Archivum Artis Lovaniense. Bijdragen tot de geschiedenis van de kunst der Nederlanden. Opgedragen aan Prof. Em. Dr. J.K. Steppe*, ed. M. Smeyers (Leuven: Peeters, 1981), p. 23; Joseph de Borchgrave d'Altena, "Vierges de Pitié de chez nous," *Annales de la Société royale d'Archéologie de Bruxelles* 46 (1942-43), pp. 266-67; and especially, Jos. Destrée, "A propos de l'influence de Roger van der Weyden (Roger de la Pasture) sur la sculpture brabançonne," *Annales de la Société royale d'Archéologie de Bruxelles* 28 (1919): 1-11. Edgar Baes, "Roger Van der Weyden," *Fédération Artistique* 29 / 3 (1901): 19. Baes mentions that Louis Maeterlinck had two articles, in the *Gazette des Beaux-Arts* and *Chronique des Arts et de la Curiosité*, about Roger's connection with sculpture, especially Tournai sculpture, as studied by des Haisnes, de la Grange, and Cloquet. Louis Maeterlinck, "Roger van der Weyden, sculpteur," *Gazette des Beaux-Arts* 43.2 / 26 (1901): 409. I wish to thank Victoria Potts for calling my attention to Maeterlinck. See also Julius Baum, "Vesperbild aus dem Kreise Rogier van der Weyden," *Pantheon* 4 (1929): 563-69, who in tracing the source of Rogier's motif, relates it to a *Pietà* in the collection of Margaret of Austria (see below, Inv. no. 145); and Lucie Van Caster-Guiette, "Réminiscences Rogériennes dans la

sculpture brabançonne," in *Mélanges d'archéologie et d'histoire de l'art offerts au Professeur Jacques Lavalleye* (Leuven: Université de Louvain, 1970): 297-304. For the *Pietà* in manuscript illumination, see the Pierpont Morgan Library's *The Golden Age of Dutch Manuscript Painting*, exh. cat. (New York: George Braziller, 1990); and Panofsky, "Reintegration of a Book of Hours Executed in the Workshop of the 'Maître des Grandes Heures de Rohan,'" in *Medieval Studies in Memory of Arthur Kingsley Porter*, vol. 2, ed. W.R.M. Koehler (Cambridge, Massachusetts: Harvard University Press, 1939), pp. 479-99.

[58] There are a great number of relationships to suggest that the "pictorial" is the dominant hermeneutic in *Pietà* studies, for example, that the anecdotal presence of persons like John and the Magdalen is important to the *Pietà*, that it came to Italy from Byzantium, that it was reinvigorated by painting, and finally that the *Pietà* completed its course in *the* most painting-emulative genre of sculpture, the narrative retable. For an excellent overview and bibliography of the relations between narrative painting and the Netherlandish retable, which adopted a narrative series or cycle approach to the sculpture, see Piotr Skubiszewski, "Le retable gothique sculpté: Entre le dogme et l'univers humain," in *Le retable d'Issenheim et la sculpture au nord des Alpes à la fin du moyen âge*, exh. cat., ed. Christian Heck (Colmar: Musée d'Underlinden, 1989): 13-48, esp. 23-30; and Robert Didier, "Sculptures et retables des anciens Pays-Bas méridionaux des années 1430-1460: Traditions et innovations pour le Haut-Rhin et l'Allemagne du Sud," in *Le retable d'Issenheim* (1989): 49-79. See also above nn. 8, 57 for a discussion of precedents in painting.

[59] A general review of mysticism is available in Peter Dinzelbacher and Dieter R. Bauer, eds., *Frauenmystik im Mittelalter*, Wissenschaftliche Studientagung der Akademie der Diözese Rottenburg-Stuttgart, 22-25 February 1984 in Weingarten, (Ostfildern: Schwabenverlag, 1985); Steven Katz, "Recent Works on Mysticism," *History of Religions* 25 (1985): 76-86; Richard Kieckhefer, "Major Currents in Late Medieval Devotion," in *World Spirituality* 17 (1987): 75-108; for the Low Countries, see "Van Hadewijch tot Maria Petyt. Vrouwen en mystiek in de Nederlanden van 13de tot de 17de eeuw," conference held in Antwerp, 5-7 September 1989, sponsored by the Ruusbroecgenootschap, with proceedings to be published by *Ons Geestelijk Erf* (in press). For mysticism and women visionaries, see Peter Dinzelbacher, *Vision und Visionsliteratur im Mittelalter,* Monographien zur Geschichte des Mittelalters 23 (Stuttgart: Anton Hiersemann, 1981).

[60] For a review of the state of the question on visions and art, see above n. 39; and Hamburger (1989), esp. pp. 165-69. The classic studies are by Ernst Benz, "Christliche Mystik und christliche Kunst (zur theologischen Interpretation mittelalterlicher Kunst)," *Deutsche Vierteljahrsschrift für Literaturwissenschaft und Geistesgeschichte* 12 / 12 (1934): 22-48 and idem, *Die Vision: Erfahrungsformen und Bilderwelt* (Stuttgart: E. Klett, 1969); see also Sixten Ringbom, "Devotional Images and Imaginative Devotions: Notes on the Place of Art in Late Medieval Private Piety," *Gazette des Beaux-Arts* 73 (1969): 159-70; C. Frugoni, "Le mistiche, le visioni e l'iconografia: rapporti ed influssi," (Todi: Accademia Tudertina, 1982): 5-45; Peter Dinzelbacher (1981) for additional bibliography. To see what the problem looks like when it functions within gendered discourse of our own day, see Caroline Walker Bynum "The Body of Christ in the Later Middle Ages: A Reply to Leo Steinberg," *Renaissance Quarterly* 39 / 3 (1986): 399-439.

[61] As quoted by Elisabeth Vavra, "Bildmotiv und Frauenmystik — Funktion und Rezeption," in Dinzelbacher / Bauer (1985): 210-30.

⁶² Angela da Foligno had a similar vision, in which she held the body of Christ as a *Pietà*. For a discussion of this part of her *vita*, see Frugoni (1982), esp. pp. 23-24, 36-37.

⁶³ See above, n. 39.

⁶⁴ This interest in a sociological and contextual approach has guided scholars to investigate, for example as Hamburger (1989) recently did, the degree of interdependency or departure from the ideal of Cistercian (male) devotion and ideology and the functioning of bizarrely innovative devotional imagery in their Cistercian nuns. See above nn. 39, 60, 61 for additional bibliography.

⁶⁵ See above nn. 39, 60.

⁶⁶ Belting (1990).

⁶⁷ Ibid., p. 189.

⁶⁸ Ibid., p. 90.

⁶⁹ Ibid., p. 84 and n. 45.

⁷⁰ Ibid., p. 90.

⁷¹ In this Belting in a sense answers Panofsky's call in 1915 for a documented art history that would be able to reconstruct objects accurately.

⁷² Ziegler, "The Medieval Virgin" (1989), pp. 251-64.

⁷³ Richard Hamann took a similar position in 1943 in an essay, now largely forgotten, dedicated to Wilhelm Worringer on his sixtieth birthday. See Richard Hamann, "Die Kategorie der Stofflichkeit in der bildenden Kunst," in *Neue Beiträge deutscher Forschung: Wilhelm Worringer zum 60. Geburtstag*, ed. Erich Fidder (Königsberg: Kanter Verlag, 1943): 143-50. Hamann says: "Da das Sichtbare allein nicht das Wesen des Stofflichen bestimmt, sondern allein die Erfahrung über Verschiebbarkeit der Teile bei Berührung mit der Hand, so spielen in der Wahrnehmung des Stofflichen auch die passiven Tastgefühle an Stelle der motorisch aktiven Formbewegungen eine Rolle, das Gefühl des Glatten und Rauhen, und bei letzterem als dem besonders Stofflichen die Annehmlichkeit auf der Haut, die wir beim Streicheln als ein bis zum Kitzel sich steigerndes Wohlgefühl erfahren. Das Stoffliche führt damit in das Gebiet des Sinnlichen hinein." (p. 146)

51

PART II

THE BEGUINES: SETTING AND AUDIENCE

CHAPTER 2

APPROACHING THE PIETA VIA THE BEGUINES
THE PATHS OF INQUIRY

The approach undertaken in these pages needs explanation. As a means for exploring the origins and popularity of the sculpted *Pietà* in the southern Low Countries during the later Middle Ages, we will examine the Beguines, women who lived together in semi-religious communities and were active promoters and users of devotional objects like the *Pietà*. It is not a history of the Beguines we are about to undertake. To be sure, it is important to review a certain amount of historical background, and we will do so momentarily. But my reason for focusing on the late medieval Beguines is this community's usefulness in explaining larger cultural and social themes characteristic of early viewers of the *Pietà*. I asked questions and pursued data not so much out of a desire for comprehensive knowledge of the Beguines as out of the belief (which in time became conviction) that the Beguines were a model society of ordinary people, a composite collective in which systems of meaning, based in everyday experience, could be observed by the modern researcher.

I am interested in probing the nature of the experience of looking at *Pietàs*. As an art historian, then, it is not viewers of the present who interest me as much as those of the past. Modern, Catholic cult practice is emerging from the domain of folklore and becoming a serious field of research among ethnographers and anthropologists, who have recently turned their attention to cultic practices in the West, investigating modern pilgrimages and modern ritual activities. [1] Their findings and the kinds of questions they ask certainly form a significant part of the conceptual and informational apparatus of this study. Yet I must stress here that my interests lie in the distant past, with viewers who cannot be observed or spoken to. Despite my historical aims, it has nevertheless been the modern devout — the Catholic woman wrapped in prayer before the image — who is so deep in my experience, so much a part of what

I know about commonplace devotion that it is she, I grant, who directed me to construct the concept of "the historical viewer" in the way that I do. Belgian women still grasp their bellies deep in prayer before old medieval *Pietàs*, their eyes fixed upon the image, absorbed in dialogue with it. This relation between woman and image is a cultural reality in many Catholic countries, despite preferences and sensibilities of the more rational members of society, who find such behavior excessive, even repugnant, in any period. [2] Women, we know, prayed to images in the fourteenth century, too. Why? Why beseech the inert matter of sculpture? Have the reasons for doing so, and the associated effect, changed distinctly with the course of time? It is the premise of this book that on the deepest level of experience, they have not.

I write from the belief — indeed it is what guided me to frame the questions of my research — that the relation between believing beholder and *Pietà* is, on one level, constant, unaffected by the time and place in which it happens. That perspective, seeking to reveal continuity across time, is challenged these days by the rise in academic inquiry of what is termed the new historicism. That view celebrates difference, the inherent and inescapable conditioning of particular times and places, and few among us would deny that cultural relativism presently wields a sovereign arm in determining the point of view scholars now take before they proceed with their interpretive tasks. No investigator (so the theory goes in simplest fashion) can escape receiving and transmitting the signs and symbols of meaning through his or her own signs and symbols of meaning. This is a reality which has been predetermined by personal and cultural forces completely out of an individual's control; we are 'of our times,' and we cannot escape that.

My approach to this topic is a result of a 'reality' born of years of visiting churches in Europe and of having been raised as a scholar by what amounts to a particular family of art historians. I cannot deny, then, that the special system of meaning I am about to explore among the Beguines arose from an interaction between it and the one resulting from my professional, and personal, reality. Standing back from it I see, for example, that the impetus to look for signs of the Beguines' ordinariness, and for how inner feeling was both conditioned and articulated, springs from present conditions. We find ourselves at a moment when the theater in which Roman Catholics enact passionate scenes with cult statues appears about to end, and when the emotive or affective messages of objects like the *Pietà*, long around us, seem about to lose their potency. [3] Another important factor shaping my viewpoint derives from the simple fact that scholars of religious art are increasingly anxious to link historical spectator-ship with something definite, that is, with the demonstrable, recorded events of the past, such as the marketing of art, the social status of patrons, the literary sources of imagery, or the rites and rituals of societies as written down at the time. [4]

A long time ago Erwin Panofsky cautioned art historians not to rely too total-ly on the object for their information. [5] Art historians should be wary, he warned, of relying on the object as evidence alone, without historically reconstructing it through written documents. Documents are the special purveyors of the precise circumstances in which an object made its original appearance; documents expose the why, for whom, and when an object was made, and what purpose it was meant originally to serve. Panofsky's words proved to be something of a prophecy. His conviction that art historians can (and should) accurately rebuild the context of an object's past is now standard practice. This has been true especially over the last two decades, when late medieval and early Renaissance scholars have turned ever more enthusiastically toward period documents for help with "decoding" an image's meaning. [6] This they have done in numerous ways, and from a variety of technical, social, literary, and theological perspectives. That approach, firmly contextual and historical, and grounded in the evidence of the written word, stands at the center of my art historical culture, the culture of the specialized interpreter.

For me to offer, as I do in the present study, an alternative to the position that meaning is always culturally constructed and historically located (and therefore profoundly altered in its substance according to time and place) is something of a conscious affirmation of the present. My desire to explore the Beguines' ordinariness as much as their spectator-feelings arose directly from the context of specialized academic discourse, from the questions that it did and did not ask, no less than from the kinds of viewing experiences that its methods can and cannot address.

I have also been prompted to test alternative approaches by something else, by what seemed to be the *Pietà's* profoundly non-discursive and wholly per-sonal, affective appeal, still manifestly at work. People come to the image, as they always have, to pray; there they activate the inner self in a non-public, in-trospective dialogue. To investigate in a scientific way the phenomenon of the continuous living bond of believer to object, admittedly gained from personal observation, art history offers no acceptable methods at present. With its com-mitment to historicism and with its central interpretive apparatus still focused on written documentation, art history is at this moment practically ineffective as a bed of interpretive models. Moreover, it is even quite consciously uninterested in the results of research studies that attempt to explore anything like "universal" realms of ordinariness, feeling, emotion, sensation, and the like. While my approach is similar to that of my colleagues in being determined by contemporary discourse and by a belief in the inescapable imposition of the cultural present upon our thinking, vast differences do arise. I have found that working within the restrictions of current methodologies has not enabled me to answer all of the questions my material poses. Although we can never escape the degree to which we are conditioned by our own time and culture, we need not deny the existence of certain universal, timeless principles.

To address questions about ordinariness and spectator-feeling, I have used other traditions of scholarship as models. Cultural anthropology and structural anthropology within it have tested a range of definitions and analytical procedures for describing social relations that are helpful for understanding the Beguines as a society — and as an ordinary society, at that. As we will see in chapter 4, anthropology helps to expose convincing evidence about the Beguines' pervasive social identity. Of central importance is an interpretation of semi-religiosity as assisted by anthropological theory. Historians have not yet explored the Beguines' social identity subtly enough or in ways that would enable scholars from other disciplines, such as art history, to profit from historical interpretation. [7] Thus, until positivist, historical research illuminates the socially complex identity of the Beguine movement, anthropology offers a helpful point of departure for interpretation rather than a fixed or final model. [8]

I have also capitalized on a body of older art historical theory in formulating my approach to the problem of spectator-feeling. That theory advances a view of artistic experience that claims the following: "Each art," as the English critic Walter Pater wrote in 1877, "has its incommunicable element, its untranslatable order of impressions. . . ." [9] The theory holds that a distinct sensation takes place in the experience of an art form and that that sensation cannot be had any place but in that particular form. Pater stressed the purity of artistic media. If, for example, the distinctive experiential impact of poetry could be either translated into or gained by looking at architecture, then poetry would cease to exist as a distinct and necessary mode of communication, inviolable and separable from the other arts. The arts, and the various media they adopt, offer unique kinds of experience, experience which is not conceptual,

58

not motivated by language, but sensory, which is to say, taken in through the senses and affecting to individuals in various ways designated as emotion, pleasure, sensation, and imagination. Pater articulates it thus:

> It is the mistake of much popular criticism to regard poetry, music, and painting — all the various products of art — as but translations into different languages of one and the same fixed quantity of imaginative thought. . . . In this way, the sensuous element in art, and with it almost everything in art that is essentially artistic, is made a matter of indifference; . . . For, as art addresses not pure sense, still less the pure intellect, but the 'imaginative reason' through the senses, there are differences of kind in aesthetic beauty, corresponding to the differences in kind of the gifts of sense themselves. [10]

This school of thought (perhaps the better term is school of criticism) has been linked with various movements in philosophy and aesthetic theory, such as formalism, empathy theory, and a kind of neo-Romanticism. [11] Its historiography lies unfortunately beyond the scope of the present undertaking. [12] What is important, however, is that there exists a great tradition of writing about spectator-feeling, once widespread if currently out-of-vogue, which has sought to link the formal properties of given media with experiences that cannot be had elsewhere, nor accurately translated, transcribed, or described via written terminology. With this book we return to some of those premises.

We may recall that, like Pater before him, William James also turned to music as an analogy of the mystical experience. Music is closest to mystical union, he claimed, because the two share an "ineffability." James was acknowledging the impossibility of expressing such a state by means of words or concepts; that state James called "immediate feeling," noting that it has "no content but what the five senses supply." James was one voice among many at the turn of the century to speak in support of the existence and fundamental human importance of non-discursive sensations. He claimed that we can savor those sensations only through certain experiences: music, art, love, and mystical union with God. Most turn-of-the-century writers hinged their understanding of (art-induced) feeling, as James did, on music. [13] The reason is that the content of music was considered indistinguishable or at least inseparable from its form:

59

It is the art of music which most completely realizes this artistic ideal, this perfect identification of matter and form. In its consummate moment, the end is not distinct from the matter, the subject from the expression; they inhere in it and completely saturate each other; and to it, therefore to the condition of its perfect moments, all the arts may be supposed to constantly tend to and aspire. [14] (Pater)

In that art form, emotions are regarded as ends in themselves. [15] The nineteenth century did profoundly believe in the sensation evoked by music's supposed subjectlessness, by its power to arouse feeling, passion, and heightened sensation, [16] although for some this was a terrifying prospect. "Music," said Tolstoy, "in general is a terrible thing. . . . Music makes me forget myself, my real situation. It transports me into a state that is not my natural one. . . . Indeed it is a terrible power to place in anyone's hands." [17] This deep cultural belief in music's power led writers dealing with the other arts, beyond music and fiction, to explore the possibility that analogous emotional responses might be happening in other artistic media as well.

This view is explored again by the present study of the *Pietà*. I attempt to disclose what the nature of "sensation" or "immediate feeling" was like when ordinary people of centuries past beheld a *Pietà*. I presume that the substance of that experience for many believers, but especially for the illiterate, unlearned, and naive, did not occur in thought or concepts about liturgical and sacramental rites, nor in reason, exegesis or comparison of texts, but in a kind of direct feeling — like being in love or being overtaken by music, to use the metaphors given us by the nineteenth century — that is nearly impossible to describe in words. And I presume that the medium (sculpture) which initiated the experience was the primary vehicle of its affect. More specifically I assert that the sculpture evoked, guided, and aroused sensations of a particular, tactile sort. [18]

The sculptural medium of the *Pietà* is a language, which like any language requires the participant to have fluency and experience to understand it. If we believe William James at all, then, we must proceed by understanding that not everyone "hears" or is moved by music, or falls in love, or unites sublimely and totally with their godhead. The sensations produced by the tactile language of the sculpted *Pietà*, and the immediate and unique feelings that its language evokes, come to those prepared, willing, and inclined to have them. What I write about here is the special culture of the Beguines that renders them especially able to pursue tactile sensations and sculptural experiences.

60

My approach to examining the proclivity of these individuals to experience special sensations in particular cultural forms in order to understand human feeling is not at all the same as investigating the psychological or cultural constructions people use to comprehend emotion and feeling. Of course, individuals conceive their emotions and express their feelings to one another differently in different cultures. As Catherine Lutz convincingly argued in *Unnatural Emotions* (1981), "Recognizing emotion is a cultural rather than natural category." [19] When we use the word *emotion* we do so according to Western ideology and its own cultural constructions. This is hardly disputable. But I am not writing here about emotion or feeling as they are used in language or speech. Nor am I concerned with how everyday people describe the states of those feelings. I am not investigating what Lutz terms "emotional concepts," nor how everyday people "indigenously conceptualize" emotions. [20]

This is not a book about the "emotional content of everyday life." [21] I write with an eye not toward everyday feelings of happiness, anger, fear, shame, or embarrassment, for example. I write about a rather separate domain of experience. The experience of which I speak is not an everyday one; it does not arise ordinarily within day-to-day social intercourse, even if "ordinary" people are precisely the ones to have it. It is a distinctive sphere of experience, generated by special categories of things. James defined those things when he likened mystical union to listening to music, in other words, when he likened the willingness and inclination to give oneself totally over to the heightened, absorptive, direct effect of sensory experience. This is not at all how we tend to define emotion and feeling today.

The separateness of such sensations has been the greatest obstacle to many an intellectual's ability to accept them, as has the notion that not everyone can or will be able to undergo them. The direct experience of feeling gained by art, music, or James's mysticism and love, is a privileged one, whose causes lie not in social class or in materialistic preparation. The sensations and feelings of which I speak could not, in that sense, be more unlike ordinary emotions. [22]

The reality of the longevity and Catholic universality surrounding the *Pietà* presses me to pursue those distinctive, sensory feelings once again in this study. I write with the belief that "aesthetic emotion," as it came to be termed in nineteenth- and twentieth-century discourse, has always been more or less a functioning part of the beholding of objects, although the terms of its happening have assumed any number of different cultural formats. Today's practioners of formalism are moved by the "magical power of art" [23] and believe in its special properties no less than did illiterate, Christian devouts some six hundred years ago. This is not to say that people back then were consciously articulating abstract (formal) values of form, line, shape, and contour, among others. Nor is this to say that people back then were not reminded when looking at *Pietàs* of immediate situations, like the yearly elevation of the Host they had just witnessed, the sermon they had heard the other day describing the gruesome horrors of Christ's torture, or possibly the physical and emotional sensation of seeing and touching the corpse of a loved one — situations that do nearly totally escape the twentieth century viewer. It would be absurd indeed to claim that the viewing consciousness could be devoid of local, indigenous, and timely references at any point in time. And part of this book, in fact, is dedicated to revealing just how imposing on meaning those local, period references can be. But viewing can, for some people, also be simply and deeply moving, and it is there, when all conscious rendering of memory and thought-references falls away and is replaced by indescribable sensation, by affect and a private, inner feeling — it is at that moment when, in any spectator of any age and from any epoch, "aesthetic sensation" arises and dominates.

I am supported in this view of "aesthetic emotion" by anthropological studies. In 1962 Claude Lévi-Strauss produced his classic, consciously scandalous work, *The Savage Mind*. The opening chapter, "The Science of the Concrete," concerns itself with that pre-eminent domain of the history of art, the "aesthetic sense," [24] called "aesthetic emotion" by Lévi-Strauss himself. [25] His aim was to establish that there are two "modes of acquiring knowledge, magic and science." [26] Lévi-Strauss argued that these modes "require the same sort of mental operations and they differ not so much in kind as in the different types of phenomena to which they are applied." [27] Magic for Lévi-Strauss, then, is a mode of scientific thought because it organizes the chaos of natural phenomena. It differs from the scientific mode not because the mind which applies it is at a different, a more primitive stage of development. Rather, magic accesses nature, according to Lévi-Strauss, on a different "strategic level," one more "adapted to perception and imagination than, as science is, removed from them." Magic is also a route to the "object of all science," but it gets there via "sensible intuition." [28]

This schema is important to us, for Lévi-Strauss elaborated his theory around a discussion of art as lying "half-way between scientific knowledge and mythical or magical thought." [29] We discover in this famous first chapter that Lévi-Strauss, one of the most influential thinkers of the twentieth century in any

62

discipline, believed in "intrinsic aesthetic quality" and "aesthetic emotion." And we discover, even more importantly, that his structuralist theory of the acquisition of knowledge pivots on the exposition of a philosophy of art within that theory.

In a brilliant, if at points rather inaccessible, analysis of the aesthetic phenomenon of miniaturization in *A Portrait of a Lady* by the French eighteenth-century painter Clouet, Lévi-Strauss showed how art holds an intermediate position between science and myth, or between structure and event. [30] Art is a balance Lévi-Strauss defined as being between "structure and event, necessity and contingency, the internal and the external, design and anecdote, being and becoming." [31] Aesthetic emotion derives from this balance:

> The aesthetic emotion is the result of this union between structural order and the order of events, which is brought about within a thing created by man and so also in effect by the observer who discovers the possibility of such a union through the work of art. [32]

The structural order in the case of miniatures, according to Lévi-Strauss, allows us to take in an object at a glance. The sheer miniature size of the thing abbreviates the time and effort of that first, crucial, cursory glance. As a result, the viewer's experience of the miniaturized object is such that the sense of sight seems intensified and concentrated, giving the viewer a sense of power or possession. Thus Lévi-Strauss says that miniatures "sustain the illusion" that we know the whole before the parts, and that this illusion "gives rise to a sense of pleasure which can already be called aesthetic on these grounds alone." [33]

Structure, to move more deeply into Lévi-Strauss's framework, is the general property or the intrinsic properties of things. For example, it is a structural quality of the lace collar on Clouet's woman which, in being hand-made, constructed, or an "artefact," [34] to use his term, leads the observer to its particulars. Merely by contemplating the object, the observer is "put in possession of other possible forms of the same work." [35] Thus the work of art takes intrinsic properties of things (the general "structure") and synthesizes them "with properties which depend on a spatial or temporal context" [36] ("events"). The instrinsic property in this case is the lace, with things like degrees of whiteness or frilliness depending on the spatial or temporal context. Aesthetic emotion thus results, in Lévi-Strauss's view, from the observer's discovering through looking at the work such a temporary, exciting union of structure and event. Art makes use of properties, in other words, by which the observer makes intelligible relations with other things.

Now this is a very particular view of art which certainly we would not apply to any period or style of art, although Lévi-Strauss would have us do so from the full range of primitive to academic art. Several points, however, do prove especially applicable to the present study of the *Pietà*. One is that structural anthropologists in the Lévi-Straussian vein argue from the belief that "aesthetic emotion" plays a fundamental part in human experience, especially in our organization of the world around us. Secondly, convinced Lévi-Straussians assert that it is the intrinsic properties of the hand-made artefact that provide the means to do so. Those properties bring about in the observer an awareness and a sense of natural phenomena as being both general and specific, and this effect is exercised uniquely by works of art. Works of art, according to Lévi-Strauss, thus organize reality according to kinds of knowledge not accessible in either of the other two modes of knowledge acquisition, myth and science. And they do so, our third point, by employing aesthetic perception, which starts from an exploitation of the sensible dimensions of the world and by engaging the observer's sensible intuition, that is, the intuition of the senses. How very like James this sounds. That engagement of the senses in turn is what gives rise to that unique mode of knowledge, aesthetic emotion.

The sensible properties of the *Pietà* have to do, as we will discover in Part II, with its sculptural qualities, those of mass, weight, and edge. Those properties are always present in the objects. The observer's sensible intuition is engaged by those properties to organize them first, and generally, as tactile properties, such as hard and soft, rounded or angular, fat or thin, rough or smooth. Following Lévi-Strauss's sequence of experiencing, those properties then put the observer in touch with other possible forms of tactility, and synthesize them with properties which depend on spatial or temporal context.

Viewers of the *Pietà* would, in this schema, have understood the particulars of the tactile in terms which their own experience of touch would have opened them to — of what they touch, perhaps by analogy with the body (the subject of the representation of the *Pietà*), perhaps with flesh itself, or maybe with linens, cloth, and other textiles, or with the foods they prepare. We shall soon link the tactile properties of the *Pietà* (structure) with the specific activities of the single group of users, the Beguines (event) to see how such Lévi-Straussian syntheses were achieved. But the point worth driving home is that the sensible dimensions of the *Pietà* (sculpture) engage the sensible intuition of the observer (touch) to give rise to a kind of experience (tactile aesthetic emotion) that cannot be had elsewhere.

Lévi-Strauss's theory of aesthetic emotion opens a great door. It encourages us to be less concerned with precise material interpretations of the *Pietà* than with the larger social issues of how it might have organized "knowledge," and perhaps still does. In other words, his definition of social and temporal context rests not so much in period or historical specificity as it does in broadly locating the interaction of science, myth, and art. This process of analysis thus seeks to go below the surface of language which, in our case, would mean going below the imagery, below that is to say, the humanity of Christ or semi-religiosity as fourteenth- and fifteenth-century phenomena, to probe the nature of the reality being organized outside such linguistic references.

One of the fascinating aspects of the *Pietà* is of course the fact that this art form appeared in the fourteenth century but did not die out then as so many religious images and structures did. It persisted as a popular object of devotion. In returning to the early period of its appearance, it becomes all the more necessary to peer below the local references and strictly period-bound events to try and locate the nerve center of the sculpture's appeal, for its roots are alive today, if but barely. From Lévi-Strauss we have learned that that fundamental discovery has to do with locating the sensible properties of an object and the sensible intuition it engages in the observer. This I propose takes place in the sculptural-tactile dialogue between *Pietà* and believer, a dialogue that began in the fourteenth century among commonplace believers, and continues today.

[1] Nolan and Nolan (1989), with excellent bibliography; see also Victor Turner and Edith Turner, *Image and Pilgrimage in Christian Culture: Anthropological Perspectives* (New York: Columbia University Press, 1978).

[2] This explains, I believe, why art historians have avoided investigating private devotions. Magic is a perfectly acceptable problem for scientific analysis, but emotional wailing and weeping before an image is not. I suspect many persons share the great German composer Richard Wagner's views on this: "The medieval poem presented Lohengrin in a mystic twilight that filled me with suspicion and that haunting feeling of repugnance with which we look upon the carved and painted saints and martyrs on the highways, or in the churches of Catholic lands." (Richard Wagner [1964], p. 26) Modern art historians may in this sense be described as perhaps "more Protestant" than old image-loving Catholics.

[3] David Freedberg's recent *The Power of Images: Studies in the History and Theory of Response* (Chicago and London: Chicago University Press, 1989) is a challenging call to art historians to reconsider their present posture vis-à-vis the power of images.

[4] The recent, free movement of historians, historians of literature, and literary criticism into the study of the history of art is especially revealing of the trends I cite here.

[5] Erwin Panofsky (1920; 1981), pp. 32-33.

[6] Insofar as late medieval, early Renaissance sculpture is concerned, Michael Baxandall has been especially exemplary. The nature of interpreting the documents is quite another matter; interpretation at least in medieval art history has become intensely neo-positivistic as archival evidence grows more important.

[7] This situation is presently being redressed by Walter Simons, most significantly in his essay, "Theoretical Issues in the Study of the Beguines" (Paper delivered at the Graduate Research Colloquium in Women's Studies, Princeton University, Princeton, New Jersey, 13 February 1991).

[8] My attempt to avoid a positivist approach to both the Beguines and the *Pietà* has been in good measure stimulated by Clifford Geertz's "Deep Play: Notes on the Balinese Cockfight" (1972), in *Interpretive Social Science: A Reader*, ed. Paul Rabinow and William M. Sullivan (Berkeley: University of California Press, 1979): 181-223; and Robert Darnton, *The Great Cat Massacre and Other Episodes in French Cultural History*, 2nd ed. (New York: Vintage Books, 1985). For a review of their approaches, see James Fernandez, "Historians Tell Tales: Of Cartesian Cats and Gallic Cockfights," *Journal of Modern History* 60 (1988): 113-27.

[9] Walter Pater, "The School of Giorgione" (1877), in *The Renaissance: Studies in Art and Poetry* (London: Macmillan and Co., Limited, 1910): 139.

[10] Ibid., p. 130.

[11] I wish to thank the students in my Worringer Seminar (College of the Holy Cross, spring 1990) for their solid research into this area, especially Patricia Pongracz ("Romanticism and Self-Alienation circa 1908: Wilhelm Worringer and Georg Lukâs", Michael Hallet ("Untimely Meditations on the Intellectual Kinship of Wilhelm Worringer and Georg Simmel"), Patricia Lawrence ("The Rise of Science and Art History"), and Laura Panzarino ("Panofsky and Worringer"). On the "presentness" of art, see David Carrier, *Artwriting* (Amherst, Massachusetts: University of Massachusetts Press, 1987). Some writers still believe in the uniqueness of artistic sensation. Saul Bellow delivered inspiring words on "esthetic bliss" during a conference on American writing in Amsterdam, summer 1990, organized by the John Adams Institute. See the report in the *Standaard der Letteren* 16 June 1990.

[12] The formalist approach is assumed to be well known and totally understood today. David Freedberg has printed numerous caustic remarks on formalism, especially in *The Power of Images* (1989) and *Iconoclasts and their Motives* (1985). Freedberg misdefines formalism, I believe, for he views it as "style," in his words, as those "intellectualizing conceptions of immanence, whether the immanence of quality, of formal relationships, or merely the fallacious assumption of emotion within the image itself." (1985, pp. 7-8) See also Arthur Danto, "Review of David Freedberg, *The Power of Images*," *The Art Bulletin* 73/2 (June 1990): 341-42. Criticism (of this sort) of the inherent message of given media centers largely on the notion that the experience of artistic phenomena changes with time and place, that the effect a work of art has on us has been so altered by changing perceptions (transformed by changing

cultural conditions) that formal components of a work of art can no longer be seen or experienced as they were in their "original" state.

13 The critic Roger Fry, for instance, had ideas similar to Pater's and James's about music, which he considered in his, "An Essay on Aesthetics" (1909), reprinted in *Vision and Design* (Cleveland: Meridian Books, 1963): 23, 29, where he wrote that ". . . . of all the arts [music] supplies the strongest stimulus to the imaginative life, and at the same time has the least power of controlling its direction. . . . We must therefore give up the attempt to judge the work of art by its reaction on life, and consider it as an expression of emotions regarded as ends in themselves."

14 Pater (1877; 1910), p. 139.

15 J.E. Ziegler, "The Emergence of a Women's Sensibility in Late Medieval Art in Northern Europe" (Paper delivered at Brown University, Providence, Rhode Island, Spring 1986).

16 For a discussion of music as the aesthetic paradigm of mid-nineteenth century France, see Kermit S. Champa, "The Rise of Landscape Painting in France," in *The Rise of Landscape Painting in France* (1991): 23-63.

17 Leo Tolstoy, *The Kreutzer Sonata*, rev. trans. Isai Kamen, (New York: Vintage Books, 1957): 90-91.

18 An interesting study of tactile evocations in art is Carlo Ginzburg, "Titian, Ovid, and Sixteenth-Century Codes for Erotic Illustration," in *Clues, Myths, and the Historical Method*, trans. John and Anne C. Tedeschi (Baltimore and London: Johns Hopkins University Press, 1989), where he says, "Only later in the sixteenth century did sight emerge slowly as a prominent erotic sense, immediately after touch. In the still unwritten history of the senses, due weight will have to be given to this eroticization of sight in respect to hearing. . . ." (p. 93) Ginzburg's statement accords well with Robert Mandrou who said in his *Introduction à la France moderne (1500-1640): Essai de psychologie historique* (Paris: Editions Albin Michel, 1961) "Jusqu'au XVIIIe siècle au moins, le toucher demeure donc un maître sense . . . ." (p. 79) See also Richard Hamann's views quoted above in chapter 1, n. 73. Hamann's understanding of touch is more like mine and differs significantly from touch as a phenomenological and philosophical category of the aesthetic. On the latter see Richard Wollheim, "On Tactile Values," in *Art and Its Objects: An Introduction to Aesthetics* (New York: Harper Torchbook Edition, 1968): 44-48.

19 Catherine A. Lutz, *Unnatural Emotions: Everyday Sentiments on a Micronesian Atoll & Their Challenge to Western Theory* (Chicago: University of Chicago Press, 1981): 81.

20 Ibid., p. 43.

21 Ibid., p. 46.

22 The history of art has witnessed the resistance of intellectuals most clearly in the attacks against formalism, the late twentieth-century inheritor and propagator of the theory of artistic sensation and emotion. Tolstoy would be in easy company today could he read the condemnations of the formalist approach to art as ridiculous, absurd to think that by *form alone* an individual, some individuals, are certain that they can experience the totality of its meaning. The attack on formalism gave "aesthetic experience," the formalist's concept of that special sensory feeling, a very bad name, which still hangs in the air.

23 Danto (1990), pp. 341-42.

24 Claude Lévi-Strauss, *The Savage Mind* (1962; Chicago: University of Chicago Press, 1966): 12.

25 Ibid., p. 25.
26 Ibid., p. 13.
27 Ibid.
28 Ibid., p. 15.
29 Ibid., p. 23.
30 Ibid., p. 25.
31 Ibid., p. 30.
32 Ibid., p. 25.
33 Ibid., p. 24.
34 Ibid.
35 Ibid.
36 Ibid., p. 25.

CHAPTER 3

THE HISTORICAL BEGUINES

The origins of the Beguine movement are obscure, making a precise definition for the early period of its history difficult to establish.[1] Beguines appeared at the end of the twelfth century in the most advanced urban areas of Europe, first in the southern Low Countries and the Rhineland, then in southern France and central and northern Italy. These first Beguines were known as *mulieres religiosae*, which in English simply means holy women. They lived either alone or as members of small, unorganized communities, dedicating themselves to live in the image of Christ. Their religious life combined a charitable and spiritual coloration. Humble of dress, living in chastity, and punctuating life with prayer, these women have been located in the tradition which scholars call ''evangelical poverty,'' a form of religious life modeled on certain beliefs about Christ's activities while on earth.

These women did not belong to an established Order, such as the Cistercians or Premonstratensians. Rather they grouped spontaneously with other women like themselves who were interested in leading a religious life of a particular sort; alternatively they situated themselves alone near male religious houses that supported their spiritual and charitable activities.[2] Consistently, their communities were found in urban milieus, not in rural or agricultural areas.

In the thirteenth century, the Beguine movement manifested itself in two different organizational forms. Some women lived together in small, isolated communities scattered about the town or under the parental roof, usually numbering but a handful of women, at most, in any given house. Those groupings have come to be known in the Low Countries as ''convent'' Beguines and elsewhere, in the Rhineland, France, and Italy, under various other names, such as Papelarde, Humiliate, Bizoke, or Coquenonne. At exactly the same time as that ''convent'' type of Beguine community arose, women were also entering into large, all-female housing settlements, known as *curtis* beguinages.

Unlike the Beguine convents, which really were nothing but Beguine residences in town, the beguinage was a town in and of itself. *Curtis* beguinages housed between twenty and perhaps as many as one thousand women at a time. The beguinage was an all-inclusive setting, enclosed by a wall or moat, where women lived, worked, and prayed. There were houses for the wealthy women, so-called convents for groups of poorer ones, a hospital, church, and cemetery. The *curtis* beguinage was an architectural complex — one not so dissimilar from the modern-day college campus or elaborate, church-run, boarding school. Only in the southern Low Countries do we find the ''convent'' Beguine residences and the *curtis* beguinages co-existing. [3]

The loose, rather *ad hoc*, ''convent'' Beguine grouping seems to have been the most frequent form in which single women who pursued charitable work and prayer took to communal living. These groups resulted from conditions probably not vastly different from those characterizing the preceding decades of the late twelfth century, when women began to group themselves outside the cloister in many a town and city across the continent. Although the early male supporters of these groups underscore in their writings the women's extreme purity, their all-consuming, spiritual devotion, their nurturing disposition, and their selfless commitment to serve God and be like Christ, one needs to be somewhat careful about accepting these accounts too literally. Women of the late twelfth century may have abandoned (or foregone) the pleasures of the conjugal bed and the comforts of domestic materiality in order to heed the call to higher spiritual goals than motherhood and marriage could offer. But the high (and growing) numbers of Beguines in this period, decidedly concentrated in the most densely populated areas of Europe, suggest that other agents, probably more social and political than religious, were also at work.

Those agents, historians now believe, were the massive changes accompanying urbanization. For example, in the rapidly growing towns of the late twelfth and early thirteenth centuries the laity emerged as a more distinct and crucial component of society than it had ever been before. Scholars find evidence of this new urban laity in a range of pious acts and public expressions of spiritual concerns; the Beguine movement has been viewed as one such manifestation. [4] Researchers have also observed socio-economic forces at work. These have thrown especially helpful light onto the central issue of Beguine recruitment: where did all the women come from, and why? [5] Various hypotheses have

70

been advanced to account for what investigators view as "the surplus of women" in the towns. Many of these "extras" became Beguines. Proposed explanations cite circumstances such as the closure of monasteries to women of anything less than proven hereditary rank,[6] and the disproportionately low ratio of marriageable males to females due to the higher mortality rate among men,[7] and guild regulations about marriage which stipulated, for example, when and how long members had to remain celibate. Also seen as crucial are dietary improvements for women and a decrease in female infanticide. Changes in population structure associated with the disruption of an agricultural society have likewise been examined,[8] along with the relative cost of entrance into religious orders as opposed to the cost of marriage.[9]

The precise religious and social stimuli for the Beguine movement are, not surprisingly, difficult to establish; they undoubtedly differed from woman to woman. In some cases a materialistic interpretation, which views the Beguine as a social solution to society's burdens, may be accurate, whereas for others, purely religious or charitable motives may have played the deciding part. Beguine settlements everywhere were no monolith; they were at one and the same time poor houses, retreats for contemplatives, sites of women workers, and havens for upper-class, single women.

In the fourteenth century, the loosely organized Beguine "convents" gradually ceased to be live conduits for women seeking a profession. Times were difficult for urban folk, especially during the first two decades of the century, when many popular, lay religious groups, such as the Beguines, were suppressed. In the Rhineland, suspicions of heresy ran particularly high. Groups of urban laity who had banded together for "religious" purposes were immediately marked in that strongly repressive atmosphere as suspect. The Beguines were not exempt from such suspicions.[10] Repressive measures of the worst sort imaginable ultimately worked to terminate the possibility for women in those many cities of the Rhineland — whatever their reasons had been for living together — to become Beguines. Elsewhere, women slipped out of their "convents" and into the protection of an approved Order such as the third Order of St. Francis and many a Beguine "convent" was simply transferred over to existing, officially-approved religious Orders.

Everywhere but in the southern Low Countries the Beguine movement dwindled precipitously in the fourteenth century. Strikingly, in one area — the southern Low Countries — the Beguine movement not only survived the fourteenth century, but reached a second zenith in the seventeenth and lasted well into the twentieth century, when Belgian women still took the call to vocation as Beguines. [11] The reasons for the continued survival of the *curtis* beguinage are important to the present study, which seeks to establish the Beguines' ordinariness. The church and civic authorities succeeded in devising a unique solution for lay women desiring to live together, whatever the motives for either party were. That solution was the *curtis* beguinage.

Curtis beguinages were first founded between 1230 and 1270 and emerged at the same time as the isolated ''convent'' Beguine houses. As an architectural solution, these two forms differed radically. [12] The beguinage is an architectural complex enclosed by a wall or moat and containing houses for Beguines, service buildings, a hospital, and a chapel. There are two types of housing within the *curtis* beguinage: convents (not to be confused with the isolated houses in town for Beguines, situated outside the beguinage) for poorer women living under the guidance of a Mistress, and detached houses for women of greater means living alone or in the company of a servant or female relative. The buildings are grouped around a chapel and, generally speaking, manifest two types of plans: a grid plan (Dutch *stratenbegijnhof*) and open courtyard plan (Dutch *pleinbegijnhof*). An all-service residential complex, the *curtis* beguinage was a virtual women's town. [13]

Once inside the *curtis* beguinage as full members of the Beguine community, the women did not, however, constitute a united Order. This means several things. A nun, for example a Cistercian, Dominican, or Premonstratensian, was bonded to her Order for eternity by a rule (Lat. *regula*) and by perpetual vows. The Beguines did not have such overarching structures. First, there was no mother Beguine house, no mother Beguine uniting them all. Each beguinage was separately governed by a Head Mistress to whom the women pledged obedience during their stay as Beguines. Second, regulations for membership were separately codified into statutes by each beguinage independently of the others. Not until the end of the sixteenth century does anything like uniformity among the rules and statutes for Beguines emerge. Third, the Beguine adopted her vocation not in perpetuity but rather only so long as she chose to do so. She was obliged to obey the Head Mistress, be humble of dress and means, and remain chaste, but only for the duration of her stay inside the *curtis* beguinage. Fourth, Beguines were only partially cloistered; they were routinely permitted to leave the complex and go into town for a variety of familial and business obligations.

72

Women from all social strata were received by the *curtis* beguinages. For wealthy women who wanted to (or whose families wanted them to) preserve capital and inheritance,[14] the solution was ideal. As Beguines, unlike nuns, they were permitted to maintain private property as long it was not displayed too openly. For poorer women, becoming a Beguine was equally ideal. Inside the beguinage there were many opportunities for work of a modest, pragmatic sort, such as cooking, cleaning, sweeping, and the like. Following the principle of economic and practical self-maintenance, Beguines worked for and supported one another by the income of personal dowries, carding wool, or washing laundry locally. The beguinage offered opportunities for social interaction, too. Group events primarily focused on the Beguines' religious and charitable obligations, such as attending Mass, singing vespers, and being gentle and caring toward one another, as well as renewing periodically their statutory obligations to the group.

The prompt success of the *curtis* beguinage and its rapid spread throughout the Low Countries is hardly surprising. In fact, so many women joined beguinages that the calculations of contemporaries, no less than those of many a modern scholar, have frequently tended to be enthusiastically rather large. The thirteenth-century Cistercian, Thomas of Cantimpré, for example, mentioned "two thousand" Beguines living in the town of Nivelles, and modern historians have averaged the numbers for St. Elisabeth's in Ghent somewhere between 800 and 1,000 women.

Historian Walter Simons has recently discovered important evidence about the actual population figures of beguinage inhabitants of the fourteenth century.[15] Working from the census of hearths for the duchy of Brabant and registers of admissions to the Beguines in Flanders and Liège, as well as from obituary lists and visitation reports, Simons offers a number of startling observations on the statistics of Beguine populations. Past scholarship has consistently held that the zenith of beguinage population levels was reached in the seventeenth century, believing that in earlier centuries the numbers of Beguines were considerably lower. In fact, Simons has shown that beguinage population levels were just as high at the beginning of the fourteenth century as in the late seventeenth.[16] He contends that populations varied from modest sizes (24 and 36 at Nivelles and Zoutleeuw, to 185 at Diest), to larger sizes, ranging from the 372 to 510 Beguines in Brussels in the late fifteenth century to St. Elisabeth's in Ghent, which peaked in 1670 at about 800, possibly even 1,000, women inhabitants. According to Simons, the inhabitants of some beguinages in the southern Low Countries "certainly outnumbered the population of even the largest women's monastery." [17]

We unfortunately know precious little about the planning stages of the *curtis* beguinages. The foremost Belgian historian to study the movement at the beginning of this century, L.J.M. Philippen, took an evolutionary approach to the problem. [18] He viewed the *curtis* beguinages as a kind of immanent or organic solution, that is, as the cumulative result of a string of different stages in the way society handled the "problem" of single women scattered about the towns. Philippen marked out four phases or stages of development, each leading immanently to the next; the final stage, in his analysis, was the *curtis* beguinage. It is certainly high time to look at those phases critically, for they have become nearly a truism of Beguine historical observation. Walter Simons postulates, accurately I believe, that the *curtis* beguinage was not a consecutive or organically developed form but a separate option, one open "to Beguines and their leaders at the same stage of development" as the isolated convent, [19] from which Philippen argued it had ultimately derived.

The leaders responsible for this remarkable innovation have been known about for quite some time: the countesses Joanna (1205-44) and Margaret (1244-78) of Flanders and Hainaut, the two dukes Henry of Brabant, I and II, and more locally Arnold IV (1227-73), count of Loon, the lords of Breda and Diest. [20] The canons regular, the Cistercians, and the Dominicans guided the course of both the women and the secular leaders. Historians have long been aware of the terms in which those individuals stated their reasons for promoting the *curtis* type of beguinage: to protect women from physical danger and exposure to heresy in the streets outside, and to offer them a quasi-isolated site to pursue spiritual goals which otherwise would be denied to them. Whatever the motives, and however the leaders may have specified them, the *curtis* beguinage was a masterful plan that worked in exemplary fashion for both sides of the equation. It got single women off the streets and out of whatever danger there might have been; perhaps it even got them 'out of sight.' And, as the numbers would seem to suggest, women, too, found it an attractive option — probably for many of the same reasons the leaders did. But for all that we understand of the range of contemporary explanations and for all that we know about the parties involved, the solution remains something of a genuine mystery in terms of precedents and immediate inspiration.

Towns and cities of the Low Countries were quick to promote the *curtis* beguinages. Whatever it was that made them work in the early days sustained its effectiveness in the centuries that followed. Surely the first women had particular reasons for forming or entering a beguinage. Did the reasons change with time? When the vocation of Beguine was re-ignited by a second wind in the seventeenth century, were women drawn to it for fundamentally different reasons than their fourteenth-century predecessors?

Part of the attractiveness, we may assume, had initially to do with the patent contrast between nuns and Beguines. A nun took her habit in perpetuity, chastity was an eternal reality, the woman's remove from the world and into the silence of the monastic choir was total. Her dedication to Christ was consummate; he remained her only possibility for conjugal union. She was his spouse, he her lover. The Beguine also was a bride of Christ, but the more worldly nature of her life, her distinctly secularized, daily routine, gave that spousal role more the bite of reality. Some Beguines were widows, who knew from experience what marriage meant. Others had never married but knew they could return to their family or marry at any point should they wish to do so. Conjugal union, the meeting of flesh to flesh, was not precluded women who became Beguines. The right to maintain one's goods and livelihood rather than abandon them to the common property of a monastery must also have been attractive to women and their families, who chose to uphold financial relations with succeeding generations of their kind. The *curtis* beguinage thus offered an opportunity for personal and material autonomy, something no woman's monastery could ever claim to do.

Beguines exercised a greater measure of both individual and collective initiative than nuns did: they had more frequent opportunity to come and go beyond the walls to visit friends and celebrate feasts with family, to live among the things of their personal material and familial identity, to maintain servants, eat at their own table, and keep at least some portion of their earnings for themselves. This aspect is what kept a Beguine with one foot firmly planted in the world of ordinary, lay people. And yet, by submitting herself to discipline, wearing a kind of habit, giving service and donations to her community, praying, fasting, meditating in common with other Beguines, preserving her chastity, and loving her sisters before all others, her life was seen equally bound to a religious one. This combination, documented in numerous ways and in a variety of primary sources, constitutes in good measure some of the reasons why contemporaries, and modern scholars of the fourteenth-century Beguines, saw them as "semi-religious."

I have sought to explore this condition of semi-religiosity, especially in contrast with women's cloistered Orders, and to offer some views about what made it attractive to leaders and women both in the fourteenth century. The following concepts are graphic reminders that both parties, the women and the authorities, stood to gain from the institution of the *curtis* beguinage: for the women it meant protection, for the authorities jurisdiction; for the women it was a site of a certain amount of autonomy, for the authorities a way to ensure supervision; it was flexible for women of different social backgrounds but could include them all; it was in large measure self-maintaining and socially expedient; it was a place for spiritual activities and practical facilities. Lastly, it was an answer or alternative to many of the problems and difficulties a woman faced when she found herself childless and husbandless, whether temporarily or permanently, allowing her to live with dignity in an urban setting. It was a kind of life that to women and authorities alike was a worthwile endeavor.

The issue for the present study now becomes this. If the terms of contract between church and society, on the one hand, and Beguines, on the other, were particular to the thirteenth and fourteenth centuries, then why did the *curtis* beguinage not die out as an organizational form, as the convent-type did? What kept it alive, if its construction as a workable system of meaning was built solely on the social foundation of that time? The answer seems to be that the *curtis* beguinage addressed women in a way that transcended historically specific terms; or, that the social and religious formulae of the *curtis* beguinage were so precocious that they could both service women *and* the socio-religious hierarchy during later centuries. It is not difficult to understand why.

The Beguine organizations combined aspects of community with personal autonomy, of collective with individual priorities — that is, of the abstract social with the personally material. The *curtis* beguinage, though a direct creation of the exigencies of a thirteenth- and fourteenth-century social and religious milieu, addressed them with remarkable success and nearly inconceivable foresight. Those same social solutions were activated by later *curtis* beguinages and their members and have remained active successfully across a good many centuries. This suggests that the women of the earlier period, in their experiences as well as their priorities, may have been conditioned not nearly as much by strictly local or time-bound factors as one might otherwise think.

The *curtis* beguinage, to summarize its role in brief, addressed a broad cross-section of the female population of urban society. All social strata as well as women of varying degrees of religiosity and intelligence were welcomed. So comprehensive was its social base that the *curtis* beguinage was able to maintain itself as a desirable placement option for women across a considerable sweep of time. Its temporal continuousness bears witness to the fact that the Beguines of whatever century are best characterized not by any eccentric, unique, or particular historical features but rather as everywoman's woman, the one who is foremost the construct and product of an urban milieu — single, religious to a greater or lesser degree, and seeking (or else driven to) the companionship of other women. The *curtis* beguinage aimed directly at that woman from the very beginning of its history. That is what I recognize as the ordinariness of the Beguines.

[1] The standard work about the Beguines in English is Ernest W. McDonnell, *The Beguines and Beghards in Medieval Culture, with Special Emphasis on the Belgian Scene* (New Jersey: Rutgers University Press, 1954). For work since McDonnell, see Kaspar Elm, "Be(g)hinen," in *Lexikon des Mittelalters*, vol. 1 (Munich and Zurich: Artemis Verlag, 1980), cols. 1799-1800; idem, "Die Stellung der Frau in Ordenswesen, Semireligiosentum und Häresie zur Zeit der heiligen Elisabeth," in *Sankt Elisabeth. Fürstin, Dienerin, Heilige*, exh. cat. (Sigmaringen: Jan Thorbecke, 1981): 7-28, with bibliography; Walter Simons, "The Beguine Movement in the Southern Low Countries: A Reassessment," *Bulletin de l'Institut Historique Belge de Rome / Bulletin van het Belgisch Historisch Instituut te Rome* 59 (1989): 63-105; idem, "Begijnen en begarden in het middeleeuwse Dowaai," *De Franse Nederlanden / Les Pays-Bas Français* 17 (1992): 92-114; M. Lauwers and W. Simons, *Béguins et Béguines à Tournai au Bas Moyen Age: Les communautés béguinales à Tournai du XIIIe au XVe siècle*, Tornacum 3 (Tournai: Archives du Chapitre Cathédrale; Louvain-la-Neuve: Université Catholique de Louvain, 1988); J.E. Ziegler, "The *curtis* beguinages in the southern Low Countries and art patronage: interpretation and historiography," *Bulletin de l'Institut Historique Belge de Rome / Bulletin van het Belgisch Historisch Instituut te Rome* 57 (1987): 31-70; and idem, "The Beguines," in *The Dictionary of Art* (London: MacMillan Publishers, Ltd., forthcoming).

[2] The paradigmatic person for this sort of Beguine is Marie d'Oignies. For a solid bibliography and good working translation of Marie's *vita* see Jacques de Vitry, *Vita Mariae Oigniacensis*, ed. D. Papebroch, *AASS*, June 23 / 5 (Paris, 1867): 542-72, translated by Margot H. King under the title *The Life of Marie d'Oignies* (Saskatoon, Saskatchewan: Peregrina Publishing Co., 1986), bibliography on pp. 139-74; and Hugh Feiss, "Supplement to *The Life of Marie d'Oignies*," *Vox Benedictina* 7 / 1 (1990): 53-72.

³ Elsewhere, in the Rhineland especially, Beguines had only one option for living together in town outside the cloister, the Beguine "convent," and it lacked the range of legal and religious benefits that the *curtis* beguinages of the southern Low Countries offered. I discuss the two different organizational forms of Beguines in Ziegler (1987), pp. 51-70.

⁴ Lester K. Little, *Liberty, Charity, Fraternity: Lay Religious Confraternities at Bergamo in the Age of the Commune*, Smith College Studies in History 51 (Northampton, Massachusetts: Smith College and Pierluigi Lubrina Editore, 1988).

⁵ Simons (1989).

⁶ J.E. Ziegler, "Secular Canonesses as Antecedents of the Beguines in the southern Low Countries: An Introduction to some Older Viewpoints," *Studies in Medieval and Renaissance History* n.s. 13 (1991).

⁷ McDonnell (1954), p. 84.

⁸ L. Milis, "Het begijnenwezen, uiting van een middeleeuwse maatschappij in de kering," in *Toespraken gehouden bij de begijnhoffeesten, Breda - Juni 1980* (N.p., n.d. [1980]): 9-29; and Simons (1989).

⁹ E. Koch, "Kloosterintrede, huwelijk en familiefortuin. De kosten van klooster en huwelijk voor adellijke vrouwen in zuidoost-Nederland in de late middeleeuwen," in *In de schaduw van de eeuwigheid. Tien studies over religie en samenleving in laatmiddeleeuws Nederland aangeboden aan Prof. Dr. A.H. Bredero*, ed. N. Lettinck and J.J. Van Moolenbroek (Utrecht: HES, 1986): 242-57; and idem, "De positie van vrouwen op de huwelijksmarkt in de middeleeuwen," *Tijdschrift voor sociale geschiedenis* 13 (1987): 150-72.

¹⁰ Jean-Claude Schmitt discusses the connotations of women attached to sorcery and heresy in *Mort d'une hérésie. L'Eglise et les clercs face aux béguines et aux béghards du Rhin supérieur du XIVe au XVe siècle*. Civilisations et Sociétés 56 (The Hague and New York: Mouton; Paris: Ecole des hautes études en sciences sociales, 1978); see also Ziegler (1987), pp. 59-64.

¹¹ Simons (1989); Bert D'Huys states that there were 25 Beguines in Ghent in 1984 in his essay, "De Gentse begijnhoven in cultuurhistorisch perspectief," in *Werken en Kerken: 750 jaar begijnhofleven te Gent*, exh. cat. (Ghent: Stad Gent, 1984): 48.

¹² For analysis of the "convent" Beguine houses of Tournai, see Simons and Lauwers (1988); and Simons (1989), p. 86.

¹³ J.E. Ziegler, "Low Country Beguinages: Women's Town Planning in the Middle Ages" (Paper delivered at the 22nd International Congress of Mediaeval Studies, Kalamazoo, Michigan, 1987).

¹⁴ Koch (1986).

¹⁵ Simons (1989).

¹⁶ Ibid., p. 100.

¹⁷ Ibid., p. 83.

¹⁸ L.J.M. Philippen, *De Begijnhoven. Oorsprong, Geschiedenis, Inrichting* (Antwerp: Veritas, 1918).

¹⁹ Simons (1989), p. 85.

²⁰ For bibliography on local lords, see Simons (1989), p. 86.

CHAPTER 4

THE ANTHROPOLOGICAL BEGUINES

In attempting to establish the Beguines as ordinary women of late medieval Low Country culture, I turn to symbolic anthropology for guidance. Scholars in that field, particularly Mary Douglas, Edmund Leach, and Victor Turner, have developed methods that aid our historical understanding of the Beguines' place in the social hierarchy. Dedicated to investigating living cultures *via* extended interaction with informants, those scholars have generated ways to think about primitive cultures that can enrich the findings of history, where the informants are no longer living. Symbolic anthropology is especially effective in shedding light on the ambiguous, part sacred, part everyday nature of the Beguines, that crucial mark of their continuity and, as I shall argue here, of their ordinariness as well.

Historians traditionally define the Beguines' ambiguity as semi-religiosity, a term that denotes the women's legal status within the church. In addition to analyzing semi-religiosity from a different set of conceptual priorities than history does, symbolic anthropology poses new directions for interpreting the spiritual and physical behavior of famous holy women in the fourteenth century. Many of these women were Beguines or have been closely linked to a Beguine environment. Indeed the central and largest body of evidence about Beguine spirituality to date has been the *vitae*, the saintly biographies of these holy women.

The *vitae* have continuously intrigued modern readers, especially because of their profuse references to a range of gruesome physical activities which the holy women seem to have engaged in routinely.[1] These range from self-mutilation to drinking off pints of leper pus. The *vitae* have therefore come to constitute the prime evidence about most forms and activities of holy women in the period; and this evidence is routinely extended to the Beguines. Historians generally accept, for example, the *vitae* as pointing to women's bodies, that is, to their essential physicality as the main instrument of feminine ideology and reality: in, with, and through the body they go to Christ. Recently, investigations of the *vitae* have focused on gender problems and suggested that such problems are ideologically linked to social history.[2] Anthropology can enlarge the scope of these views substantially, for it encourages the written records to be approached more as social and symbolic systems of meaning than as repositories of chronological, economic, and gender data. Anthropology also has tools that can dig beneath historically grounded concepts, like semi-religiosity, to locate broader social patterns of thought and meaning. These patterns help illuminate the Beguines as viewers of *Pietàs*.

ANTHROPOLOGY

Encompassing a wide range of approaches, symbolic anthropology, broadly defined, analyzes symbols and their uses. Some specialists in the field explore the role of cultural symbols in social life, while others attempt to interpret the logic of symbol systems. Its practitioners, especially in the branch of the anthropological study of religion, examine religious belief and thought. They try to define how religion fulfils sociological and psychological functions as well as how a society expresses and structures religion in language, thought, rituals, and belief. When applied to the problem at hand, symbolic anthropology is especially helpful in deciphering the reality of the Beguines as a viewing audience of the *Pietàs*, an audience made up of ordinary women. The approaches range from studying the process by which symbols acquire social meaning to examining the nature of meaning conveyed and constructed in symbolic classification systems. As a means of supplementing rather than supplanting historical analysis, the methods of symbolic anthropology aid us in understanding the Beguines.

Reading the written evidence of the Beguines the way a symbolic and structuralist anthropologist would, we learn that the Beguines are a cosmos, a kind of enclave or extra-industrial, primitive society. In anthropological terms, the

80

patterns of social organization in the *curtis* beguinage were not vague or open as they are in modern industrial societies, but rather fixed, stable, precise, and very detailed as well as ritualized. Those patterns have remained that way until the present day. In point of fact, throughout their history the Beguines maintained strict rules for organizing social life within the *curtis* beguinages. An anthropological analysis of the rules governing dress, drink, food, work, prayer, sex, comradeship, discipline, and the architectural site makes it clear that the *curtis* beguinage constituted a miniature world, one that was very nearly a full-dressed society, with the systems and patterns of organization that operate in all small-scale societies. The rules and the physical setting of the *curtis* beguinage towns complemented one another in organizing the community. Although the beguinages matured in — and were eventually surrounded by — a mature, urban, industrial culture, they preserved their internal mechanisms of patterning social relations for the women who lived within. This consistent social framework to every *curtis* beguinage is what allows us to characterize them in anthropological terms as a social microcosm and to treat them as manifesting certain general social principles.

Let us turn first to the ways in which the earliest centuries classified the status of Beguine society. We may isolate three areas of classification from the official documentary sources, the foundation charters of *curtis* beguinages, and the reports of ecumenical councils and hearings, among others:

(1) the Beguines were temporarily religious women

(2) their social status as women was indeterminate

(3) the architectural site of the beguinage was physically de-centered, i.e., physically removed from the city center.

Monastic life was the first classification contemporaries viewed in the context of the officially accepted form of religious life for women. Beguines did not adapt their religious life in perpetuity, as nuns did. Although the majority of the women concerned may have actually lived out their lives within the *curtis* beguinage, nothing like a vow obliged them to do so. A nun was a nun not only because her vows defined her as such, but because the terms of her commitment dictated that she stay that way for all eternity. The nun was therefore an unmovable essence, a fixed being, unchanging in her status, at least according to the law of vows. The religious life of Beguines, who entered a religious setting but took no vows, was thus transient, provisional, and able at least in theory to be revoked at any point. It might be revealing to learn that the thirteenth-century *jongleur*, Rutebeuf, in satirizing the beguinage, described it as a "waiting room" [for marriage].[3] Life as a Beguine, without irrevocable vows, meant that as a religious woman one was mutable, inconstant, and provisional. This contemporaries interpreted in various ways: at best, the Beguine was capricious or insincere, at worst, she was uncommitted religiously. More important than the bite of criticism, however, is the word used to describe the Beguines' social status, temporary.

The first category has something in common with our second, that the Beguines' social status as women is indeterminate. Let us begin with the women from the upper strata of society, those with a sufficient dowry to maintain themselves financially and to own a private residence, frequently outfitted with a servant.[4] Such women were financially able to marry but, according to the sources, were apparently not marriageable. For women of certain upper levels of society there were no men of suitable rank available to marry them. By the same token, although the dowry may have been large enough to gain them entry to an official religious Order, certain women from this level could not bear the strict discipline required of them in a religious Order. Two documents testify plainly to both situations. The first is a section of the general statutes for Beguines in the diocese of Liège written in 1246 for Bishop Robert of Thorote:

> Therefore so many of you, virgins and women, who have been unable to find completely the access to obedience, or were able to do so without being able to bear the strictness of the Orders, have wisely and prudently chosen this way — that you prefer to preserve in the company of respectable and humble people the virginity and modesty of purity in your courts[5] and houses rather than to live in the dwellings of sinners. Therefore whenever it was possible you have left of old your paternal house and the temporal joys to come to Liège and to other villages and towns in our diocese in order that you might have more freedom and more time for works in the service of the Lord.[6]

The next document is a portion of a Memorandum dated 14 May 1328, drafted by the delegates of the bishop of Tournai, Guillaume de Ventador (1326-33), and describing the Beguines of St. Elisabeth's in Ghent:

> Johanna and her sister Margaret, ladies of blessed memory, succeeding each other as countesses of Flanders and Hainaut, taking into account that the aforesaid county abounds in women who, because of their own condition and that of their friends, were shut off from a decent marriage, and that daughters of honest men,

82

both of the nobility and of the middle classes, if they wanted to live in chastity, could not easily gain (admittance) to religious convents, owing to their multitude or to the poverty of their parents; also that honest and noble but impoverished young ladies would have to beg or to lead a life reflecting disgrace on themselves and on their own people unless a suitable remedy were provided; by divine inspiration, as one may piously believe, after having obtained the advice and the assent of *diocesani* and of other upright men, founded in various parts of Flanders spacious quarters, that are called beguinages . . . [7]

Women as Beguines of a higher social status were thus in an anthropological sense captured between the only options then open to them, marriage or entering a nunnery.

The status of poorer women operated slightly differently. The impoverished woman who became a Beguine was expected not to become a burden to anyone, and the language of the rules often makes this clear. [8] For poor Beguines there should be no outward sign of poverty, such as begging for alms or wandering the streets. The poor woman, once a Beguine, had become, in other words, a non-entity to society, a person to be removed and saved from disgrace. The 1328 Ghent Memorandum says expressly that the spacious quarters of the beguinages of Flanders were founded so that honest but impoverished women, daughters, and young ladies could live "without disgrace on themselves or on their friends." [9] *Inconspicuous* is the term used to describe the lower class women in the *curtis* beguinages, a term that stresses an element of indeterminacy, of vacuousness, and of insubstantiality.

Another category of ambiguity surrounding the Beguine, in addition to her economic, social, and religious status, was that she was single and childless, either by choice or by chance, permanently or temporarily. The Beguine as a woman was therefore neither fully worldly (married to a man) nor fully religious (perpetually the bride of Christ). The conjugal state and motherhood were experiences she either had known as a reality or knew was still a real possibility. Contemporaries addressed those conditions explicitly and repeatedly in the rules for becoming a member of a *curtis* beguinage. A woman had to move herself out of the Beguinage of Sint-Truiden if she thought of "marrying or having a man;" [10] as a member of the Antwerp Beguinage (1323) to enter the conjugal state you "forfeit your house or chamber and retain no title to them." [11] There are strong prohibitions against letting men into one's bed chamber at night, and copious references to sins against chastity, including pregnancy while a member of the beguinage. [12] The single and childless woman, concretized as a Beguine, became the target of suspicion, as she was seen perpetually ready to cross over the sinful edge of temporary chastity into sex, prostitution, and pregnancy. Such women, as contemporary criticism implies, fell between the clear social classifications of contemporary society, for they were chaste but not necessarily perpetual virgins (like nuns), widows but ready and able to pursue the ends of conjugal union; childless but not barren, and childless sometimes, I suspect, even by choice. To interpret the situation theoretically, female chastity was an indeterminate state, if one chose to practice it as a Beguine. [13]

The third and final classification of the Beguines has to do with their physical remove from the town or city center. On the one hand, the microtown of the *curtis* beguinage was enclosed, walled off by moats and walls. Presumably the authorities supported the beguinage in part because of its architectural separability and self-containment. [14] The founding documents refer time and again to the *curtis* beguinage as one or a single place (Lat. *sub una loca, sub una clausura*), for it gathered women up and put them into single, separate, and isolated architectural units. [15] The beguinage was linked to nothing, above all, not to any other beguinage. It was a self-contained unit, not a satellite of a centralized religious institutional network. In the beguinage's tightly-circumscribed setting, individual societies of women flourished. But the setting itself, a contained unit to be sure, was frequently pushed to the edge of town, beyond the city walls. Moreover, although the walls and moats enclosed the inhabitants, Beguines had the freedom to come and go with considerable frequency, routinely penetrating the envelop of the beguinage enclosure; and under certain conditions, they were allowed to receive visitors in the beguinage.

BEGUINES: CLASSIFICATION AND MEANING

Structuralist and symbolic anthropologists study the systems of classification by observing relations between the categories they contain in order to locate

84

social meaning. In 1966 Mary Douglas in her seminal study, *Purity and Danger*, [16] explored the related concepts (or categories) of dirt, pollution, and taboo at work in Leviticus in relation to prohibitions against eating certain animals. She found that dirt "is not in itself dirt" but is rather the way a culture deals with anomaly, with what "confuses and contradicts" its classifications. [17] Prohibition and taboo for Douglas are ritual ways of confronting the undefinable — the undefinable being synonymous with the dangerous. Thus prohibition and taboo are a ritualized way of preserving order by reaffirming order.

Douglas calls for specialists to pay attention to manifestations of what is dirty, polluting, or tabooed, for when they do so they will be able to locate where a culture is pointing to itself, anxiously. In Douglas's system of analysis, dirt, prohibition, and taboo are a sort of ritual horror, a culture gawking at what cannot fit neatly and safely within its system of classification.

Nature, in this theoretical view, is undifferentiated and unclassified. It is we who classify and separate, we who in our social interactions and language separate fish from fowl, man from God. To use a frequently cited example, not all cultures have the range of names for the color spectrum that English does. These names are not merely labels for things but actually govern our ability to think and conceptualize as well as reflect the systems by which we do so. Douglas hypothesizes that social beings fit their observations into the extant structure of their language and, hence, when something falls outside those readymade structures, or in between them, the response is equally important: we fear what we cannot name or place. The result (and this is important to stress) is that given cultures will react to this obstruction by sacralizing or tabooing the thing. Douglas scrutinizes, for example, the dietary laws of Jews and attempts to inquire into them by probing beneath the surface of medical materialism. She does not accept, for instance, the face value interpretation — the materialistic one based on the physiological practice of avoiding certain meats in excessive heat — of Jewish dietary laws; rather, she attempts to show that the unclean animal is "contrary to holiness":

The last kind of unclean animal is that which creeps, crawls, or swarms upon the earth. This form of movement is explicitly contrary to holiness (Levit. XI, 41-44) . . . . Whether we call it teeming, trailing, creeping, crawling or swarming, it is an indeterminate form of movement. Since the main animal categories are defined by their typical movement, 'swarming,' which is not a mode of propulsion proper to any particular element, cuts across the basic classification. Swarming things are neither fish, flesh nor fowl. Eels and worms inhabit water, though not as fish; reptiles go on dry land, though not as quadrupeds; some insects fly, though not as birds. There is no order in them. . . . The prototype and model of the swarming thing is the worm. As fish belong in the sea so worms belong in the realm of the grave, with death and chaos. [18]

I have spent time with Douglas's theories because they can prove useful to historians of Beguines. Douglas prompts us to look for evidence of anomaly and ambivalence in things that resist classification. Edmund R. Leach, testing this theory in another situation, provides further evidence of its utility. Leach applied Douglas's procedures to his analysis of food taboos, especially those of contemporary English society and its prohibitions against eating reptiles, insects (they live between land & sea *and* land & air), and dogs. The English prohibition against eating dogs Leach interprets as showing relative distance from the self, a "graduated scale close / far, more like me / less like me." [19] Social classification Leach views as "a matter of language and culture, not of nature" [20] and he uses edible substances to demonstrate that food taboos and animal-abuse language — Frenchmen as "frogs" and "sons of bitches" — point to special attitudes in a culture about what it holds to be firm, right, superior, and correct. Such linguistic usages and attitudes, Leach says, have a social origin and enforce social assumptions, such as that Englishmen find eating dog quite as objectionable as Jews do pork, though in some parts of the world both are considered perfectly edible.

The three classifications used above to describe the Beguines bear striking resemblance to the ones isolated by the structural anthropologists, Douglas and Leach. They linguistically mark the Beguines as falling between categories or lying absolutely outside them, evidence that, were we writing anthropology, could be used to signal the crucial anthropological element of anomaly. Taken on purely historical grounds semi-religiosity does point to the women's special legal status within the church at a particular point in time. Yet the terms which define that status manifest the salient linguistic hallmarks that social anthropologists view as being associated with anomaly and undifferentiation. Nuns and married women had both taken vows that bound them until death. Historically, Beguines are neither / nor: neither perpetually inside nor outside, neither chaste nor sexually active, "married" to neither man nor Christ. The architectural site of the beguinage was enclosed but permeable; it was a self-

86

functioning, internal mechanism, separate from other urban or religious organisms but was able to converse with both urban and religious institutions.

Historians of the Beguines have long recognized that semi-religiosity is the central factor in interpreting Beguine status. Anthropology deepens this awareness by pointing out that semi-religiosity is a social classification, linguistically manifested, and crucial because it focuses precisely on the paradox, contradiction, and anomaly of Beguine status. Semi-religiosity is a social and religious definition which recognizes, cites, and points to the Beguines as inherently outside, or at least in between, fixed categories of social and religious classification. The Beguines are "out of order." When anthropology provides the interpretive model that phenomenon can be used to show that the Beguines conversely are central to the culture's understanding of itself. Like taboos and food prohibitions, the Beguines enforce cultural rules and confirm accepted classifications, by standing apart from them. To use Victor Turner's phrase, they "expose the building blocks of culture." [21] The Beguines manifest the central beliefs and assumptions of late medieval urban culture. This is witnessed by the urban culture, then no less than now, that distanced them and classified them consistently according to a terminology of ambiguity.

Our language has exercised this operation of classification on the Beguines for centuries. Modern scholars still define the Beguines as semi-religious, although they do so in the form of modern scholarly writing rather than the medieval one of legal contract. Using anthropology's approach to the symbolic analysis of language, we can interpret the Beguines as a primary social structure, one that functioned to enforce the moral, social, and spiritual order. In making the Beguines the object of intense anomaly (*via* their semi-religiosity) social relations emerge as fundamental to defining and dealing with women, in general.

Chastity for women is one such fundamental social relation. For the later Middle Ages chastity seems to have been either confirmed as a perpetual enactment of a religious vow or negated by an ongoing conjugal relationship with husband (or, conversely, by prostitution). Semi-religiosity points out this binary opposition by which chastity was defined and recognized. It points out that a woman was chaste or not chaste — classified within the social realm according to whether she was either a spouse, a widow, a nun, or a prostitute. Prostitution stood outside the "acceptable" social roles for women, but did so definitively. The Beguines, who had chosen the limbo of temporary chastity, had failed, in society's eyes, to make a commitment to any of the acceptable social and sexual norms. Semi-religiosity, in its historical manifestations and contemporaneous reactions, indicates that acceptable women were classified and hence defined socially this way: as fixed, closed, and immutable entities. Beguines challenged this social and cultural assumption in many ways.

Scholars have demonstrated that in the period of the Beguines' emergence, Low Country towns and cities could not guarantee a sufficient number of places for women to locate themselves with any security.[22] There was not a wide enough variety of social slots. Some women sought and gained entry to monasteries or marriage contracts. Others, however, were not so fortunate in finding a place. Many women who became Beguines could not — or, more reprehensibly perhaps, would not — locate themselves in one of society's accepted religious or conjugal frames of fixed, clear, and delimited social reference.[23]

Beguines from the start were the products of an urban society. That society, as historians have demonstrated elsewhere, grew anxious in the thirteenth and fourteenth centuries about how to deal with the many unattached women in its midst. In the worst of terms, society was faced with the problem of getting them off the streets and out of sight.[24] Historians have analyzed this as largely the manifestation in urban settings of feminine piety and social standing, often referred to in the scholarly literature as the *Frauenfrage*.[25] The situation of women in the towns may also be interpreted, however, as a social process quite different from those historians have identified thus far.

The complex linguistic and social relations between society and the Beguines may be evidence that these women were vital, central, and fundamental to society in that they affirmed and clarified the accepted and acceptable identities for women in an urban culture. Adopting a structuralist point of view, we see that Beguines had possibly enforced the official, legal, and social definitions of marriage, religiosity, widowhood, of the social strata of wealth and poverty, and of motherhood. They did so because they were all of those states and none: Beguines were the women who fell outside the structural order of nunneries and active marriage and even of promiscuity. That is what the criticism and cynicism of contemporaries revealed in descriptions of the Beguines' status as semi-religious.

Thus, the anthropological approach inverts the terms of interpretation. The women who became Beguines did fall outside the accepted social structures for women. This has led many an historian to interpret them, as contemporaries did, as eccentric, peripheral, or marginal in any number of ways. The inter-

88

pretative prompts from anthropology suggest other ways to analyze this pattern, especially considering the numbers and types of women involved: widows, the never-married, the not-yet married, old abandoned wives (and young ones, too), the impoverished, devout, sick, and terminally ill, those without family or children, and the barren, ugly, or deformed. Such women were indeed, and remain, the ordinary women of western urban culture, to a very great extent. They are ordinary for the same reason that historians have not yet quite been able to access them. This is because these are the women who fell between the tidy social slots into which western society tends to organize — and recognize — women's social roles and contributions, and has for quite some time.

Returning the Beguines to their proper historical setting in the later Middle Ages, one last note of anthropological interest can be introduced. We have been exploring semi-religiosity as a linguistic classification of women's social roles. The fourteenth century defined those roles in one additional way, by calling attention to their potency and their danger. Two sources contain suggestive evidence that contemporaries were concerned with substances considered dangerous and unclean.

The *vitae* of holy women contain excessive references to women's fluids and other exudations of their bodies: blood, sweat, tears, nail parings, hair clippings, and spittle. One need only peruse Caroline Walker Bynum's *Holy Feast and Holy Fast: The Religious Significance of Food to Medieval Women* to see how plentiful those references are. [26] Whoever reads for themselves the *vitae* will not quickly forget the women, a number of whom were Low Country Beguines, who drank the pus of lepers and ardently kissed their sores. Vomiting, hacking off pieces of the flesh, bleeding, excreting spittle, weeping oceans of tears — these are the ways the Beguines' contemporaries describe the spiritual activities of the great holy women of the fourteenth and fifteenth centuries.

Recent historians have tended to view these written glimpses of the feminine spirituality of the fourteenth century in terms of gender tensions and conflicts. Because of their eccentric behavior and the excessively physical autograph of their spirituality as recorded in the *vitae*, women, so the position goes, "claimed 'clerical' power for themselves, or by-passed the power of males, or criticized male abuse of priestly authority." [27] There may indeed have been political motives at work; but such feminist interpretations do not address squarely the

89

full social significance of the language used to describe the women's behavior. It is perhaps less revealing to determine whether the actions of the women were accurately described, or even whether they were true, and what the motives might have been. More suggestive is the fact that whoever wrote the actions down (or made them up, as the case may be) was using striking and consistent kinds of language classification by citing particular kinds of substances.

The substances are fluids and body parts. Like feces, urine, and menstrual blood, these are things that anthropologists agree to be almost universally the objects of intense taboo. Such substances, when approached as symbolic and linguistic categories, are both us and not us; they are at once contained and at the same time spilling out and over into the beyond. They are marginal, ambiguous substances that defy being tied to definite categories. Is menstrual blood, for example, within or outside the body? Is it me or not me? This is what anthropologists call boundary- or border-crossing, and it serves to explain why such substances are almost always either tabooed or sacralized. These substances are unclassifiable; they lie "betwixt and between" categories. They therefore are potent stuff that must be dealt with in some way. As specialists have contended, such substances are manipulated (and thus controlled) by being feared or worshipped or by being tabooed.

That the *vitae* of holy women set such substances in the foreground of description is intriguing. Considering the suggestions of anthropology, alternative interpretations of the *vitae* arise. The recurrent emphases and types of description suggest that the women described in the *vitae* had been powerful social beings, who in excessive fluid-production of blood and tears, among other things, gave visible form to what contemporaries probably understood as manifesting an image of states that are neither / nor, in anthropological terms, as anomalous states. [28] The *vitae* of holy women and the Beguines, when viewed this way, reveal quite strikingly similar situations — these women were potent because, in anthropological terms, they were anomalous, continually resisting the clarification of being one state or another. By supplementing historical interpretation with a structuralist model of anthropological analysis, it becomes possible to hypothesize that the women of the *vitae* had in their resistance to classification helped their society to conceptualize and define what was fixed and clear about women's status: chastity, motherhood, and marriage.

The *vitae*, importantly, are not the only sources to reveal a concern with substances or activities society considered especially potent or threatening. The beguinage rules and related Beguine sources contain terms similar to those in

90

the *vitae*. There are accounts of ordinary Beguines, whom scholars generally consider to be of lesser spiritual rank than the stupendous women of the *vitae*, caring for the sick, the lepers, and victims of plague, who themselves were enveloped in dangerous fluids and bodily excretions. There are prohibitions against the Beguines "playing" during the wake of dead (and hence potentially unclean) sisters they are guarding.[29] There are copious references to pregnancies and impoverished women who become "structurally invisible"[30] because once within the beguinage, they are no longer a burden to society. The frequent emphasis on such activities and substances in the written sources of the Beguines, when combined with the analysis of their intermediary social status, reveals a symbolic description of a kind of social reality. That reality is ambivalent and anomalous and therefore (following the interpretive processes of anthropology) dangerous. That holy women of the *vitae* drank the pus of lepers may or may not be true; but there is nothing fictional about analogous daily happenings among the Beguines.[31] Beguines really did partake of dangerous substances and fluids. They did so by being women, that is, by being the ones who menstruate and nurse the bodies of their sick and dying sisters. And what is more, they did this daily.

CONCLUSION

Society, according to anthropology, showed its anxiety toward women in its classification of the Beguines' status as semi-religious and in the identification of their activities with ambiguous substances and dangerous fluids. Both operations reveal crucial attitudes at work, for they reveal how the mature female was conceptualized in the system of social meanings. Linguistic concepts show that the Beguines fell clearly outside the established roles for women. Moreover, the categories of religious women's actions (spiritual, practical, and personal) were described in the *vitae* as calling into play powerful substances of blood, spittle, and leper pus, and occasionally in the rules of the beguinages by making references to pregnancy and other forms of improper bodily conduct. This two-

91

fold construct of classification and identification, based in status and action, enhances our understanding of the women who lived as Beguines. The Beguines enforced fixed categories of social definition for women and became a central social structure by falling on the boundaries of those categories.

Beguines were something to be manipulated, repressed, isolated, controlled, or removed. That they were has been proven from one perspective or another by historians many times before. [32] Their ambiguousness, in some ways, placed them at the center of urban culture. Beguines were urban culture's everywoman, the one who, for any number of reasons having to do with health, age, social status, physical deformity, or even freedom of choice, threatened to escape the predetermined social categories for women in the urban order. From this point of view it becomes possible, and indeed effective, to interpret the Beguines as ordinary.

The beguinage had the capacity (both physically and sociologically) to accomodate widely diverse groups of women. It is precisely the Beguine's diversity that precludes simple classification of these women as one or another social type. [33] But the limitations or bias of their society's classification system should not be a reason for us to continue to view these women as eccentric, out-of-the-ordinary personalities. They were ordinary women — their sheer numbers and the longevity of the beguinage testify to this — whose identities or own social needs were best addressed by an ''alternative'' communal life. It has been anthropology, not history, that allows us to discern the ordinary in the Beguines. This operation is valuable, for it gives us access to the audience of ordinary viewers of the *Pietà*, which was composed, at least in part, of women who were Beguines.

[1] The most comprehensive study of these *vitae* remains Simone Roisin, *L'hagiographie cistercienne dans le diocèse de Liège au XIIIe siècle*, Université de Louvain, Recueil de travaux d'histoire et de philologie, 3e ser., fasc. 27 (Leuven: Bibliothèque de l'Université, 1947). *Vox Benedictina: Women and Monastic Spirituality*, a journal published four times a year by Peregrina Publishing Co. under the editorship of Margot H. King, has been concerned with providing working translations into English of the *vitae*.

[2] Caroline Walker Bynum, *Holy Feast and Holy Fast: The Religious Significance of Food to Medieval Women* (Berkeley: University of California Press, 1987); Rudolph Bell, *Holy Anorexia* (Chicago: University of Chicago Press, 1985).

92

3 McDonnell (1954) p. 470.

4 **Lier** (1401), p. 340.

5 *Hoven* or courts may be translated as beguinages.

6 See **Liège** (circa 1246), pp. 303-04.

7 **Ghent Memorandum** (1328), p. 74. Walter Simons addresses the general implications of this famous account in his "Een zeker bestaan: de Zuidnederlandse begijnen en de *Frauenfrage*, 13de-18de eeuw," *Tijdschrift voor Sociale Geschiedenis* 17 / 2 (1991): 125-46.

8 "Similarly, if they can satisfy their need of bread or possess enough other rents or fortune not to become a burden to the beguinage [nyet]..." [**Antwerp** (1323), p. 336]; "Nevertheless they are no burden to anybody," [**Ghent Memorandum** (1328) p. 74]; "...if they possess at least so much that they will not become, during the next three years, a burden [niet en dorve sijn] to the beguinage," [**Lier** (1401), p. 340].

9 **Ghent Memorandum** (1328), p. 74.

10 **Sint-Truiden** (fourteenth century?), p. 309.

11 **Antwerp** (1323), p. 337; see also **Lier** (1401), p. 340.

12 **Lier** (1401), 341; **Sint-Truiden** (fourteenth century?), p. 309.

13 Virginia Burrus, *Chastity as Autonomy: Women in the Stories of the Apocryphal Acts* (Illinois: Edwin Mellen Press, 1989). Also see Sally L. Kitch, *Chaste Liberation: Celibacy and Female Cultural Status* (Chicago: University of Illinois Press, 1991); Schmitt (1978), pp. 96-114 and 195-202, discusses the connotations of women attached to sorcery and heresy.

14 Ziegler (1987); Simons (1989).

15 Ziegler (1987), esp. pp. 51-70.

16 Mary Douglas, *Purity and Danger: An Analysis of the Concepts of Pollution and Taboo* (1966; London: Ark Paperbacks, 1988).

17 Ibid., p. 36.

18 Ibid., p. 56.

19 Edmund R. Leach, "Anthropological Aspects of Language: Animal Categories and Verbal Abuse" (1964), in Lessa / Vogt (1979), p. 166.

20 Ibid., p. 156.

21 Victor Turner, "Betwixt and Between: The Liminal Period in *Rites de Passage*" (1964), in Lessa / Vogt (1979), p. 243. For Turner's consideration of liminality in other works, see Victor Turner, "Passages, Margins, and Poverty: Religious Symbols of Communitas" (1972) in *Dramas, Fields, and Metaphors: Symbolic Action in Human Society* (Ithaca: Cornell University Press, 1974): 231-71; and idem, *The Ritual Process: Structure and Anti-Structure* (Chicago: Aldine Publishing Company, 1969).

22 For different approaches to the documentary and demographic evidence of the surplus of women, which is where one can discern the social units into which women fit, see Ludo Milis (1980); Simons (1989), esp. pp. 70-78; and idem (1991).

23 Perhaps the situation, and the results, can best be conveyed by considering our own society at present, whose members feel tremendous discomfort by an unmarried woman or a childless spouse — and this they do even though the social categories for women, no less than our consciousness about them, appear so much more expanded and freer than they have ever been before.

24 Schmitt (1978); Simons (1989), pp. 89-92.

25 Simons (1989), p. 77.

26 Bynum (1987).

27 Caroline Walker Bynum, "Women Mystics and Eucharistic Devotion in the Thirteenth Century," *Women's Studies* 11 (1984): 179-214, esp. p. 193.

28 Victor Turner has contributed most to the discussion of similar phenomena in anthropology. He calls such persons "liminal personae," or transitional beings, who are in the process of passing out of one clearly defined social status and into another, as neophytes do, for example, or adolescents, as they pass through puberty and into maturity. While the terminology of liminality may not be especially suitable, Turner's conclusion remains crucial to interpreting the Beguines nonetheless: ". . . it is these [the phenomena and the processes of mid-transition], I hold, that paradoxically expose the basic building blocks of culture just when we pass out of and before we reenter the structural realm." (Turner [1964] in Lessa / Vogt [1979], p. 243) For a critique of Turner, see Caroline Walker Bynum, "Women's Stories, Women's Symbols: A Critique of Victor Turner's Theory of Liminality," in *Anthropology and the Study of Religion*, ed. Robert L. Moore and Frank E. Reynolds (Chicago: Center for the Scientific Study of Religion, 1984): 105-25. When Bynum claims, "But that which characterized the beguines . . . was exactly *lack* of leaders, rules, detailed prescriptions for the routine of the day or for self-regulation, *lack* of any over-arching governmental structures" (p. 116) she is inaccurate. The Beguines did in fact have rules and prescriptions for everyday life and behavior, which are treated comprehensively below in chapter 5.

29 **Bruges** (circa 1290), p. 62-63.

30 Turner (1964) in Lessa / Vogt (1979), p. 237.

31 See Gananath Obeyesekere, *Medusa's Hair: An Essay on Personal Symbols and Religious Experience* (Chicago: University of Chicago Press, 1981), who takes us beyond the basic "tabooed dirt" argument and into the inner psychological lives of ordinary women. Obeyesekere argues from a Freudian perspective that the expression of public symbols (such as dread locks) in religious virtuosi, in individual women, is a transformation of personal states of deep emotional pain having to do with sex and marriage.

32 Ziegler (1987), esp. pp. 51-68.

33 Simons (1989), pp. 77, 98.

CHAPTER 5

MATERIALITY AND TACTILITY
SOCIAL FACTS AND EXPERIENTIAL ESSENCES OF THE BEGUINES

Earlier in this book, I introduced the idea that the *Pietà* communicated its message by stimulating the viewer's sense of touch. We now turn our attention to the particular conditions of Beguine life that gave these women fluency in the language of sculpture. The discussion that follows does not try to offer psychological or physiological insights into the relation between the emotions and the world at the level of the sense of touch. [1] Nor does it probe philosophical issues, recently reviewed and investigated by David Summers around the role of the senses in apprehending art. [2] These have been developed in other contexts many times before. From Aristotle onwards the domains of philosophy, theology, and aesthetics have disputed the matter of sense perception as a fundamental factor in our knowledge and apprehension of the world. Aristotle claimed that touch is the basic sense, and that we ought grant it a special status in human apprehension. For without touch, he reasoned, "there can be no other sense." [3]

My focus on tactility does not participate in the predominantly philosophical discourse on the nature of sense perception in the arts. [4] Rather, it arose as a result of quite different concerns. It materialized during art historical research as an attempt to gain insight into the factors conditioning the "feeling spectator." My discussion of the tactile therefore centers on a specific historical example, exploring the ways in which the tactile sense functioned in human nature, and how it played into the viewing (and, by extension, the extraordinary popularity) of *Pietàs*.

I explore tactility rather as an influence factor in organizing ordinary women's behavior and aesthetic feeling. I do so in one group only — the Beguines, a group of ordinary women about whom we have an exceptional amount of documentation. These women had a special fluency in the language of touch, a fluency that enabled them to be especially discerning spectators of sculpture, receptive and sensitive to the instrinsic message of the *Pietàs*. I contended above in my discussion of aesthetic emotion that some individuals are more sensitive than others to the special effects of certain artistic media, and that fluency with the language of a medium was a determining factor in one's ability to experience a work in that medium as pure feeling or aesthetic sensation. In the case of medieval sculpture, and specifically the *Pietà*, the language of spectatorship was pre-eminently one of touch, that is, one demanding fluency in tactile matters. In this chapter the mechanisms by which women as Beguines acquired this fluency will be explored in order to disclose the sensory logic behind the artistic system of the sculpted *Pietà*.

BEGUINE RULES

The Beguines offer an unusual opportunity to observe the formation and routine use of the tactile language in ordinary women. Generally, there are very few written sources referring to or stemming from ordinary folk of the fourteenth and fifteenth centuries.[5] People of that time did not write about themselves in autobiographies, diaries, and the like. Nor were there any scholars or anthropologists who sought to record the activities, interests, and aspirations of ordinary people. Most of the documentation that remains to tell us of ordinary people in this period is legalistic and prescriptive, not personal or psychological. We know next to nothing about the thoughts and feelings of ordinary individuals; inner reflection only began to emerge in writing of the fifteenth and sixteenth centuries.[6] Self analysis and introspection are not yet matters of record in the Middle Ages. To compound the difficulties of modern scholars, most of the written evidence that does remain was written by men about men. Excepting the legendary holy women, whose stories are often exaggerated, we do not know what women of this period thought and did — and this holds particularly true of women from the middle and lower strata of society.

96

The *curtis* beguinages in the Low Countries, however, left surprisingly rich records about the lives and customs of their inhabitants in the fourteenth and fifteenth centuries. The records bring us into the lives of women in both the public and private spheres. They shed light on the everyday activities and concerns of an entire portion of late medieval society (ordinary women) which until now has been well beyond the historian's reach.

The *curtis* beguinages owe this rich documentary life to their pluralistic nature. The women inhabitants came from various social backgrounds, and the institution itself had several identities, some domestic, some civic, and others religious. In the first place, as institutions in the legal sense of the term, beguinages had standard financial obligations, religious dealings, and civic relations, all of which necessitated the drafting of various types of written contracts. Donations of money and land to the *curtis* beguinages, for example, were recorded, as were activities such as the founding and fixing of settlement locations, rights to cultivate fields and grind grain,[7] the payment of taxes, and stipulations about the level of Beguine participation permissible in the wool trade.[8] Non-secular matters were also recorded, such as the nomination duties, the supervision of the pastor, indulgences, the paying of tithes, the building and dedicating of chapels, and, in certain cases, the establishment of the *curtis* beguinage as an independent parish.

The community itself kept internal records in addition to those required by outside civic and religious administrations. They maintained inventories of the communal goods (especially those of the infirmary and chapel), payments to workers and clergy, records of the alms-giving services (the Table of the Holy Ghost), and occasionally (routinely after the sixteenth century) inscription registers and obituaries. Individual Beguines also left records in the form of personal wills and testaments, as well as records of endowments to pay for burning candles and saying masses.

Yet for learning about ordinary women, for learning about what they did and how they acted, the rules for membership in the *curtis* beguinage (sometimes called statutes) are uniquely revealing. The rules were a contract between the individual woman and her community. They dictated the terms that regulated her entry and ensured her continued membership in a given community. They are evidence (sometimes direct, sometimes indirect) of how women acted and behaved, for they tell us precisely to what extent actions and behavior were formulated by the authorities and adopted by the women. In many cases, the prohibitions and warnings that appear in the rules are undoubtedly indicative of abuses that went on in the beguinage community. The rules stipulate, often in exacting detail, what was expected of the women upon entering the beguinage, what licensed them to stay there, and under what circumstances they would be forced to leave. Stipulations ranged from dress, the manner of taking meals, and the performance of other mundane activities to property rights and spirituality. The rules are ''how to do it'' manuals — how to be an acceptable Beguine.

To achieve their function, the rules structured social relations for the women in nearly every conceivable way. The rules formulate women's relations with the world of people. They dictate how, when, and in what manner the Beguines can associate with men, with women who are not Beguines, with people outside the beguinage, with one another, and even with God. The rules classify relationships according to gender, type, and location and they designate how the women will behave in those relationships by defining the time, place, dress, and demeanor of their meetings and conversations. For modern scholars, the Beguine rules throw open the doors to a reality that would otherwise be entirely obscured from view. [9]

The Beguine rules reveal that touch was the primary category organizing the women's social relations. Although, as Aristotle observed, all people certainly have the sense of touch, the rules point to a context in which that sense went beyond common experience to emerge as the central means by which Beguines understood and structured their reality.

Let us begin by setting forth the basic chronological and typological characteristics of Beguine rules. R.M. Quintijn's unpublished thesis of 1984 remains the principal and most comprehensive source of information about Beguine rules of the southern Low Countries. [10] Quintijn divides the rules into four successive chronological periods. The first stage endures until circa 1300, and this she refers to as the stage of foundation or organizing rules, when the earliest prescriptions were drawn up by founders or benefactors, such as by the countess Joanna of Flanders, her sister Margeret, [11] Jacques Pantaleon of Liège, [12] and by the Cistercians and Dominicans. [13] Phase two, the fourteenth century, Quintijn characterizes as a period of more, better, and defensive rules. This period witnessed an increase of written prescriptions and the emergence of what Quintijn calls ''a sort of filiation of Beguine rules.'' [14] Quintijn sees in this period a continuity with the thirteenth century in terms of the persons involved and some of the motives for writing the rules, but also discerns that new, largely defensive, reasons for organizing the communities had come into play. [15] The third phase, the fifteenth century, Quintijn sees as marked by a growing diversity among the rules, largely documented by events surrounding civic interference, and by an emerging "conservativism." [16] Phase four, the sixteenth and seventeenth centuries, is a period of tightening up the rules generally against abuses, and of unifying and specifying governance and law within the beguinages. [17]

Although geographical and chronological factors produced minor differences among beguinages, the rules exhibit a remarkable consistency across an extensive area (the southern and northern Low Countries) for seven centuries. [18] Quintijn astutely warns that a "comprehensive enumeration of all articles of a beguinage rule (contingent on area and period) will thus be no more than a repetition, in so many words, of what can be observed just as well by reading one or more representative rules." [19] The types of issues and elements covered and the terms used to describe them are similar enough from one beguinage to another to permit generalizations. A composite picture of Beguine life can be assembled from discrete elements in the rules of several *curtis* beguinages, [20] the statutes for congregations of Beguines in the diocese of Liège (1246), [21] and a report drafted for the bishop of Tournai on the organization and conduct of the Beguines of St. Elisabeth's in Ghent (1328). [22] Consistent themes of governance, spirituality, chastity, labor, clothing, household goods, and charity recur, allowing us to recognize certain underlying principles of Beguine life.

Items contained in the rules never address or describe the private and introspective life of the women inhabitants, but this is not to say that the rules ignore inner states. The classic Christian ideals of chastity, poverty, humility, and charity are present, but they are rephrased. The rules of the beguinages were patterns women were required and expected to imitate, patterns exemplified by the female saint, on the one hand, and the ideal Beguine, on the other. To be successful at imitation the Beguines employed particular methods and material forms that could be recognized externally, that is, by regulating and dictating the women's material appearance. The women's appearance as a material entity, for instance in the fabric of their dress, in their conspicuous behavior, and in their bodily demeanor, was understood as a manifestation of inner virtues. Material appearance was the means by which they displayed the virtues of their adopted life to the world outside and ensured continuation of

99

group membership. The rules are formulae of appearance; in the Beguine world view material appearance equaled inner virtue.

For the Beguines, social action and behavior were processed through material and bodily categories. To be a Beguine was ultimately a simple matter: the woman was called to accept or reject the material appearance and activities of Beguine life. The Beguine identity was something objective and objectifiable — that is to say, something largely extrinsic. Thus material appearance was the key constituent of women's social reality as Beguines, and was central to interpreting the experience of Beguine selfhood in general. In fact appearance was arguably so fundamental to Beguine reality that by tracing it in the rules we are drawn, I believe, into the orbit of "the experiential" — into the realm where we begin to understand how these women experienced and understood their everyday world.

Before examining specific evidence of this principle in the rules, we need to examine more precisely the concept of appearance. Its meaning in this book requires some explanation. Everyday language, and certainly art historical usage, often assigns a strictly visual connotation to the term appearance, without considering the full meaning of the term or the full impact of the visual image. Visual imagery can be an extraordinarily powerful tool for appealing not only to the sense of sight, but to all the senses, as any observer of modern advertising techniques can confirm. The specific, intense language of the visual — that is, *appearance* — refers to and calls upon all the senses, concerning itself with the entirety of material experience. [23] In Beguine reality, appearance communicated the existence of virtues and other phenomena through physical properties. Although these properties were first received through sight, their communicated values are, I would argue, intrinsically tactile rather than visual ones. When people saw a Beguine, they understood her virtuousness through what her appearance told them of her material existence.

Let us look first at how the Beguines imitated the model of the female saint. [24] It comes as little surprise that the rules should prescribe, albeit in very broad terms, how Beguines should maintain the basic virtues of saintly women and cloistered nuns. In adopting a mode of the religious life Beguines were expected, however moderately, to manifest the virtues expected of good religious women everywhere: [25] chastity, poverty, humility, and charity. The external display or manifestation of virtue was in some ways more important for Beguines than it was for nuns, since Beguines lived in the world. [26] Yet still more important for the purpose of the present study is that even in this, the

100

most common arena of imitation, the terms by which women activated the religious virtues as Beguines was through outwardly visible signs, through *appearing* to be saintly.

Simplicity and humility, for instance, were conveyed in part by the fabric of a woman's dress. The visual appearance of a fabric communicates its tactile qualities and thus its richness or simplicity. For any Beguine, fabric was a thing whose value (literally and figuratively) was known through its tactile nature — through its texture, its warmth, and its fineness. The visitation report of the Beguines in Ghent noted that "none of them was allowed to possess anything conspicuous or exquisite."[27] At Sint-Truiden, the Beguines were not allowed to wear silk gloves, dyed stockings, bonnets, or fur- and velvet-lined clothes (among other finery);[28] at Bruges, their clothing was to be simple, "such that no one can remark that it is beautiful and expensive."[29] Humility was also conveyed by how a woman held herself, to whom she spoke, and her manner of speech. The rule of Bruges indicated that her gait should be dignified and her eyes fixed while walking; her voice should not be raised and her face should be kept joyful, serious, and modest (or humble).[30] Even the topics of conversation were addressed by the rules; Beguines were not to discuss the news of the world or to gossip, or to boast.[31]

Chastity, too, was recognized by pre-specified actions, such as moving about the town in groups of two with heads veiled and eyes cast downward. As we know, for Beguines chastity was a temporary state, one to which the women agreed to abide for the duration of their stay in the beguinage. How, then, were authorities to secure for the women, and for those with whom they routinely came in contact, the recognition of a virtue which women in the official Orders preserved inwardly and for eternity within the cloister walls? They did it by regulating the outward show of chastity. They stipulated the external signs (the things) by which society distinguished the chaste from the unchaste woman.

For Beguines chastity, like simplicity and humility, was conveyed in material terms such as dress and demeanor. It was seen as a public act, a condition readily discerned by those with whom they met in public and with whom they spoke. The Beguines of Bruges were cautioned not to speak to anyone without a witness present.[32] The Ghent rule called up Beguines to shun all suspect places and gatherings of companions with persons of the opposite sex, both ecclesiastics and laymen that might raise suspicion and affect their names and reputations.[33] It was considered an offense, according to the statutes of Liège,

101

if a Beguine talked "too long to any unreliable man," "if she has clothes that are too vain or showy," or if she "was found in suspicious places or at suspicious homes to be talking to a man or to be doing something else that might seem suspicious or shady." [34] Naturally, the rules also forbade Beguines to have men stay overnight in their home.

Charity is rather less comprehensively covered by the rules. It is not fully addressed as alms-giving or compassion, except in the rule for Bruges. [35] There is, however, an emphasis on charitable treatment of one's companions and superiors, especially through speech, and in one's manners and consideration for others. The rule of Bruges directs the Beguines to care for the sick by making them soft beds, preparing their food properly, and washing their feet; they are also instructed to "console those who are in temptation and melancholy." [36]

To imitate the ideal Beguine, a woman was similarly guided by the rules of her beguinage. The model of the ideal Beguine was spelled out in specific, materially oriented, essentially mundane terms. Rather than extolling modesty or humility in conceptual terms, for instance, the rules stipulated how a woman should walk, how she should dress, and what her facial expression should be. Even the volume of her voice, as well as the topics for her conversation, were taken into account. There are, for instance, references to Beguine's speech and to the fact that they shall not make noise, [37] either by gossiping, quarreling, shouting or hurling invectives and the like, [38] that they shall be tranquil of sound and quiet of demeanor. [39] Indeed the property of "silence" looms large in the rules but that, too, I attribute to materiality and appearance. Sound, as depicted in the rules, is materialized noise, that which is concretely heard, whether gossip, laughter, loud sounds, clogs or metal slippers worn when entering church, [40] or slander. Even Beguine spirituality was articulated in concrete terms. Devotion to the Passion, for example, was quantified by how frequently Beguines went to Mass, took communion, recited the offices, and said their prayers. [41] Punishments for sins are defined by the rules in terms of public actions — kneeling on the ground, flagellation with palm switches, and fasting on coarse bread. [42]

We now examine how the rules point to the primacy of the sense of touch in Beguine experience. Historians have traditionally understood the Beguines' manual labor as part of the indigenous concept of apostolic poverty, believing that work with the hand had both a spiritual and practical role to play. Manual labor earned one one's daily bread in appropriately harsh fashion and, at the

102

same time, hard work kept one's spirit, mind and body in the penitential state. So it did for the Beguines. The Bruges rule states, ''They will be constant and true to their work, since it is by this work that they will earn their bread; by it they perform penitence; thanks to it they resist temptation and the weakness of the body that leads astray the soul; by it after all they please God and acquire grace on earth and glory in the next life.''[43] Beguine manual labor is also commonly associated with the active and contemplative life, with Martha and Mary, the two poles of practical and spiritual experience which working with the hands made manifest in the later Middle Ages.

Manual activities of various sorts were characteristic of the Beguines from the early days. This was especially true of the treatment of cloth and the routine of manual labor (for instance, nursing and doing laundry). Beguine commitment to handwork is a long tradition, an attribute of their activities throughout their history. These women were always engaged most heavily in what people consider the quintessentially female occupations of clothmaking and nursing, although the precise forms of these occupations did change with time (for example, from bleaching and carding wool in the fourteenth century to making lace and embroidering vestments in the modern period).[44]

My view of handwork is different, and somewhat more comprehensive than a strictly historical one. I wish to consider more that just the accepted categories of manual labor and manual activities for Beguines by looking into the rules controlling such activities, keeping in mind the importance of materiality and appearance as established in the preceding pages. Handwork, the manual, and the tactile were all part of the broader experience of imitation and appearance for the Beguines. There are two components of this experience: the hand itself (the receiver and transmitter of the system of tactile values) and the articles and forms (the objects and symbols) in which tactile expression most frequently took place. We will see later on in this book that the *Pietà* can be placed into the latter category.

In Beguine reality the hand was the primary tool that made the connection between the virtue expressed and the material manifestation of that virtue. Returning to the example of a fabric of a Beguine's clothing, it is the hand (and its sensitivity) that connects the fabric to the virtue of humility. The hand was what coupled the Beguine to the world around her, for she routinely touched sick bodies, carded wool, and kneaded bread. Her communal life, and her life of service and obedience, her life of *imitatio Christi*, was firmly grounded in material experience. In routine and ritualized ways Beguines gave with the

103

hand (in alms and compassion) and lived by the hand (in making and wearing cloth, sweeping floors, and nursing, among other things). The Beguine's sense of touch, exercised and refined by her day-to-day activities, must surely have reached an exceptionally developed state. Beguines were governed especially by a language in which the tactile sense communicated and carried the meaning of day-to-day experience. But while those manual emphases originated in a fourteenth-century environment (in *imitatio Christi* and the Beguines' servicing of social needs), they remained fairly constant to Beguine life across the centuries. Nursing, knitting, cleaning, lace-making, and cutting out devotional cards are pre-eminent Beguine occupations which have changed only in type, not in genuine substance, across the centuries.

The research that went into this part of the study, and the conclusions I reached from analyzing the rules of late medieval beguinages, were confirmed by my conversations with two Beguines in the summer of 1989.[45] I spoke with a former Beguine from the Lier Beguinage and with another still living as a Beguine in St. Amandsberg's Beguinage in Ghent. What these women said confirmed that my findings in the rules need not be isolated to the fourteenth and fifteenth centuries. The principles I had isolated about how the rules structured social relations for Beguines of the late Middle Ages appear, at least from these sessions, to be still operative today.

When questioned about her life in the beguinage the Beguine from Lier focused predominantly on her work, i.e. cutting out hosts and baking them. She could rehearse, with remarkable specificity for a woman of nearly eighty years, her daily routines as a young Beguine of washing, baking, laundering, and other manual tasks. When questioned about special church holidays or preparations for the feast days, her response was always the same: ironing, baking, washing. When there was a procession she had to wash and iron the special garments of the religious sculptures and take care that everything was in order. She had to attend Mass daily and had to rise early in the day and say her prayers before Mass because "we had no time. We had to bake the hosts and eat while they were baking. I never went out." She remarked repeatedly that she was "always working." Even on Sundays, they could not go out, she said, because they had to bake hosts for the week. Interestingly, she described her work in specifically tactile terms — kneading the dough into big and little shapes in the cellar, so as to make it crisp; and then counting all the hosts; and saying three rosaries a day, fondling the beads:

104

’K moest altijd maar hosties tellen en bakken. We konden niet vertellen he, het enige dat we konden, dat was drie rozehoedjes bidden op een dag, dat deden we, dan moesten we dat zo een beetje arrangeren dat we dat konden. Als we wat uitstaken, dan konden we dat. Dan leesde de overste voor en wij antwoordden dan; maar als we aan het tellen waren, dan konden we dat niet.

[I was always counting and baking hosts. We had no time to talk [about the past], all we could do was to say three rosaries a day. We were able to do so if we were careful to organize our work well. When we were cutting out hosts, we could do that. Thus, the mistress would lead in prayer and we would respond. But when we were counting hosts, we could not do that.]

The relationship between Beguine ideology and daily routine is complex. The specific format that ideology takes as daily routine both expresses the ideology and constructs it. [46] The tactile may have arisen for Beguines as an indigenous social fact of fourteenth-century life. Manual labor may well have been the norm for the majority of fourteenth-century women, in general. But tactile emphases evolved, as my recent conversations with Beguines testify, into the central constituent of human experience if one were a Beguine in any period. The primacy of touch for Beguines, therefore, was an experiential constant rather than something particular to the fourteenth century.

As the longevity of the beguinages proves, women from all walks of life and all stations have been able to conform to the model of imitating the virtues of a good Beguine. The rules reveal, I believe, that authorities were cognizant of the principle of imitation as an effective means of social organization. The authorities seem to have been aware that by propounding a material definition of a good Beguine *via* appearances in dress, walk, and action, they provided the terms which best facilitated the adoption of this way of life. [47]

The way Beguines viewed images could not escape being conditioned by the material nature of their lives. It seems highly unlikely that their private introspective feelings, their prayers, and their petitions to the holy figures of Christ and Mary would have gone untouched by the comprehensive range of structures and experiences ordering the entirety of their lives. Given the Beguines' heightened sensitivity and active engagement in matters of touch, surely they discerned the instrinsic content of the religious sculpture with which they came in contact (the most tactile of all religious imagery) with nearly excessive ease. As they conceptualized virtues, actions, and identity in external forms, and as they spent their daily lives touching bodies, things, and cloth,

105

so too would Beguines have easily apprehended the full range of meanings carried by the religious sculpture ever present in the beguinages. Religious imagery communicated itself and was conceptualized the same way their other experiences were — with a foundation in and appeal to the tactile sense. The Beguines could grasp the subtleties of this tactile language almost intuitively. Their system of sensory logic prepared the Beguines to receive (and embrace) the intrinsically tactile content of the sculpted *Pietà*.

¹ For this approach, see William Schif and Emerson Foulke, *Tactile Reception: A Sourcebook* (Cambridge: Cambridge University Press, 1982); and Ashley Montagu, *Touching: The Human Significance of the Skin* (New York: Columbia University Press, 1971).

² For a discussion of the role of the senses and aesthetics, especially Renaissance aesthetics and theories of beauty, see David Summers, *The Judgment of Sense: Renaissance Naturalism and the Rise of Aesthetics* (Cambridge: Cambridge University Press, 1987). For two different examinations of the theological implications of the theory of touch for the Middle Ages, see John Giles Milhaven, "Thomas Aquinas on Sexual Pleasure," *Journal of Religious Ethics* 5 / 2 (1977): 157-81; and idem, "A Medieval Lesson on Bodily Knowing: Women's Experience and Men's Thought," *Journal of the American Academy of Religion* 57 / 2 (1989): 341-72.

³ Quoted and discussed by Summers (1987), p. 103.

⁴ As an exception to the philosophical and aesthetic discourse governing discussion of the senses thus far, one may consult Hamann (1943), pp. 143-50. Hamann's discussion is quoted at length above in chapter 1, n. 73.

⁵ For useful discussions of sources and historiography with bibliography, see Stanley Chojnacki, ed., "Recent Trends in Renaissance Studies: The Family, Marriage, and Sex," *Renaissance Quarterly* 40 / 4 (1987): 660-751; and Martha Howell with Suzanne Wemple and Denise Kaiser, "A Documented Presence: Medieval Women in Germanic Historiography," in *Women in Medieval History & Historiography*, ed. Susan Mosher Stuard (Philadelphia: University of Pennsylvania Press, 1987): 101-31. Although his views of the Beguines do not coincide with mine, Peter Biller raises important problems in the accessing of ordinary women in the Middle Ages in his "The Common Woman in the Western Church in the Thirteenth and Early Fourteenth Centuries," in *Women in the Church*, Studies in Church History 27, ed. W.J. Sheils and Diana Wood (Oxford: Basil Blackwell, 1990): 127-57.

⁶ There are two great examples and exceptions to the rarity of autobiography in the Middle Ages, even among the upper strata: Augustine's *Confessions* and the Memoirs of Abbot Guibert of Nogent (1064?-circa 1125). The nineteenth-century historian Jacob Burckhardt centered his great thesis, portrayed in his *Civilisation in the Renaissance* (1865; rev. ed. New York: Harper & Row, 1958), around the discovery of the individual in the fifteenth century. For a review of the development of autobiography, see Rudolf Dekker, "Egodocumenten: Een literatuuroverzicht," *Tijdschrift voor Geschiedenis* 101 (1988): 161-89.

106

⁷ See McDonnell (1954), p. 483, regarding Brussels.

⁸ On the Beguines' involvement in the production of cloth, seen n. 29 below.

⁹ Studying everyday reality as far back as the fifteenth century is rather new to the discipline of history. The realm of commonplace experience is presently being addressed by scholars of a new branch cultural history known as gesture studies. During this research, I have been especially interested in Robert Darnton, *The Great Cat Massacre and Other Episodes in French Cultural History*, 2nd ed. (New York: Vintage Books, 1985). For a slightly earlier period I found Herman Pleij, *De sneeuwpoppen van 1511: literatuur en stadscultuur tussen middeleeuwen en moderne tijd* (Amsterdam: Meulenhoff; Leuven: Kritak, 1988) and Paul Vandenbroeck, *Jheronimus Bosch: Tussen volksleven en stadscultuur* (Berchem-Antwerp: EPO, 1987); idem, *Over wilden en narren, boeren en bedelaars. Beeld van de Andere, Vertoog over het Zelf*, exh. cat. (Antwerp: Koninklijk Museum voor Schone Kunsten, 1987); and idem, "Zwischen Selbsterniedrigung und Selbstvergottung. Bilderwelt und Selbstbild religiöser Frauen in den südlichen Niederlanden. Eine erste Erkundigung," *De zeventiende eeuw* 5/1 (1989): 67-88 (especially useful for imagery). Gesture studies and similar new cultural methods have been slow to make discernable headway into mainstream medieval history, which is still dominated by positivism in many ways. One may consult the innovative works on medieval problems by Richard Trexler, "Ritual Behavior in Renaissance Florence: The Setting," *Medievalia et Humanistica* 3 (1972): 125-44 and other historians in Jean-Claude Schmitt, ed. *Gestures, History and Anthropology*, vol. 1 (Great Britain: Harwood Academic Publishers, 1984). The articles there are not precisely cultural history of the Darnton sort, but they gesture, as it were, in that direction. These approaches are put into a methodological context by Lynn Hunt, "Introduction: History, Culture, and Text," in Lynn Hunt, ed., *The New Cultural History* (Berkeley: University of California Press, 1989): 1-22.

¹⁰ R.M. Quintijn, "Normen en normering van het begijnenleven: vergelijkende studie van de begijnenregels in de Nederlanden van de XIIIe tot de XVIIIe eeuw" (Master's thesis, University of Ghent, 1984). For an earlier discussion of the rules, see Philippen (1918), pp. 336-39.

¹¹ Quintijn (1984), p. 26; For St. Elisabeth's Beguinage in Ghent, also see Jeannine Baldewijns, "Organisatie van het begijnhofleven," *Werken en Kerken*, exh. cat. (Ghent: Stad Gent, 1984): 93-106.

¹² Quintijn (1984), p. 27.

¹³ Ibid., pp. 28-29 and n. 37; for bibliography and a brief discussion of the propagators of the movement by the religious Orders, see Simons (1989), pp. 87-89.

¹⁴ Quintijn (1984), p. 30.

¹⁵ Those reasons largely had to do with helping Beguines fend off criticism and attacks on their existence, especially in the wake of the persecutions following the Council of Vienne (1311-12). For a discussion of that Council, see Ziegler (1987), pp. 31-70, esp. p. 51ff.; and Simons (1989), pp. 96-99. The fourteenth century was when rules also first emerged for Beguines in Holland and Zeeland. See Quintijn (1984), p. 31; Florence W.J. Koorn, *Begijnhoven in Holland en Zeeland gedurende de middeleeuwen* (Assen: Van Gorcum, 1981), with English summary. Review of Koorn's book by David Nicholas, "Review of Florence W.J. Koorn, *Begijnhoven in Holland en Zeeland gedurende de middeleeuwen*," in *Speculum* 58/2 (1983): 494-96; and J.E. Ziegler, "Review of Florence W.J. Koorn, *Begijnhoven in Holland en Zeeland gedurende de middeleeuwen*," *Mystics Quarterly* 15/2 (1989): 103-05.

[16] The documentary sources are based on complaints against the Beguines and on the stipulations for governance of the beguinage and relations with locals, relations which differed from town to town. In this phase, one sees a greater number of references in the rules to bishops, dukes, and city magistrates.

[17] Quintijn (1984), p. 35.

[18] Ibid., p. 43.

[19] Ibid.

[20] **Antwerp** (1323), **Bruges** (circa 1290), **Ghent Rule** (before 1354), **Leuven** (Small Beguinage), **Lier** (1401), and **Sint-Truiden** (fourteenth century?).

[21] **Liège** (circa 1246).

[22] **Ghent Memorandum** (1328).

[23] Hamann (1943).

[24] For a discussion of comparisons between hagiographical sources and Beguine rules, see J.E. Ziegler, "Reality as Imitation: The Dynamics of Imagery Among the Beguines," in *Maps of Flesh and Light: New Perspectives on the Religious Experience of Medieval Women*, ed. Ulrike Wiethaus (Syracuse, New York: Syracuse University Press, 1992).

[25] **Ghent Rule** (before 1354), pp. 5-7; **Bruges** (circa 1290), p. 74.

[26] To my knowledge there has not been a comprehensive study of the rules and customaries of nuns that addresses this issue. A useful introduction to the material is provided by Micheline de Fontette, *Les religieuses à l'âge classique du droit canon. Recherches sur les structures juridiques des branches féminines des ordres*, Bibliothèque de la Société d'Histoire Ecclésiastique de la France (Paris: J. Vrin, 1967). For the daily life in the women's convents of Windesheim, see E. Persoons, "Het dagelijks leven in de Windesheimse vrouwenkloosters," *Spiegel Historiael* 15 (June 1980): 342-49, 383.

[27] **Ghent Memorandum** (1328), p. 75.

[28] **Sint-Truiden** (fourteenth century?), pp. 310-12; also **Lier** (1401), pp. 339-40.

[29] **Bruges** (circa 1290), p. 70. The frequency with which cloth and fabric are mentioned in the rules may likely derive from the fact that many beguinages were involved in the manufacture of cloth. The Beguines in Ghent, for example, cleaned wool sent to them from the town [**Ghent Memorandum** (1328), p. 74]. And the Beguines at Sint-Truiden were permitted to make cloth or clothes only if the court authorities authorized them to; those same authorities also forbade them, under penalty of expulsion from the beguinage, from working in town and earning a living by either tailoring or burling [**Sint-Truiden** (fourteenth century?), p. 312]. For further study of the Beguine participation in the manufacture of cloth, see the chapter entitled "The Extraregular in Industry," in McDonnell (1954), pp. 270-77; and Simons (1989), p. 96.

[30] ". . . har ansichte blide, swaer end scamel." [**Bruges** (circa 1290), p. 28].

[31] **Bruges** (circa 1290), pp. 74-75.

[32] **Bruges** (circa 1290), p. 28; **Sint-Truiden** (fourteenth century?), p. 312, says that "they shall not hold any meeting with anybody on any day in the streets or before the gates of the beguinage, but remain in their house or their chamber."

[33] **Ghent Rule** (before 1354), p. 6.

[34] **Liège** (circa 1246), pp. 306-07.

[35] Under the heading of "Van ghenadichheden ende alemoessene te gheven," **Bruges** (circa 1290), pp. 76-77.

³⁶ **Bruges** (circa 1290), p. 77.

³⁷ The Liège statutes cite as a "slight offense" "if a beguine, whilst service was held in the church of God, made noise or behaved turbulently." [**Liège** (circa 1246), p. 305]. "Similarly, as talking in church, according to the Holy Fathers, is talking with the devil, they shall preserve or keep silence except in case of necessity . . . " [**Sint-Truiden** (fourteenth century?) p. 313].

³⁸ According to **Liège** (circa 1246), p. 306, it was a slight offense "if she is in the habit of swearing or denying; if she is in the habit of slandering or speaking vainly"; more serious offenses were "if she is at strife or quarreling or breaking in upon another woman's peace, or if she confuses or disturbs"; most serious is "if she indulges in indecent invective against the rector or the mistress." The **Bruges** (circa 1290) rule dedicates an entire section to *About Keeping Quiet* ("from complines until prime and on feast days until after mass; and always in their church . . . unless their mistress has something to say. If something is missing from the table, they will hit the table with a knife and the server will make haste." pp. 29-30). The **Ghent Rule** (before 1354) states: "They shall be on their guard against all licentiousness in speech, against idle words, shouting and laughing, against bad manners in speaking and in other matters; they shall also abstain from spreading rumors, from casting aspersions on a person's name or reputation, from divulging somebody's offenses, out of disdain or for any other reason, whoever may be concerned. Nor shall they mock or ridicule anybody for any reason, however little grace God may seem to have granted to the person in question." (p. 9) See also **Lier** (1401), p. 342.

³⁹ See also **Bruges** (circa 1290), p. 77. **Sint-Truiden** (fourteenth century?), p. 313, adds: "In that case [of necessity of talking] they shall talk in a lowered voice or with laywomen, at their request."

⁴⁰ **Sint-Truiden** (fourteenth century?), p. 313.

⁴¹ For Beguines attending Mass, see **Antwerp** (1323), p. 336; **Bruges** (circa 1290), p. 53; **Ghent Rule** (before 1354), pp. 7, 11; **Lier** (1401), p. 341; **Sint-Truiden** (fourteenth century?), p. 313. For receiving the sacrament of communion, see **Bruges** (circa 1290), pp. 32-33; **Lier** (1401), p. 341. Beguines were instructed when and how often to say the offices and recite certain prayers, for example, at **Antwerp** (1323), p. 338; **Ghent Rule** (before 1354), pp. 7-8; **Lier** (1401), p. 341; **Sint-Truiden** (fourteenth century?), pp. 312-13.

⁴² For kneeling, see **Bruges** (circa 1290), p. 57; **Liège** (circa 1246), p. 307; **Sint-Truiden** (fourteenth century?), p. 313. The use of palm switches is noted in **Bruges** (circa 1290), p. 36 and scourging in **Sint-Truiden** (fourteenth century?), p. 308. Coarse bread is referred to in **Bruges** (circa 1290), p. 37; and **Ghent Memorandum** (1328), p. 75.

⁴³ **Bruges** (circa 1290), pp. 75-76.

⁴⁴ For the Beguine participation in the manufacture of cloth, see n. 29 above.

⁴⁵ I withold the names of the Beguines I interviewed to respect their desire for privacy. For a deep understanding of Beguine life in its entirety, consult Frans Verachtert, André Gailliaerde and Frans Vervoort, *Voorsale des Hemels ofte het begijnhof in de XVII Provinciën in woord en beeld gebracht* (Retie: Kempische Boekhandel, 1973). This book is itself a Beguine treasury! The author makes a sort of "living history" out of Beguine documents (including rules, ordinances, necrologia, a.o.), books, newspaper clippings, letters, poems, works of art, bits of property, and other articles.

⁴⁶ Here we find guidance toward understanding how daily life contructs and manifests social concepts and meaning from the distinguished American novelist Saul Bellow, who recently

discussed the ideology governing our own culture. He termed it "detachment." He considered the ways in which detachment is communicated and made to maintain its substance as an ideology — its delivery system, essentially. Bellow located those ways in television, MTV [music videos], movies, and televised international news. The cool production and proliferation of violence on television, which began with the reporting of the war in Vietnam, is the vehicle that for Bellow gives particular character to the pervasive but generic ideology of detachment. The interactive relationship between ideology (detachment) and particular manifestation (cool violence) *via* a symbolic vehicle (television reportage) differs from what occurred in the fourteenth century in type, but not in the general operation of such a cultural ideology. Conference on American writing in Amsterdam, summer 1990, organized by the John Adams Institute. See the report in the *Standaard der Letteren* of 16 June 1990.

[57] Susan Rodgers (Department of Sociology and Anthropology, Holy Cross College, Worcester, Massachusetts) noted that the "extrinsicness" seems very similar to the "object-fascination" and "thinginess" of primitive art worlds.

CONCLUSION

Social action and social behavior were structured in the founding period of the *curtis* beguinages through the general principle of *imitatio Christi*. This process of knowledge by identification shaped, and was shaped by, the particulars of particular settings. And yet for all that we now perceive to be its local character, there was probably no single category of social experience and religious knowledge more common to more people on the western European continent than that of identification *via* the imitation of Christ.

The Beguines and their authorities manifested a deep and lively commitment to this general category of pious identification by imitation. The rules reveal that it functioned always on two levels, the Beguines were expected to model themselves on — that is, to imitate — the virtues of saintly women and nuns (external) and to model themselves on one another (internal). At the same time, Beguines were expected to make those properties recognizable as Beguineness to outsiders as well as insiders. This happened because of the abject regulation of explicit materiality and physical appearances of dress, action, and behavior. All states of saintliness, Beguine-ness, chastity, respectability, simplicity, work, and compassion were *described, recognized*, and *defined* by explicit and detailed materiality.

Identity and imitation (*via* materiality and physical appearance) played a truly profound part, therefore, in the apprehension, indeed the structuring, of reality for these communities. The women defined and described the "self" by imitation; and they identified with one another also by materially recognized examples. The women recognized others as like or unlike, as good or bad examples, according to how closely they measured up to the requisite material and physical manifestations of the model.

Self and other, the very nerve center by which reality is shaped and expressed in any culture, were thus constructed not on unknowable (meaning, unconcrete) abstractions or unfamiliar virtues or morals, but on explicit materiality. The Beguines had no ideal prototype on which to model themselves. They were not exposed either by their preachers or their regulations to imaginary foreign conceptions; nor were they instructed to reach toward unknown and unseen

111

goals. There is no evidence of ecstasy as a routine feature of religious life in the beguinages. Abstractions and aberrations were kept out of most women's spiritual activities and thus the beguinage is a kind of counter-example to the *vitae* of the great holy women. Many of the ecstatics, it is true, lived among the Beguines but the connection between the extraordinary and ordinary women remains puzzling, and difficult to document. An interesting case study is the rejection and attempted dissociation of the stigmatized Beguine, Gertrude of Oosten, by her Beguine sisters.[1] The Beguines' model was no queen of heaven or triumphant Virgin enthroned at the right hand of God the Father, nor was it the swooning ecstatic female saint exuding putrid odors or perfumed smells.[2] Those images are abstractions, which demand as such that the believer transcend herself and, guided by the way of faith, grope for, and try to attain, a different, otherworldly, spiritual state of being. Moreover, these other models are deeply literate ones; the Beguines, by contrast, were intensely worldly in their assumptions and experiences.

Transference, not transcendence, is the key premise underlying Beguine identity. Transference happens *via* identity — but we must be prepared to interpret this sensitively and subtley. Reality for women as Beguines was structured by the process of knowledge through material identification and identity, or by a process of transference. The instruments of transference shape, define, describe, guide, coax, and control actual experience and thus they are what gives actual substance to it. The instruments of transference, in other words, are the things that actually construct reality — they are the codes, the non-spoken language, that classify the identity and existence of things and how they are conceptualized.

The instruments of Beguine transference (the codes of knowledge as imitation) are explicitly material ones, instruments of the hand, as demonstrated above. Those instruments and codes, materially explicit and physically recognizable, construct the bridge between the individual and her reality. Through the tactile sense primarily the Beguine is linked to her collective social universe. That bridge — the sense of touch and tactility — is her reality; it is her realism.[3]

Tactile realism is a process of transference, grounded in recognizable identity *via* explicit materiality; and it is deeply personal, even if initially grounded in the institutional and collective social systems of the time.

Only after reading the Beguine rules this way can the question of how things generated feelings in Beguine viewers be responded to confidently. With a fresh view onto those rules we now can proceed by saying that whatever the Beguines felt, it did not occur as a process of transcending the reality of the senses the way it did for the more familiar western European medieval mystics. Rather, feeling took place in their conscious awareness of bridging themselves over to actual substances, of recognizing those substances as qualities, and of identifying with them by imitating them. Those are the processes of Beguine realism, mobilized in the tactile sphere, and conveyed by the instruments and codes of touch, things, and transference. Those are probably the most fertile sources of feeling (aesthetic and otherwise) in ordinary women viewers, the Beguines.

[1] See A.H. Bredero, ''De Delftse begijn Gertrui van Oosten (ca. 1320-1358) en haar niet-erkende heiligheid,'' in *De Nederlanden in de Late Middeleeuwen*, ed. D.E.H. de Boer and J.W. Marsilje (Utrecht: Het Spectrum, 1987): 83-97.

[2] Sweet odor is a *topos* of saintly behavior at St. Elisabeth's Beguinage in Ghent, in the legendary miracle (c. 1470) of the pleasing smells issuing from the tomb of a young Beguine named Matteken (*seer aengename reuk uyt quam*), who died on her knees praying. See Johan van Mechelen, *Vlaamse Begijnhoven. In Schemelheyt der Maechtlykheydt* (Tielt: Lannoo, 1973): 18-19; and *Werken en Kerken* (1984), pp. 22-23, and cat. no. 17 (the Matteken Crucifix).

[3] The use of the word realism is not intended to suggest an imitation of nature or a duplication of natural phenomena. That view has nothing to do with realism as I define it here. Rather, tactile realism is a term useful for evoking the ways Beguines structured, and hence understood, their reality.

PART III

THE PIETA

CHAPTER 6

DOCUMENTING SETTING AND USE

Establishing a corpus of *Pietàs* from the southern Low Countries, or present-day Belgium, is a complicated task. There is no way to confirm the number of *Pietàs* that may belong to private collectors *via* purchase or inheritance; nor is there any way to confirm the possessions of the various religious Orders and charitable houses in Belgium which may prefer not to make public the nature of their artistic inventories.[1] To gain an accurate picture of the date and provenance of the bulk of *Pietàs* from the southern Low Countries is thus quite difficult, for the documentation is sparse.

The state of documentary information on these *Pietàs* raises several important points. The first point has to do with the nature of the historical records themselves. The sources, where extant, may document who owned a given object, the miracles it worked, its architectural placement, who made it, or who inherited it; or, in still rarer cases, they may even convey something of the changing situation of a *Pietà* (for instance, the date and perhaps the reason for payment, an endowment of clothes to dress it or gold to adorn it,[2] a confraternity's weekly gatherings and prayers to it, or the consecration of benefices and altars to support it).[3] The sources at their richest, when they are most comprehensive, tell about an object's use and how that use metamorphosed across time.[4] But none of the remaining sources describes how ordinary people *felt* as they looked at *Pietàs*. They itemize people's actions and bear witness to the user's social status and religious occupation, or the artist's mode of production.[5] Yet I know of not a single document which records the feelings of an ordinary individual upon, or after, the act of beholding.[6]

We have two ways to proceed to interpret this omission. Either we can decide that feelings played no part in use, which is to say that individuals were motivated to look at *Pietàs* because of liturgical requirements or other forms of collective stimulation, and not by inner feelings; or we can conclude that feel-

117

ing in the later Middle Ages was not yet transferred, or transferable, to the given written structures of the time. That is to say, medieval concepts of self were not yet at that state of ego awareness where writers would see it fitting or relevant to report such personal inner feelings.[7] I take the latter hypothesis to be more nearly the case.

The sources of documentation on *Pietàs* are official records, wills and testaments listing ownership of goods, notarized acts of endowment, statutes of sculptors' guilds (and marks),[8] acts of founding chaplaincies, the dedications of altars, and the statutes regulating confraternal and other activites. Such records are the output of the civic and ecclesiastical legal system of a given society at a particular point in time; in the later Middle Ages such texts certainly accorded no place for the expression of personal sentiment and the like. Documentary sources of *Pietàs* are of a juridical and material nature; they are civic or religious actions or lists of property. Even if modern scholars were able to discover a full range of documentary sources for all of the extant *Pietàs*, the riddle of the object's meaning to believing individuals would still remain very far from solved.[9] In other words, more documentation will yield, in a positivist sense, more data of a quantifiable, chronological, and material sort, but it will never provide access to what with simple common sense we suspect to have been the case — that ordinary people were inwardly "moved" by viewing *Pietàs*.[10]

This brings us directly to our second point, the investigatation of the realm of ordinary feeling in private women viewers of *Pietàs*. To take up the task of exploring the feeling spectator is to venture a comment on current art historical uses of historical sources. It is to attempt to fuse two extremes of the processes of investigation, the one starting from the demonstrably certain and the other from the commonsense notion that sacred sculpture aroused a person's feelings. I believe that there exists a critical gap between what is demonstrable (legal actions, and religious and practical behavior) and what is not. In that gap are found ordinary people, their attitudes and feelings, and commonplace events. This gap can be filled only by supplementing the demonstrable evidence with a network of circumstantial evidence. The aim of an investigation such as this calls upon scholars to set aside momentarily certain presumptions about what is demonstrable *and* where such information is found and to replace those procedures with other modes of locating and structuring evidence. Those modes I developed by looking at the interstices between recorded use, action, and behavior and unrecorded feeling.[11]

This raises the third and final point having to do with the types of evidence presented here. The nature of my data in many ways was clarified by living, researching, and reading in that gap between use and feeling. The findings are best classified as pertaining to two types of records. The first have to do with use and site. The documentation discovered in the process of investigating the *Pietàs* is sufficient to permit a number of generalizations to be made. More than 25 percent of the *Pietàs*, for example, addressed women in some way or other — either they were owned by a beguinage, convent, or hospital, or they were at some time the focus of widespread public veneration. Of those, nine *Pietàs* almost certainly had a Beguine setting at some point in their history. In examining the importance of the *Pietà* image for the Beguines we must consider the following: (a) Beguines attended services and visited local parish churches[12] which today contain over 75 percent of the *Pietàs*; (b) individual Beguines very likely passed on their sculpture to family members without recording such;[13] (c) Beguines gave religious objects to their confessors or other members of the clergy;[14] (d) much of the sculpture of the southern Low Countries has been lost, stolen, or sold off, especially during the French Occupation at the end of the eighteenth century;[15] and (e) few of the *Pietàs* are documented at all. [Figures 1 and 2] When the above items are taken into account, the number of *Pietàs* attached to Beguines at some point or other in their history is in fact remarkably high. Considered in the context of the known extant *Pietàs* in general, those still found in beguinages form a considerably large proportion indeed.

In addition to the documentary evidence about *Pietàs*, we have a second type of record that can tell us about these objects, one that has to do with personal feeling. This evidence rests with the objects themselves. The *Pietà*, many scholars would probably claim, is one of the more formulaic and monotonous of the sculpture types to emerge during the Middle Ages.[16] Yet as David Freedberg has recently shown, the variations in limited types, such as the *Pietà*, or mass-produced devotional prints, are precisely what "ensures proper distinctions between one object and another."[17] Those distinctions, such as the formal specifications of the figures, their scale and surface treatment, the role of exaggeration and simplification, to name but a few, I take to be the factors that generate feeling in particular ways.[18] In fact, the culture seems to have discovered and sustained, as popular, an object type that consistently aroused the same range of strong feelings. Therefore the variations in the formal properties of *Pietàs* will not be treated here, as they have by art historians in the past, as records of geographical and regional style, of particular workshops, or of the manifestations of local workshops. [19] The variations in the *Pietà* type will not be analyzed in terms of style, but rather in relation to the way they focus and arouse specific feelings in the spectator. Variations will be looked at as evidence that viewing responses were not independent of the form.

The *Pietàs* are themselves historical records, *things* that document the conventions and expectations of the forms. These forms, then, act as a mode of accessing an aspect of reality as constructed by the community. People would not have been drawn to the sculptures had the formal properties not been able to unite spectator with sacred representations in a host of meaningful ways. To observe the factors underlying that union is to expose, on the one hand, what the anthropologist, Victor Turner, has termed, "the symbolic template of the whole system of beliefs and values in a given culture" [20] and to reveal, on the other, what is inherent to the forms, and thus culturally non-specified. To approach formal variations of given *Pietàs*, in other words, and to grasp the character of single features, enables us at once to locate symbols and themes indigenous to the fourteenth century (the *Pietà*, for example, as a reference to the Eucharist) and, at the same time, to indicate the source of continuously affective appeal. What I mean by "source" is that there is something present, only in the object, that continues to reverberate, as it were, to produce feelings in individual viewers across a succession of epochs and in many diverse Catholic cultures.

Our investigation of the *Pietàs* is not so constrained by a lack of sources as it might appear, especially when we proceed more openly in the ethnographic grain. We might say that the written sources (no matter how complete they may seem to be for a given object) give access to a discrete and incomplete historical reality, for it is a reality that is specified by written contents as predicated on the nature of the type of source at a given historical moment. To base an interpretation of *Pietàs*, for instance, on the sculptures' presence, descriptive character, and/or absence from wills and testaments is to learn much more about the reality of legal documentation and inheritance systems, and of how objects were cited and "valued," than about the meaning of *Pietàs* to the viewers they serviced.

Writing in the first decade of this century a German art historian and medievalist, Wilhelm Worringer, identified these issues clearly when he quoted the perspicacious philosopher and sociologist Georg Simmel: [21]

History cannot be a replica of events 'as they actually were,' but only a remodelling of the actual events determined by the constructive aims of knowledge and *a priori* categories, a remodelling which makes the form, that is, the actual essence, of this kind of knowledge no less than of the knowledge of natural science, a product of our synthetic energies. [22]

Simmel's position pertains to our discussion, especially when we consider the disjunction between the *Pietàs* in the written records and those outside them. When mentioned in written records *Pietàs* can contribute to our understanding of the larger hierarchies of values embedded both in what can and what cannot be written down. Yet the actual, lived meaning of *Pietàs,* their "historical truth," to borrow the description from Worringer, happened in areas of personal experience that until the eighteenth century were almost nowhere written down — and even at those rare times when they were, it was not ordinary people who took up the pen to do so. Beguine statutes have guided my analysis, but the items they contain are not reducible (or equivalent) to the full substance of what they mean. I might say the same for the miracle legends, the *vitae* of holy women, the foundation documents of lamps to altars of *Pietàs,* the transfer of objects from one owner to another. For this author, the objects and their formal variations are the *central components* of a unique experience, a unity of spectator to object; they are themselves the genuine record of feeling-experience.

In the following pages we reconstruct the bond between the two types of records (documents and *Pietàs*). First, we will look at the evidence in the written sources. This will tell us something about the events or situations that might have conditioned the spectator to unite, to put this in metaphorical terms, emotionally with the *Pietà*. Secondly and finally, we will explore how the object itself (to continue the metaphor) controlled her doing so. I have selected five objects on which to focus this discussion. Each has either been documented to a specific beguinage or Beguine or was part of a female context closely affiliated with the Beguines. In other words, I have attempted to develop the spectatorship of ordinary women by discussing in the text only those objects which we can be comparatively certain arose in or nearby a Beguine environment. We now turn to the *Pietàs*.

Let us begin our examination of the objects with the *Pietà* of the beguinage in Diest. (Inv. no. 116, plate 101) In 1988 it was exhibited and catalogued for an exhibition of treasures from that beguinage. [23] Yet our knowledge of its role within the community of Beguines remains limited to a few simple facts. It originally came from the church of the beguinage, but its precise location therein is not known. [24]

Scholars have not neglected to write about this elegant piece of sculpture, but they have focused their investigations exclusively on issues of composition, type, and style. In fact, a date of the first quarter of the fifteenth century has been proposed solely on the basis of the object's stylistic features and how they compare with similar *Pietàs* elsewhere. [25] The type from which Diest's *Pietà* is postulated to have derived was first described in 1924 by Walter Passarge in his *Das deutsche Vesperbild im Mittelalter* as the *Horizontaltyp* [26] and it offered him, as it did scholars thereafter, a way to date *Pietàs* which due to a lack of documentation would otherwise have been undatable.

Although the Diest *Pietà* is believed to have always belonged to the Beguines of Diest, discussions have brought to light no information about its use in the community's rituals.

We may consider the *Pietà* formerly at the beguinage of St. Catherine in Tongeren for which such use is better documented. (Inv. no. 84, plate 77) The product of an unknown workshop, this oak sculpture has several characteristics worth noting. First, Mary is crowned and seven swords pierce her heart; these additions show how this object has been materially altered to meet the needs of the new devotional expectations for the treatment of Mary in the fifteenth century. This is the *Virgin of the Seven Sorrows*, a type that accompanied devotion to the suffering Mary which became popular in the later fifteenth century in the Low Countries. [27] We know that there was a devotion to the *Noet Gods* in Tongeren in 1379. [28] Although this *Pietà* has not been subjected to a rigorous material analysis, it is not unlikely that the swords and crown were added to the Mother and Son group sometime after the initial production, to accomodate or respond to changing practices of devotion to the Seven Sorrows of Mary in the fifteenth century; [29] perhaps these changes occurred in the seventeenth century, when these kinds of additions to the core figures had their greatest popularity. [30] (Plates 51-52, 107-108) Second, the polychromy is modern. This demonstrates the continuous devotional importance of the object, for it has been modified according to the dictates stemming from changes in taste for heightened realism. Third, this *Pietà* formerly stood in the niche of a gable of a Beguine house, now disappeared, in the Bredestraat of the beguinage of St. Catherine in Tongeren. [31] This is a potentially important indicator of the sites for *Pietàs* and their use.

In the sixteenth century it became customary for Beguine houses and Beguine convents to be dedicated to a patron saint or similar theme which served to protect the inhabitants and remind them of the centrality of the devotion to their daily existence.[32] The house of this *Pietà* had most likely been dedicated to the Seven Sorrows of the Virgin. The site and the probable function suggest the meaning of the image to the Beguines. Just as importantly, opportunities for viewing the object arose daily, indeed as often during the day as the women came and went. Fourth, and perhaps most revealing for the process of tracing the paths of *Pietàs*, this *Pietà* was transferred before 1913 to the Franciscan convent in Tongeren, in whose collection it is currently maintained.[33]

Like the Tongeren *Pietà*, the *Pietà* of Mechelen also seems to have been sited outdoors. (Inv. no. 131, plate 112) It is believed to have once stood in a niche of a house[34] on the corner of the Tuinstraatje in Mechelen [Fr. Malines] dedicated to *de Nood Gods* [Dutch for *Pietà*].[35] The object is wood and is in a poor state of preservation (further evidence of its original placement out-of-doors).

In his invaluable documentary and stylistic study of the *Pietà* from Onze-Lieve-Vrouw van Ginderbuiten in Leuven (Inv. no. 123, plates 107, 108) published in 1981, the American art historian John Steyaert related the Mechelen *Pietà* to a group of "Netherlandish" *Pietàs*, versions of the German *Steilsitz* type[36] and examples of a "shift of emphasis" (the Virgin gazes outward) and a "softening of expression . . . typical of a general development in the treatment of this subject in Northern Europe after 1350."[37] The *Steilsitz* type, proposed by Wolfgang Krönig in 1962,[38] is based on the handling of compositional motifs: the type shows Mary sitting on a bench-like throne and holding Christ in an upright, almost seated position. Krönig's typology ultimately derives from Passarge's 1928 classification of *Pietà* groups and, like Steyaert's analysis, aims to illuminate typological filiations with a German ancestry. The Mechelen *Pietà* has thus far primarily been viewed within the geographical orbit of Mosan sculpture, an orbit which is interpreted by art historians as a fundamentally German production point. Like the Beguine *Pietà* currently housed in the Franciscan convent in Tongeren, this object probably had as its context a house dedicated to the suffering Christ.

As Steyaert has demonstrated, stylistic analysis has proven vital to situating this object within a family of similar date and similar compositional motifs. That this *Pietà* probably belongs to the earliest of such groups (circa 1375 in the southern Low Countries) might be crucial evidence for more than sculpture classification schemes, however; it may reveal, along with further archival research, that devotion to the suffering Christ had been strongly extra-liturgical, not confined to the dedicated liturgy and spaces (altars) of an official, religious realm. Integrated within the wall of a building on a city street, this image had been a public one. Moreover, as this *Pietà* was situated on the Tuinstraatje, a street that immediately abuts the western side of the Mechelen Beguinage, it was surely viewed daily by the Beguines, who walked through such streets as frequently as other townsfolk did as they went about their business in the town.[39] The display of *Pietàs* or other free-standing sacred objects (sculpture) in the secular realm (street) may have been formulated as a type of public address analogous to exterior portal programs, but intended to be less monumental and symbolically intricate than dedicated sacred sculpture on churches. At the same time however, this new type is less ornamental than the figurines carved over doors and onto exterior walls of the cloth and town halls.

In the following *Pietàs*, there are strong indications of an original setting in women's cloisters with Beguine antecedents. There are striking similarities between them in terms of dimensions (96 vs. 104 cm), material (lindenwood), composition (*Steilsitz*), and proposed date (around the end of the fourteenth century). The first *Pietà*, now in the Bonnefanten Museum in Maastricht, has been traced to a Franciscan convent in Heythuizen. (Inv. no. 130) We may recall that the *Pietà* of St. Catherine's Beguinage in Tongeren was transferred before 1913 to the Franciscan convent there; further archival research may reveal that the Bonnefanten *Pietà* underwent a similar transfer.

Another *Pietà* in the Tongeren City Museum very definitely belonged originally to a house of semi-religious women. (Inv. no. 136, plates 116, 117) These women began as a community of Beguines and in 1438 adopted the rule of the Third Order of St. Francis. Before 1796 (that is, until the French Occupation of the Low Countries) this *Pietà* stood in the church of the St. Agnes Convent in Tongeren.[40] Little documentation has emerged to clarify the inventories of sales during the French Occupation. In certain cases objects came into private hands. In others they were taken over by the secularized administration of charitable houses.[41] The properties of the Convent of St. Agnes appear to have been confiscated by the State and sold publicly in Maastricht in 1798. How the *Pietà* was acquired by Tongeren's City Museum is unknown.

The St. Agnes Convent was closely linked to the Beguines of Tongeren, and was itself probably a Beguine "convent" before Prince-Bishop Jan van Heinsberg of Liège allowed the women in 1438 to adopt the rule of the Third

124

Order of St. Francis.[42] The community originated in 1418[43] and soon thereafter the sisters may have purchased their *Pietà*, although there is no document to confirm this. The women were living immediately next to the St. Catherine Beguinage, not as members of it but rather as "convent" Beguines living together in their own house.[44] The Sisters of St. Agnes were prohibited in 1434 from begging for alms (which had probably been their way of supporting themselves) but they were allowed to support themselves by handwork.[45]

With the approval of their profession according to the rule of the Third Order, the sisters received permission to put up one or two altars and to enlarge their convent. A fire destroyed the church and part of the convent in 1500, but according to a seventeenth-century source, an "image of Our Lady and one of St. Agnes" were spared. This image of the Virgin can probably be identified as the *Pietà* now in the City Museum collection.

From 1438 the sisters were under the spiritual guidance of the Chapter and Congregation of the Beghards (Bogards) of Zepperen, a congregation of the regular Third Order of St. Francis. The Beghards in the fifteenth century probably worked from the cloth of the St. Agnes sisters.[46] In 1719 the Convent had a special veneration to the Immaculate Conception of Mary, although nothing is known about the ritual or cult objects and practices employed for such.

This evidence raises additional questions about the role of sacred sculpture in women's communities: was this *Pietà* made to order in the second decades of the fifteenth century for the newly established community of St. Agnes? It is quite likely that there is a connection with the devotion to the Sorrows of Mary that became active elsewhere in Tongeren at that same time.[47] Finally, how did the sisters, with their emphasis on handwork, but strongly cloistered, exercise their devotions to the old image of Mother and Son?

Similar observations may be made on the *Pietà* from the St. Agnes Convent of Dominican nuns in Sittard, founded in the seventeenth century.[48] (Inv. no. 81, plates 73, 74) There is almost no scholarship on this *Pietà*, however, and what does exist centers on issues of style. D. Bouvy related the Sittard *Pietà*, which he dates to the sixteenth century, to *Pietàs* in Oldenzael and the Cathedral of Roermond, the latter of "better quality and more organized composition."[49] In 1980, J.J.M. Timmers dedicated but a single sentence to the Sittard *Pietà* in his monumental study, *De Kunst van het Maasland*: "another fine and sensitive (late fifteenth century) rendering of the theme from the chapel of the former Dominican cloister of Sint-Agnes in Sittard."[50]

The location remains intriguing, especially in light of the previously examined *Pietàs* which have been relocated. As the Sittard *Pietà*, which is now kept in the convent, was certainly made before the seventeenth century, it evidently was not made for the nuns of Sittard. Their convent was founded only in 1649 and was destroyed by a storm in 1662; the new church, which was called the "begijnenkerk," was built in 1699.[51] We may have here another *Pietà* miraculously transferred and saved from fire.

Finally a sixteenth-century oak *Pietà* now in the Helshoven Chapel of Groot-Gelmen is not directly linked to a Beguine context and yet it offers exciting prospects for scholars to discover links between context and female spectatorship of sacred sculpture. (Inv. no. 32, plate 34) There are no documents linking the Helshoven *Pietà* with its present site, but tradition holds that it always stood in the Mary Chapel of Helshoven, an old pilgrimage site with a history of continuous and evolving devotions to Mary. The Mary Chapel lies on the border of several parishes and administrative communities. It is directly on the old Roman high road that links Belgium's oldest (Roman) city of Tongeren with Tienen and its environs. The place itself, in a rural part of Belgium, has been known as a "miracle site" for more than seven hundred years, which gives witness to the thousands of pilgrims who travelled there in the course of the centuries to implore the Mother of God. And, the nature of the cult, especially as it later evolved into one spiritually blessing stillborn children, was such that women were probably a major constituency of the pilgrims who visited there.

Historian Walter Simons indicates that "there is considerable evidence that great numbers of the women populating the beguinages were of rural origin."[52] In Sint-Truiden, not far from Helshoven, the percentage of women of "non-local origin" was as high as 62 percent in 1780.[53] Furthermore, although Simons states that "further research is . . . needed into the usual age of entry into the beguinage[54] . . . contemporary views continuously emphasized the large number of women of nuptial age who sought refuge in the beguinage after failing to marry properly."[55] Simons's discussion is suggestive of the female visitors to Helshoven, who may have implored the Virgin while living in the region before becoming Beguines. Although it cannot be proven, we ought not exclude the likelihood that women of many ages and all sorts of professions visited miracle-working shrines, like Helshoven, dedicated to Mary. Women entering the beguinage of Sint-Truiden may have been among them.

The first chapel at Helshoven was built in 1254 by the Knights of Saint John, who erected a hospice on the other side of the high road in order to accomodate

126

pilgrims with food and shelter. [56] In an inscription on a tombslab, currently housed on the west wall of the Helshoven Chapel, it is said that on 4 July 1255 Bishop Henry of Guelder permitted mass to be said along with grants to those who gave alms to the hospice. In the course of the fourteenth century, the Order of Saint John sold the property at Helshoven to the Teutonic Order at Bernissem near Sint-Truiden, which had Mary as its protector. The Chapel burned around 1574 during the Eighty Years War. Whether the *Pietà* was already in place then is impossible to ascertain. [57]

The Chapel was rebuilt in 1661. (plate 33) In 16 April 1674, the hermit Gerardus van Deventer received permission to build a hermitage next to the Chapel. Between 1674 and 1908, there were fourteen holy men in succession who consecrated their lives to the devotion of Mary, to the preparation of medicinal herbs, and the care of the sick. The last hermit died in 1908. During the time of Petrus Petri's hermitage remarkable events happened: in 1750, stillborn children were brought to the Chapel and laid near the altar. [58] After five days of novenas, the infants came back to life, were baptised by the hermit, and then died again. Mention was made in the eighteenth century by pastor Bartholeyns of a "miraculous image" — the period of great pilgrim traffic to the Chapel and the second peak period at the beguinages.

The *Pietà*, part of a fascinating repository of cult images dating over several centuries and displayed throughout the interior of the little Chapel, has not yet been examined for the specific role it may have played in women pilgrims' visitations. [59] Visitors coming to invoke Mary would not have missed the sculpture of Mother and dead Son. One is led to wonder whether the sculpture had not been implored to help the mothers of stillborn children or pregnant women from an early date. Although we cannot be certain of its use, we can surmise that the *Pietà* was at the center of a miracle-working shrine in the countryside, visited by believers from far and wide, especially female, in the efficacy of Mary.

The five case studies presented here indicate that *Pietàs* were housed in a variety of settings: in churches, chapels, convents, and pilgrimage oratories. One place for viewing *Pietàs* was the quintessential religious setting, the altar. But such official religious settings such as this were not the only ones available. *Pietàs* were also installed outdoors, in gables and niches of houses in the beguinage and on the city streets. Moreover, by the nineteenth century a Beguine community of Ghent, for example, had a large-scale *Pietà* placed at street level by the church. [Figure 3] The beguinage of Lier placed theirs in an

127

enclosed garden, where it remains in use today. [Figure 4] Although it is impossible to confirm at present, the tradition of placing *Pietàs* outside probably dates back to well before the nineteenth century. As the discussion that follows should reveal, there is sufficient evidence to indicate that the ritual of viewing *Pietàs* often took place out-of-doors and was not dictated by any formal or liturgical rites.

When placed in churches, they were probably not located on the high altar but on a subsidiary one, most likely on altars dedicated to the *Pietà* [Dutch *Nood Gods*] or to the Virgin of the Seven Sorrows [Dutch *Onze Lieve Vrouw van de Zeven Weeën*].[60] In 1423, for example, Jan van Heinsberg, prince-bishop of Liège, installed a chaplain for the altar of the *Noet Gods* in the beguinage church in Tongeren.[61] In 1394, the Beguines, Cristine and Margareta Anthonis, endowed a yearly *rente* for a perpetual lamp to burn (a candle) before the statue [*bijlde*] in the new chapel of the Church of Our Lady in Sint-Truiden. Here great miracles and favors *of God and his mother* purportedly happened on a daily basis [*en welker Capellen daechlics grote ghenade ende myracule Van Gode ende siinre liver moder gheschijt*].[62] There was a calvary, a scene of the crucifixion that included a *Pietà* in the beguinage church in Brussels, along the side aisles.[63] Documented evidence such as this suggests that the time of viewing was not dictated by the official liturgy and cultic rite, and that viewing was not restricted to the times of day when Beguines were statutorily required to be in the church to attend mass or to recite their daily offices.

Viewing was not officially part of the standard rite of the Mass, but rather one of the extra-liturgical rituals in church. Notably, many Beguine communities were required, it seems, to gather in the church daily to recite the hours. The rule for Bruges states, for example, that "All other hours of the office [except Nones] they will say in church unless they have a serious reason like a malady, great labor or other reasonable ground and notably holidays. Complines can be said at home, when this hour is said late or when it is dark in the winter."[64] At Lier, "every beguine received in the court shall hear every day a complete mass . . .; similarly, all beguines who have been received are obliged to observe the seven hours of the day; similarly all beguines on Sundays and Saints' days shall also hear High Mass and vespers in their parish church and not omit to do so except in case of great necessity. . . "[65] The Ghent Memorandum (1328) describes their "working usages and habits [are] as follows: they get up very early in the morning, gather together in the church,

128

each of them taking her proper place . . . . During the evening, however, they
enter the church after vespers and apply themselves to prayers and meditation
until the sign is given to go to bed. On Sundays and holidays they apply
themselves to masses, sermons, prayers and meditation and show the Lord their
complete devotion and servitude. . .'' [66] Vespers was the hour traditionally
reserved for contemplating the events of the crucifixion, and it may be the case
that during vespers the women took to saying the office before the statue of a
Pietà. [67]

Beguines maintained sacred statues in other indoor settings. It is recorded
that Bernard Pilate, a citizen of Douai, had bought two houses in the city for
ten poor Beguines and instructed them on his death bed, presumably before
1282, to pray daily for his soul before the Virgin in their hospital. [68] Wealthier
Beguines most likely had sacred statues in their private chambers, too, although
documenting this phenomenon remains difficult. [69] The custodian of the
church of the Madeleine of Tournai gave, for example, a ''crucifit en pitet''
from above his bed in 1349 to Maigne dou Cange. [70] This term likely refers
either to a *Pietà* or to a crucifix with a *Pietà* below; [71] in 1349 the Beguine
Maigne Au Poch of Tournai gave to Colle, the daughter of Henri de Maude,
a leather box filled with ''ymages.'' [72] The will of a Leuven Beguine reveals
that on 18 October 1625 she bequethed, among other things, a small statue of
Our Lady which hangs on the mantelpiece. [73]

First, any of these records may be referring to a *Pietà* since there was not yet
a standard terminology to denote this object type. [74] Moreover, it is impossible
to confirm how old the 'ymages' or sculpture mentioned were. Also, references
to women in wills and testaments often do not specify whether or not an individual was a Beguine. An overview of the documents does prove, however,
that Beguines owned sacred statuary privately. [75] Lastly, as the objects from the
Tongeren Beguinage and Mechelen prove, *Pietàs* were placed out-of-doors on
individual houses. And if nineteenth-century customs are continuous with those
of earlier days, *Pietàs* may have been in graveyards (plate nos. 41, 42, 85)
gardens (figure 4), in gateways (Inv. no. 3), on chapel and church walls (figure
3; plate 43), and in various other non-liturgical places within the beguinages.

When we look to the evidence of private ownership, there are clear indications that viewing was not formalized at all. Rather, we find that meditation
on the sculpture in the privacy of one's own chamber or the light of day along
the beguinage street seems to have been a function of a daily routine, regulated

by an individual's habits of praying and moving about the streets in pursuit of chores, visits, and other forms of everyday activities.

The fact that the settings for *Pietàs* were diverse helps us to characterize the structure and ritual of viewing. Primarily, viewing was not regularized or methodical, except in cases when linked to saying vespers; nor was viewing — and this is important to stress — necessarily a group or collective activity. Mass and the recitation of the Chapter rules and the hours were prescribed — and indeed strenuously enforced — as predictable, daily group activities. Thus far, however, there is no evidence that attests to the fact that viewing of sacred statuary was a communal event, except when images of Our Lady were carried in procession during feast days. It appears that viewing sacred imagery as a ritual structure was determined, and made routine, more by the individual than by the group. This point was reinforced by the Beguines I spoke to in 1989:

> "Ge mocht doen wat ge wilde. Ja, in uw kamer, daar mocht ge beelden zetten of portretten, dan mocht ge doen wat ge wilde he." [76]

> [You could do as you pleased. Yes, in your room, there you could put sculpture or photographs, then you could do as you liked.]

> "Hun eigen privédevotie, dat was meer op hun kamer he, elk had haar eigen devotie." [77]

> [Their own private devotion — that happened more in their room; each [Beguine] had her own devotions.]

The moments at which one came to beseech an image were therefore self-chosen and the method of devotion largely self-executed. This is important because it points to the personalized nature of viewing and to its autonomous structure as a ritual determined by the individual. These conditions, then, permit us to identify within the beguinage walls the phenomenon of the private, ordinary woman viewer of sacred objects.

The medium of the image played a part in enabling this phenomenon to come to the fore. [78] The Low Country *Pietàs* in the following Inventory are sculpted, mostly wood, and carved in the round. They are produced as free-standing groups conceived to be independent of monumental programs such as portals or large-scale altarpieces and retables. [79] As autonomous sculptures which, like the free-standing figures of saints that were emerging at the same

130

time, *Pietàs* are free agents, portable for the most part, and therefore able to be installed by owners in a variety of settings, indoors and out. The latter feature is crucial. *Pietàs* are religious objects; yet they are able and in fact conceived to function outside of liturgy. They are therefore one of the earliest and most numerous manifestations of the new genre of independent sculpture that emerged in the fourteenth century. This genre, because of its inherently simplified and flexible nature, would soon occupy a central place in the formation of private secular collections of religious art by many sectors of society.[80] The *Pietà* played a crucial role in this development.

Art historians understand that the emergence of free-standing sculpture marks a radical departure from the monumental architectural sculpture on the doors and choirs of Romanesque and Gothic churches or the liturgy-dependent, so-called "minor arts" of the preceding epochs. They tend to view the new genre as a response to the more privatized devotional practices generally, or as a result of local markets in the north yielding to the new production and taste for up-to-date sculpture types being exported from sculpture workshops in the Rhineland. Studying the *curtis* beguinage as a context for the sculpture suggests an additional factor in the emergence of free-standing sculpture: the new habitat for lay religious women, with its comprehensive union of sacred with secular and public with private architecture, was sufficiently unprecedented as a sculpture site to have made novel demands on the production of sacred sculpture in terms of scale and iconographical treatment.

Once inside the beguinage, sacred objects no longer fall within a vast superstructure of official churchly rite or as part of the common property of cloisters and monasteries. In earlier centuries sacred objects had been the purview of male monastery, cloister, and cathedral, where they were used and enjoyed collectively. Both features, the gender-specific product and the collective ownership, gave way in the fourteenth century and in the institution of the beguinage to a more open-ended set of functional and decorative priorities. Especially worth noting is that sacred objects could be common or personal property, and that this difference seems to have been totally irrelevant to their function.

This randomly personal and collective feature marks a radical change from the sacred art of the preceding epoch with its predictable patronage sources and patterns of architecturally and liturgically conditioned use. Considering the nature of previous contexts, it seems quite possible that free-standing figures, those like the *Pietà* which were carved in the round, had arisen to fulfill real-

131

ly quite practical demands. These were sometimes decorative and at other times efficacious, and were demands that were asserted by the unprecedented architectural settings of the women's beguinage towns, settings in which all aspects of life, prayer, and material things (like sacred statues) were both private *and* collective. [81]

[1] It has been quite customary in Belgium for banks to support exhibitions in their branches. These little showings of objects are accompanied by illustrated catalogues, in which the objects are undated, and presented without provenance or bibliography; objects included therein are therefore totally untraceable. See, for example, the catalogue which includes four *Pietàs* without citing provenance or bibliography or ownership: Bernard Blondeel, ed., *Gotische groepen uit Antwerps privé-bezit*, exh. cat. (Antwerp: Bank Brussel Lambert, n.d.), cat. nos. 17, 30, 31, and 51; also C. Engelen, ed., *Passie*, exh. cat. (Hasselt: Generale Bank, 1988). In the summer of 1988 I visited a hospital in which the nuns, pleased to have present the cleric who accompanied me, revealed their "hidden" treasures of approximately twenty *besloten hofjes*, from the Beguines, of the fifteenth and sixteenth centuries.

[2] A.R.A., Openbare Onderstand Leuven, no. 4984 makes frequent reference to clothes and crowns to dress images of Mary, St. Anne, and Christ [inventory of the chapel of the Small Beguinage in Leuven, 1617-1625]. For specific payments, see also Robert Van de Ven, "De Kunstinboedel van de Sint-Catharina- of Begijnhofkerk tijdens de 15de en 16de eeuw," in *Kunstschatten uit het Diestse Begijnhof*, exh. cat. (Diest: Stedelijk Museum, 1988): 129-38, nos. 14 and 15, which cites payment for a cloak and metal crown for the statue of Onze Lieve Vrouw of the beguinage of Diest.

[3] Ziegler (1989).

[4] Ibid.

[5] See the excellent exhibition catalogue, with scholarly essays on the production of sculpture and the Leuven *ateliers*, in *Het Laatgotische Beeldsnijcentrum Leuven*, exh. cat., ed. J. Crab and M. Smeyers (Leuven: Stedelijk Museum, 1979).

[6] I do not take the reactions of the great women mystics of the medieval west to be typical, but rather exceptional. Such would be Margery Kempe's hysterical outpourings at the sight of a *Pietà*. These are quoted in Edmund Colledge, O.S.A. and James Walsh, S.J., *A Book of Showings to the Anchoress Julian of Norwich*, part 1 (Toronto: The Pontifical Institute of Mediaeval Studies, 1978), p. 53. Until we understand the actual function of women's *vitae*, we cannot legitimately hold them to be representative of ordinary behavior. See Walter Simons, "The Hidden Language of Dance in Women's *Vitae*," (Paper delivered at the International Congress of Mediaeval Studies, Kalamazoo, Michigan, 1991); and Mark A. Abdoo, "Women's *Vitae*: A Response to Thomistic Eucharistic Theology" (unpub. paper, Holy Cross College, Worcester, Massachusetts, fall 1990).

[7] Dekker (1988).

132

⁸ J.M. Montias, "Socio-Economic Aspects of Netherlandish Art from the Fifteenth to the Seventeenth Century," *The Art Bulletin* 72 / 3 (September 1990): 358-72, esp. 369 for the southern Netherlands. For another view of the marketing situation, see Els Cornelis, "De Kunstenaar in het Laat-Middeleeuwse Gent," in *Handelingen der Maatschappij voor Geschiedenis en Oudheidkunde te Gent*, n.s. 41 (1987): 97-128 and n.s. 42 (1988): 95-138; and *Het Laatgotische Beeldsnijcentrum Leuven* (1979). While finishing the editing of this book an important article appeared by Dan Ewing, "Marketing Art in Antwerp, 1460-1560: Our Lady's *Pand*," *The Art Bulletin* 72 / 4 (October 1990): 558-84. See especially p. 560, where he writes: "The earliest reference to uncommissioned art being offered for sale at the Antwerp fairs comes from the *Chronicle of the New Church* in Delft, which records the visit of an out-of-town artist and master who stopped in Delft several years before 1411 while en route to the fairs of Antwerp and Bruges to market his works, one of which was a sculptured *Pietà*." Check against J. Leeuwenberg, "Een nieuw facet aan de Utrechtse beeldhouwkunst," *Oud Holland* 77 (1962), p. 99, n. 21, who records a text of circa 1380 referring to the passage through the city of Delft of a sculptor who wishes to sell his works, including "een beeld van onser liever Vrouwen in der Noodt" in Antwerp or Bruges. Cited in Steyaert (1981), p. 19, n. 12.

⁹ Historians are now exploring methods for retrieving from official, legalistic documents the more personal, subjective responses of ordinary individuals. In this regard see especially Darnton (1985). He reveals the method after recounting the trial and massacre of hundreds of cats by the workers in a print shop. The event stood out to them as the "most hilarious experience" in many of their careers: "By getting the joke of the great cat massacre, it may be possible to 'get' a basic ingredient of artisanal culture under the Old Regime." (p. 78)

¹⁰ For a compelling description of the use of documentation as a kind of archaeology, see Podro (1982), especially his Introduction. The discussion of sources and what they contain necessarily raises questions about the role of positivism as an historical approach. I claimed in Part II that conclusions drawn from circumstantial evidence (the history of gestures, as it was referred to by nineteenth-century cultural historians) would be cast into doubt by the positivist shadow looming over the doing of medieval history. One can see it forming in the methodological contributions of the German historian and classical philologist Leopold von Ranke (1795-1886), who turned scholars to the archives to use the sources. He sought objectivity in historical science, grounded in the foundation of the sources alone. 'Rarely has a phrase been so often and approvingly quoted as Ranke's declaration that he wanted not to pass judgment on the past but simply to report 'wie es eigentlich gewesen' [how it actually was]." Quoted in Ernst Breisach, *Historiography: Ancient, Medieval, & Modern* (Chicago and London: University of Chicago Press, 1983): 233.

¹¹ By this I mean to advance one more step beyond Richard Trexler who said, so inspiringly, in "Ritual Behavior in Renaissance Florence" (1972): "In order to correctly evaluate the relevance of religious behavior, the modern scholar must free himself from certain preconceptions. Easily the most confining is the assumption that religious behavior is less pious than contemplation, action less dignifed than sensibility." (p. 133) To which I would append, "and feeling less interesting than action."

¹² The rules regulated visits to local churches by Beguines: "If they go out of town or elsewhere, the mistress shall, at her own discretion, instruct someone to accompany them on their journey." [**Ghent Rule** (before 1354), p. 8] 'Similarly . . . no more than 12 shall go to somebody's first mass or to a funeral service . . ." and, "Similarly, as often as they can do so,

they shall hear mass in their parish and they shall not look for any useless opportunity to run without good reason to other churches . . .'' [**Sint-Truiden** (fourteenth century?), p. 310].

13 Conversations with Beguines (summer 1989): both said that the sculptures Beguines owned were inherited from the family and went back to the family after death.

14 In the inventory of goods of Catherine Simons, a Beguine in the Great Beguinage in Leuven, mention is made of a painting left to her confessor [A.R.A., Openbare Onderstand Leuven, no. 3071/64, n.d.]. The Virgin of Spermalie in Bruges was moved to the beguinage by the last surviving Cistercian nun of Spermalie. See M. English, ''Middeleeuwsche Mariabeelden te Brugge,'' *Kunst Adelt Peer* 7/3-4 (15 April 1929): 1-36.

15 For instance, an alderman of Bruges, J. Van Heurne, took a great deal of art out of the cloisters and convents in Bruges for his own collection in the last decades of the eighteenth century. See English (1929), pp. 16-17.

16 For how formulaic the type can be, see Inventory below for the southern Low Countries and for Germany, see *Stabat Mater: Maria unter dem Kreuz in der Kunst um 1400*, exh. cat. (Salzburg: Salzburger Cathedral, 1970), with hundreds of *Pietàs* illustrated.

17 Freedberg (1989), pp. 113, 115.

18 An additional thesis about the duplication of various *Pietàs* has been proposed in *Plastik am Mittelrhein ca. 1400: Ein Teil der Wirklichkeit*, exh. cat. (Frankfurt am Main: Liebieghaus, 1974), which claimed that duplication is indicative of the participation of the lower levels of society.

19 Consult the Inventory below for bibliography of specific objects.

20 Victor Turner (1964), in Lessa/Vogt (1979), p. 24.

21 Relations between Worringer and Simmel were explored during a symposium on Worringer at Hofstra University (April 1991). I wish to acknowledge here the research and writing of my seminar students (Holy Cross College, spring 1990) on Worringer: M. Hallett especially, with P. Lawrence, L. Panzarino, K. Pineo, and P. Pongracz.

22 Wilhelm Worringer, *Form in Gothic* (1911-12), trans. and ed. Herbert Read (London: Schocken Paperback, 1964). By using Simmel, Worringer was reacting against the von Ranke approach to history. See n. 10 above.

23 *Kunstschatten uit het Diestse Begijnhof*, exh. cat. (Diest: Stedelijk Museum, 1988), pp. 73-75, cat. no. 45.

24 There is a little modern *Pietà*, in a niche, still there on the north aisle of the nave of the Church. The other fine object from the beguinage of Diest is a standing Virgin and Child. There are documents (rare for the period) attached to this object, revealing its date of 1344 and its placement in the choir of the church. See *Rhin-Meuse* (1972), cat. no. 379.

25 In 1941, de Borchgrave d'Altena related this *Pietà* to a ''type popular in Germany'' in his *Notes pour servir à l'inventaire des oeuvres d'art du Brabant: arrondissement de Louvain* (Brussels: Ballieu, 1941), p. 209.

26 Passarge (1924), pp. 56, 68. Passarge contended that the type appeared ''fully new'' in the first decade of the fifteenth century, especially in eastern and southeastern Germany, and is denoted by the horizontal position of the Christ and the soft style (*der weiche Stil*) rhythm of the drapery folds.

27 B.A.O.C.M.W., Begijnhof van de Wijngaard, H. 794/1: accounts with information for expenses paid for the feasts of the Seven Sorrows and Seven Joys of Mary [Beguinage of the Vineyard in Brussels, 1579-80]; A.R.A., Openbare Onderstand Leuven, no. 2723: reference to

an altar of the Virgin of Sorrows in the Great Beguinage in Leuven (eighteenth century); A.R.A., Openbare Onderstand Leuven, 4034, nr. 9: will of Maria Horion, 17 November 1679 [Great Beguinage, Leuven]: she wished to be buried *"omtrent den autaer der Seven Weeden van Onze Lieve Vrouwe, in kercke van voorseide begijnhove."* For secondary sources, see Ed Speelman (1859); Joseph Witlox, *Belgium Marianum. Marias heiligdommen in woord en beeld* (Antwerp: Opdebeek, 1912); Abbé H. Mayo, *Le Belgique à Marie* (Brussels: Bieleveld, 1929); and "De Maria Vereering in Brabant," special issue of *Eigen Schoon en de Brabander*, n.s. 9, 17 / no. 3-4 (1934). Ed Speelman (1859), p. 47, on 7 March 1313 notes a diploma according indulgences to the faithful who visit the Oratory of the Seven Sorrows or Schreyboom in Ghent. For devotions to Seven Sorrows of Mary in Leuven, see Steyaert (1981), p. 23, n. 25; and W.A. Olyslager, *Het Groot Begijnhof van Leuven* (Leuven: Great Beguinage, 1978), p. 193, where the statutes (1791) regulate the eighth hour of the evening with the Seven Sorrows. The Beguines at St. Elisabeth's now have a *Pietà* in the hallway of the Head Mistress's residence perhaps associated with the Schreyboom (see Inv. no. 29, plate 30). For devotion to the suffering Mary east of the Rhine, see Lionel Rothkrug (1979), pp. 20-86.

[28] See the will of Ricald de Luyke of 29 August 1379: *Item legavit sepedictus testator altari ab ipso testatore fundato et in honore Passionis Domini nostri Jesu Christi vulgariter dicto der Noet Gods consecrato in ecclesia beate Catherine Beghinagii Tongrensis sito duos modios siliginis...* in Jean Paquay, *Cartulaire de la collégiale Notre-Dame à Tongres, jusqu'au XVe siècle*, vol. 1 (Tongeren, 1909), p. 507, no. 240. See also E. Persoons, "Prieuré de Ter-Nood-Gods à Tongres," *Monasticon Belge*, vol. 6: *Province de Limbourg* (Liège: Centre national de Recherches d'histoire religieuse, 1976): 267-76; and Tongeren, Stadsarchief, Begijnhof, Oorkonden, no. 90 [1423].

[29] See the *Pietàs* in Bellaire, Leuven, the Eglise Saint-Denis in Liège, and Winterslag with and without crowns (Inv. nos. 4, 46, 51, 104; plates 3-4, 45-46, 51-52, 91-93).

[30] Ziegler (1989).

[31] *Het Catherinabegijnhof te Tongeren*, exh. cat., Kunst en Oudheden in Limburg, no. 11 (Sint-Truiden: Provinciaal Museum, 1975), p. 21, cat. no. 17, illus. no. 6.

[32] Olyslager (1978), esp. pp. 102-58, for the specific dedications of the houses in the Great Beguinage in Leuven and Bijlage 6, p. 187, for payment for sculpture.

[33] See n. 31 above. Such moves from one location to another are rarely documented.

[34] See below Inv. no. 131. There are no museum records on file to confirm this but verbal communication with a museum administrator indicates that the piece was sited outdoors. For others similarly sited out-of-doors, see Inv. nos. 84, 99, 143.

[35] For the Dutch terminology see J.K. Steppe, "Het paneel van de Triniteit in het Leuvense Stadsmuseum. Nieuwe gegevens over een enigmatisch schilderij," *Dirk Bouts en zijn tijd*, exh. cat. (Leuven: Stedelijk Museum, 1975): 452-53; and for a documented use of *Noet Gods* as *Pietà*, see J. Duverger, *Brussel als kunstcentrum in de XIVe en de XVe eeuw. Bouwstoffen tot de Nederlandsche kunstgeschiedenis* (Antwerp: De Sikkel, 1935): 26-27.

[36] See below for comparision the *Pietàs* of Bellaire (Inv. no. 4, plates 3-4), Bree (Inv. no. 15, plate 17), and the Tongeren City Museum (Inv. no. 136, plates 116-117).

[37] Steyaert (1981), p. 20.

[38] Krönig (1962), pp. 133-34.

39 I cannot resist including here the comment by one of my readers, who wondered whether this wasn't the way to get a quick "suffering fix" as they go about their shopping. Intriguing thought.

40 Stedelijk Museum Tongeren, *Handout*, cat. no. 45.

41 In Leuven, for example, the church of the Small Beguinage (*Het Klein Begijnhof*) was closed in 1797 and sold off in 1798; its furniture was bought by individuals and its houses changed over to "Les Hospices Civils de Louvain." (Olyslager [1978], p. 212) For additional examples of *Pietàs* now in the possession of O.C.M.W. or other secular institutions, see Inv. nos. 61, 114, 116 below.

42 *2000 jaar Tongeren, 15 voor Christus tot 1985*, exh. cat. (Hasselt: Uitgeverij Concentra, 1985).

43 Gilbert Remans, "Twee Franciskaansche Instellingen te Tongeren," *Bulletin de la Société Scientifique & Littéraire du Limbourg* 42 (1928): 127-36, esp. p. 129.

44 Ibid., p. 129. This situation was similar to that in Leuven, where the Black Sisters, although not belonging to the Great Beguinage, had been connected to it architecturally — they were joined by a common wall. The Leuven community originated in 1438, only two decades after the St. Agnes Convent in Tongeren, when Elisabeth Ymbrecht of Liège, a convert from Judaism, rented a house in Leuven to care for the sick; she wore Beguine clothes. Before long, other young women came to help her, and she bought a house to start a cloister; her community adopted St. Augustine's rule, quickly enlarged and became a vast organization of women caring for the sick at home. The cloister in Leuven was expropriated under the French regime and today serves as a psychiatric institute for women. See Olyslager (1978), p. 150.

45 Remans (1928), p. 130.

46 Ibid., p. 136.

47 Persoons (1976).

48 J.H.H. Sassen, "Register en memorieboek van het Dominicanessenklooster St. Agnetenberg te Sittard," *Publications de la Société Historique et Archéologique dans le Limbourg* n.s. 29 (1913): 161-304; and Michael Schoengen, *Monasticon Batavum*, vol. 2, *De Augustijnsche Orden* (Amsterdam: Noord-Hollandsche Uitgevers Maatschappij, 1941): 174-75.

49 D.P.R.A. Bouvy, *Middeleeuwsche Beeldhouwkunst in de Noordelijke Nederlanden* (Amsterdam: A.A. Balkema, 1947): 186-87.

50 J.J.M. Timmers, *De kunst van het Maasland*, vol. 2 (Assen: Van Gorcum, 1980): 159.

51 A.M. Bogaerts, ed., *Historische beschryvinghe der cloosters van het order van den H. Dominicus, geschreven in 't jaer 1715 door Pater Bernardus de Jonghe, predikheer*, vol. 1, *Bouwstoffen voor de geschiedenis der dominikanen in de Nederlanden* (Brussels: Dominikaans Archief, 1965): 211-18. An interesting link with Tongeren is that in the second half of the seventeenth century, according to Bogaerts (p. 214), at least one of the confessors at Sittard was Raymundus a Campo, a member of the Dominican convent of Tongeren, who seems to have been instrumental in the rebuilding of the convent in 1662-63. It remains a mystery why the church of St. Agnes is called "begijnenkerk." There was a beguinage in Sittard by 1276. See R.R. Post, *Kerkgeschiedenis van Nederland in de Middeleeuwen* (Utrecht and Antwerp, 1957), p. 228.

52 Simons (1989), p. 73.

53 Ibid., p. 74.

54 Ibid., p. 75.

55 Ibid.

56 All information is taken from Fons Appermans, *Kapel Helshoven 13de eeuw: Genadeoord van Maria van de Blijde Vrede* (N.p., n.d.); and "De kapel van Helshoven," in *Grepen uit het verleden van Hoepertingen* 12 (1988): 751-58, which summarizes and repeats the content of Appermans's handout.

57 This *Pietà* has been published with and without polychromy. See Inv. no. 32 for location of the photographs. Perhaps the *Pietà* there today is a replica. This is important, as it suggests a history of continuous devotion.

58 See the Vreren *Pietà* (Inv. no. 99, plate 86), which was also reputed to bring stillborn children back to life.

59 Michael P. Carroll, *The Cult of the Virgin Mary: Psychological Origins* (Princeton: Princeton University Press, 1986), pp. 111 and 221, claimed that the Mary cult was not inherently female, but rather depends on regional location.

60 See, for instance A.R.A., Openbare Onderstand Leuven, no. 2723: *cum in ecclesia majoris begguinagii Lovaniensis variae reperiantur statuae seu imagies B. Mariae Virginis...adeo...tres ad idem altare Septem Dolorum Beatae Mariae Virginis..., quarum medio in altari collocata Matrem Dolorosam representat* [Great Beguinage in Leuven, eighteenth century]; no. 3071/13: *kiesende haere begraeffenisse inde kercke van dit begijnhof omtrent den autaer van Seven Weeuen* [will of a Beguine of the Great Beguinage in Leuven, 1701]; see above n. 28 for the citation of the will of a Beguine of the Great Beguinage Leuven, 1679, who wishes to be buried near the altar of the Seven Sorrows of the Virgin; no. 4682, fol. 2v: *Item sal de huysmeesteresse mette conventualen schuldich sijn behoorlijck te palleren ende vercieren den autaer van Onse Lieve Vrouwe Seven Weeden inde kercke vanden voors. beghijnhove naer het saisoen van tijdt ende heysch der heylighe kercke* [foundation of the convent of the Virgin of the Seven Sorrows in the Great Beguinage of Leuven, 1662].

61 Tongeren, Stadsarchief, Begijnhof, Oorkonden, no. 90; see also *Het Catharinabegijnhof te Tongeren*, exh. cat., Kunst en Oudheden Limburg, no. 11 (Sint-Truiden: Provinciaal Museum, 1975), no. 46.

62 J. Moors, *De oorkondentaal in Belgisch-Limburg van circa 1350 tot 1400* (Brussels: Belgisch Inter-Universitaire Centrum, 1952), no. 148. pp. 301-02. It is impossible to tell which "bijlde" is being named, but the suggestion provided by "God and his mother" that it may be the *Pietà* is intriguing. The practice began earlier: in 1279 the will of a Beguine of Tongeren endows income for candles given to the church of the Beguinage *ante ymaginem beate maria e virginis in eadem ecclesia* [Tongeren, Stadsarchief, Begijnhof, Oorkonden, no. 6].

63 B.A.O.C.M.W., Begijnhof van de Wijngaard, H 794/2B, fol. 8r [1744].

64 **Bruges** (circa 1290), pp. 53-54.

65 **Lier** (1401), p. 341.

66 **Ghent Memorandum** (1328), p. 75.

67 That the *Pietà* was beheld during vespers is the reason for the origin of the German word for *Pietà, Vesperbild*. See Panofsky (1939), p. 490.

68 Douai, Archives municipales, GG 191 [seventeenth-century copy]. See also B.A.O.C.M.W., Begijnhof van de Wijngaard, H 764/1, fol. 2r: accounts for the "Convent of the Calvary" in the Brussels Beguinage, 1676-1780, citing expenses for candles on the altar of Our Lady (in the church of the beguinage?). It proves to be nearly impossible to trace the objects owned by such hospitals, especially if they have been sold. For example, the inventory

137

of goods of the chapel of the infirmary of the Great Beguinage in Leuven mentions the sale of two objects in 1659, but does not specify what kind of objects they were or to whom they were sold [A.R.A., Openbare Onderstand Leuven, no. 3477].

69 To document private ownership and placement requires a more comprehensive understanding than we possess at present of the pattern of recording images in personal wills.

70 A. de la Grange, "Choix de testaments tournaisiens antérieurs au XVIe siècle," *Annales de la Société Historique et Archéologique de Tournai*, n.s. 2 (1897): 70. In the inventory of goods left by Catherine Simons, Beguine in the Great Beguinage in Leuven: *item een crucifix met voet* [A.R.A., Openbare Onderstand Leuven, no. 3071/64].

71 See Alexandre de Laborde, *Les Miracles de Nostre Dame compilés par Jehan Miélot* (Paris: Société française de reproductions de manuscrits à peintures, 1929), p. 174, chapter 34 for the Jesus and the oath of the crucifix, where the crucifix is illustrated as a *Pietà*. I wish to thank A. De Schryver, University of Ghent, for this reference and for informing me that in texts of the later Middle Ages, crucifix simply means crucified man, not cross. This view is supported by a document of 21 April 1520 in which Margaret of Austria pays Bernard van Orley for polychroming a *Pietà*. The object is described in her account books as, "Et pour avoir coulouré une grande ymaige de bois à la remenbrance [sic] de nostre Dame de pitié tenant le crucifix devant elle . . ." Jos. Duverger, *Conrat Meijt (ca. 1480-1551)*, Académie royale de Belgique, Classe des Beaux-Arts, Mémoires in -4, no. 5 (Brussels, 1934), p. 75. The *Pietà* is perhaps the same as the one by Conrat Meijt discussed in Inv. no. 145 below.

72 de la Grange (1897), p. 72.

73 A.R.A., Openbare Onderstand Leuven, no. 3494/26.

74 For definitions of *Pietà*, see K. Smits, *De Iconographie van de Nederlandsche Primitieven* (Amsterdam: De Spieghel, 1933), pp. 106-13; Duverger (1935), pp. 26-27; Kalinowski (1953), pp. 106, 108; Steppe (1975); Belting (1990), pp. 84, 172-73, 191.

75 This practice was confirmed in 1989 *via* my conversation with the Beguines of Lier and Ghent: wealthier Beguines had statuary in their private chambers, which they believed had been inherited from and passed back into the family without a record of such.

76 Conversation with a Beguine from Lier, 1989.

77 Conversation with a Beguine from Ghent, 1989.

78 For a theoretical discussion of the emanicipation of sculpture from the cult ritual to "unspecific functions," see Bernhard Decker, *Das ende des mittelalterlichen Kultbildes und die Plastik Hans Leinbergers*, Bamberger Studien zur Kunstgeschichte und Denkmalpflege (Bamberg: Lehrstuhl für Kunstgeschichte und Aufbaustudium Denkmalpflege an der Universität Bamberg im Selbstverlag, 1985), esp. pp. 92-98.

79 Some *Pietàs* housed in museums are obvious fragments of retables. For an illuminating discussion of the figurally autonomous image within the retable, see Skubiszewski (1988), p. 24ff.

80 Ringbom (1969) illustrates several images of aristocrats and clerics praying before images and reading from psalters; art historians have thus far concentrated on the better-documented, high level patronage of the arts in this time period — by well-placed clergy, nobles, court functionaries, and so on. See, for example, Craig Harbison, "Secularity and Social Standing in Jan van Eyck's Arnolfini Double Portrait," *Renaissance Quarterly* 43/2 (1990): 249-91. An important exception, unfortunately treating only household works and private devotion in Italy, is Roland G. Kecks, *Madonna und Kind. Das häusliche Andachtsbild im Florenz des 15.*

Jahrhunderts (Berlin: Gebr. Mann Verlag, 1988). As discussed above, the wills and testaments of ordinary women demonstrate, however, that in the southern Low Countries people from a variety of social strata owned sculptured images — in contrast to texts, whose owners and users were far more restricted to higher levels of society. Evidence of book possession by individual Beguines is found in wills. Some data have been collected on this point by Lauwers and Simons (1988), pp. 33-34. A lack of sources, however, makes it difficult to generalize about their ownership of texts. Moreover, most Beguines had little time for activities such as reading. Beguine psalters have recently been studied by Judith Oliver, *Gothic Manuscript Illumination in the Diocese of Liège (c.1250-c.1330)*, in Corpus van verluchte handschriften uit de Nederlanden / Corpus of Illuminated Manuscripts from the Low Countries, vols. 2-3 (Leuven: Peeters, 1988) and idem, *In beeld geprezen. Miniaturen uit Maaslands devotieboeken 1250-1350*, exh. cat. (Leuven: Peeters, 1989). Walter Simons's review of these two studies in *Ons Geestelijk Erf* 65 / 1 (1991): 23-30 probes further the historical premises still needed to establish whether the psalters were actually owned by and made for Beguines.

[81] This interpretation is substantially different from previous ones that have sought a textual source for these late medieval sacred images. We do not need, I believe, to find a text as source.

CHAPTER 7

THE "PERIOD" *PIETA*

INTRODUCTION

Let us stand back from the particulars and talk about the *Pietàs* as a group, especially about their subject matter and the readings it may have received in the later Middle Ages. A woman holds the body of a half-naked man on her lap. That, simply put, is the subject of the *Pietà*, even though across the centuries audiences never doubted the identity of the figures as being the Virgin Mother with her Son, Jesus Christ, after his crucifixion.

During the peak period of production between the early fourteenth and mid-sixteenth centuries, the treatment saw numerous changes and transformations, which scholars have scrupulously classified according to type, date, and regional point of origin. During the late fourteenth and early fifteenth centuries, for example, a popular type of *Pietà* depicted the Christ as a full-grown man but with a small, diminutively scaled body. This gives the appearance, scholars have argued, that the Virgin holds a child's body, not that of an adult or of a man of the age Christ was when crucified. [1] [Inv. nos. 22, 130, 131, 136] Types have been classified according to the facial expression of the Virgin, which in some examples is joyful, in others sorrowful. Types have also been categorized according to the positioning of Christ's body: whether it is upright, on a diagonal, horizontal, or on the ground in front of the Virgin at her feet. [2] As has often been noted, stylistic details evolved with time from figures whose drapery folds look back to a Gothic mode or forward to the voluminous billowing quality of the Baroque style. Regional preferences have also been considered important explanations of variations in style. Sculptors from certain regions, such as Bohemia, left vigorous signs of local workshop preferences in the handling of the Virgin's veil or the layering of relief in her drapery. [Inv. nos. 57,

104, 116 and plates 91-93, 101, 116] Iconographical and stylistic details such as these have been comprehensively investigated for more than a century because they help modern scholars establish dates, places, affiliations among sculptors, and export patterns. The near total absence of documentation about the objects would otherwise leave them groping in the dark for chronological certainty.

The present approach owes a great deal to those findings. Indeed the tradition of art historical connoisseurship has secured so many *Pietàs* in terms of date and regional point of origin that Low Country examples, by comparison, may be situated fairly easily. We are therefore able to turn to other concerns. I wish to take up issues of the subject matter of the *Pietà*, especially those concerning the representation of the two figures as an ensemble. There are two categories of meaning in the *Pietà* which do not depend on our apprehending the stylistic or morphological details. To gain insight to this level of meaning necessitates setting aside the variations of drapery treatment and stylistic details for the moment. Rather we must put the following in view: semantically, all *Pietàs* work outward from an identical kernel formed by the human, crucified Christ alone with his Mother. That is what makes a *Pietà* a *Pietà*. Differences in date or workshop cannot and do not fundamentally alter the essentials of that relationship — indeed they serve to enhance and elaborate it. From this premise it becomes possible, by isolating the Beguines in the period of the later Middle Ages, to generalize about the ways that ordinary women were likely to have ''seen'' the essentials, the kernel of the *Pietà*. Here I am interested first in establishing a local reading, that is to say, in establishing the indigenous meaning of *Pietàs* to Beguines of the fifteenth and sixteenth centuries. Indigenous meanings are the ones that arose, lived, and died in the particular ambience of past times, in specific times and places. Those are the meanings that constitute what I have called the *Pietà's* ''period'' iconography rather than its more ''universal'' meaning. This study ultimately wants to illuminate the sources of the *Pietà's* universal meaning; but the meaning of the *Pietà* in its own time must be clarified before we can distinguish it from the nature of its appeal as a universal one.

THE "PERIOD" PIETA

There are two categories of period meaning in the *Pietà* in the time from the late fourteenth through the sixteenth centuries: the practical and the sacramental. We turn first to the practical aspect of the iconography as conveyed by the specific imaging of woman in the *Pietà*.

Mary — she is woman, mother, chaste wife, consoler, nun, mourner and guardian of the body, a husbandless woman and, as a result of the crucifixion, a childless one. Working from the simplest level of the representation, a striking concordance emerges between the representation of Mary and the actual woman as Beguine. Like the Beguine, Mary herself was not a nun: she was a lay woman and a holy one, but never a cloistered member of a religious Order. Like the Beguine, Mary could have known the pleasures of the conjugal bed had she chosen to; chastity was her want. Beguines were without child and husbandless, all of them alone, isolated. Nursing was a Beguine vocation; they ministered to one another and, as documented in Tournai and Bruges, guarded the corpses, prayed for them [3] and escorted the dead to the burial ground. [4] The *Pietà* images the kind of woman a Beguine was, in her maturity, in her painful relation to children, in her self-imposed chastity, and in the active pastoral role as consoler to the dying and guardian of the dead, and in her independence. In their imaging of woman, if in no other way, *Pietàs* do mirror the material characteristics of Beguines.

I do not intend to claim that Beguines were alone in perceiving self-references to Mary's identity. For, as I have stressed from the beginning of this study, the Beguines are but the rare documented examples of ordinary women. What is central to our interpretation of them as viewers, however, is that they have been documented as experiencing the same actions and conditions as those imaged by the *Pietà*-Mary.

Beguines were prepared to access this practical category of meaning by the principle of imitation. This was the process by which women's experience as Beguines was structured; they assumed that they should model themselves on the virtues of saintly women as well as on the exterior conditions of one another. As women routinely schooled in the process of identification, or of knowledge by identification, the Beguines would have been sensitive to the Virgin's call to imitate herself, the call to *imitatio Beate Virginae*: to be like,

143

act like, look like Mary. [Plates 34, 101] There in the *Pietà* she sits, veiled in the widow's hood or nun's habit, her head always covered (as Beguine statutes prescribe), her facial expression composed in grief or joy.[5] The *Pietà*-Mary is prescriptive and didactic. She is a virgin wife, a chaste and isolated woman. Her image calls for the viewer to be like her and act like her, for it is good to nurse, to show compassion, to pray over the corpses of the dead; and to look like her, cover the head with a veil and carry the body always in a dignified manner.

Those operations call to mind the characteristics of an *exemplum*, a recipe or formula which preachers and writers employed when constructing sermons or saintly biographies in order to aim these verbal texts directly at local audiences by the use of readily comprehensible anecdotes. Lascivious clerics, promiscuous widows, and all versions of the 'birds 'n bees' are the humorous side of the powerful rhetorical device of anecdote, known as an *exemplum*.[6] Although scholars have largely confined their explorations of *exempla* to their verbal manifestations in sermons and *vitae*, visual imagery comes very close indeed to the spirit and objective of that narrative device. *Exempla* seek to drive home general principles to specific audiences by ornamenting them with vivid and explicit features that render intelligible the abstractions of a moral lesson or other significant points. *Exempla* have an explicit moral and religious significance.[7] Clearly visual imagery served similar exemplary purposes. Beguine audiences, given the probable low level of literacy, had likely been more active in shaping the meaning of visual things to meet their own ends (and in making them conform to particular purposes) than in hearing the anecdotes presented audibly in a sermon.[8] The Mary of the *Pietà* probably functioned as an *exemplum*, one which in the later Middle Ages imaged for the Beguines the practical model of Mary, a simple recipe supplementing, codifying, and reinforcing the particular features that comprise the ideology of imitation.[9]

The second category of period meaning in the *Pietà* is sacramental, by which specifically I mean eucharistic. The crucified body of Christ represented in the *Pietà* — the *corpus Domini* — in and of itself signals the presence of the redeemer in the most complexly historical, sacramental, and symbolic modes. In 1981, Hans Belting published a categorical account of the "language of the image" [of the body of Christ], revealing what the images communicated and the contemporary conditions of cultic practice and reception of relevant imagery which enabled them to do so.[10] Belting was primarily interested in the sacramental references to the body of Christ and in how viewers came to decode

144

them.[11] Although he did not include northern *Pietàs* in his investigation, Belting's claims are applicable to them nonetheless.[12] Especially relevant are the ones that assert that the viewer must be "prepared to experience" the "sacramental reality" of the image in order for it to be "visible" or "recognizable" at all.

Beguines were as prepared as any of the laity to decode the eucharistic references in the *Pietà*.[13] It must be remembered that the Feast of Corpus Christi [1264] — a special feast day "dedicated exclusively to the celebration of the real presence of Christ's body in the consecrated sacramental elements"[14] — arose in a female and Beguine ambience, and (importantly) arose specifically and uniquely in the southern Low Countries.[15] The Feast and its associated cultic rituals Belting finds important for exciting the popular imagination about the sacramental references in imagery to the body of Christ.[16] Even so, Belting neglects to make the point that it was a woman, Juliana of Cornillon (1193-1258), who promoted the founding of the Feast Day.

This legendary woman was, moreover, an integral part of the everyday Beguine milieu in the Low Countries.[17] Juliana had numerous friends among the Beguines, and between 1240 and 1244 she even lived in a beguinage.[18] Likewise, she had friends among the Cistercians, such as the abbess of Salzinnes and the abbots of Villers, who were themselves vigorously involved in promoting and protecting the Beguines of the area.[19] It is thus not surprising to discover that some beguinages required Beguines to take the sacrament at least four times a year;[20] or that Beguines mounted their own ceremonies for the Feast Day, including processions;[21] and that individual women made donations of candles to be burned for the sacrament on the high altar.[22] Beguines thus received the sacramental Christ as the Host in the Eucharist *and* as an object of ritual exhibition, two of the components that Belting claims must be present for the viewer to receive the image of the body of Christ visibly as a sacramental one.[23]

There is no need, then, to turn for further proof to accounts of bleeding and flying Hosts, however abundant or prevalent they may have been in the *vitae* of women or in the narratives describing the theatrical spectacles of elevation and reception of the Host in the North.[24] The textual records of little bits of Christ's body winging through the air or its pregnancy-stimulating effects on women's bellies which swelled as they approached receiving it — those legends are so miraculous and fantastic that they are as "live" in the popular imagina-

145

tion now as they were then. These narratives are stunning depictions of women's reaction to the sacramental body of Christ, to be sure. But the *vitae* are not nearly so dependable as records of ordinary women's real and habitual eucharistic activities as are the comparatively prosaic and mundane documents about beguinages and about the Beguines' routines of receiving and honoring the Host with candles, processions, and other sorts of predictable feast day activities.

Nor is there need of delving into theoretical debates over the belief in the "real presence" of Christ in the Host and how this belief gave rise to the many manifestations of "passive" or "spiritual" Communion. Scholars have speculated that the fear of being in a state of sin upon receiving the sacrament produced in people the fear of subjecting the Christ in the Host — the "real presence" — to the indignities of the crucifixion again. And this fear, they argue, in turn produced an intensification of visual rather than actual reception of the Host. [25] Despite speculation about people's awareness of the profound theological mystery of Transubstantiation, these remain impossible to confirm as an actual, functioning reality among ordinary Beguines.

By following Belting's line of interpretation more closely, it becomes possible to view the Beguines as finding in the *Pietà* an equal emphasis on the sacramental nature not only of Christ, but of Mary, too. Belting says, "As is well known, the *Pietà* group consists of a figure bearing and a figure being borne, of Mother and Son. Mary is, so to speak, the monstrance for the exhibition of the sacrificed Christ whom she displays, and with whose piteous appearance she awakens the pity of the viewer." [26] The woman takes unto herself the body; the woman "receives" the crucified Christ. In this sense, the *Pietà* is re-enacting the First Communion of the Virgin. The image of the Virgin's "reception," I would emphasize, is more active in the strictly female context of the beguinage than is Belting's proposed image of "presentation." The process of identification with Mary, and of modeling on and learning from her example, was already well in place before the Beguines would have viewed the image. That process was ensured by the Beguines' institutional ideology of material appearance. If a sacramental reality existed in the image at all, it did so by proceeding from the (Beguine) viewer's practical identity with Mary first. The *Pietà* images the way the women of the later Middle Ages shall "have" the body of Christ, first by identity as mother, nurse, consoler, guardian of the dead, mourner, and only after, as a sacramental image of Mary taking onto and into herself the crucified body of Christ.

146

The *Pietà's* emphasis on Mary raises a number of intriguing issues about the deepest levels of engagement between the object and the woman viewer. We hear often from feminist scholars of the Middle Ages that women generally took the prevalent desire to live in imitation of Christ much farther than men did. [27] Descriptions of extreme bodily reactions abound in that scholarship, of women excreting bodily fluids, bleeding, routinely undergoing the stigmata, vomiting, crying oceans of tears and the like. Drawn from the *vitae* and convent chronicles, these narratives suggest to modern scholars that for a variety of reasons, which can only be speculated on, women's tendency to imitate in those reactions the humanity of Christ was very widespread indeed. Important for this study is the suggestion, too, that this pattern was present some time before the founding of the beguinages in the mid-thirteenth century. To what extent those narratives reflect any degree of historical truth we are not at this moment in any position to determine.

It is clear nonetheless that at least the principle of *imitatio Christi* — and of imitation generally — was the foothold upon which the rules of the beguinages and hence of women's most predictable common experience did rest. The *Pietà* had an especially suggestive part in the program of imitation. Mary touches the body of a half-naked Christ. This is puzzling. Authorities were otherwise careful to regulate and control women's codes of actions and behavior and were otherwise fully aware, as I have argued elsewhere, [28] of exploiting women's inclination to imitate *via* material and physical substances. How could those same authorities permit those same women to gaze upon the quintessential female model engaged in overtly physical dealings with the body of Christ? [29]

It is well to remember how explicit the beguinage rules were concerning women's sexual activities. For Beguines, unlike nuns, the conjugal state and hence physical knowledge of a man was always before her as a possibility. Whether in fact the possibility was likely is quite beside the point. The rules also give witness, as might be expected, to the fact that Beguines were preoccupied with the day-to-day workings and desires of the flesh. [30] Additionally, historians have been quick to point out that the Beguines believed in Christ as the Heavenly Bridegroom, their spiritual spouse, companion, and lover. [31] The statutes of Bruges go so far as to direct the women after prayers to go ''to bed and rest with God.'' [32] These conditions are an illuminating backdrop for characterizing the social-psychological reality of the women viewers when they were Beguines.

147

One final and crucial aspect of the women should be recalled. Generally speaking, most Beguines were not great intellects, visionaries, or towering mystics. While scholars keep these figures vividly in the foreground today, such women (some of whom it is true were Beguines) were exceptions in society, not the rule. They were the subject of written biographies, the friends and intimates of male clerics, even of aristocrats. [33] The Beguines who are known by name, such as Ida of Louvain or Hadewijch of Brabant, are the hagiographical Beguines who stood apart from and — we must be prepared to grant — above the ordinary Beguine. The latter was occupied not by extremes of asceticism or piety but by going about her daily chores of cooking, doing laundry, washing floors, making cloth, and cleansing the sores of sickly souls. As the Beguine of Lier recently put it, ''We had no time. We had to bake hosts and even eat while they baked. We were always working.'' [34]

I am not the first scholar to contend that exceptional holy women probably had little need of concrete images of Christ and Mary, so powerful was their ability to summon visions at will and at least to envision a mental picture of him with some predictable frequency. Ordinary women, like many lay folk, had greater need of upward assistance from the world of visual imagery.

Tying these strands together — the rules' evidence of fleshly wonderings, imitation, and the call for concrete, visual imagery — it would seem likely that the more ordinary women living together, alone, and without men would have been preoccupied with carnal desire — with sex, to put it bluntly. While we must be careful not to read twentieth-century notions of sexuality back into the medieval records, the past is not without its signals in this respect. The Beguines were simple-minded, less theologically literate than the great learned women of the *vitae*. Thus it is not so anachronistic to speculate that such women were likely to have indulged fantasies on Christ of an explicit, credible, earthy, material sort, especially since those images like the Heavenly Bridegroom were authorized and even encouraged by their preachers and confessors.

Visual imagery would have served two functions in this ordinary women's reality: acting, on the one hand, as a target for fantasies and, on the other, as a mode of control by the clerical hierarchy. [35] Mary touches Christ, and the woman who models herself on Mary may have aroused herself to displace similar desires onto that image. There in the *Pietà*, after all, was their Christ, bridegroom, man, and lover. The Christ figure combined baby, lover, and God in a single category. The image of the naked, crucified body was not a call to necrophilia; that is too modern a concept to be of much use when talking

148

about fourteenth- and fifteenth-century religious reality. Rather what seems more likely to have been the case is that the image of the naked dead man became a licence for viewers to join that body as something spiritual and salvific. The *Pietà* thus offered women an opportunity to house, own, and behold the human Christ in a cognitive format different from the one that "special" women mystics had. Mystics engaged the body of Christ in more literal and physical ways by imitating the extremes of its humanity, and by undergoing all modes of ecstasy and all sorts of fantastically "real" visions. The *Pietà*, on the other hand, provided women an object with which, clearly from the hierarchy's perspective, they could safely and appropriately arouse themselves to various kinds of physical union with the body of Christ. It allowed for a motherhood type union with Christ, which would have pleased the hierarchy. And for the female viewer, it also had that additional element of making present a "lover." The *Pietà* did so as an object by offering a material substitute, one effecting union by outer (sensory) devotion rather than inner (spiritual) ecstasy.

In ushering forth an image of Christ as man, the *Pietà*, and other sacred subjects like it, go far toward suggesting why authorities permitted them. It seems that such images were a means of gaining control of women's tendencies to spiritually induced physical excesses by channeling those tendencies into more controllable reactions. At the same time the images were ones that could specify the models to be imitated and guide the viewer's reactions into a limited range of predictable responses.

In the following pages, those responses will be considered. They were grounded in the tactile sense and arose fundamentally because of the sculpture medium in which the *Pietà* typically appeared. A kind of transference took place between beholder and object around the humanity of Christ as that humanity was expressed in *physical* and material terms. Transference was already present as a key premise of Beguine identity. When it came to sculpture, the three-dimensional essence again called this premise actively into play. Materiality and three-dimensionality in the *Pietà* became the source of its affective appeal. That appeal played a role in meaning far beyond the later Middle Ages, with its local iconography of the Eucharist, and well into the Modern period, with its contemporary, western Catholic meanings and experiences.

149

[1] The diminutive Christ type will be discussed in the text below. For a discussion of the so-called corpusculum type see, Kalinowski (1952), p. 108; Panofsky (1939), pp. 479-99; and Dobrzeniecki (1967), p. 24.

[2] For a review of these types, see Krönig (1962), pp. 97-110. For the joyful *Pietà*, see Dobrzeniecki (1967), p. 24; and Elisabeth Reiners-Ernst (1939). For the sorrowful type, see Dobrzeniecki (1967), p. 24; Kurt Gravenkamp, *Marienklage: Das deutsche Vesperbild im 14. und im frühen 15. Jahrhundert* (Aschoffenburg: Paul Pattloch, 1948); and Passarge (1924).

[3] **Bruges** (circa 1290), p. 63; **Ghent Memorandum** (1328), p. 75.

[4] de la Grange (1897), p. 10, n. 2; p. 15, n. 1.

[5] German *Pietàs* tend to be much more dramatic and extreme in representing the facial expressions of the Virgin.

[6] J. Berlioz, "Le Récit efficace: *l'exemplum* au service de la prédication (XIIIe-XVe siècle)," *Mélanges de l'Ecole français de Rome. Moyenâge-temps modernes* 92 (1980): 113-46; Claude Brémond, Jacques Le Goff and Jean-Claude Schmitt, *L'"Exemplum",* Typologie des sources du moyen âge occidental (Turnhout: Brepols, 1982).

[7] Alan E. Bernstein, "The Exemplum as 'Incorporation' of Abstract Truth in the Thought of Humbert of Romans and Stephen of Bourbon," in *The Two Laws: Studies in Medieval Legal History Dedicated to Stephan Kuttner*, ed. Laurent Mayali and Stephanie A.J. Tibbets (Washington, D.C.: Catholic University of America Press, 1990): 82-96.

[8] In this I agree with Michael Camille. Marrow (1979), for example, attributed the growing importance of *visual* anecdote to the proliferation of written Passion tracts, with their emphasis on gruesome details. The rhetorical devices of *exempla* which I see at work in *Pietàs* are not, however, a problem of "sources" but rather one much closer to "visual speech," aimed toward, and thus understood in a particular way by, what Michael Camille has termed, the "totally illiterate who must rely on the literacy of another for access to written transmission," whether artist or spectator. See Camille (1985), pp. 26-49.

[9] Ziegler, "Reality as Imitation."

[10] Belting (1990).

[11] Ibid., p. 68ff.

[12] Ibid., p. 85.

[13] Studies basic to understanding the veneration of the Eucharist among Belgian Beguines are Stephanus Schoutens, *Geschiedenis van den eeredienst van het allerheiligste sacrament des altaars* (Antwerp, 1902); Simone Roisin, "L'efflorescence cistercienne et le courant féminin de piété au XIIIe siècle," *Revue d'histoire ecclésiastique* 39 (1943): 342-78; A. Mens, "De Verering van de H. Eucharistie bij onze vroegste Begijnen," in *Studia Eucharistica* (Antwerp, 1946): 157-86; idem, *Oorsprong en betekenis van de Nederlandse begijnen- en begardenbeweging. Vergelijkende studie: XIIde-XIIIde eeuw*, Verhandelingen van de Koninklijke Vlaamse Academie voor Wetenschappen, Letteren en Schone Kunsten van België. Klasse der Letteren 9 / 7 (Antwerp: Standaard-Boekhandel, 1947); McDonnell (1954), pp. 299-319; J. Van Herwaarden, "Geloof en geloofsuitingen in de veertiende en vijftiende eeuw: Eucharistie en lijden van Jezus," *Hoofsheid en devotie in de middeleeuwse maatschappij: De Nederlanden van de 12e tot de 15e eeuw*, Handelingen van het Wetenschappelijk Colloquium te Brussel, 21-24 oktober 1981 (Brussels, 1982), 175-207; Dennis Devlin, "Feminine Lay Piety in the High Middle Ages: The Beguines," in *Distant Echoes: Medieval Religious Women*, ed. John A. Nichols and Lillian Thomas Shank, Cistercian Studies Series 71, vol. 1 (Michigan: Western Michigan Univer-

sity, 1984): 183-96; and idem, "Eucharistic Devotion Among Beguines in the Thirteenth Century" (Paper delivered at the 21st International Congress of Mediaeval Studies, Kalamazoo, Michigan, May 1986). For a general discussion of medieval women, in which Beguines are included, see Bynum (1984), pp. 179-214, and idem, "Fast, Food and Flesh: The Religious Significance of Food to Medieval Women," *Representations* 11 (1985): 1-25; Dennis S. Devlin, "*Corpus Christi*: A Study in Medieval Eucharistic Theory, Devotion and Practice," Ph.D. diss., University of Chicago, 1975; and Miri Rubin, *Corpus Christi: The Eucharist in late medieval culture* (Cambridge, England: Cambridge University Press, 1991).

[14] Devlin (1975), p. 266, as in n. 13 above.

[15] McDonnell (1954), pp. 299-319.

[16] Belting (1990), p. 81.

[17] For Juliana see the *Vita sanctae Julianae virginis*, ed. G. Henschenius and D. Papebroch, *AASS*, April 5 / 1 (Paris, 1865): 435-75; an English translation with introduction appears in *The Life of Juliana of Mont Cornillon*, trans. Barbara Newman, Peregrina Translations Series 13 (Toronto, Ontario: Peregrina Publishing Co., 1988). See also n. 13 above and G. Simenon, "Les origines liégeoises de la Fête-Dieu," *Studia Eucharistica* (Antwerp, 1946): 1-19.

[18] Devlin (1975), p. 281, as in n. 13 above.

[19] See McDonnell (1954), pp. 299-319; E. de Moreau, S.J., *L'Abbaye de Villers aux XIIe et XIIIe siècles. Etude d'histoire religieuse et économique* (Brussels: Librairie Albert Dewit, 1909), p. xlix; H. Schuermans, *L'Église de L'Abbaye de Villers* (Brussels: Van Langhendonck, 1984), esp. pp. 2-3; and E. Brouette, "L'Abbaye de Villers à Tilly," *Monasticon Belge* 4 / 2 (1968): 341-405, 376, esp. n. 4, for bibliography relative to Juliana. Olyslager (1978), pp. 72, 221; Juliana visited Tongeren, which had a sizeable Beguine community at that time, to pray for the Feast Day (Ziegler, "Reality as Imitation," p. 259). One wonders if she visited the Beguines there.

[20] "Similarly all beguines shall feel honored to partake of the Holy Communion at least four times a year." [**Lier** (1401), p. 341]. "They shall receive Communion at least on all high days and on the feasts of Our Lady." [**Ghent Rule** (before 1354), p. 20]. "One will see to it that all the daughters take Communion at Easter, at Pentecost, at Christmas, at Candlemas, unless they absent themselves on counsel from their confessor. They can also take Communion seven times during the year: Easter, Pentecost, mid-August, All Saints Day, Christmas, Candlemas, and on the Annunciation of Our Lady." [**Bruges** (circa 1290), pp. 33-34].

[21] Numerous references in archives establish this. B.A.O.C.M.W., Begijnhof van de Wijngaard, H. 794 / 1: Information on the ceremonies for the special feasts [Beguinage of the Vineyard in Brussels, accounts 1579-80]; B 1750, fol. 11r°: expenses for making two crowns of flowers to be offered to the Sacrament, for the procession on Sacrament's day, and other ornaments for the choir; fol. 12v°: payment to the Beguine who carries the cross during procession throughout the year. [Accounts of "de Kiste," 1563-64]; A.R.A., Openbare Onderstand Leuven, no. 3070, fol. 9r°: foundation of a rent of 60 guilders per year, to be used for distributions among the Beguines on the days of the processions of the Sacrament and of another feast day (text illegible) [will of Marie Cloetinckx, 31 March 1571, Great Beguinage in Leuven]; no. 3214-3254: accounts for Dominicans preaching there and going in procession [1416-17].

[22] A.R.A., Openbare Onderstand Leuven, no. 3071, fols. 2r°, 4v° and 7r°: Beguine wills include donations for candles to be burned for the Sacrament on the main altar, which seems

to have been done on Sundays and Feast days throughout the year [register with extracts from wills concerning the Great Beguinage of Leuven, 1436-1636].

23 Belting (1990), p. 68.

24 A number of such eucharistic spectacles are examined in the publications of Caroline Walker Bynum (see bibliography).

25 Devlin (1975), pp. 137-71, esp. p. 154ff.; Bynum (1987), p. 57.

26 Belting (1990), p. 84.

27 Bynum (1984), p. 205.

28 Ziegler, ''Reality as Imitation.''

29 Help in answering this question may come from anthropology; many anthropologists believe that religious rituals often seem to break the major taboos set up in the doctrines of the religion. See Mary Douglas (1966; 1988).

30 See chapter 5 above.

31 L. Breure, ''De hemelse bruidegom,'' *Spiegel Historiael* 15 (1980): 149-56, discusses the Heavenly Bridegroom and the Modern Devotion sisters, with a good general bibliography listed on p. 191. Ludo Milis suggested in private correspondence that the Beguines may be fantasizing, using the Heavenly Bridegroom, over a mortal marriage which they cannot obtain.

32 **Bruges** (circa 1290), p. 57.

33 For a specific example of an exceptional woman (possibly a Beguine), who was sought after by clerics and kings, see W. Simons and J.E. Ziegler, ''Phenomenal Religion in the Thirteenth Century and Its Image: Elisabeth of Spalbeek and the Passion Cult,'' in *Women in the Church*, Studies in Church History 27, ed. W.J. Sheils and Diana Wood (Oxford: Basil Blackwell, 1990): 116-26.

34 Conversation with Beguine from Lier, 1989.

35 Ziegler, ''Reality as Imitation.''

CHAPTER 8

THE "UNIVERSAL" *PIETA*

INTRODUCTION

The practical and sacramental components of the meaning of the *Pietà* were necessarily modified with (as well as by) successive generations of believers. Women of the fourteenth century, especially those of the first and second generation, witnessed events that conditioned their understanding of their lives as Beguines that later generations did not.[1] The fourteenth-century persecutions of semi-religious groups, the legendary fame of ecstatic women, the emergence of particular customs around the sacrament of the Eucharist, the overarching presence of the mendicants in the north,[2] the rapidly expanding numbers of plague victims, the social customs of marriage and inheritance — all were dominant factors of life at that particular time. The close-up view of the events described in the preceding pages must now be set aside if we hope to illuminate why the *Pietà* exerted an appeal continuously beyond those times, and how it did so. In addition to that close, historical and contextual reading, I now introduce a less culture-specific mode of proceeding, one I have loosely termed a comparativist, anthropological approach.

There are three axiomatic principles at work in the *Pietà* in any given period, which may be classified as: (1) what is shown; (2) when it is shown; and (3) how it is shown.[3]

"What is shown" touches upon the subject matter of the Virgin holding the crucified Christ, but on the anthropological level of interpretation the subject is enlarged to encompass a broader conception of mother and son. Scholars have often remarked on the links between the *Pietà* and the Great Mother goddesses of ancient times.[4] The English ethnographer, Sir James Frazer, in his classic

153

study of 1911-15, *The Golden Bough: A Study in Magic and Religion*, forcefully commented on the analogy between the dying Greek gods and Jesus in the following way: ''The type, created by Greek artists, of the sorrowful goddess with her dying lover in her arms, resembles and may have been the model of the *Pietà* of Christian art.'' [5] In her splendid study of the myth and cult of the Virgin Mary, Marina Warner reconsidered the parallels Frazer and other scholars found between pagan and Christian mythology. She concentrated in particular on the similarities between the Great Mother worship of the Middle East and the Christian theme of the *Pietà*. [6]

Warner cites a Sumerian liturgical poem, *Inanna's Journey*, 5,000 years old, in order to express that '' . . . it is startling and profoundly moving when the words of the oldest surviving literature — the liturgies of Sumer, written around 3000 B.C. — correspond so closely to Christian cult that an actual historical chain of descent can be postulated.'' [7] Warner traces the Sumerian liturgy to the Akkadian and Babylonian empires and into Egypt and the cult of Isis and even suggests that the *Pietà* ''may have been influenced by'' the image of the goddess with the ''miniature mummy of the dead Osiris across her knees.'' [8] Warner quickly traces into the Middle Ages the texts of this theme, their Christian form as the Virgin of Sorrows, the *Mater Dolorosa*, which she describes as the myth of Mary as the ''nodal point of [Christ's] passion.'' [9] Thus does Warner view Mary as ''belonging to a tradition of the all-devouring and savage goddess of myth . . . .'' [10]

So startling is the concordance between the subject matter of the *Pietà* and the Great Mother goddesses of Near Eastern mystery religions that Camille Paglia recently used it to affirm her views, springing from both Freudian and Jungian grounds, of the recurrent force of mother as a pagan, earthbound incestuous persona. [11] The immense, world-wide popularity of Michelangelo's *Pietà* she ascribes, for example, not at all to any of the late-fifteenth century conditions on which art historians perennially hang their interests; in fact, she never even mentions its date. Rather, the sculpture's popularity has to do, Paglia claims, with its resonance, ''partly because of its pagan evocation of the archetypal mother-son relation.'' For Paglia, that great Christian ''artistic'' version of the pagan cult symbol of the Great Mother continually bursts forth in marriage as a social reality, in literature as a *topos*, and in modern show business as the female ''mother-father'' superstar, who like Judy Garland is made of ''cold male will and sexual ambiguity.'' [12]

154

At the emotional heart of every marriage is a pietà of mother and son. I will find traces of the archaic incest of mother-cults in Poe and James and in Tennessee Williams' *Suddenly Last Summer*, where a queen mother, ruling a brutal primeval garden, marries her homosexual aesthete son, who is ritually slain and murdered. Female dynamism is the law of nature. Earth husbands herself. [13]

What these examples show is that the *Pietà* fascinates writers who take the bird's-eye view of things, the ahistorical view from afar, where culture-bound, local conditions and all specificity of detail can no longer be perceived. Taking the bird's-eye view, the mother-son relationship of the *Pietà* will emerge as clearly as that of the more historical and sacramental relationship between Virgin and Christ. The view from afar helps explain the continuous, affective appeal of the *Pietà*. Ordinary women spectators today have no need of knowing — nor any way to do so, for that matter — the history of controversies of Mariology, or the stimulus to the cult of the mourning mother provided by the Eastern liturgy, eucharistic conventions, or Cistercian and mendicant theological catalysts, to be affected by the *Pietà* as imaging a mother with her son.

We might compare this view of the universality of the subject with Rodney Needham's hypothesis of the affective appeal of percussion. [14] "Admittedly," noted Needham, "society . . . conditions its members to respond to certain sounds rather than others . . . but practically everywhere it is found that percussion is resorted to in order to communicate with the other world." [15] We may just as easily replace the words, and say instead that admittedly a society conditions its members to respond to certain meanings of the *Pietà* (the practical and sacramental, for example) rather than others, and that each chooses its own form of psychologically appropriate symbol (Isis, Earth Mother, *Pietà*). But practically everywhere in Christianity and at all times it is found that the mother-son relationship is a constant image resorted to by believers seeking to express and aim personal feelings outside of the realms of liturgical or public ritual action.

The second principle concerns "when the *Pietà* is shown." Whether it is on a side altar in a parish church, in a rural wayside chapel, in a garden or a graveyard, or in the niche of a residential gable, the *Pietà* is there to be seen at any moment of the day. Unlike many a medieval object, its viewing is not necessarily tied to the customs of the liturgy or other public celebratory events. Works held in church treasuries, such as monstrances and other eucharistic vessels, processional crosses, and the vestments of the mass, were "occasional pieces," seen by a viewing public only during rites which specifically called upon them to be used. The winged altarpiece and the book of hours, ever present and accessible to individuals as we may think they had been, had their visual content regularized according to pre-specified liturgical or calendrical usage. Whether the wings of a retable were opened or closed or to what page the pious reader could turn the book were not matters determined at will by individual owners. The *Pietà*, like other free-standing figural sculpture of the saints or of the Virgin with Child, however, was by contrast available at every moment of the day for one to stop in front of, beseech, implore, pray to, or simply gaze upon spontaneously, involuntarily.

Its open-ended "when-it-is-shown" character indicates that the *Pietà* occupied a central place in the emergence of a truly secular art. It stands firmly on the margins of all of the features that scholars traditionally depend upon to distinguish the sacred from the secular, and public from private art. Its subject is religious, but its function is not determined primarily by ecclesiastical or other churchly rites. Its sites are public and often consecrated, yet it is individuals and not groups who more often than not visited them. What kind of classification, then, suits the *Pietà*, when its sites are consecrated (sacred) *and* public (secular) and when the ritual is largely not liturgical, structured, or formalized? And how should scholars interpret the fact that believers undertake to view the object, each according to her personal need? The ritual space of enactment is a public one, yet what compels the believer to enter it arises primarily from inner force. By considering "when it is seen" some of the complexity of the *Pietà's* symbolic structure is disclosed. This is a structure which inhabits sacred and secular realms and which is ritualized as much by personal, inner, genuinely private motivation as by the dictates of public, group religion — if not more so.

The third principle of "how it is seen" will finally bring us into contact with the distinguishing feature of the *Pietà*. When the *Pietà* first appeared in the north just around 1300,[16] it did so predominantly as sculpture rather than painting. In the fifteenth century, the great Flemish painters and illustrators of the Passion often incorporated the theme of the *Pietà* into their paintings, and by the seventeenth century it was a common *topos* of pictorial treatment. Strictly speaking, however, the great majority of these examples are not *Pietàs* but Lamentations. The Lamentation depicts Mary grieving among a group of onlookers over the dead body of Christ, and it is but one narrative scene among a sequence of scenes that constitutes the Lord's Passion. The historical and formal relations between sculptured and painted *Pietàs* is a subject too broad to study here. Yet the point may be made nonetheless that the *Pietà*, the complete isolation of Mary and Christ from the narrative context of the Passion, is accurately defined as a sculptural, not a pictorial theme. [17]

In the first two centuries of its origin and popularity, the *Pietà* group of mother and son was carved, not painted, as a representation, especially in the north. The medium of sculpture — and this is the point to note — is, along with the subject matter, the key factor for classifying it. In fact, the premise of this book is that the *Pietà* is defined as precisely the combination of subject (mother and son) and medium (sculpture).

The medium is central to the communication of the subject. Sculpture is three-dimensional by its very nature. It inhabits space, occupies and displaces it. Sculpture *is* material substance in the round. It thus proceeds from premises that are unique to itself as a medium, especially in the free-standing type of sculpture which re-emerged after centuries of dormancy in the later Middle Ages with the *Pietà* and other such figure group types. [18] Those premises, to generalize about them as formal properties, concern weight, mass, and edge: that is, the constituents of three-dimensional substances. Sculpture has ''body,'' for it has material three-dimensionality. Sculpture as a medium stands distinct, then, both from painting with its inherent flatness (two-dimensionality) and from architecture with its inherent space (or intangible three-dimensionality).

How the *Pietà* theme arose in those first decades definitively as a sculptured product remains one of the more compelling art historical mysteries. The research undertaken here has not unearthed anything like a prototype or model to explain it. Consider for a moment two textbook cases in the history of sculpture. Behind the *Prima Porta Augustus*, that glorious, declamatory sculptured figure of the first emperor of Rome, visibly stands its Greek prototype, the *Spear Carrier* (*Doryphorus*). This is true in terms of form if not totally in terms of iconography. Later, that incomparable creative titan, Michelangelo, referenced antique models for many a formal solution to his sculpture. Yet no such model, let alone the process of working from a prototype, has been securely identified for the *Pietà*. Indeed nothing about the *Pietà* has puzzled so many scholars and for so long as has the object's genesis and origin. [19] Those will probably remain exercises in speculation rather than demonstration.

Yet the third axiomatic principle, "how it is shown," offers a number of compelling insights into the *Pietà's* symbolic and aesthetic functions, if not into its place within the hierarchy of sculptural evolution in general. The medium is fundamentally appropriate to the subject. The *Pietà* is at most about the humanity of Christ, at least about the humanity of man; in either case the bodiliness of sculpture represents the bodiliness of the subject matter in appropriately analogous terms.[20] Sculpture's three-dimensionality *is* the meaningful content of the *Pietà*: sculptural bodiliness *is* bodiliness. No medium is better suited than sculpture to describing the properties of the physical world, the medium singularly possessed of three-dimensional matter and physical form. The medium of sculpture is ideally suited to engaging the beholder in appropriate, experiential ways. Sculpture does more than represent the illusion, as two-dimensional painting does, of Christ's humanity as man and bodily presence on earth as the son of Mary. Sculpture, by its own overtly physical properties of mass, weight, and edge, can exaggerate the factors of humanity — of the living flesh and blood of the subject. In its materiality and three-dimensionality, sculpture does not merely imitate nature; it is in essence a physical reality, not merely the painted or graphic illusion of such, but by inhabiting the very space the viewer inhabits. In its overt materiality — its own physical body — sculpture engages more than the eyes, for it demands the sensitivity of the hands and fingers as well, of the sense of touch — the tactile — the one sense above the others that can access the physical world and the properties that are unique to it.[21]

"How the *Pietà* is shown," the third axiomatic principle, is thus of central importance if we wish to comprehend this image's function at the deepest level of experience — its meaning, that is, as content and spectator-engagement. The subject matter cannot be dislodged from the form of its conveyance: humanity and sculpture are of one and the same essence, an essence fundamentally and totally material and physical, because they are three-dimensional. In the following pages we explore that essence, as well as the generalities and particulars of the quintessential physical medium, in order to approach the domain of spectator-engagement more closely. By sight alone, the overtly material and physical constituents of the medium located the beholder's experience in the tactile sense and that experience — "seen touch" bridging beholder to *Pietà* — is where "feeling" in ordinary people happened.

158

THE *PIETA*: ANTHROPOLOGY, SYMBOL, AND AESTHETIC

The *Pietà* concerns itself primarily with two objectives: the representation of humanity in analogously three-dimensional terms and the sensory engagement of the spectator. We have just introduced these terms by noting three axiomatic principles at work in the *Pietà*-type. The medium of sculpture is key, for the matter and substance of sculpture express the physical properties and actual states of the figures. As we now turn to observing the objectives at work specifically in our five case study objects, let us keep active the first two principles of "how" and "what" is shown — the free-standing, ever present, non-liturgical object representing a mother and son group. These principles confronted all sculptors of *Pietàs* with a single, artistic challenge, that of "sculptural time." There, in individual sculptor's solutions to that challenge, is where each *Pietà* gains and manifests its particular identity: every *Pietà* exhibits a different interpretation of the general problem of how to represent sculptural time.

The free-standing and three-dimensional nature of the *Pietà* conditions the character of represented time. The *Pietà* is not a story about Christ and Mary; it is a relationship or set of relationships placed against one another, such as mother-son, dead-living. But it is not a narrative, if by that we mean the representation and isolation of one segment from among the many unfolding continuously and cumulatively across time. Wrested from the narrative context of the crucifixion or the entombment, the *Pietà* vigorously resists being integrated into a larger narrative setting or receiving reading-based devices having to do with sequence and dramatic culmination. [22] The properties of wood and/or stone also contest pictorial narrative time, so few are the devices available to the carver for rendering or even evoking the illusion of multiple and causally related events. Because of their medium, painters employed and invented illusionistic devices almost naturally. [23]

Sculptors were not less concerned with time than painters, but the time they addressed was of a different narrative conception altogether. [24] In the *Pietà* it is time suspended, not time unfolding; time stopped, not sequential or cumulative time. The two figures of Christ and Mary can be represented in a variety of physical states, but in only one state per figure in each *Pietà*; they are held frozen in those states. Christ, for example, can be depicted as dead or still in the process of dying. Mary can appear to be young, mature, or aged. The variations are endless for representing the physical and developmental status of the figures, but only one status per figure is possible, and that state must be isolated and stopped, fixed forever in time.

This discussion should point out the degree to which the objective of representing humanity is profoundly conditioned by the problem of sculptural time and by each sculptor's interpretation of that problem. Time, because of the properties of the sculpture medium, must be manifested — and arrested — as the specific attributes of life or death at a single stage of its development. Also, Mary as mother holds a grown Christ on her lap. This is a throwback to his infancy, which is a mixup of time conception in that same regard. [25] The sculptor thus shows Mary's experience and her psychic state as a cumulative, distilled experience, not as a sequential narrative. Indeed, it appears in looking back on *Pietàs* that the conception of sculptural time was creatively defined as the representation of mortality, that is, as a particular stage of physical life manifested analogously in the physical substance and properties of the sculptural form and frozen in the manipulated sculptural substance.

Christ emaciated or Christ muscular are not minor tonal accents. They are the very essence of the content of humanity as represented and, at the same time, they are the guide which the spectator must follow in order to experience the fullness and richness of the content of a given *Pietà*. Thus the representation of mortality — in its essence a physical, material state — is a prime constituent of the meaning of the *Pietà*.

The other constituent, the sensory engagement of the ordinary spectator, is also a function of sculptural time. The representation of physical states frozen in time is the spectator's only point of access to the particular content of a particular *Pietà*. A bony and emaciated Christ, whose fragile, angular, sculptural substance evokes images of a terrible and long suffering, will engage the spectator's tactile feeling differently than will a full-bodied, muscular Christ, whose bulging and curving sculptural forms pulse with hot-blooded life. The sculptural representation of Mary equally guides the spectator's tactile feeling, echoing it as a kind of antiphonal emotional process. Her sculptural substance and how it acts over and against the body of the son she holds becomes a form of psychological and emotional response. In other words, it is crucial to the expression whether Mary contains and encloses Christ or functions in isolation from him.

160

Spectators, then, have two points of sculptural access to the content of given *Pietàs*: through the body of the son and through the concretized response of his mother. The representation of humanity and the sensory engagement of the spectator hinge on the sculptor's interpretation of sculptural time — on the representation, in the physical substance of matter, of fixed properties of the physical world. Those properties are there not only to be seen but to be "felt." After and as a result of sight, the spectator's sense of touch plays the dominant part; one "feels" as one "sees" the particulars and varieties of the human condition.

THE OBJECTS

In the Diest *Pietà* [Plate 101], the sculptural content is conveyed by the exaggerated opposition of axes, weight, and edge. The mother sits upright, looking ahead, her torso leans slightly, her head is gently inclined to her right. The body of the son she holds on her knees, which are visibly spread apart. Her right knee supports his upper torso, her left, his upper thighs. His left hand rests on hers, which is placed close to his genitals. This is a grown man and a mature woman, ages expressed by the similar scale of the two figures.

The juxtaposition of the axes is striking: the mother occupies and asserts the primary vertical axis of the group, her body and drapery form a stable pyramid around that axis, culminating at a point in her head. The body of the son marks out an equally strong horizontal accent, an accent which is articulated and emphasized by the fact that it breaks sharply out of the firm controlling contour of the mother's pyramidal shape.

In its sharp angular projection, violently cutting across the center of the group, the body of the son levitates weightlessly. The head and knees suspended in mid-air at either side appear not to exert the gravitational weight one would expect from a full-grown man lying in this position. The narrow, angular, weightless torso juxtaposes the fullsome, stable, contained bulk of the mother's pyramidal shape.

161

The oppositions of mother and son, of vertical and horizontal axes, of stable and suspended weight, of contained contour and broken edge, are sculptural ones. They define in their material balance physical equivalents. One ''feels,'' as values of touch, that the figures are inherent equals, in the counter-balance of similar age and size, of physical assertiveness *versus* physical absence of weight, of grave serenity *versus* weightless serenity. The general propositions of the *Pietà* — mother and son humanity — have in the Diest example been specified because of the sculptural handling as attributes in the stages of the life cycle.

The spectator enters those propositions of mortality by way of similarly experiential means of axis, weight, and edge. The broken contour — the sculptural edge — guides the viewer's experience. It frames and gives meaning to the opposition of axes, the weight and weightlessness; it is where the tactile experience comes into play, for the edge moves out of the realm of outline and into becoming a physical property of the ''natural'' three-dimensional world. Edge calls attention to the specific concordances (age and size) and oppositions (assertiveness) of the mother and son. And, therefore, broken edge particularizes the humanity and specifies the process of our engagement and understanding of that humanity.

When such a synthesis occurs as between the general proposition of humanity and its specific description, the act of beholding is at its most profound. Individual spectators may have personalized this object differently at different points in time. Yet the concordance and opposition as generated by the sculptural edge calls attention to a level of reality between the figures that, if understood as touch, has to do with the detachment and isolation of one figure from the other.

At quite the other end of the spectrum of sculptural propositions lies the Helshoven *Pietà* [Plate 34],[26] where the content is conveyed by a closed contour and an overtly rhythmical presentation of the son's body as shape and weight. Mary sits upright, looking straight ahead and slightly to her right. The Helshoven mother supports the torso of the son with his head to her right. The torso lays on and across the figure of Mary in a complex way, as placement, shape, and distribution of mass.

All is different here from the clear, weightless, suspended horizontality of the Diest *Pietà*. The Helshoven Christ builds in kinetic weight and physical density from its feet to its head. The body is placed in a step-like series of ascents from feet, placed on the ground horizontally, up to the lower limbs to knees,

162

across to groin. The chest is thrust over the mother in an arching curve to the head, thrown backwards lifelessly. The right arm descends, seemingly on its weight, so that even the tips of the fingers are forced to bend as they touch the ground.

The body of the son is a complex sculptural event, a set of contrasting shapes (step-like lower limbs against the arched and curving torso) and weights (the self-supportiveness of the limbs and the dropped gravitational force of the head and limbs). In combination these form something of a rhythm or pulse of shape and mass. The body of Christ, however, is framed and constrained by the bulky mass of the mother, the complexity of shape and mass never breaking the edge or penetrating beyond the clear borders of her figure, although much of the Virgin's body is obscured by the scale and intensity of the sculptural intricacy of the corpse.

The Helshoven *Pietà* does not manifest any of the sculptural propositions of the Diest *Pietà*. The grown man and mature woman are depicted, but the handling calls attention not to specific concordances and oppositions as it does in Diest's. Equivalents of scale and axes are not present here, and the edges are not broken but contained. The Helshoven *Pietà* is about the contained frame of the Virgin's body and the overtly rhythmical distribution of weights and shapes of Christ's body. Those are sculptural proclamations, or emphases, about the son over the mother, of naked male body over clothed woman's form. The physical attributes and distribution of the masses *via* the carving assert the primacy of death, its movemented sensual quality and its prominence over life, which softly recedes to enclose it.

The spectator gains insight to those propositions *via* the tactile messages as communicated by the shapes and distribution of the masses, all of which call attention to a certain level of reality. That level is a kind of flip-flop, an inversion of life, one in which death holds primacy, one in which death is more movemented than life, one in which the dead naked male is more vital than woman is in life. The sculptural propositions of the Helshoven *Pietà* point the way to an intriguing thought about spectator-engagement, that the tactile sculptural features constitute a pulsing rhythm and vitality in the dead son, which are enclosed and controlled by the body of the mother. The sculptural features act as symbols and as avenues to those potent, sometimes social, sometimes inner, psychological feelings.

The Sittard *Pietà* is related to the Helshoven *Pietà* in the kinetic weight and physical density of the body of Christ. [Plate 73] Here, his corpse is turned out-

163

ward to face the viewer, the body more of a single, unified shape, less complicated by steps and patterns than Helshoven's. Christ's right arm marks out the only clear vertical axis of the group; his hand hangs just above the ground line from the shoulder as though it were pulled downward by an immense weight inside his palm, around which fingers curl.

This arm is a tense form, rigid, erect, powerful, the only form the sculptor permits the illusion of gravity to occupy. The mass of the group is weighted toward that side. The line from his feet to his armpit forms one side of an irregular triangle, which is filled by the mother's knees. Her knees follow the direction of his body; her hand at his wound occupies the apex of the triangle. She leans to one side toward his body, which leans outward. Her ample veil echoes the path of the leaning corpse.

These forms, unlike Helshoven's, move as weight and in density in parallel. Their directionality acts in unison. There is harmony, then, between the living and the dead, not isolation of one from the other (Diest) or absorption of one by the other (Helshoven). All three *Pietàs* represent a grown naked man and a mature woman, but the relationship between the dead and the living as fixed status could not be more different than it is among the three objects. The sculptural features of the Sittard *Pietà* call our attention at once to lifelessness in that erected arm of Christ, with its sense of *rigor mortis*, and at the same time to the dynamic, living relationship the Virgin captures. Her form looms larger than his, but it echoes and repeats it, fills in and accentuates its marginal status between life and death. In this harmonious, repetitious distribution of dynamic diagonal forms, the sculptor advances something of the literal takeover, the subsuming of the dead (the male cadaver) by the living (movemented body of woman). The sculptural premises of the Sittard *Pietà* exaggerate the physical union of two bodies.

Sculptors of *Pietàs*, especially during the first decades of this image's production, did not always start from age similarities of the sort observed in the objects presented above. The Tongeren St. Agnes *Pietà* represents the mother, seated on a bench, holding a small-scale model of a grown man. [Plates 116, 117] Like the *Pietàs* of Mechelen [Plate 112] and Maastricht [Inv. no. 130],[27] the Tongeren St. Agnes *Pietà* has the son seated upright, his face bearded and aged, his body manifesting the marks of the crucifixion, his head crowned with thorns. Yet were it not for the specific signs of the Passion, the scale of the figure would indicate that the mother holds on her lap a late adolescent boy, who waits to be told a story or some such form of familial interaction.

164

Numerous scholars have explored this anomaly of the tiny body of the crucified Christ and have accounted for it as a compositional transposition of the sculptured type of the *Seated Virgin with Infant* [28] or as a sculptural link, in the handling of the body of Christ, between the infancy and the Passion of Christ, the latter aspect containing symbolic reference to the Redemption. [29] The particular treatment of this group suggests, however, that even the unlearned — even those not cognizant of the artistic prototypes or of the biblical nuances of the Redemption — could gain access to the Redemptive content *via* the sculptural handling alone. [30]

A comparison between the Sittard and Helshoven *Pietàs* and the Tongeren St. Agnes *Pietà* reveals how all three objects isolate the weighted and erect right arm of Christ and keep the two figures more or less contained within an unbroken frame, unifying the group. This is very different from the Diest *Pietà*, where the body of Christ punctures and opens the outline of the group. Yet the Tongeren St. Agnes *Pietà* differs in the distribution of masses and the relations between the two figures as forms, and that is precisely where the particular meaning, with its references to the Redemption, comes to life.

The contrast of scale is not nearly as important as the concordance of shape and mass between the mother and son. The *Pietà* from Onze-Lieve-Vrouw van Ginderbuiten presents the two figures as being of the same scale, yet many iconographers tend to read the son as younger and childlike. [31] [Inv. no. 123, Plates 107, 108] This is not because of scale but because of a concordance of shape and mass between the two figures, similar to that of the Tongeren St. Agnes *Pietà*. The Tongeren St. Agnes *Pietà* breaks both sets of masses at the knees; each figure sits on a horizontal plane. The hands, left to left especially, echo and repeat themselves; heads incline toward or away from one another, with their ovals culminating in the more rigid and planar distributions of the bodies' masses. The body of the son is indeed a miniature of the mother, a proposition that stems not from the contrast of scale but from the particulars of shape and mass, so that what is known from the one figure is known of as well as from the other.

As the French structural anthropologist, Lévi-Strauss, wrote in *The Savage Mind*, miniatures draw a constant virtue not just as a matter of scale but by constituting a "real experiment" with the object they represent. This experiment is at work in the Tongeren St. Agnes *Pietà* (as well as in the others included here of this type) in its reversal of the process of understanding the humanity. The mother is the totality — the living creature of apparently "real

165

dimensions.'' To understand her, as happens in real life, we need to work by breaking that totality down into parts, into her pose, shape, edge, inclines and so on. There in Christ is ''the whole'' who gives us *at a single glance* the knowledge of her. The totality we gain by working from her parts, we get through him as a whole. He offers us, as Lévi-Strauss said, because of his ''apparent'' miniaturization, no resistance — for his form simplifies, diminishes, and extends our understanding over the larger thing. What is important is that, first, the totality, the ''larger thing of real dimensions'' is the mother; and, second, the proclamation of her as such is made in sculptural terms alone. This is a striking declaration, accessible to all, of the Incarnation and the Redemption.

[1] I have developed a model for analyzing the ''generational'' theory in, ''On the Textuality of Architecture: Building the Abbey Church of Villers in Brabant,'' *Cîteaux* (in press).

[2] For a central study of the mendicants in the Low Countries, see Walter Simons, *Stad en apostolaat. De vestiging van de bedelorden in het graafschap Vlaanderen (ca. 1225-ca. 1350)*, Verhandelingen van de Koninklijke Academie voor Wetenschappen, Letteren en Schone Kunsten van België, Klasse der Letteren 121 (Brussels: Paleis der Academiën, 1987).

[3] These principles I have adapted from Victor Turner's fascinating characterization of ''sacra.'' See Turner (1964), in Lessa / Vogt (1979), p. 239.

[4] For the cult of the Mother Goddess and its relations with Christianity, see Gananath Obeyesekere, *The Cult of the Goddess Pattini* (Chicago: University of Chicago Press, 1984), esp. pp. 474-82.

[5] James Frazer, *The Golden Bough: A Study in Magic and Religion*, vol. 5, 3rd ed., revised and enlarged (New York, 1925): 256-57. See also Kalinowski (1952), p. 107; and Carroll (1986), p. 111. Regarding Frazer's method as ethnographer, see George E. Marcus and Michael M.J. Fischer, *Anthropology as Cultural Critique: An Experimental Moment in the Human Sciences* (Chicago: University of Chicago Press, 1986), esp. pp. 7-16.

[6] Marina Warner, *Alone of All Her Sex: The Myth and Cult of the Virgin Mary* (1976, New York: First Vintage Books Edition, 1983), esp. pp. 206-23; and Sheila Bonde, ed., *Survival of the Gods: Classical Mythology in Medieval Art*, exh. cat. (Providence, Rhode Island: Brown University, 1987). Carroll (1986), p. 111 disagrees with Warner's emphasis on Isis and Mary connections and argues instead for the Cybele cult as precursor.

[7] Warner (1983), p. 208.

[8] Ibid., pp. 208-09.

[9] Ibid., p. 211.

[10] Ibid., p. 221.

166

[11] Camille Paglia, *Sexual Personae: Art and Decadence from Nefertiti to Emily Dickinson* (New Haven: Yale University Press, 1990): 52-53.

[12] Ibid., p. 54.

[13] Ibid., p. 53.

[14] Needham (1967), in Lessa / Vogt (1979).

[15] Ibid., p. 315.

[16] For a long time, German art historians claimed that the first *Pietà* appeared in Cologne in 1298 in a Carmelite convent (Dehio [1923], p. 120; Passarge [1924], p. 34). No record of this object appears in L. Arntz et al., eds., *Die ehemäligen Kirchen, Klöster, Hospitaler und Schulbauten der Stadt Köln*, vol. 2 (Düsseldorf, 1937). I am grateful to Kathryn Brush for this reference. The prospect of unlocking the evolutionary puzzle of the "Ur-Pietà" does not engage scholars the way it once did.

[17] See especially the treatment of Dehio in chapter 1 above.

[18] For a discussion of free-standing sculpture in the Middle Ages, see M.F. Hearn, *Romanesque Sculpture* (Ithaca, New York: Cornell University Press, 1981). There he is interested in the tenth- and eleventh-century Virgin seated with Child not for its precedence as free-standing sculpture, reviving an antique tradition of carving figures in the round, but for its influence on monumental portal sculpture of the Gothic period. A related point was made by Kurt Weitzmann, *The Icon: Holy Images, Sixth to Fourteenth Century* (New York: Braziller, 1978), pp. 9, 3, namely that pagans preferred sculpture in the round for cult objects, but that painted panels depicting gods and goddesses were more popular especially with the Eastern mystery religions because of those religions' "transcendental outlook."

[19] The evolutionary approach dominates the scholarship of *Pietàs*: where did it come from, what is its source (textual or pictorial) and so on. The genetics of the species — archetype and prototype — is, however, a "classical" theoretical approach, better applied to classic and Renaissance sculpture than to medieval examples. The Darwinian path illuminates little about the *Pietà*.

[20] Many *Pietàs* are smaller than life size but not yet miniatures. See Inventory for dimensions.

[21] See chapter 5, pp. xx-xx on definition of appearance — touched values seen.

[22] See Marrow (1979) for a discussion of reading-based viewing of the Passion scenes. Marrow's study is treated in chapter 1 above.

[23] Ernst Murbach, *Form und Material in der spätgotischen Plastik*, Baseler Studien zur Kunstgeschichte 1 (Basel: Birkhäuser Verlag, 1943).

[24] In 1961 Edmund Leach proposed a rethinking of the "representation of time" in primitive ritual and mythology that is quite relevant (especially his views on "oscillation and alternation") in his "Two Essays Concerning the Symbolic Representation of Time" (1961) in Lessa / Vogt (1979), pp. 311-17.

[25] This infant Christ of the crucifixion has been treated many times before by art historians but as a theological issue, not a sculptural or temporal one, by Kalinowski (1952), p. 108; Panofsky (1939), pp. 479-99; Dobrzeniecki (1967), p. 24; and Von Simson (1953), pp. 9-16.

[26] Compare the Tongeren Beguinage *Pietà*, which is not going to be discussed in the text at this point. See Inv. no. 84, plate 77.

[27] See also Bonnefanten *Pietà*, Inv. no. 130.

[28] Pinder (1919 and 1922); Passarge (1924), pp. 50-55.

[29] Swarzenski (1935), pp. 141-44; Millard Meiss, *Painting in Florence and Siena After the Black Death: The Arts, Religion, and Society in the Mid-Fourteenth Century* (1951; reprint New Jersey: Princeton University Press, 1978), p. 127; Panofsky (1939); and Kalinowski (1952).

[30] A feminist reading might offer that scale here asserts women's power in relation to that of men. This is, I believe, an anachronistic interpretation.

[31] For the corpusculum type of *Pietà*, see n. 1 above.

CONCLUSION

The analysis set forth in the preceding pages may be categorized in art historical terms as an iconology of sculptural substances. My claim all along has been that the sculptural properties of the *Pietà* are its meaning. We have learned that the *Pietà* had a cultic context, on the altar, in the gable, in church and in the domestic residence. Yet the cultic site appears to explain precious little about the particular formal and sculptural properties of the objects it contains. The Helshoven *Pietà*, for example, was part of a public pilgrimage site concerning stillborn children, and yet the *Pietà* closest to it formally and compositionally was housed within the walls of a women's convent in Sittard. Ritual site is important for helping to account for the audience, especially for its gender, but it does not fully explain why certain patterns of sculptural handling obtain over others.

I have claimed here that an examination of the particular characteristics of the medium of sculpture will expose more of the experienced meaning and continued life of the *Pietà* than strictly contextual information can. The particular phraseology of the sculpture initiated an experience unique to itself; indeed the sculptural properties of particular *Pietàs* evoked and guided sensations of a particularly undiscursive sort. Those sensations I have described as tactile in point of origin, because they are conditioned by the inherent properties of the medium of sculpture, especially by mass, weight, and edge.

The Beguines have offered us an exemplary group because they left the records that allow us to analyze them as ordinary women spectators. I have therefore attempted to identify them as the earliest, certain audience for the *Pietà* in the southern Low Countries. Moreover, I have cited the things that conditioned its tactile fluency, especially the Beguines' structure of experience and reality. The Beguines described, recognized, and defined states of being according to explicit materiality, and they recognized the identity of both "self" and "other" in material terms. They encoded and decoded reality through the vehicle of explicit materiality. This structure, through which all reality was filtered and defined, explains their readiness to receive the material, sculptural meanings of the *Pietà*. Knowledge by identification with explicit material

169

references readied them to engage meanings of the material substance of the *Pietà* — its iconology.

The bridge between object and viewer in the case of the *Pietà* is tactility. That bridge is where the synthesis of the general property of humanity and its particular content (as detachment, lifelessness, rhythmicality, referentiality) takes place. This experience — the synthesis which Lévi-Strauss termed as one of structure and event — is an aesthetic one. By this I mean that it produces "feeling," that ineffable thing, that thing which is nearly impossible to convert into rational and discursive terms. Sculpturally induced sensation is a separate domain of sensation, guided by the sense of touch as it responds to the particularities of sculptural events in given *Pietàs*.

Seen as a viewing audience, the Beguines have given us the opportunity to suggest that tactile experience, the reality gained through explicit materiality and the sense of touch, was an integral component of their lives. Knowing this about them explains, I believe, the decided absence of ecstasy, rapture, and mysticism in the great majority of the women who were Beguines. Touch and materiality tied them vigorously to the sensible world, the world of things. Touch is the most obviously material of the five senses, which explains why medieval philosophers and theologians considered it to be the lowest among them. Beguines did not transcend the sensible world; they did not rise above it as mystics did, who superseded the senses. They were tied to the sensible world experientially. The primacy of the sense of touch does not serve to abstract the meaning of things or to cause the participant to transcend them. The sense of touch serves rather as a bridge, allowing the participant to identify with material things. The primacy of materiality and touch among the Beguines, the *Pietà* as a private and non-liturgical object, its material (sculptural) premises conveying physical content: these are the things that in combination raise compelling issues about the nature of feeling and the role of art in the later Middle Ages.

In 1989 theologian John Giles Milhaven responded to my discussion of the primacy of sculpture and the *Pietà* by proposing that we view it as related to Christian and Greek epistemology.[1] He showed how the sense of touch pervades the ecstatic experiences of later medieval women mystics and goes on to reveal the problems that it presented to theologians who, like Thomas Aquinas, considered that sense the least like reason, and hence the lowest of the senses. Milhaven gives us the background for this view in Greek (male) philosophy which conditioned Western culture to elevate one pole of human knowing, that

170

of reason and rationality, above the other. For Milhaven the sense of touch is an epistemology — a "bodily knowing" to use his words — that Western culture, culminating in the Christian thinkers of the Middle Ages, identified as inferior. [2] Milhaven claims that two "polar kinds of knowing" exist, the rational and "the sensory," the latter form of knowing belonging to women, women's history, and the women mystics. I do not know whether sensory knowing belongs essentially to women. And I am not a philosopher or a theologian. I remain therefore indebted to Milhaven's interpretation of the problem, the same one as I have undertaken to investigate in this book.

In pursuing another course I have located in the Beguines an example of women whose day-to-day reality was manifested in the tactile domain. They were, as I have argued throughout this study, ordinary women; and thus they probably reflect much of the structure of common experience. Whether the nature of that experience was predominantly Beguine or even predominantly female can only be answered once scholars explore examples of tactility among other groups of ordinary women and men with similarly rich documents.

The Beguines, then, do not advance the proposition that tactile experience is female. Rather, the Beguines give insight into how sculptured *Pietàs* might have been accessed by an audience particularly receptive to tactile messages. Among those women the experience of viewing was one bridged by the sense of touch. By the sculptural properties of mass, weight, and edge, the believer was engaged in a form of sensory identification, in which the sense of touch "knew" the range of material appearances. And the sense of touch induced the beholder to experience not a transcendence but a transference between beholder and object. This is a crucial point.

Transference, the key relationship between (Beguine) user and (*Pietà*) object, accounts for a number of profound changes that took place in the role of art at the end of what has come to be known as the "medieval" period. First, it suggests a level of self-consciousness at work in the spectator, at least on the level of sensory identification. Second, it suggests a sort of realism operating not on the level of artistic imitation of "natural" subject matter, but in the fact that spectators experienced whatever was conceived as reality directly, in material and tactile terms.

The call to represent the humanity of Christ in the *Pietà* is probably at the heart of the emergence of a sculptural realism. There was, after all, no subject that challenged artists to transfer the concept of humanity into artistic (visual and tactile) terminology more explicitly than the humanity of Christ did. These

171

contextual, social, and artistic phenomena culminated and exchanged forces in the fifteenth century. They gave rise to a form of realism, by which I mean an exchange of identity between beholder and object *via* the sense of touch. That exchange came as a sculptural experience of the actuality of material humanity. This realism did not encourage the beholder to transcend the sensory world but to transfer herself with it.

Such transference is at base an aesthetic experience. It is one which is so tied to phenomenal (sensory) reality and sensory experience that it can shed light on those aesthetic experiences that abstract the beholder from the here and now and guide her or him to transcend the object and venture into less explicit realms, into pure abstractions. The transference between object and beholder I have been discussing is also an inner experience, an ineffable feeling, and a non-discursive event. Although users of *Pietàs* did not participate in the other, arguably purer level of aesthetic experience — that is, in the other pole of ineffable, instrinsically aesthetic experience — there is always present in viewing *Pietàs* a core of ineffability. An aesthetic experience of a sort, then, endured. For believers fluent in tactile experiences, *Pietàs* are there to arouse "feelings." Perhaps those feelings are not transcendent or purely artistic ones, but they are formed nonetheless of distinctly aesthetic material. That is why the tactile realism of the *Pietà* — despite as well as because of its subject matter — advanced the role of art into autonomous, personal and secular categories, categories that will increasingly dominate the value structure of imagery in the coming of modern times.

[1] John Giles Milhaven, "A Medieval Lesson on Bodily Knowing: Women's Experience and Men's Thought," *Journal of the American Academy of Religion* 57 / 2 (1989): 341-72.
[2] Ibid., pp. 362-68.

GENERAL BIBLIOGRAPHY

UNPUBLISHED ARCHIVAL MATERIALS

Brussels, Algemeen Rijksarchief / Archives générales du Royaume
Openbare Onderstand Leuven / Assistance publique de Louvain
Nos. 2678-4863: Great Beguinage of Ten Hove in Leuven
Charters, wills, inventories of goods, accounts, chronicles, 14th-18th centuries
Nos. 4923-5072: Small Beguinage of Saint Gertrude in Leuven
Charters, wills, inventories of goods, accounts, 15th-18th centuries
Kerkelijk Archief van Brabant / Archives ecclésiastiques du Brabant
Nos. 13700-14157: Beguinage of Saint Catherine in Diest
Charters, wills, inventories of goods, 13th-18th centuries
No. 14722: Beguinage of Zoutleeuw
Description of the church, 1550

Brussels, Archief van het Openbaar Centrum voor Maatschappelijk Welzijn / Archives
du Centre public d'aide social
Begijnhof van de Wijngaard / Béguinage de la Vigne
Great Beguinage of the Vineyard in Brussels
B 1452: wills, 1288-1588
B 1689-1863: accounts 1401-1798
H 262: statutes and ordinances, 1270, 1372
H 277: wills, 1369-1753
H 528-714: accounts of the infirmary, 1385-1517
H 744-774: documents concerning foundations, 16th-18th centuries
H 794: documents concerning the church, 1579-1742
H 795: report on the finances of the beguinage, 1773

Douai, Archives municipales
GG 191
documents concerning the Beguine convent of Bernard Pilate

Ghent, Rijksarchief
Bisdom
E 374: cartulary of the Great Beguinage of Saint Elisabeth in Ghent, 1402

Sint-Elisabethbegijnhof Gent, Oorkonden
Charters of the Great Beguinage of Saint Elisabeth in Ghent, 1233-1796

Ghent, Stadsarchief
Reeks LXXVIII, Oorkonden Béthune
Charters of the Great Beguinage of Saint Elisabeth in Ghent, 13th-18th centuries

Hasselt, Rijksarchief
Begijnhof Sint-Truiden, Oorkonden
Charters of the Beguinage of Saint Agnes in Sint-Truiden, 13th-18th centuries

Leuven, Universiteitsbibliotheek, Archief
Collectie Philippen, XVI
Charters and wills of the Beguinage of Saint Catherine in Diest, 13th-16th centuries

Tongeren, Stadsarchief
Begijnhof Tongeren
Charters, wills and inventories of the Beguinage of Saint Catherine in Tongeren, 13th-18th centuries

174

PRIMARY AND SECONDARY SOURCES

Appermans, Fons. *Kapel Helshoven 13de eeuw: Genadeoord van Maria van de Blijde Vrede*. N.p., n.d.

Arasse, Daniel. "Entre dévotion et culture: fonctions de l'image religieuse au XVe siècle." In *Faire croire: modalités de la diffusion et de la réception des messages religieux du XIIe au XVe siècle*. Table ronde, Rome, Ecole française de Rome, 22-23 juin 1979, pp. 131-46. Turin: Bottega d'Erasmo, 1981.

Ars Sacra Antiqua (exh. cat.). Leuven: Stedelijk Museum, 1962.

L'Art Mosan. Journées d'Etudes, Paris, Février 1952. Edited by Pierre Francastel. Bibliothèque générale de l'Ecole Pratique des Hautes Etudes, VIe Section. Paris: Armand Colin, 1953.

Asche, Sigfried. "Das Vesperbild in Waischenfeld — ein unbekanntes Werk Peter Breuers." *Pantheon* 26 (1968): 115-21.

Ashley, Kathleen M., ed. *Victor Turner and the Construction of Cultural Criticism: Between Literature and Anthropology*. Bloomington: Indiana University Press, 1990.

Aspekten van de Laatgotiek in Brabant (exh. cat.). Leuven: Stedelijk Museum, 1971.

Baes, Edgar. "Roger Van Der Weyden." *Fédération Artistique* 29 / 3 (1901): 19.

Baldewijns, Jeannine. "Organisatie van het begijnhofleven: De Begijnhofregel als spiegel van het dagelijks leven in het hof." In *Werken en Kerken* (exh. cat.), pp. 93-105. Ghent: Stad Gent, 1984.

Baum, Julius. *Gotische Bildwerke Schwabens*. Augsburg and Stuttgart: Benno Filser, 1921.

—. "Die Lütticher Bildnerkunst im 14. Jahrhundert." Vol. 1, *Belgischer Kunstdenkmäler*, edited by Paul Clemen. Munich: Bruckmann, 1923.

—. "Vesperbild aus dem Kreise Rogier van der Weyden." *Pantheon* 4 (1929): 563-69.

Baxandall, Michael. *Painting and Experience in Fifteenth-Century Italy: A Primer in the Social History of Pictorial Style*. London: Oxford University Press, 1972.

—. *The Limewood Sculptors of Renaissance Germany*. New Haven: Yale University Press, 1980.

175

Beelden uit Brabant: Laatgotische kunst uit het oude hertogdom 1440-1520 (exh. cat.). 's-Hertogenbosch: Nordbrabants Museum 's-Hertogenbosch, 1971.

Beinert, W., and H. Petri. *Handbuch der Marienkunde*. Regensburg: Friedrich Pustet, 1984.

Bell, Rudolph. *Holy Anorexia*. Chicago: University of Chicago Press, 1985.

Belting, Hans. *The Image and its Public in the Middle Ages: Form and Function of Early Paintings of the Passion*. 1981. Translated by Mark Bartusis and Raymond Meyer. New Rochelle, New York: Aristide D. Caratzas, 1990.

Benjamin, Lloyd. "Disguised Symbolism Exposed and the History of Early Netherlandish Painting." *Studies in Iconography* 2 (1976): 11-24.

Benz, Ernst. "Christliche Mystik und christliche Kunst. (zur theologischen Interpretation mittelalterlicher Kunst)." *Deutsche Vierteljahrsschrift für Literaturwissenschaft und Geistesgeschichte* 12 / 12 (1934): 22-48.

—. *Die Vision: Erfahrungsformen und Bilderwelt*. Stuttgart: E. Klett, 1969.

Bergmann, Ulrike. *Die Holzskulpturen des Mittelalters (1000-1400)*. Cologne: Schnütgen Museum, 1989.

Berliner, R. *Die Weihnachtskrippe*. Munich: Prestel Verlag, 1955.

—. "Bemerkungen zu einigen Darstellungen des Erlösers als Schmerzensmanns." *Das Münster* 9 (1956): 96-117.

Berlioz, Jacques. "Le Récit efficace: *l'exemplum* au service de la prédication (XIIIe-XVe siècle)." *Mélanges de l'Ecole française de Rome. Moyenâge-temps modernes* 92 (1980): 113-46.

—. "La lactation de Saint Bernard dans un *Exemplum* et une miniature du *Ci Nous Dit* (début du XIVe siècle)." *Cîteaux* 39 / 3-4 (1988): 270-83.

Bernstein, Alan E. "The Exemplum as 'Incorporation' of Abstract Truth in the Thought of Humbert of Romans and Stephen of Bourbon." In *The Two Laws: Studies in Medieval Legal History Dedicated to Stephan Kuttner*, edited by Laurent Mayali and Stephanie A.J. Tibbets, pp. 82-96. Washington, D.C.: Catholic University of America Press, 1990.

Béthune, J. *Cartulaire du béguinage de Sainte Elisabeth à Gand*. Bruges: Aimé De Zuttere, 1883.

Bialostocki, Jan. "Erwin Panofsky (1892-1968): Thinker, Historian, Human Being." *Simiolus* 4 (1970): 68-89.

Bierens de Haan, J.C.J. *Het houtsnijwerk in Nederland tijdens de Gotiek en de Renaissance*. 1921. Reprint. The Hague: Martinus Nijhoff, 1977.

Biller, Peter. "The Common Woman in the Western Church in the Thirteenth and Early Fourteenth Centuries." In *Women in the Church*, Studies in Church History 27, edited by W.J. Sheils and Diana Wood, pp. 127-57. Oxford: Basil Blackwell, 1990.

Blank, W. "Umsetzung der Mystik in den Frauenklöstern." In *Mystik am Oberrhein und in benachbarten Gebieten* (exh. cat.), pp. 25-36. Freiburg im Breisgau: Augustinermuseum Freiburg im Breisgau, 1978.

Blondeel, Bernard, ed. *Gotische groepen uit Antwerps privé-bezit* (exh. cat.). Antwerp: Bank Brussel Lambert, n.d.

Bolton, Brenda M. *"Mulieres Sanctae."* In *Sanctity and Secularity: The Church and the World*, Studies in Church History 10, edited by Derek Baker, pp. 77-96. Oxford: Basil Blackwell, 1973.

—. *"Mulieres Sanctae."* In *Women in Medieval Society*, edited by S.M. Stuard, pp. 141-58. Philadelphia: University of Pennsylvania Press, 1976.

—. *"Vitae matrum, a Further Aspect of the Frauenfrage."* In *Medieval Women. Dedicated and presented to Professor Rosalind M.T. Hill on the occasion of her seventieth birthday*, edited by Derek Baker, pp. 253-73. Oxford: Basil Blackwell, 1978.

Bonde, Sheila, ed. *Survival of the Gods: Classical Mythology in Medieval Art* (exh. cat.). Providence, Rhode Island: Brown University, 1987.

de Borchgrave d'Altena, Joseph. *Notes et Documents pour servir à l'histoire de l'art et de l'iconographie en Belgique. 1re série: Sculptures conservées au Pays Mosan.* Verviers: G. Leens, 1926.

—. "La Sculpture gothique à l'exposition d'art religieux de Liège." *Bulletin de la Société royale d'Archéologie de Bruxelles* 77 (1930): 77-87.

—. "Notes au sujet de sculptures conservées à Wellen." *Leodium* 26/1 (1933): 5-14.

—. *A propos de l'exposition 'Les Madones du Limbourg.'* Brussels: Ballieu, 1936.

—. *Notes pour servir à l'inventaire des oeuvres d'art du Brabant: arrondissement de Louvain.* Brussels: Ballieu, 1941.

—. *De l'influence de l'art brabançon dans l'ancien comté de Looz: Retables, statues, statuettes.* Brussels: Ballieu, 1942.

—. "Vierges de Pitié de chez nous." *Annales de la Société royale d'Archéologie de Bruxelles* 46 (1942-43): 263-70.

—. *Oeuvres de nos imagiers romans et gothiques. Sculpteurs, ivoiriers, orfèvres, fondeurs: 1025 à 1550.* Brussels: Raymond Dupriez, 1944.

—. *Madones anciennes conservées en Belgique 1025-1425.* 2nd ed. Brussels: Editions du Cercle d'Art, 1945.

—. *La Passion du Christ dans la Sculpture en Belgique du XI au XVIe S.* Paris and Brussels: Editions du Cercle d'Art, 1946.

—. *Notes pour servir à l'inventaire des oeuvres d'art du Brabant: arrondissement de Bruxelles.* Brussels: Lesigne, 1947.

—. "Notes pour servir à l'étude des oeuvres d'art du Limbourg, 1ère partie." *Bulletin de la Société d'Art et d'Histoire du Diocèse de Liège* 43 (1963): 67-181.

—. "Vierges de Pitié." Offprint. Virton: Michel Frères, 1965. Originally published in *Le pays gaumais* 26 (1965): 87-105.

—. "Notes pour servir à l'étude des oeuvres d'art du Limbourg, 2e partie." *Bulletin de la Société d'Art et d'Histoire du Diocèse de Liège* 48 (1968): 1-21.

—. *Sculptures du moyen âge conservées dans les collections privées belges* (exh. cat.). Laarne: Kasteel Laarne, 1969.

de Borchgrave d'Altena, Joseph, and Josée Mambour. *La Passion dans la sculpture en Hainaut de 1400 à 1700, troisième et dernière partie* (exh. cat.). Charleroi: Imprimerie Provinciale du Hainaut, 1974.

de Bosschere, Jean. *La Sculpture Anversoise aux XVe et XVIe Siècles.* Brussels: G. Van Oest & Cie, 1909.

Bouvy, D.P.R.A. *Middeleeuwsche Beeldhouwkunst in de Noordelijke Nederlanden.* Amsterdam: A.A. Balkema, 1947.

—. *Beeldhouwkunst, Aartsbisschoppelijk Museum Utrecht.* Utrecht: Aartsbisschoppelijk Museum, 1962.

Brandenbarg, Ton. "Ste.-Anna en haar familie. De Anna-verering in verband met opvattingen over huwelijk en gezin in de vroeg-moderne tijd." In *Tussen heks en heilige: het vrouwbeeld op de drempel van de moderne tijd, 15de / 16de eeuw* (exh. cat.), edited by Petty Bange et al., pp. 101-28. Nijmegen: SUN and Nijmeegs Museum 'Commanderie van Sint-Jan,' 1985.

Bredero, A.H. "De Delftse begijn Gertrui van Oosten (ca. 1320-1358) en haar nieterkende heiligheid." In *De Nederlanden in de Late Middeleeuwen*, edited by D.E.H. de Boer and J.W. Marsilje, pp. 83-97. Utrecht: Het Spectrum, 1987.

Bréhier, Louis. *L'Art chrétien: son développement iconographique des origines à nos jours.* 2nd ed. Paris: H. Laurens, 1928.

Breisach, Ernst. *Historiography: Ancient, Medieval & Modern.* Chicago and London: University of Chicago Press, 1983.

Brémond, Claude, Jacques Le Goff, and Jean-Claude Schmitt. *L'"Exemplum". Typologie des sources du moyen âge occidental.* Turnhout: Brepols, 1982.

Breure, L. "De hemelse bruidegom." *Spiegel Historiael* 15 (1980): 149-56.

Brouette, E. "L'Abbaye de Villers à Tilly." *Monasticon Belge* 4 / 2 (1968): 341-405.

Burckhardt, Jacob. *Civilisation of the Renaissance*. 1865. Rev. ed. New York: Harper & Row, 1958.

Burrus, Virginia. *Chastity as Autonomy: Women in the Stories of the Apocryphal Acts*. Illinois: Edwin Mellen Press, 1989.

Bynum, Caroline Walker. "Women Mystics and Eucharistic Devotion in the Thirteenth Century." *Women's Studies* 11 (1984): 179-214.

—. "Women's Stories, Women's Symbols: A Critique of Victor Turner's Theory of Liminality." In *Anthropology and the Study of Religion*, edited by Robert L. Moore and Frank E. Reynolds, pp. 105-25. Chicago: Center for the Scientific Study of Religion, 1984.

—. "Fast, Food and Flesh: The Religious Significance of Food to Medieval Women." *Representations* 11 (1985): 1-25.

—. "The Body of Christ in the Later Middle Ages: A Reply to Leo Steinberg." *Renaissance Quarterly* 39/3 (1986): 399-439.

—. *Holy Feast and Holy Fast: The Religious Significance of Food to Medieval Women*. Berkeley: University of California Press, 1987.

—. "The Female Body and Religious Practice in the Later Middle Ages." Vol. 1, *Fragments for a History of the Human Body*, edited by Michel Feher, pp. 160-220. New York: Zone, 1989.

Camille, Michael. "Seeing and Reading: Some Visual Implications of Medieval Literacy and Illiteracy." *Art History* 8/1 (1985): 26-49.

Campbell, Lorne. "The Art Market in the Southern Netherlands in the Fifteenth Century." *Burlington Magazine* 118 (1976): 187-98.

Caron, M.L. "Ansien doet gedencken; de religieuze voorstellingswereld van de Moderne Devotie." In *Geert Grote en de Moderne Devotie* (exh. cat.), pp. 12-24. Utrecht: Het Catharijneconvent, 1984.

Carrier, David. *Artwriting*. Amherst, Massachusetts: University of Massachusetts Press, 1987.

—. "Circa 1640." *New Literary History* 21 (1989-90): 649-70.

Carroll, Michael P. *The Cult of the Virgin Mary: Psychological Origins*. Princeton: Princeton University Press, 1986.

Champa, Kermit S. *The Rise of Landscape Painting in France: From Corot to Monet* (exh. cat.). Manchester, New Hampshire: The Currier Gallery of Art, 1991.

Chatellier, Louis. *The Europe of the Devout: The Catholic Reformation and the Formation of a New Society*. 1987. Translated by Jean Birrell. 2nd ed. Cambridge: Cambridge University Press, 1989.

Chojnacki, Stanley, ed. "Recent Trends in Renaissance Studies: The Family, Marriage, and Sex." *Renaissance Quarterly* 40 / 4 (1987): 660-751.

Clemen, Paul, ed. *Belgische Kunstdenkmäler*. 2 vols. Munich: Bruckmann, 1923.

Coenen, J. "Limburgsche Beelden uit de XVIe eeuw." *Kunst Adelt Peer* 5 / 1-2 (15 July and 15 October 1926): 3-29.

Colledge, Edmund, O.S.A., and James Walsh, S.J. *A Book of Showings to the Anchoress Julian of Norwich*, part 1. Toronto: The Pontifical Institute of Medieaval Studies, 1978.

Cornelis, Els. "De Kunstenaar in het Laat-Middeleeuwse Gent." *Handelingen der Maatschappij voor Geschiedenis en Oudheidkunde te Gent* n.s. 41 (1987): 97-128; n.s. 42 (1988): 95-138.

Crab, J., P.-V. Maes, and L. Van Buyten. *Kerk van het Groot Begijnhof*. Bronnen voor de kunstgeschiedenis van het arrondissement Leuven. ser. A: Inventaris, vol. 1. Leuven: 1966.

Danto, Arthur. "Review of David Freedberg, *The Power of Images*." *The Art Bulletin* 72 / 2 (June 1990): 341-42.

Daris, J. *Notices historiques sur les églises du diocèse de Liège*, vol. 15. Liège: Demarteau, 1894.

Darnton, Robert. *The Great Cat Massacre and Other Episodes in French Cultural History*. 1984. 2nd ed. New York: Vintage Books, 1985.

Davis, Natalie Zemon. "Some Tasks and Themes in the Study of Popular Religion." In *The Pursuit of Holiness in Late Medieval and Renaissance Religion*, edited by Charles Trinkaus with Heiko A. Oberman, pp. 307-36. Leiden: E.J. Brill, 1974.

De Backer, Chr. "Beklede Devotieprenten uit het Klooster der Penitenten bij St.-Jacobs te Gent." *Volkskunde* 84 / 1 (1983): 1-10.

Decker, Bernhard. *Das ende des mittelalterlichen Kultbildes und die Plastik Hans Leinbergers*. Bamberger Studien zur Kunstgeschichte und Denkmalpflege. Bamberg: Lehrstuhl für Kunstgeschichte und Aufbaustudium Denkmalpflege an der Universität Bamberg im Selbstverlag, 1985.

De Coo, J. *Museum Mayer van den Bergh*. Vol. 2, *Beeldhouwkunst, Plaketten, Antiek*. Antwerp: Museum Mayer van den Bergh, 1969.

Dehio, Georg. "Andachtsbilder." Vol. 2, *Geschichte des deutschen Kunst*, pp. 117-23. 3rd. ed. Berlin and Leipzig: Walter De Gruyter & Co., 1923.

Dekker, Rudolf. "Egodocumenten: Een literatuuroverzicht." *Tijdschrift voor Geschiedenis* 101 (1988): 161-89.

Delmaire, B. "Les béguines dans le Nord de la France au premier siècle de leur histoire (vers 1230-vers 1350)." In *Les religieuses en France au XIIIe siècle*, edited by Michel Parisse, pp. 121-62. Nancy: Presses universitaires de Nancy, 1985.

Demmler, Theodor. *Die Bildwerke des Deutschen Museums*. Vol. 3, *Die Bildwerk in Holz, Stein und Ton, Grossplastik*. Berlin and Leipzig: Walter de Gruyter & Co., 1930.

De Munter, Longinus. "'De Nood Gods' bij ons Primitieven." *Kunst Adelt Peer* (15 July 1925): 3-20.

Destrée, Jos. *Etude sur la sculpture brabançonne au moyen âge (première partie)*. Brussels: Vromont, 1894.

—. "A propos de l'influence de Roger van der Weyden (Roger de la Pasture) sur la sculpture brabançonne." *Annales de la Société royale d'Archéologie de Bruxelles* 28 (1919): 1-11.

Devigne, Marguerite. *La Sculpture mosane du XIIe au XVI siècle. Contribution à l'étude d'art dans la région de la Meuse moyenne*. Paris and Brussels: G. Van Oest, 1932.

De Vis, H. "De Mariavoorstellingen in Vlaamsch Brabant." *Eigen Schoon & De Brabander* n.s. 9, 17/3-4 (1934): 117-67.

Devlin, Dennis. "*Corpus Christi*: A Study in Medieval Eucharistic Theory, Devotion and Practice." Ph.D. diss., University of Chicago, 1975.

—. "Feminine Lay Piety in the High Middle Ages: The Beguines." Vol. 1, *Distant Echoes: Medieval Religious Women*, edited by John A. Nichols and Lillian Thomas Shank, pp. 183-96. Cistercian Studies Series 71. Michigan, Western Michigan University, 1984.

Devotionalia: Periodiek voor verzamelaars van devotionalia. Issued quarterly since 1981 by Stichting Devotionalia, 5625 CP Eindhoven, the Netherlands.

D'Huys, Bert. "De Gentse begijnhoven in cultuurhistorisch perspectief." In *Werken en Kerken* (exh. cat.), pp. 13-48. Ghent: Stad Gent, 1984.

Didier, Robert. "Christ attendant la mort au Calvaire et Pieta, deux sculptures anversoises conservées à Binche: problèmes de datation et d'iconographie." *Bulletin de la Commission royale des Monuments et des Sites / Bulletin van de Koninklijke Commissie voor Monumenten en Landschappen* 14 (1963): 53-75.

—. "Sculptures mosanes des années 1400-1450." In *Clio et son Regard: Mélanges d'histoire, d'histoire de l'art et d'archéologie offerts à Jacques Stiennon à l'occasion de ses vingt-cinq ans d'enseignement à l'Université de Liège*, edited by Rita Lejeune and Joseph Deckers, pp. 143-73. Liège: Pierre Mardaga, 1982.

—. "Sculptures et retables des anciens Pays-Bas méridionaux des années 1430-1460: Traditions et innovations pour le Haut-Rhin et l'Allemagne du Sud." In *Le retable* d'Issenheim et la sculpture au Nord des Alpes à la fin du moyen âge (exh. cat.), edited by Christian Heck, pp. 48-79. Colmar: Musée d'Unterlinden, 1989.

Didier, R., and H. Krohm. *Duitse middeleeuwse beeldhouwwerken in Belgische ver- zamelingen. Les sculptures médiévales allemandes dans les collections belges* (exh. cat.). Europalia 77 Bundesrepublik Deutschland. Brussels: Generale Bankmaat- schappij / Société Générale de Banque, 1977.

Dilly, Heinrich. "Review of Marlite Halbertsma, *Wilhelm Pinder en de Duitse kunstgeschiedenis.*" *Kunstchronik* 40 (September 1987): 444-50.

Dinzelbacher, Peter. *Vision und Visionsliteratur im Mittelalter*. Monographien zur Geschichte des Mittelalters 23. Stuttgart: Anton Kiersemann, 1981.

Dinzelbacher, Peter, and Dieter R. Bauer, eds. *Frauenmystik im Mittelalter*. Wissenschaftliche Studientagung der Akademie der Diözese Rottenburg-Stuttgart, 22-25 February 1984, Weingarten. Ostfildern: Schwabenverlag, 1985.

—. *Religiöse Frauenbewegung und mystische Frömmigkeit im Mittelalter*. Beihefte zum Archiv für Kulturgeschichte 28. Cologne and Vienna: Böhlau, 1988.

Dirk Bouts en zijn tijd (exh. cat.). Leuven: Sint-Pieterskerk, 1975.

Dobrzeniecki, Tadeusz. "Mediaeval Sources of the Pietà." *Bulletin du Musée National de Varsovie* 8 (1967): 5-24.

Douglas, Mary. *Purity and Danger: An Analysis of the Concepts of Pollution and Taboo*. 1966. London: Ark Paperbacks, 1988.

Duggan, Lawrence G. "Was art really the 'book of the illiterate'?" *Word & Image* 5 / 3 (1989): 227-51.

1000 Jaar kerkelijke kunst in Limburg (exh. cat.). Hasselt: Provinciaal Begijnhof, 1961.

Dusar, Albert. *Limburgs kunstbezit: van prehistorie tot classicisme*. Hasselt: Heideland- Orbis N.V., 1970.

Duverger, J. *Brussel als kunstcentrum in de XIVe en de XVe eeuw. Bouwstoffen tot de Nederlandsche Kunstgeschiedenis*. Antwerp: De Sikkel, 1935.

Eisler, Colin. "Kunstgeschichte American Style." In *The Intellectual Migration. Europe and America 1930-1960*, edited by Donald Fleming and Bernard Bailyn, pp. 544-629. Cambridge, Massachusetts: Belknap Press, 1969.

—. "Review of Sixten Ringbom, *Icon to Narrative.*" *The Art Bulletin* 51 / 2 (1969): 186-88.

Elm, K. "Be(g)hinen." Vol. 1, *Lexikon des Mittelalters*, cols. 1799-1800. Munich and Zurich: Artemis Verlag, 1980.

—. "Die Stellung der Frau in Ordenswesen, Semireligiösentum und Häresie zur Zeit der heiligen Elisabeth." In *Sankt Elisabeth. Fürstin, Dienerin, Heilige* (exh. cat.), pp. 7-28. Sigmaringen: Jan Thorbecke, 1981.

Engelen, C. *Passie* (exh. cat.). Hasselt: Generale Bank, 1988.

English, M. "Middeleeuwsche Mariabeelden te Brugge." *Kunst Adelt Peer* 7 / 3-4 (15 April 1929): 1-36.

Erbstösser, Martin. *Sozialreligiöse Strömungen im späten Mittelalter. Geissler, Freigeister und Waldenser im 14. Jahrhundert.* Forschungen zur mittelalterlichen Geschichte 16. Berlin: Akademie Verlag, 1970.

Erbstösser, Martin, and E. Werner. *Ideologische Probleme des mittelalterlichen Plebejertums. Die Freigeistige Häresie und ihre sozialen Wurzeln.* Forschungen zur mittelalterlichen Geschichte 7. Berlin: Akademie Verlag, 1960.

Escherisch, M. "Eine mittelrheinische Pietà auf hollandischem Boden." *Zeitschrift für christliche Kunst* 33 (1920): 52.

Ewing, Dan. "Marketing Art in Antwerp, 1460-1560: Our Lady's *Pand.*" *The Art Bulletin* 72 / 4 (1990): 558-84.

Feiss, Hugh. "Supplement to the *The Life of Marie d'Oignies.*" *Vox Benedictina* 7 / 1 (1990): 53-72.

Fernandez, James. "Historians Tell Tales: Of Cartesian Cats and Gallic Cockfights." *Journal of Modern History* 60 (1988): 113-27.

Flanders in the Fifteenth Century: Art and Civilization (exh. cat.). Detroit: Detroit Institute of Arts, 1960.

Foerster-Nietzsche, Elizabeth, ed. *The Nietzsche-Wagner Correspondence.* New York: Liveright, 1949.

de Fontette, Micheline. *Les religieuses à l'âge classique du droit canon. Recherches sur les structures juridiques des branches féminines des ordres.* Bibliothèque de la Société d'Histoire Ecclésiastique de la France. Paris: J. Vrin, 1967.

Ford, James B., and G. Stephen Vickers. "The Relation of Nuno Gonçalves to the Pietà from Avignon, with a Consideration of the Iconography of the Pietà in France." *The Art Bulletin* 21 / 1 (1939): 4-43.

Fotorepertorium van de Belgische Bedehuizen, Provincie Limburg, Kanton Beringen. Kanton Bilzen. Kanton Borgloon. Kanton Bree. Kanton Genk. Kanton Hasselt. Kanton Maaseik. Kanton Maasmechelen. Kanton Neerpelt. Kanton Sint-Truiden. Kanton Tongeren. 12 vols. Brussels: Ministerie van Nederlandse Cultuur, Koninklijk Instituut voor het Kunstpatrimonium; Sint-Truiden: Provinciale Dienst voor het Kunstpatrimonium, 1972-1979.

Frankl, Paul. *The Gothic: Literary Sources and Interpretations through Eight Centuries.* Princeton: Princeton University Press, 1960.

Frazer, James. *The Golden Bough: A Study in Magic and Religion.* 12 vols. Revised and enlarged. London: Macmillan, 1911-15.

Fredericq, Paul. *Corpus documentorum inquisitionis haereticae pravitatis Neerlandicae.* 2 vols. Ghent: J. Vuylsteke, 1889-1906.

Frederiks, J.A., J. Kalf, and W. Vogelsang. *De oude kerkelijke kunst in Nederland.* On the occasion of the national exhibition in 's-Hertogenbosch, 1913. 's-Hertogenbosch: C.N. Teulings, 1914.

Freedberg, David. "The Problem of Images in Northern Europe and its Repercussions in the Netherlands." *Hafnia: Copenhagen Papers in the History of Art* (1976): 25-45.

—. *Iconoclasts and Their Motives.* Maarssen: Gary Schwartz, 1985.

—. "Art and Iconoclasm, 1525-1580: The Case of the Northern Netherlands." In *Kunst voor de Beeldenstorm: Noordnederlandse Kunst, 1525-1580,* edited by J.P. Filedt Kok, W. Halsema Kubes, and W.T. Kloek, pp. 39-84. Amsterdam: Rijksmuseum, 1986.

—. *Iconoclasm and Painting in the Revolt of the Netherlands, 1566-1609.* New York: Garland Press, 1987.

—. *The Power of Images: Studies in the History and Theory of Response.* Chicago and London: University of Chicago Press, 1989.

Frijhoff, Willem. "Het votiefschilderij als historisch object." *Volkskundig Bulletin* 11 / 1 (1985): 34-43.

Frugoni, G. "Le mistiche, le visioni e l'iconografia: rapporti ed influssi." Offprint. Todi: Accademia Tudertina, 1982, pp. 5-45. First published in *Temi e problemi nella mistica femminile trecentesca (Todi, 14-17 ottobre 1979),* pp. 139-79.

Fry, Roger. "An Essay on Aesthetics." 1909. Reprint in *Vision and Design,* pp. 16-38. Cleveland: Meridian Books, 1963.

Geert Grote en de Moderne Devotie (exh. cat.). Utrecht: Het Catharijneconvent, 1984.

Geertz, Clifford. "Deep Play: Notes on the Balinese Cockfight." 1972. In *Interpretive Social Science: A Reader,* edited by Paul Rabinow and William M. Sullivan, pp. 181-223. Berkeley: University of California Press, 1979.

Gent duizend jaar kunst en cultuur (exh. cat.). Ghent: Museum voor Schone Kunsten, 1975.

Gerits, T.J. "Inventaris van het meubilair in de pastorie en kapelanie van het Begijnhof te Diest (XVIde eeuw)." *Ons Heem* 19 (1965): 55-58.

Gewijde kunst in Limburgs bezit (exh. cat.). Hasselt: Provinciaal Begijnhof, 1966.

Ghent, Musée des Beaux-Arts / Museum voor Schone Kunsten. *Catalogue du Musée des Beaux-Arts de la ville de Gand, précédé d'un plan des salles et d'une notice historique par L. Maeterlinck.* Ghent: F. Meyer & Van Loo, 1905.

Ghent, Musée des Beaux-Arts / Museum voor Schone Kunsten. *Museum voor Schone Kunsten / Musée des Beaux-Arts*. Ghent: Ad. Hoste, 1915.

Gillet, Louis. *Histoire artistique des ordres mendiants*. Paris: H. Laurens, 1912.

Ginzburg, Carlo. "Titian, Ovid, and Sixteenth-Century Codes for Erotic Illustration." In *Clues, Myths, and the Historical Method*, translated by John and Anne. C. Tedeschi, pp. 77-95. Baltimore and London: Johns Hopkins University Press, 1989.

Godenne, W. "Christ de pitié. Sculptures diverses." *Handelingen van de Koninklijke Kring voor Oudheidkunde, Letteren en Kunst van Mechelen* 74 (1970): 115-23.

The Golden Age of Dutch Manuscript Painting (exh. cat.). New York: George Braziller, Inc., 1990.

Gorissen, F. *Die klevischen beeldensnijder. Meisterwerke niederrheinländischer Holzbildnerei der Jahre 1474-1508 im Städtischen Museum Haus Koekkoek* (exh. cat.). Kleef, 1963.

Die Gottesmutter, Marienbild in Rheinland und in Westfalen (exh. cat.). 2 vols. Recklinghausen: Aurel Bongers, 1974.

de la Grange, A. "Choix de testaments tournaisiens antérieurs au XVIe siècle." *Annales de la Société Historique et Archéologique de Tournai* n.s. 2 (1897): 1-365.

Gravenkamp, Kurt. *Marienklage: Das deutsche Vesperbild im 14. und im frühen 15. Jahrhundert*. Aschoffenburg: Paul Pattloch Verlag, 1948.

Grundmann, Herbert. *Religiöse Bewegungen im Mittelalter*. 2nd ed. Hildesheim: G. Olm, 1961.

Gysseling, M. "De oudste statuten van het Groot Begijnhof." *Jaarboek van de Heemkundige Kring de Oost-Oudburg* 21 (1984): 2-20.

Halbertsma, Marlite. *Wilhelm Pinder en de Duitse Kunstgeschiedenis*. Groningen: Forsten, 1985.

Hamann, Richard. "Die Kategorie der Stofflichkeit in der bildenden Kunst." In *Neue Beiträge deutscher Forschung Wilhelm Worringer zum 60. Geburtstag*, edited by Erich Fidder, pp. 143-50. Königsberg: Kanter Verlag, 1943.

Hamburger, Jeffrey. "The Visual and the Visionary: The Image in Late Medieval Monastic Devotions." *Viator* 20 (1989): 161-82.

Harbison, Craig. "Secularity and Social Standing in Jan van Eyck's Arnolfini Double Portrait." *Renaissance Quarterly* 43/2 (1990): 249-91.

Hearn, M. F. *Romanesque Sculpture*. Ithaca, New York: Cornell University Press, 1981.

Heck, C. "La Vierge de pitié de Sigolshein." *Cahiers alsaciens d'archéologie, d'art et d'histoire* 25 (1982): 81-86.

Heckscher, William S. "Erwin Panofsky, A Curriculum Vitae." In *Art and Literature, Studies in Relationship*, edited by Egon Verheyen, pp. 339-62. Durham, North Carolina: Duke University Press; and Baden-Baden: Valentin Koerner, 1985.

Helbig, Jules. *L'Art mosan depuis l'introduction du Christianisme jusqu'à la fin du XVIIIe siècle*, vol. 1. Brussels: C. van Oest, 1906-11.

Hemsterhuis, Franz. "Lettres sur la sculpture." 1765. New ed. In *Oeuvres philosophiques de François Hemsterhuis*, edited by Louis Susan Pedro Meyboom. Leeuwarden: W. Eekhoff, 1846-50.

Henschenius, G., and D. Papebroch, eds. *Vita sanctae Julianae virginis*. In *AASS*, Apr. 5 / 1 (Paris, 1865): 435-75. Also translated by Barbara Newman, Peregrina Translations Series 13. Toronto, Ontario: Peregrina Publishing Co., 1988.

Herbst des Mittelalters. Spätgotik in Köln und am Niederrhein (exh. cat.). Cologne: Kunsthalle, 1970.

's-Hertogenbosch. *Catalogus der Nationale tentoonstelling van oude kerkelijke kunst te 's-Hertogenbosch* (exh. cat.), edited by Jan Kalf, with J.A. Frederiks, J.M. Hillesum et al. 's-Hertogenbosch: Teuling, 1913.

Holly, Michael Ann. *Panofsky and the Foundations of Art History*. New York: Cornell University Press, 1984.

Hommage à Roger de la Pasture-Van der Weyden 1464-1964 (exh. cat.). Brussels: Dereume, 1964.

Honderd Limburgse Madonnas in de Romaanse Kloostergang van de O.-L.-Vrouw-Basiliek (exh. cat.). Tongeren: O.-L.-Vrouw-Basiliek, 1953.

Hoornaert, R. "La plus ancienne Règle du Béguinage de Bruges." *Annales de la Société d'Emulation de Bruges* 72 (1929): 17-79.

Howell, Martha, with Suzanne Wemple and Denise Kaiser. "A Documented Presence: Medieval Women in Germanic Historiography." In *Women in Medieval History & Historiography*, edited by Susan Mosher Stuard, pp. 101-31. Philadelphia: University of Pennsylvania Press, 1987.

Huizinga, Johan. *The Waning of the Middle Ages*. 1924. Reprint. Translated by F. Hopman. Harmondsworth, England: Penguin Books, 1968.

Hunt, Lynn. ed. *The New Cultural History*. Berkeley: University of California Press, 1989.

James, William. *The Varieties of Religious Experience: A Study in Human Nature*. 1901-02. Reprint. New York: NAL Penguin, 1958.

Jansen, Jaak. *Het Kunstpatrimonium van het Begijnhof te Turnhout*. Brussels: Ministerie van Onderwijs, Koninklijk Instituut voor het Kunstpatrimonium and Turnhout: Vrienden van het Begijnhof, 1988.

Kalinowski, L. *Geneza Piety Średniowiecznej*. Polska Akademia Umiejętności. Cracow: Krakowska Drukarnia Naukowa, 1953. Originally published as "Geneza Piety Średniowiecznej." *Prace Komisji Historii Sztuki* 10 (1952): 135-257.

Katz, Stephen. "Recent Works on Mysticism." *History of Religions* 25 (1985): 76-86.

Kecks, Roland. *Madonna und Kind. Das häusliche Andachtsbild im Florenz des 15. Jahrhunderts*. Berlin: Gebr. Mann Verlag, 1988.

Kieckhefer, Richard. *Unquiet Souls: Fourteenth-Century Saints and their Religious Milieu*. Chicago: University of Chicago Press, 1984.

—. "Major Currents in Late Medieval Devotion." *World Spirituality* 17 (1987): 75-108.

Kitch, Sally L. *Chaste Liberation: Celibacy and Female Cultural Status*. Chicago: University of Illinois Press, 1990.

Klapisch-Zuber, Christine. "Holy Dolls: Play and Piety in Florence in the Quattrocento." In *Women, Family and Ritual in Renaissance Italy*, pp. 310-29. Chicago: University of Chicago Press, 1985.

Koch, E. "Kloosterintrede, huwelijk en familiefortuin. De kosten van klooster en huwelijk voor adellijke vrouwen in zuidoost-Nederland in de late middeleeuwen." In *In de schaduw van de eeuwigheid. Tien studies over religie en samenleving in laatmiddeleeuws Nederland aangeboden aan Prof. Dr. A.H. Bredero*, edited by N. Lettinck and J.J. Van Moolenbroek, pp. 242-57. Utrecht: HES, 1986.

—. "De positie van vrouwen op de huwelijksmarkt in de middeleeuwen." *Tijdschrift voor sociale geschiedenis* 13 (1987): 150-72.

Konrad, Martin. *Meisterwerke der Skulptur in Flandern und Brabant*, vol. 1. Berlin: Imago, 1928.

Koorn, Florence W.J. *Begijnhoven in Holland en Zeeland gedurende de middeleeuwen*. Assen: Van Gorcum, 1981.

—. "Ongebonden vrouwen: overeenkomsten en verschillen tussen begijnen en Zusters des Gemenen Leven." *Ons Geestelijk Erf* 59 / 2 (1985): 393-402.

Krohm, H. "Zwei neuerwobene Alabasterarbeiten des 15. Jahrhunderts in der Skulpturengalerie." *Jahrbuch der Preussischer Kulturbesitz* 13 (1976): 249-52.

Krönig, Wolfgang. "Rheinische Vesperbilder aus Leder und ihr Umkreis." *Westdeutches Jahrbuch für Kunstgeschichte* 24 (1962): 97-191.

Kubler, George. *The Shape of Time*. New Haven: Yale University Press, 1962.

Künstle, Karl. *Ikonographie der christliche Kunst*, vol. 1. Freiburg im Breisgau: Herder, 1926-28.

Kunstschatten uit het Diestse begijnhof (exh. cat.). Diest: Stedelijk Museum, 1988.

Kunze, Herbert. *Die gotische Skulptur im Mitteldeutschland*. Bonn: Friedrich Cohen, 1925.

Küppers, Leonhard. "Marienklage." Vol. 1, *Die Gottesmutter, Marienbild in Rheinland und in Westfalen* (exh. cat.), pp. 277-90. Recklinghausen: Aurel Bongers, 1974.

Kutsch, K.J. "Spätgotische Schnitzkunst zwischen Maas und Ruhr." *Selfkantia* 64 (1956): 49-103.

Het Laatgotische Beeldsnijcentrum Leuven (exh. cat.). Leuven: Stedelijk Museum, 1979.

Laat-gotische beeldsnijkunst uit Limburg en Grensland (exh. cat.). Sint-Truiden: Provincie Limburg Culturele Aangelegenheden, 1990.

de Laborde, Alexandre. *Les Miracles de Nostre Dame compilés par Jehan Miélot*. Paris: Société Française de Reproductions de Manuscrits à Peintures, 1929.

La Faoia, Louis. *The Man of Sorrows: Origin and Development in Florentine Trecento Painting*. The Hague: Sangreis, 1980.

Lauwers, M. "Testaments inédits du chartrier des Dominicains de Liège (1245-1300)." *Bulletin de la Commission royale d'Histoire* 154 (1988): 158-97.

—. "Expérience béguinale et récit hagiographique: à propos de la 'Vita Mariae Oigniacensis' de Jacques de Vitry (vers 1215)." *Journal des Savants* 1-2 (1989): 61-103.

Lauwers, M., and W. Simons. *Béguins et Béguines à Tournai au Bas Moyen Age: Les communautés béguinales à Tournai du XIIIe au XVe siècle*. Tornacum 3. Tournai: Archives du Chapitre Cathédrale; Louvain-la-Neuve: Université Catholique de Louvain, 1988.

Leach, Edmund R. "Two Essays Concerning the Symbolic Representation of Time." 1961. In *Reader in Comparative Religion: An Anthropological Approach*, 4th ed., edited by William A. Lessa and Evon Z. Vogt, pp. 311-17. New York: Harper & Row, 1979.

—. "Anthropological Aspects of Language: Animal Categories and Verbal Abuse." 1964. In *Reader in Comparative Religion: An Anthropological Approach*, 4th ed., edited by William A. Lessa and Evon Z. Vogt, pp. 153-66. New York: Harper & Row, 1979.

Leeuwenberg, Jaap. "Een nieuw facet aan de Utrechtse beeldhouwkunst." *Oud Holland* 77 (1962): 99.

Leeuwenberg, Jaap, ed., with Willy Halsema-Kubes. *Beeldhouwkunst in het Rijksmuseum: Catalogus*. Amsterdam: Rijksmuseum, 1973.

Legros, Elisée. "Sur les 'repos de Jésus' tournaisiens (et sur quelques autres faits attestés par les testaments de Tournai)." *La Vie Wallonne* 33 (1959): 212-17.

Lehrs, Max. *Geschichte und kritischer Katalog des deutschen, niederländischen und französischen Kupferstichs im XV. Jahrhundert*. Vienna: Gesellschaft für Vervielfältigende Kunst, 1908-34.

Leisenheimer, Bernhard. "Ehrenstein 500 years." *Crosier Heritage* 16 (special issue, July 1985): 1-12.

Lessa, Evon Z., and William A. Vogt. *Reader in Comparative Religion: An Anthropological Approach*. 4th ed. New York: Harper & Row, 1979.

Lessing, Gotthold Ephraim. *Laocoön: An Essay on the Limits of Painting and Poetry*. 1766. Translated by Edward Allen McCormick. Baltimore: Johns Hopkins University Press, 1984.

Lévi-Strauss, Claude. *The Savage Mind*. 1962. Chicago: University Press, 1966.

Liège, Musée d'Art religieux et d'Art mosan. *Oeuvres maîtresses du Musée d'Art religieux et d'Art mosan*. Liège, 1980.

Lies, Dagmar Editha. "Plastik als Gestaltung: Wilhelm Pinders Aussagen zur deutschen Plastik in den Jahren 1914-1930." Inaugural dissertation, Rheinischen Friedrich-Wilhelms-Universität Bonn, 1980.

Lipphardt, W. "Studien zu den Marienklagen." *Beiträge zur Geschichte der deutschen Sprache und Literatur* 58 (1934): 390-444.

Little, Lester K. *Liberty, Charity, Fraternity: Lay Religious Confraternities at Bergamo in the Age of the Commune*. Smith College Studies in History 51. Northampton, Massachusetts: Smith College and Pierluigi Lubrina Editore, 1988.

Lüthgen, Eugen. *Die niederrheinische Plastik von der Gotik bis zur Renaissance. Ein entwicklungsgeschictlicher Versuch*. Strassburg: Heitz & Mundel, 1917.

Lutz, Catherine A. *Unnatural Emotions: Everyday Sentiments on a Micronesian Atoll & Their Challenge to Western Theory*. Chicago: University of Chicago Press, 1981.

Maes, S.F., and J. Dreesen. *De geschiedenis van Bree: de parochie-de oude kloosters*. Bree: "Ons Erf," Gewestelijke Kring voor Geschiedenis en Heemkunde te Bree, 1946-52.

Maeterlinck, Louis. "Roger van der Weyden, sculpteur." *Gazette des Beaux-Arts* 43.2 / 26 (1901): 265-84; 399-411.

Mâle, Emile. "Le renouvellement de l'art par les mystères à la fin du moyen âge." *Gazette des Beaux-Arts* 46.1 / 31 (1904): 89-106; 215-30; 283-301; 379-94.

—. *L'Art religieux de la fin du moyen âge en France*. 4th ed. Paris: Armand Colin, 1931.

—. *L'Art religieux de la fin du moyen âge*. 5th ed. Paris: Armand Colin, 1949.

Mandrou, Robert. *Introduction à la France moderne (1500-1640): Essai de psychologie historique*. Paris: Editions Albin Michel, 1961.

Marcus, George E., and Michael M.J. Fischer. *Anthropology as Cultural Critique: An Experimental Moment in the Human Sciences*. Chicago: University of Chicago Press, 1986.

Maria in de Kunst (exh. cat.). Maastricht, 1947.

"De Mariavereering in Brabant." Special issue of *Eigen Schoon en de Brabander*, n.s. 9, 17 / 3-4 (1934): 97-179.

Maris, A. "De Nood Gods te Rupelmonde." *Heemkundige Kring 'Wissekerke.' Bazel en Omstreken, driemaandelijks tijdschrift* 11 (June 1986): 39-43.

Marrow, James H. *Passion Iconography in Northern European Art of the Later Middle Ages and Early Renaissance: A Study of the Transformation of Sacred Metaphor into Descriptive Narrative*. Courtrai: Van Ghemmert, 1979.

—. "Symbol and Meaning in Northern European Art of the Late Middle Ages and early Renaissance." *Simiolus* 16 / 2-3 (1986): 150-69.

Mayo, Abbé H. *La Belgique à Marie*. Brussels: Bieleveld, 1929.

McDonnell, Ernest W. *The Beguines and Beghards in Medieval Culture, with Special Emphasis on the Belgian Scene*. New Jersey: Rutgers University Press, 1954.

Meier, P.J. "Das Goslarer Vesperbild." *Zeitschrift für bildende Kunst* 32 / 2 (1921): 33-36.

Meiss, Millard. *Painting in Florence and Siena After the Black Death: The Arts, Religion, and Society in the Mid-Fourteenth Century*. 1951. Reprint. New Jersey: Princeton University Press, 1978.

Mens, A. "De Verering van de H. Eucharistie bij onze vroegste Begijnen." In *Studia Eucharistica*, pp. 157-86. Antwerp, 1946.

—. *Oorsprong en betekenis van de Nederlandse begijnen- en begardenbeweging. Vergelijkende studie: XIIde-XIIIde eeuw*. Verhandelingen van de Koninklijke Vlaamse Academie voor Wetenschappen, Letteren en Schone Kunsten van België. Klasse der Letteren 9 / 7. Antwerp: Standaard-Boekhandel, 1947.

—. "De 'kleine armen van Christus' in de Brabants-Luikse gewesten (einde 12de, begin 13de eeuw)." *Ons Geestelijk Erf* 36 (1962): 282-331; 37 (1963): 129-69; 38 (1964): 113-44; 39 (1965): 225-71.

Mesnil, Jacques. *L'Art au Nord et au Sud des Alpes à l'époque de la renaissance: études comparatives*. Brussels: Van Oest, 1911.

Meurer, Heribert, ed. *Die mittelalterliche Skulpturen*. Vol. 1, *Stein und Holzskulpturen 800-1400*. Stuttgart: Württenbergisches Landesmuseum, 1989.

Middeleeuwse Kunst der Noordelijke Nederlanden (exh. cat.). Amsterdam: Rijksmuseum, 1958.

Milhaven, John Giles. "Thomas Aquinas on Sexual Pleasure." *Journal of Religious Ethics* 5 / 2 (1977): 157-81.

—. "A Medieval Lesson on Bodily Knowing: Women's Experience and Men's Thought." *Journal of the American Academy of Religion* 57 / 2 (1989): 341-72.

Milis, L. "Het begijnenwezen, uiting van een middeleeuwse maatschappij in de kering." In *Toespraken gehouden bij de begijnhoffeesten, Breda - Juni 1980.* N.p., n.d. [1980]: 9-29.

—. "De Kerk tussen de Gregoriaanse hervorming en Avignon." Vol. 3, *Algemene Geschiedenis der Nederlanden*, pp. 166-211. Haarlem: Fibula-Van Dishoeck, 1982.

Millet, Gabriel. *Recherches sur l'iconographie de l'Evangile aux XIVe, XVe, et XVIe siècles d'après les monuments de Mistre, de la Macedoine, et du Mont-Athos.* Paris: Fontemoing, 1916.

Montagu, Ashley. *Touching: The Human Significance of the Skin.* New York: Columbia University Press, 1971.

Montias, J.M. "Socio-Economic Aspects of Netherlandish Art from the Fifteenth to the Seventeenth Century." *The Art Bulletin* 72 / 3 (1990): 358-72.

Moors, J. *De oorkondentaal in Belgisch-Limburg van circa 1350 tot 1400.* Brussels: Belgisch Inter-Universitaire Centrum, 1952.

de Moreau, E., S.J. *L'Abbaye de Villers aux XIIe et XIIIe siècles. Etude d'histoire religieuse et économique.* Brussels: Librairie Albert Dewit, 1909.

Muller, Ellen. "Heilige maagden. De verering van maagdheiligen in religieuze vrouwengemeenschappen." In *Tussen heks en heilige: het vrouwbeeld op de drempel van de moderne tijd, 15de / 16de eeuw* (exh. cat.), edited by Petty Bange et al., pp. 83-100. Nijmegen: SUN and Nijmeegs Museum 'Commanderie van Sint-Jan,' 1985.

Müller, T. *Sculpture in the Netherlands, Germany, France and Spain, 1400 to 1500.* The Pelican History of Art. Harmondsworth: Penguin Books, 1966.

Murbach, Ernst. *Form und Material in der spätgotischen Plastik.* Baseler Studien zur Kunstgeschichte 1. Basel: Birkhäuser Verlag, 1943.

Needham, Rodney. "Percussion and Transition." 1967. In *Reader in Comparative Religion: An Anthropological Approach*, 4th ed., edited by William A. Lessa and Evon Z. Vogt, pp. 311-17. New York: Harper & Row, 1979.

—. *Circumstantial Deliveries.* Berkeley: University of California Press, 1981.

Neff, Amy. "The 'Dialogus Beatae Marie et Anselmi de Passione Domini.' Toward an Attribution." *Miscellanea Francescana* 86 / 1 (1986): 105-08.

Neri, Guido. "The Artistic Theory of Erwin Panofsky." *Architectural Design* 51 / 6-7 (1981): 30-34.

Nietzsche, Friedrich. "The Birth of Tragedy out of the Spirit of Music." 1872. In *The Birth of Tragedy and the Case of Wagner*, translated by Walter Kaufmann. New York: Random House, 1967.

Nimal, H. *Les Béguinages*. Nivelles: Lanneau et Despret, 1908. Also published in *Annales de la Société Archéologique de l'arrondissement de Nivelles* 9 (1908): 1-126.

Nodelman, Sheldon. "Structural Analysis in Art and Anthropology." In *Structuralism*, edited by Jacques Ehrmann, pp. 79-93. Garden City, New York: Doubleday, 1970.

Nolan, Mary Lee, and Sidney Nolan. *Christian Pilgrimage in Modern Western Europe*. Chapel Hill: University of North Carolina Press, 1989.

Obeyesekere, Gananath. *Medusa's Hair: An Essay on Personal Symbols and Religious Experience*. Chicago: University of Chicago Press, 1981.

—. *The Cult of the Goddess Pattini*. Chicago: University of Chicago Press, 1984.

Oliver, Judith Hathaway. "The Lambert-le-Bègue Psalters: A Study in Thirteenth-Century Mosan Illumination." Ph.D. diss., Columbia University, 1976.

—. "Medieval Alphabet Soup: Reconstruction of a Mosan Psalter-Hours in Philadelphia and Oxford and the Cult of St. Catherine." *Gesta* 24 / 2 (1985): 129-40.

—. *Gothic Manuscript Illumination in the Diocese of Liège (c.1250-c.1330)*. Vols. 2-3, Corpus van verluchte handschriften uit de Nederlanden / Corpus of Illuminated Manuscripts from the Low Countries. Leuven: Peeters, 1988.

—. *In beeld geprezen. Miniaturen uit Maaslandse devotieboeken 1250-1350*. (exh. cat.). Leuven: Peeters, 1989.

Olyslager, W. A. *Het Groot Begijnhof van Leuven*. Leuven: Groot Begijnhof, 1978.

Ooms, Hedwig. *Onze-Lieve-Vrouw in Limburg*. Tournai: Casterman, 1959.

Paglia, Camille. *Sexual Personae: Art and Decadence from Nefertiti to Emily Dickinson*. New Haven: Yale University Press, 1990.

Panofsky, Erwin. "Das Problem des Stils in der bildenden Kunst." *Zeitschrift für Ästhetik und allgemeine Kunstwissenschaft* 10 (1915): 460-67.

—. "Der Begriff des Kunstwollens." 1920. English translation by Kenneth J. Northcott and Joel Snyder, "The Concept of Artistic Volition: Erwin Panofsky." *Critical Inquiry* 8 (autumn 1981): 17-33.

—. "'Imago Pietatis.' Ein Beitrag zur Typengeschichte des 'Schmerzensmanns' und der 'Maria Mediatrix.'" In *Festschrift für Max J. Friedländer zum 60. Geburtstag*, pp. 261-308. Leipzig: E.A. Seemann, 1927.

—. "Reintegration of a Book of Hours Executed in the Workshop of the 'Maître des Grandes Heures de Rohan.'" Vol. 2, *Medieval Studies in Memory of Arthur Kingsley Porter*, edited by W.R.M. Koehler, pp. 479-99. Cambridge, Massachusetts: Harvard University Press, 1939.

—. *Early Netherlandish Painting*. Cambridge: Harvard University Press, 1953.

Paquay, Jean. *Cartulaire de la collégiale Notre-Dame à Tongres, jusqu'au XVe siècle*, vol. 1. Tongeren, 1909.

Die Parler und der Schöne Stil 1350-1400: Europäische Kunst unter den Luxemburgen (exh. cat.). 3 vols. Cologne: Museen der Stadt Köln, 1978.

Parshall, Linda, and Peter Parshall. *Art and the Reformation. An Annotated Bibliography*. Boston: G.K. Hall, 1986.

Passarge, Walter. *Das deutsche Vesperbild im Mittelalter*. Cologne: F.J. Marcan, 1924.

Pater, Walter. "The School of Giorgione." 1877. In *The Renaissance: Studies in Art and Poetry*. London: Macmillan and Co., Limited, 1910.

Pennings, Joyce. "Semi-Religious Women in 15th-century Rome." *Mededelingen van het Nederlands Historisch Instituut te Rome* 47, n.s. 12 (1987): 115-45.

Persoons, E. "Prieuré de Ter-Nood-Gods à Tongres." *Monasticon Belge*. Vol. 6, *Province de Limbourg*, pp. 267-76. Liège: Centre national de Recherches d'histoire religieuse, 1976.

—. "Het dagelijks leven in de Windesheimse vrouwenkloosters." *Spiegel Historiael* 15 (June, 1980): 342-49, 383.

Philippen, L.J.M. *De Begijnhoven. Oorsprong, Geschiedenis, Inrichting*. Antwerp: Veritas, 1918.

—. "Begijnen-werkzaamheden naar een schilderij in 't Mechelsch begijnhof." *Prosper Verheyden gehuldigd* (1943): 51-70.

Pinder, Wilhelm. "Marienklage." *Genius* 1 (1919): 200-08.

—. "Die dichterische Wurzel der Pietà." *Repertorium für Kunstwissenschaft* 42 (1920): 145-63.

—. *Die Pietà*. Leipzig: A. Seemann, 1922.

—. *Die deutsche Plastik von ausgehenden Mittelalter bis zum Ende der Renaissance*. Potsdam: Akademische Verlagsgesellschaft Athenaion, 1924.

Pit, A. "De verzameling Hollandsch beeldhouwwerk in het Nederlandsch Museum te Amsterdam." *Bulletin van den Nederlandschen Oudheidkundigen Bond* 1 (1899-1900): 148-154; 2 (1900-01): 6-17.

—. *Catalogus van de beeldhouwwerken in het Nederlandsch Museum voor Geschiedenis en Kunst te Amsterdam*. Amsterdam: Van Rijkom Frères, 1904; 1915.

Plastik am Mittelrhein ca. 1400. Ein Teil der Wirklichkeit (exh. cat.). Frankfurt am Main: Liebieghaus, 1974.

Pleij, Herman. *De sneeuwpoppen van 1511: literatuur en stadscultuur tussen middeleeuwen en moderne tijd.* Amsterdam: Meulenhoff; Leuven: Kritak, 1988.

Podro, Michael. *The Critical Historians of Art.* New Haven: Yale University Press, 1982.

Potts, Alex. "The Verbal and the visual in Winckelmann's analysis of style." *Word & Image* 6 / 3 (1990): 226-40.

Publications du Comte J. de Borchgrave d'Altena 1924-1949. N.p, n.d.

Quintijn, R.M. "Normen en normering van het begijnenleven: vergelijkende studie van de begijnenregels in de Nederlanden van de XIIIe tot de XVIIIe eeuw." Master's thesis, University of Ghent, 1984.

Réau, Louis. *Iconographie de l'art chrétien.* Vol. 1, *Introduction générale.* Paris: Presses Universitaires de France, 1955.

Reiners-Ernst, Elisabeth. *Das freudvolle Vesperbild und die Anfänge der Pieta-Vorstellung.* Abhandlung der Bayerischen Benediktiner-Akademie 2. Munich: Neuer Filser-Verlag, 1939.

Reinle, A. "Andachtsbild." Vol. 1, *Lexikon des Mittelalters,* cols. 582-88. Munich and Zurich: Artemis Verlag, 1980.

Remans, Gilbert. "Twee Franciskaansche Instellingen te Tongeren." *Bulletin de la Société Scientifique & Littéraire du Limbourg* 42 (1928): 127-36.

Rhin-Meuse: Art et Civilisation 800-1400 (exh. cat.). Cologne and Brussels: Kunsthalle and Musées Royaux d'Art et d'Histoire à Bruxelles, 1972.

Ringbom, Sixten. *Icon to Narrative: The Rise of the Dramatic Close-up in Fifteenth-Century Devotional Painting.* 1965. 2nd rev. ed. Doornspijk: Davaco, 1984.

—. "Devotional Images and Imaginative Devotions: Notes on the Place of Art in Late Medieval Private Piety." *Gazette des Beaux-Arts* 73 (March 1969): 159-70.

—. "Review of Hans Belting, *Das Bild und sein Publikum.*" *The Art Bulletin* 65 / 2 (1983): 339-40.

Roisin, Simone. "L'efflorescence cistercienne et le courant féminin de piété au XIIIe siècle." *Révue d'Histoire Ecclésiastique* 39 (1943): 342-78.

—. *L'hagiographie cistercienne dans le diocèse de Liège au XIIIe siècle.* Université de Louvain, Recueil de travaux d'histoire et de philologie, 3e ser., fasc. 27. Leuven: Bibliothèque de l'Université, 1947.

Rothkrug, Lionel. "Popular Religion and Holy Shrines: Their Influence on the Origins of the German Reformation and Their Role in German Cultural Development."

In *Religion and the People, 800-1700*, edited by James Obelkevich, pp. 20-86. North Carolina: University of North Carolina Press, 1979.

—. "Holy Shrines, Religious Dissonance, and Satan in the Origins of the German Reformation." *Historical Reflections / Réflexions Historiques* 14 / 2 (1987): 143-286.

—. "German Holiness and Western Sanctity in Medieval and Modern History." In *Culture, Society and Religion in Early Modern Europe: Essays by the Students and Colleagues of William J. Bouwsma*, edited by Ellery Schalk. Special issue of *Historical Reflections / Réflexions Historiques* 15 / 1 (Spring 1988): 161-250.

Rubin, Miri. *Corpus Christi: The Eucharist in late medieval culture*. Cambridge, England; New York: Cambridge University Press, 1991.

Sassen, J.H.H. "Register en memorieboek van het Dominicanessenklooster St. Agnetenberg te Sittard." *Publications de la Société Historique et Archéologique dans le Limbourg*, n.s. 29 (1913): 161-304.

Schif, William, and Emerson Foulke. *Tactile Reception: A Sourcebook*. Cambridge: Cambridge University Press, 1982.

Schiff, Gert, ed. *German Essays on Art History*. New York: Continuum, 1988.

Schmitt, Jean-Claude. *Mort d'une hérésie. L'Eglise et les clercs face aux béguines et aux béghards du Rhin supérieur du XIVe au XVe siècle*. Civilisations et Sociétés 56. Sponsored by l'Ecole des hautes études en sciences sociales, Paris. The Hague and New York: Mouton, 1978.

Schmitt, Jean-Claude, ed. *History and Anthropology*. Vol. 1, *Gestures*. Great Britain: Harwood Academic Publishers, 1984.

Schmitz, K.J. et al. *Gotische Vesperbilder. Diocësanmuseum Paderborn, Sauerland-Museum Arnsberg* (exh. cat.). Paderborn: Erzbischöfliche Diocësanmuseum, 1980.

Schoengen, Michael. *Monasticon Batavum*. Vol. 2, *De Augustijnsche Orden*. Amsterdam: Noord-Hollandsche Uitgevers Maatschappij, 1941.

Schoutens, Stephanus. *Geschiedenis van den eredienst van het allerheiligste sacrament des altaars*. Antwerp, 1902.

Schuermans, H. *L'Eglise de L'Abbaye de Villers*. Brussels: Van Langhendonck, 1904.

Schulte van Kessel, Elisja, ed. *Women and Men in Spiritual Culture. XIV-XVII centuries. A Meeting of North and South*. The Hague: Netherlands Government Publishing Office, 1986.

Schwabe, Ute. *Zwei Frauen vor dem Tode*. Verhandelingen van de Koninklijke Academie voor Wetenschappen, Letteren en Schone Kunsten van België. Klasse der Letteren 132. Brussels: Paleis der Academiën, 1989.

Shorr, Dorothy C. "The Mourning Virgin and Saint John." *The Art Bulletin* 22 / 2 (1940): 61-69.

Simenon, G. *Visitationes archidiaconales archidiaconatus Hasbaniae in dioecesi Leodiensi ab anno 1613 ad annum 1763*, vol. 1. Liège: Dessain, 1939.

—. "Les Origines Liégeoises de la Fête-Dieu." *Studia Eucharistica*, pp. 1-19. Antwerp, 1946.

Simons, Walter. *Stad en apostolaat. De vestiging van de bedelorden in het graafschap Vlaanderen (ca.1225-ca.1350)*. Verhandelingen van de Koninklijke Academie voor Wetenschappen, Letteren en Schone Kunsten van België. Klasse der Letteren 121. Brussels: Paleis der Academiën, 1987.

—. "The Beguine Movement in the Southern Low Countries: A Reassessment." *Bulletin de l'Institut Historique Belge de Rome / Bulletin van het Belgisch Historisch Instituut te Rome* 59 (1989): 63-105.

—. "Begijnen en begarden in het middeleeuwse Dowaai." *De Franse Nederlanden / Les Pays-Bas Français* 17 (1992): 96-114.

—. "Een zeker bestaan: de Zuidnederlandse begijnen en de *Frauenfrage*, 13de-18de eeuw." *Tijdschrift voor sociale geschiedenis* 17/2 (1991): 125-46.

Simons, W., and J.E. Ziegler. "Phenomenal Religion in the Thirteenth Century and Its Image: Elisabeth of Spalbeek and the Passion Cult." In *Women in the Church*, Studies in Church History 27, edited by W.J. Sheils and Diana Wood, pp. 116-26. Oxford: Basil Blackwell, 1990.

Skubiszewski, Piotr. "Le retable gothique sculpté: Entre le dogme et l'univers humain." In *Le retable d'Issenheim et la sculpture au Nord des Alpes à la fin du moyen âge* (exh. cat.), edited by Christian Heck, pp. 13-47. Colmar: Musée d'Unterlinden, 1989.

Smeyers, M. "De Kapel van de H. Drievuldigheid in de Sint-Pieterskerk te Leuven en het geslacht van Baussele." In *Dirk Bouts en zijn tijd* (exh. cat.), pp. 506-08. Leuven: Stedelijk Museum, 1975.

Smeyers, M., and L. Van Buyten. "De oudste statuten van het Klein-Begijnhof te Leuven." *Mededelingen van de Geschied- en Oudheidkundige Kring voor Leuven en omgeving* 7 (1967): 10-26.

Smith, John E. "William James's Account of Mysticism; A Critical Appraisal." In *Mysticism and Religious Traditions*, edited by Steven T. Katz, pp. 247-79. Oxford: Oxford University Press, 1983.

Smits, K. *De Iconographie van de Nederlandsche Primitieven*. Amsterdam: De Spieghel, 1933.

Sobré, Judith Berg. *Behind the Altar Table: The Development of the Painted Retable in Spain, 1350-1500*. Columbia, Missouri: University of Missouri Press, 1989.

Soil de Moriamé, E.J. *Inventaire des objets d'art et d'antiquité existant dans les édifices publics des communes de l'arrondissement judiciaire de Tournai*. 5 vols. Charleroi: Imprimerie Provinciale, 1926.

Speelman, Ed. *Belgium Marianum. Histoire du culte de Marie en Belgique*. Paris and Tournai: Casterman, 1859.

Spieser, Jean-Michel. "Review of Hans Belting, *Das Bild und sein Publikum*." *Burlington Magazine* 143 / 4 (1985): 371-77.

Stabat Mater: Maria unter dem Kreuz in der Kunst um 1400 (exh. cat.). Salzburg: Salzburg Cathedral, 1970.

Stalpaert, H. "Bij een eeuwfeest: Lootens-Feys' Liederenbundel 1879-1979. Een Onderzoek van de Passieliederen." *Volkskunde* 3-4 (June-December 1979): 183-98.

Steppe, J.K. "Het paneel van de Triniteit in het Leuvense Stadsmuseum. Nieuwe gegevens over een enigmatisch schilderij." In *Dirk Bouts en zijn tijd* (exh. cat.), pp. 452-53. Leuven: Stedelijk Museum, 1975.

Steyaert, John. "Some Observations Concerning the Pietà from O.-L.-V.-van-Ginderbuiten in Leuven." In *Archivum Artis Lovaniense. Bijdragen tot de geschiedenis van de kunst der Nederlanden. Opgedragen aan Prof. Em. Dr. J.K. Steppe*, edited by M. Smeyers, pp. 15-28. Leuven: Peeters, 1981.

Sticca, Sandro. *The 'Planctus Mariae' in the Dramatic Tradition of the Middle Ages*. Translated by Joseph R. Berrigan. Georgia: University of Georgia Press, 1988.

Summers, David. *The Judgement of Sense: Renaissance Naturalism and the Rise of Aesthetics*. Cambridge: Cambridge University Press, 1987.

Swarzenski, Hans. "Quellen zum deutschen Andachtsbild." *Zeitschrift für Kunstgeschichte* 4 (1935): 141-44.

Tarrant, J. "The Clementine Decrees on the Beguines: Conciliar and Papal Versions." *Archivum historiae pontificae* 12 (1974): 300-08.

Tentoonstelling van Noord-Nederlandsche schilder- en beeldhouwkunst voor 1575 (exh. cat.). Utrecht: Gebouw voor Kunsten en Wetenschappen, 1913.

Terme, G. *Exposition de l'art ancien au Pays de Liège: Catalogue générale*. 2 vols. Liège: Aug. Bénard, 1905-1907.

Thode, Henry. *Franz Van Assisi und die Anfänge der Kunst der Renaissance in Italien*. Berlin: G. Grote'sche Verlagsbuchhandlung, 1885.

Thys, Ch. *Histoire du béguinage de Ste. Catherine à Tongres*. Tongeren: M. Collée, 1881.

Timmers, J.J.M. *Houten beelden. De houtsculptuur in de Noordelijke Nederlanden tijdens de late middeleeuwen*. Amsterdam and Antwerp: Contact, 1949.

—. "Achtenveertig eeuwen beeldhouwkunst in hout." Vol. 2, *Hout in alle Tijden*, edited by W. Boerhave Beekman, pp. 597-772. Deventer: E. Kluwer, 1949-55.

—. *De kunst van het Maasland*. 2 vols. Assen: Van Gorcum, 1980.

—. *Oude Schoonheid van Limburg*. Maastricht: Corrie Zelen, n.d.

Tinsely, E.J. "The Coming of a Dead and Naked Christ." *Religion: A Journal of Religion and Religions* 2 (1972): 24-36.

2000 jaar Tongeren, 15 voor Christus tot 1985 (exh. cat.). Hasselt: Uitgeverij Concentra, 1985.

Tolstoy, Leo. *The Kreutzer Sonata*. Revised translation by Isai Kamen. New York: Vintage Books, 1957.

Toussaert, Jacques. *Le Sentiment religieux en Flandre à la fin du moyen âge*. Paris: Librairie Plon, 1963.

Trexler, Richard C. "Le célibat à la fin du Moyen Age: Les religieuses de Florence." *Annales: Economies, Sociétés, Civilisations* 27 (1972): 1329-50.

—. "Ritual Behavior in Renaissance Florence: The Setting." *Medievalia et Humanistica* 3 (1972): 125-44.

Turner, Victor. "Betwixt and Between: The Liminal Period in *Rites de Passage*." *The Proceedings of the American Ethnological Society* (1964): 4-20. Reprint in *Reader in Comparative Religion: An Anthropological Approach*, 4th ed., edited by W.A. Lessa and E.Z. Vogt, pp. 234-42. New York: Harper & Row, 1979.

—. *The Ritual Process: Structure and Anti-Structure*. Chicago: Aldine Publishing Company, 1969.

—. "Passages, Margins, and Poverty: Religious Symbols of Communitas." *Worship* 46 (1972): 390-412; 432-94. Reprint in Victor Turner, *Dramas, Fields and Metaphors: Symbolic Action in Human Society*, pp. 231-71. Ithaca and London: Cornell University Press, 1974.

Turner, Victor, and Edith Turner. *Image and Pilgrimage in Christian Culture: Anthropological Perspectives*. New York: Columbia University Press, 1978.

Tussen heks en heilige: het vrouwbeeld op de drempel van de moderne tijd, 15de / 16de eeuw (exh. cat.). Edited by Petty Bange et al. Nijmegen: SUN and Nijmeegs Museum 'Commanderie van Sint-Jan,' 1985.

Utrecht's kunst in opkomst en bloei, 650-1650 (exh. cat.). Utrecht: Centraal Museum, 1948.

Van Caster-Guiette, Lucie. "Réminiscences Rogériennes dans la sculpture brabançonne." In *Mélanges d'archéologie et d'histoire de l'art offerts au Professeur Jacques Lavalleye*, pp. 297-304. Leuven: Université de Louvain, 1970.

Vandamme, Erik. *De Polychromie van gotische houtsculptuur in de Zuidelijke Nederlanden: materialen en technieken.* Verhandelingen van de Koninklijke Academie voor Wetenschappen, Letteren en Schone Kunsten van België. Klasse der Schone Kunsten 44 / 35. Brussels: Paleis der Academiën, 1982.

Vandenbroeck, Paul. *Jheronimus Bosch: Tussen volksleven en stadscultuur.* Berchem-Antwerp: EPO, 1987.

—. *Over wilden en narren, boeren en bedelaars. Beeld van de Andere, Vertoog over het Zelf* (exh. cat.). Antwerp: Koninklijk Museum voor Schone Kunsten, 1987.

—. "Zwischen Selbsterniedrigung und Selbstvergottung. Bilderwelt und Selbstbild religiöser Frauen in den südlichen Niederlanden. Eine erste Erkundigung." *De zeventiende eeuw* 5 / 1 (1989): 67-88.

Vandeput, E. *De Sint-Leonarduskerk. Hart van Zoutleeuw.* 1978. 2nd ed. Zoutleeuw, 1986.

Vanderbrugge, J. "Een Pieta van de Mechelse beeldsnijder Nicolaas Vander Veken (1637-1709)." *Antiek* 27 / 10 (May 1983): 529-30.

Van de Ven, Robert. "Beeldsnijders vermeld in de Diestse archieven gedurende de XVe en XVIe eeuw." *Arca Lovaniensis* 2 (1973): 309-19.

—. "Een inventaris van de infirmerie van het begijnhof te Diest (1636)." *Oost-Brabant* 16 (1979): 33-39.

—. "De Kunstinboedel van de Sint-Catherina- of Begijnhofkerk tijdens de 15de en 16de eeuw." In *Kunstschatten uit het Diestse begijnhof* (exh. cat.), pp. 129-38. Diest: Stedelijk Museum, 1988.

Van Eeckhoudt, L. "Enkele gegevens over het begijnhof van Edingen." *Het Oude Land van Edingen en omliggende* 11 (1983): 8-12.

Van Engen, John. *Devotio Moderna: Basic Writings.* New York: Paulist Press, 1988.

Van Even, Edward. *Louvain monumental ou description historique et artistique de tous les édifices civils et religieux de la dite ville.* Leuven, 1860.

—. *Louvain dans le passé et dans le présent.* Leuven: Auguste Fonteyn, 1895.

"Van Hadewijch tot Maria Petyt. Vrouwen en mystiek in de Nederlanden van 13de tot de 17de eeuw." Conference held in Antwerp, 5-7 September 1989. Sponsored by the Ruusbroecgenootschap. Proceedings in press with *Ons Geestelijk Erf.*

Van Herwaarden, J. "Geloof en geloofsuitingen in de veertiende en vijftiende eeuw: Eucharistie en lijden van Jezus." In *Hoofsheid en devotie in de middeleeuwse maatschappij: De Nederlanden van de 12e tot de 15e eeuw,* edited by J.D. Janssens, pp. 175-207. Handelingen van het Wetenschappelijk Colloquium te Brussel, 21-24 oktober 1981. Brussels, 1982.

Van Mechelen, Johan. *Vlaamse Begijnhoven. In Schemelheyt der Maechtlykheydt.* Tielt: Lannoo, 1973.

Van Os, H. "Review of Hans Belting, *Das Bild und sein Publikum.*" *Simiolus* 14/3-4 (1984): 225-27.

Van Uytven, R., ed. *Leuven, 'De beste stad van Brabant'.* Vol. 1, *De geschiedenis van het stadsgewest Leuven tot omstreeks 1600.* Arca Lovaniensis 7. Leuven: Vrienden Stedelijke Musea, 1980.

Vavra, Elisabeth. "Bildmotiv und Frauenmystik — Funktion und Rezeption." In *Frauenmystik im Mittelalter,* edited by Peter Dinzelbacher and Dieter R. Bauer, pp. 210-30. Wissenschaftliche Studientagung der Akademie der Diözese Rottenburg-Stuttgart, 22-25 February 1984, Weingarten. Ostfildern: Schwabenverlag, 1985.

Verachtert, Frans, André Gailliaerde, and Frans Vervoort. *Voorsale des Hemels ofte het begijnhof in de XVII Provinciën in woord en beeld gebracht.* Retie: Kempische Boekhandel, 1973.

Vermeersch, Valentin. *Gids Gruuthuse Museum.* Stedelijk Museum voor Oudheidkunde en Toegepaste Kunsten. Bruges: Gruuthuse Museum, 1979.

Vitry, Jacques de. *Vita Mariae Oigniacensis.* Edited by D. Papebroch. *AASS,* June 23/5 (Paris, 1867): 542-72. Also translated by Margot H. King, Matrologia Latina Translation Series, Saskatoon: 1987.

Vogelsang, W. "De Nederlandsche Beeldhouwkunst." *Elsevier's geïllustreerd maandschrift* 31 (1906): 367-80.

—. "De Noord-Nederlandsche Beeldhouwkunst van de 12de tot de eerst helft der 16de eeuw." 1935. In *Kunstgeschiedenis der Nederlanden,* 3rd ed., edited by H.E. van Gelder, pp. 120-50. Utrecht, 1954.

Vogelsang, W., with M. van Notten. *Die Holzskulptur in den Niederlanden.* Vol. 2, *Das Niederländische Museum zu Amsterdam.* Berlin: Julius Bard; and Utrecht: A. Oosthoek, 1912.

Vols, J. "Maria-vereering te Tongeren door de eeuwen heen." *Limburg* 26 (1946): 131-40.

Von der Osten, Gert, and Horst Vey. *Painting and Sculpture in Germany and the Netherlands, 1500 to 1600.* The Pelican History of Art. Harmondsworth: Penguin Books, 1969.

Von Simson, Otto G. "*Compassio* and *Co-Redemptio* in Roger van der Weyden's *Descent from the Cross.*" *The Art Bulletin* 35 (1953): 9-16.

Wagner, Georg. "Maria in der Not: Passionsfrömmigkeit um das mittelalterliche Vesperbild." *Theologie und Glaube* 71 (1981): 354-63.

Wagner, Richard. "The Origins of Modern Opera, Drama, and Music." 1846-1879. In *Wagner on Music and Drama: A Compendium of Richard Wagner's Prose Works*, edited by A. Goldman and E. Sprinchorn, translated by H. Ashton Ellis, pp. 95-178. New York: Da Capo Press, 1964.

Wallfahrt kennt keine Grenzen, edited by Lenz Kriss-Rettenbach and Gerde Mohler. Munich and Zurich: Schnell & Steiner, 1984.

Warffemius, A.A.M. "Het voormalige Dominicanenklooster te Sittard." *Koninklijke Nederlandse Oudheidkundige Bond* 85 / 5 (1986): 210-24.

Warner, Marina. *Alone of All Her Sex: The Myth and Cult of the Virgin Mary.* 1976. Reprint. New York: First Vintage Books Edition, 1983.

Weitzmann, Kurt. *The Icon: Holy Images, Sixth to Fourteenth Century.* New York: Braziller, 1978.

Werken en Kerken: 750 jaar begijnhofleven te Gent (exh. cat.). Ghent: Stad Gent, 1984.

Het werk van Roger de la Pasture Van der Weyden 1399-1400 / 1464 (exh. cat.). Leuven: S.L. Laconti N.V., 1964.

Werner, Johannes. "Frauenfrommigkeit: zur Entstehung der mittelalterlichen Andachtsbilder." *Münster* 35 / 1 (1982): 21-6.

Wilm, Hubert. *Die gotische Holzfigur. Ihr Wesen und ihre Entstehung.* Revised ed. Stuttgart: J.B. Metzlar, 1940.

Witlox, Joseph. *Belgium Marianum. Marias heiligdommen in woord en beeld.* Antwerp: Opdebeek, 1912.

Witsen Elias, J.S. "De Pietà's te Blaricum en te Eemnes." *Mededeelingen van het Museum voor het Gooi en omstreken* (1942): 42-48.

Witte, Fritz. *Tausend Jahre deutscher Kunst am Rhein.* Leipzig: H. Schmidt & C. Günter, 1932.

Wolfs, S.P. *Middeleeuwse Dominicanessenkloosters in Nederland.* Maastricht: Van Gorcum, 1988.

Wollheim, Richard. *Art and Its Objects: An Introduction to Aesthetics.* 1968. Reprint. New York: Harper & Row, 1971.

Worringer, Wilhelm. *Form in Gothic.* 1911-12. Translated and edited by Herbert Read. London: Schocken Paperback, 1964.

Ziegler, J.E. *The Word Becomes Flesh: Radical Physicality in Religious Sculpture of the Later Middle Ages* (exh. cat.). Worcester, Massachusetts: Cantor Art Gallery, College of the Holy Cross, 1985.

—. "The *curtis* beguinages in the southern Low Countries and art patronage: interpretation and historiography." *Bulletin de l'Institut Historique Belge de Rome / Bulletin van het Belgisch Historisch Instituut te Rome* 57 (1987): 31-70.

—. "The Medieval Virgin as Object: Art or Anthropology?" *Historical Reflections / Réflexions Historiques* 16 / 2-3 (1989): 251-64.

—. "Review of Florence W.J. Koorn, Begijnhoven in Holland en Zeeland gedurende de middeleeuwen." *Mystics Quarterly* 15 / 2 (1989): 103-05.

—. "Secular Canonesses as Antecedents of the Beguines in the southern Low Countries: An Introduction to some Older Viewpoints." *Studies in Medieval and Renaissance History* n.s. 13 (1991).

—. "The Beguines." *The Dictionary of Art*. London: MacMillan Publishers, Ltd., forthcoming.

—. "Reality as Imitation: The Dynamics of Imagery Among the Beguines." In *Maps of Flesh and Light: New Perspectives on the Religious Experience of Late Medieval Women*, edited by Ulrike Wiethaus. Syracuse, New York: Syracuse University Press, 1992.

PART IV

INVENTORY

ABBREVIATIONS / INVENTORY

comm. = commune

arr. = arrondissement

prov. = province

B. = Belgium

Nl. = Netherlands

A.C.L. = Inventory number of the photographic archives at the Institut Royal du Patrimoine Artistique / Koninklijk Instituut voor het Kunstpatrimonium, Brussels

de Borchgrave d'Altena (1942-43) = Joseph de Borchgrave d'Altena, "Vierges de Pitié de chez nous," *Annales de la Société royale d'Archéologie de Bruxelles* 46 (1942-43): 263-70.

de Borchgrave d'Altena (1965) = idem, "Vierges de Pitié" (Virton: Michel Frères, 1965); originally published in *Le Pays gaumais* 26 (1965): 87-105.

de Borchgrave d'Altena and Mambour (1974) = Joseph de Borchgrave d'Altena and Josée Mambour, *La Passion dans la sculpture en Hainaut de 1400 à 1700, troisième et dernière partie*, exh. cat. (Charleroi: Imprimerie Provinciale du Hainaut, 1974).

Devigne (1932) = Marguerite Devigne, *La Sculpture mosane du XIIe au XVIe siècle. Contribution à l'étude d'art dans la région de la Meuse moyenne* (Paris and Brussels: G. Van Oest, 1932).

Dusar (1970) = Albert Dusar, *Limburgs kunstbezit: van prehistorie tot classicisme* (Hasselt: Heideland-Orbis N.V., 1970).

Laat-gotische beeldsnijkunst (1990) = *Laat-gotische beeldsnijkunst uit Limburg en Grensland*, exh. cat. (Sint-Truiden: Provincie Limburg Culturele Aangelegenheden, 1990).

Ooms (1959) = Hedwig Ooms, *Onze-Lieve-Vrouw in Limburg* (Tournai: Casterman, 1959).

Steyaert (1981) = John Steyaert, "Some Observations Concerning the Pietà from O.-L.-V.-van-Ginderbuiten in Leuven," in *Archivum Artis Lovaniense. Bijdragen tot de geschiedenis van de kunst der Nederlanden. Opgedragen aan Prof. Em. Dr. J.K. Steppe*, edited by M. Smeyers (Leuven: Peeters, 1981): 15-28.

PREAMBLE

PURPOSE OF THE INVENTORY

An attempt has been made here to list sculpted *Pietàs* dating between c. 1300 and c. 1600 from the southern Low Countries (present-day Belgium) and to provide a small sample of those *Pietàs* now housed in collections outside but definately originating in the region. The geographical limits have been established by the area where Catholicism has been dominant more or less continuously since medieval times and where the population of *curtis* Beguines was densest. The inventory attempts to provide a preliminary corpus of *Pietàs*, which future investigations should supplement by extending the geographical boundaries to include the northern Low Countries (present-day Netherlands), parts of northern France, and the extended Mosan region.

CHARACTER OF THE ENTRIES

The primary goal is to present and illustrate (wherever possible) the considerable number of *Pietàs* in the southern Low Countries, which remain largely unknown to historians of art outside Belgium, and to elucidate their ritual history. The entries contain mainly information about placement, provenance as it illuminates the ritual activities (such as miracles, clothing, restoration, theft and destruction of the objects), and bibliographical data. Issues of style are mentioned only insofar as they have a bearing on comparative ritual patterns. Dating is also not mentioned in the entries, but all sculptures that the published sources cited as dating between the fourteenth and seventeenth centuries have been included. The bibliographical sources attached to each entry cover the stylistic, chronological, and iconographical issues.

ARRANGEMENT OF THE ENTRIES

The entries are divided into two main categories: *Pietàs* on location in religious institutions (Inv. nos. 1-110) and other (Inv. nos. 111-147). The last category is further subdivided into *Pietàs* in museums and city collections, such as those owned by the local O.C.M.W. / C.P.A.S. (Inv. nos. 111-137), private collections (Inv. nos. 138-144), and by sculptor, when the work has been cited but is lost (Inv. nos. 145-147). All entries are arranged alphabetically. For *Pietàs* on location in churches, chapels, beguinages,

207

and other religious institutions (Inv. nos. 1-110), the place name is followed by the commune, arrondissement, province, and country to facilitate locating the site.

BIBLIOGRAPHY AND REFERENCES

Entries distinguish bibliography (where the *Pietà* is discussed) from references, which treat the *Pietà's* location, associated miracles, and other ritual events without discussing the object itself. The bibliography cited in the Inventory has not been included in the general bibliography of this book except where the titles are of general interest to study of the *Pietà*. Titles frequently consulted in the Inventory are cited in abbreviated form, for example, thus: de Borchgrave d'Altena (1942-43). In such cases, a list of abbreviations has been provided at the front of this Inventory.

INVENTORY

No. 1   *Pietà*   Plate 1

Aldeneik / comm. and arr. Maaseik / prov. Limburg / B.
Sint-Annakerk
wood, with polychromy

Bibliography
J. Coenen, "Limburgse Beelden uit de XVIe eeuw," *Kunst Adelt Peer* 5 / 1 & 2
(1926), p. 24.
de Borchgrave d'Altena (1942-43), p. 270.
Fotorepertorium, Maaseik (1975), p. 25.

No. 2   *Pietà*   Plate 2

Antwerp / comm., arr., and prov. Antwerpen / B.
Klooster Gasthuiszusters Augustinessen
oak
h. 67 cm

Bibliography
Sint-Laurentius parochie 1659-1959: "Laus Laurentio" (exh. cat.) (Antwerp, 1959),
cat. no. 62.

No. 3   *Pietà*

Ath / comm. and arr. Ath / prov. Hainaut / B.
In niche over entrance gate

Bibliography
Julius Baum, "Die Lütticher Bildnerkunst im 14. Jahrhundert," in *Belgischer
Kunstdenkmäler*, vol. 1, edited by Paul Clemen (Munich: Bruckmann, 1923), fig.
191.

de Borchgrave d'Altena (1942-43), p. 266, fig. 4.
de Borchgrave d'Altena (1965), p. 8.

No. 4   *Pietà*   Plates 3-4

Bellaire / comm. Beyne-Heusay / arr, Liège / prov. Liège / B.
Eglise de la Visitation (no longer in place)

De Borchgrave d'Altena (1942-43) compares this *Pietà* with the earliest (circa 1350ff.) in the southern Low Countries; Steyaert (p. 20) compares it with others of the German *Steilsitz* type. Photographs indicate the Virgin had been clothed before 1974 when the A.C.L. photographed the object again.

Bibliography
Julius Baum, "Die Lütticher Bildnerkunst im 14. Jahrhundert," in *Belgischer Kunstdenkmäler*, vol. 1, edited by Paul Clemen (Munich: Bruckmann, 1923), p. 177.
de Borchgrave d'Altena (1942-43), p. 266.
de Borchgrave d'Altena (1965), p. 6.
Steyaert (1981), p. 20.

No. 5   *Pietà*   Plates 5-6

Beringen / comm. Beringen / arr. Hasselt / prov. Limburg / B.
Kerk van Sint-Pieters-Banden (originally in Onze-Lieve-Vrouwekapel or Smeedskapel) polychromed oak, with modern overpainting; original polychromy still present (gold, blue, red, ivory); some deep cracks; paint flaking (Kunst en Oudheden)
h 63.5 cm

Formerly placed in the Smeedskapel (Chapel of the Forgers), which was built in the second half of the seventeenth century, this *Pietà* is now in the church of Sint-Pieters-Banden in Beringen (*Beeldsnijkunst*). It has been placed as a south Netherlandish work and has been dated to the mid-fifteenth century (Kunst en Oudheden). De Borchgrave d'Altena (1963) compared the drapery to the *Pietà* type found in Germany at the end of the fourteenth century, a type which he also considered influential on the *Pietàs* of Diest and Maastricht (Inv. nos. 116 and 57). The entry of the 1953 exhibition *Honderd Limburgse Madonnas* states that the figure of Christ seems less old than that of Mary.

Bibliography
Honderd Limburgse Madonnas (1953), p. 23, cat. no. 65.

de Borchgrave d'Altena (1942-43), p. 268, fig. 13.
de Borchgrave d'Altena (1963), pp. 90-93, esp. 93.
de Borchgrave d'Altena (1965), pp. 6 and 7.
Dusar (1970), p. 169.
Fotorepertorium, Beringen (1977), p. 17.
Kerkelijk kunstbezit van de Sint-Pieters-Bandenparochie van Beringen (exh. cat.),
Kunst en Oudheden in Limburg, no. 20 (Sint-Truiden: Provinciaal Museum, 1978),
pp. 22-23, cat. no. 6.
Laat-gotische beeldsnijkunst (1990), inv. no. 12.

No. 6   *Pietà*   Plates 7-9

Berlingen / comm. Wellen / arr. Tongeren / prov. Limburg / B.
Kluiskapel Onze-Lieve-Vrouw van Zeven Smarten te Oetsloven
wood with modern polychromy; clothed
h. 95 cm

The Chapel is dedicated to Our Lady of the Seven Sorrows. Ooms claims it was
dedicated on 20 March 1423 (p. 16), the same date he ascribes to the *Pietà*. Daris is
more circumspect about the dedication, suggesting that it arose perhaps as a result of
a provincial council held at Cologne in 1423 that prescribed the clergy of the province
to celebrate the Feast of the Seven Sorrows of the Virgin.
Daris holds that the Chapel was a hermitage since 1177 when the Lord of Berlingen
permitted a hermit to build a chapel; the last hermit died in 1985. He says that the
pilgrimage to Oetsloven flourishes as it did in past centuries (p. 274). As for the *Pietà*,
an archdeaconal visitation of 1624 reports on the Chapel: "invenit vacuam ab omni
ornatu" (p. 52), which may imply that it was not present at that time. In 1980 the
Pietà was stolen, along with a sculpture of St. Joseph, found very damaged in a ditch
in Leuven, conserved, and put back in the Chapel (Buyle, 1982). Ooms and de Borchgrave d'Altena illustrate the *Pietà* but it wears no garments.

Bibliography
de Borchgrave d'Altena (1942-1943), fig. 13.
Ooms (1959), pp. 14-16.
Fotorepertorium, Borgloon (1975), no. 9250, inv. no. 556.
M. Buyle, "Werkzaamheden van de conserveringsploeg," in *Monumenten en Land-
schappen* 1 / nr. 5 (1982), p. 8.
Laat-gotische beeldsnijkunst (1990), inv. no. 630.

References
G. Simenon, *Visitationes archidiaconales archidiaconatus Hasbaniae in dioecesi Leodiensi ab anno 1613 ad annum 1763*, vol. 1 (Liège: H. Dessain, 1939), p. 52.
Joseph Daris, *Notices historiques sur les églises du diocèse de Liège*, vol. 15 (Liège: Demarteau, 1894), pp. 270-74.

No. 7   *Pietà* by Conrat Meijt

Besançon, France
Cathédrale Saint-Jean
alabaster

Duverger, No. LII: on 20 June 1532 a *Pietà* was ordered on command of Antoine de Montcut, court chaplain of Margaret of Austria, to be placed in the Abbey of Saint-Vincent in Besançon.

Bibliography
Jos. Duverger, *Conrat Meijt (ca. 1480-1551)*, Académie royale de Belgique, Classe des Beaux-Arts, Mémoires in -4, no. 5 (Brussels, 1934), pp. 22, 53, 93, 109.
Gert von der Osten and Horst Vey, *Painting and Sculpture in Germany and the Netherlands 1500 to 1600* (Harmondsworth: Penguin Books, Ltd, 1969), pp. 238-39.

No. 8   *Pietà*

Bilzen / comm. Bilzen / arr. Tongeren / prov. Limburg / B.
Kerkhofkapel (formerly in the Convent of the Sisters of the Third Order of Saint Francis in Bilzen)

A miraculous statue of "Onze-Lieve-Vrouw van Bijstand" was kept in the Convent of the Sisters of the Third Order of Saint Francis since 1638. According to a seventeenth-century chronicle of the Convent, it had originated in the Sint-Martinuskerk of Groningen (Netherlands) where it had been venerated since 1463 as "Onze-Lieve-Vrouw ter Nood." Apparently the statue was moved from Groningen to Bilzen at the end of the sixteenth century. It was placed on the main altar of the Convent chapel and supposedly exercised miraculous powers throughout the seventeenth and eighteenth centuries. During the French occupation when the Convent was closed and the church demolished, this statue was moved to a chapel outside the town, previously known as the Chapel of Our Lady of the Seven Sorrows, and since 1851 used as a cemetery chapel. The statue continued to draw pilgrims who would visit it in the

212

chapel for nine consecutive days to pray for the terminally ill. Another statue of Our Lady of the Seven Sorrows was placed next to it in 1924.

Bibliography
Chronique du Couvent de Notre-Dame des Anges à Bilsen (Liège: L. Grandmont-Donders, 1877).
A.P., *Het oude zusterenklooster van den Derden Regel te Bilzen* (N.p., 1896), pp. 21-24.
Jean Paquay, *Bilsen voorheen* (N.p., 1926), pp. 223-27.
J.-B. Paquay, ''Geschiedenis van het Wonderbeeld O.L.Vr. van Bijstand,'' in *Luister-rijke Feesten ter eere van Onze Lieve Vrouw van Bijstand 1638 Bilzen 1938* (N.p., n.d. [1938]), pp. 2 and 3.

No. 9   *Pietà*   Plate 10

Binche / comm. Binche / arr. Thuin / prov. Hainaut / B.
Eglise Saint-Ursmer
oak
h. 102 cm

The most complete discussion of the *Pietà* is by Didier (1963). He notes that until some years ago the sculpture was in the Chapel of Saint-André in the old cemetery which originally had two chapels. The one that contained the *Pietà* was dedicated to the Virgin of the Seven Sorrows. After demolition of the chapel (date unknown, probably early nineteenth century) the *Pietà* was transferred to the Chapel of Saint-André. It was incorporated into an eighteenth-century altar and removed at the time of the restoration of the chapel in 1898 (Didier 1963, p. 72).
Didier places the type as belonging to a group of Lamentations which seem to appear at the end of the fifteenth century or beginning of the sixteenth century, comparable to *Pietàs* from Onze-Lieve-Vrouwekerk in Diest and the Musée archéologique of Nivelles (Inv. nos. 19 and 134). The close comparison with the *Pietà* from the Ursulinenkloster in Erfurt is illustrated by Passarge. Didier notes for the first time two imprints of an Antwerp ''hand'' on the front face of the base of the statue (Didier 1963, p. 72).

Bibliography
Joseph de Borchgrave d'Altena, ''Les Sculptures de la chapelle de l'ancien cimetière de Binche,'' *Annales du 27e Congrès de la Fédération archéologique et historique de Belgique* (1928), pp. 3-4.

Cinq siècles d'art. Exposition universelle et internationale de Bruxelles (exh. cat.), vol. 3 (Brussels: Musées royaux d'art et d'archéologie, 1935), p. 95, cat. no. 1556.
de Borchgrave d'Altena (1942-43), p. 267, fig. 8.
Exposition des arts religieux anciens et modernes (exh. cat.) (Tournai, 1949), p. 21, cat. no. 6.
Trésors d'art du Hainaut (exh. cat.) (Mons, 1953), p. 78, cat. no. 106; p. 79, cat. no. 107.
Exposition Mariale du Hainaut, art ancien (exh. cat.) (Mons: Delporte, 1954), p. 5, cat. nos. 75 and 76.
La Madone dans l'Art en Hainaut, 2nd ed. (Tournai: Cathédrale de Tournai, 1960), pp. 24 and 25, cat. no. 44, plate IX. (1st ed., cat. no. 43.)
Robert Didier, "Christ attendant la mort au Calvaire et Pieta, deux sculptures anversoises conservées à Binche: problèmes de datation et d'iconographie," *Bulletin de la Commission royale des Monuments et des Sites / Bulletin van de Koninklijke Commissie voor Monumenten en Landschappen* 14 (1963), pp. 71-75 with bibliography p. 71, n. 48.
Robert Didier, "Contribution à l'histoire de la sculpture gothique en Hainaut: Le maître de la Mise au tombeau d'Hautrage et du Calvaire d'Isières," *Mélanges d'archéologie et d'histoire de l'art offerts au professeur Jacques Lavalleye* (Leuven: Publications Universitaires de Louvain, 1970), p. 55, n. 10.
Aspekten van de laatgotiek in Brabant (exh. cat) (Leuven: Stedelijk Museum, 1971), pp. 299-300, cat. no. AB / 9.
de Borchgrave d'Altena and Mambour (1974), p. 15.

References
Walter Passarge, *Das Deutsche Vesperbild im Mittelalter* (Cologne: F.J. Marcan Verlag, 1924), p. 145, plate 39.

No. 10   *Pietà*   Plate 11

Bocholt / comm. Bocholt / arr. Maaseik / prov. Limburg / B.
Sint-Laurentiuskerk
wood, with modern polychromy
h. 98 cm

Bibliography
Fotorepertorium, Bree (1977), pp. 13-16.
de Borchgrave d'Altena (1963), pp. 165-66.
Laat-gotische beeldsnijkunst (1990), inv. no. 43.

214

No. 11   *Pietà*   Plate 12

Bombaye / comm. Dahlem / arr. Liège / prov. Liège / B.
Chapelle de la Sainte-Croix
wood
h. 44.5 cm

Bibliography
Exposition Abbaye de Val-Dieu (exh. cat.) (Charneaux, 1966), cat. no. 265.

No. 12   *Pietà*   Plates 13-15

Borgloon / comm. Borgloon / arr. Tongeren / prov. Limburg / B.
Kapel van Onze-Lieve-Vrouw van Smarten
wood, with overpainting
h. 102 cm

Comparison with *Pietà* of Eglise Saint-Pierre in Waremme suggested (*Beeldsnijkunst*).
See Inv. no. 101.

Bibliography
de Borchgrave d'Altena (1942-43), pp. 268-69, plate 17.
Honderd Limburgse Madonnas (1953), p. 24, cat. no. 71.
Laat-gotische beeldsnijkunst (1990), inv. no. 66.

No. 13   *Pietà*   Plate 16

Bovigny / comm. Gouvy / arr. Bastogne / prov. Luxembourg / B.
Eglise Saint-Martin
oak with overpainting (two vertical blocks, feet of Christ have been restored)
h. 62 cm

Bibliography
A.C.L. 1275 N, Notes on file.

No. 14   *Pietà*

Brasschaat / comm, arr., and prov. Antwerpen / B.
Instituut Maria-ter-Heide

stone
h. 75 cm

R. Op de Beeck discusses the stylistic origin, provenance, and restorations of this *Pietà*, in the collection of the Marist Sisters Institute (Maria-ter-Heide) since their foundation in 1924. He suggests influences from southern Champagne or the Franche-Comté.

Bibliography
Roland Op de Beeck, *Une sculpture champenoise inédite du XVI siècle: La 'Piétà' de N.D. des Bruyères à Brasschaat-lez-Anvers* (N.p., n.d. [1974]).

No. 15   *Pietà*   Plate 17

Bree / comm. Bree / arr. Maaseik / prov. Limburg / B.
Sint-Michielskerk, on the altar of the chapel on the northeastern end of the nave
polychromed wood, clothed
h. 105 cm

This *Pietà* is considered one of the oldest in the southern Low Countries of a type marked by Rhenish and German influences. Baum described it as a *Gnadenbild*, comparable in type to the Bellaire *Pietà* (Inv. no. 4), and without any of the "fresh air of Burgundian art."
Ziegler (1990) discusses this *Pietà* at length, especially its miraculous transfer by oxen to Bree and the history of its devotions (confraternities, clothes, and gifts), which have been remarkably continuous until the present day. The rituals and legends are comparatively well-documented.

Bibliography
Julius Baum, "Die Lütticher Bildnerkunst im 14. Jahrhundert," in *Belgischer Kunstdenkmäler*, vol. 1, edited by Paul Clemen (Munich: Bruckmann, 1923), p. 177.
de Borchgrave d'Altena (1942-43), p. 266, fig. 3.
S.F. Maes and J. Dreesen, *De geschiedenis van Bree*, vol. 1: *De parochie-de oude kloosters* (Bree: "Ons Erf," Gewestelijke Kring voor Geschiedenis en Heemkunde te Bree, 1946), pp. 15-40.
Ooms (1959), pp. 37-40.
de Borchgrave d'Altena (1963), pp. 98-100.
de Borchgrave d'Altena (1965), pp. 6 and 7.
Fotorepertorium, Bree (1977), pp. 19-20.
Steyaert (1981), pp. 19-20.
Jozef Neyen, *Maria in de kerk van Bree* (Brussels: Carto, 1989), pp. 6-18.

J.E. Ziegler, "The Medieval Virgin as Object: Art or Anthropology?" *Historical Reflections / Réflexions Historiques* 16 / 2-3 (1989), pp. 251-64.

No. 16   *Pietà*   Plate 18

Bruyelle / comm. Antoing / arr. Tournai / prov. Hainaut / B.
Notre-Dame d'Espoir, aedicule
wood

Bibliography
Trésors sacrés des églises et couvents de Tournai (exh. cat.) (Tournai: Trésor et Archives de la Cathédrale, 1973), cat. no. 161.

No. 17   *Pietà*   Plate 19

Bütgenbach / comm. Bütgenbach / arr. Verviers / prov. Liège / B.
Eglise Saint-Etienne
wood, with polychromy
h. 87 cm

Bibliography
A.C.L. 7319 A, Notes on file.

No. 18   *Pietà*   Plate 20

Dendermonde / comm. and arr. Dendermonde / prov. Oost-Vlaanderen / B.
Onze-Lieve-Vrouwekerk
oak, with neo-Gothic polychromy (Gent 1975)
h. 95 cm

Dhanens states that this *Pietà* stands in the right niche of the burial chapel and was originally from a chapel in the Bogaardstraat.

Bibliography
Elisabeth Dhanens, *Inventaris van het Kunstpatrimonium van Oost-Vlaanderen*, vol. 4: *Dendermonde* (Ghent: Kunstpatrimonium, 1961), p. 101, cat. no. 141, fig. 116.
de Borchgrave d'Altena (1965), p.14.

Gent duizend jaar kunst en cultuur (exh. cat.) (Ghent: Museum voor Schone Kunsten, 1975), p. 468, cat. no. 546.

No. 19   *Pietà*, copy of 1944   Plates 21-24

Diest / comm. Diest / arr. Leuven / prov. Brabant / Belgium
Onze-Lieve-Vrouwekerk
oak
h. 100 cm

A.C.L. records that in 1942 the *Pietà* was no longer in place. The present *Pietà* is a copy dating from 1944. The plates in this book illustrate the original sculpture clothed *in situ* before 1942 (131889 A; photographic negative by D. Hendrix, Antwerp); the original sculpture without clothes (53732 A); and the 1944 copy (173283 M). De Borchgrave d'Altena published the pre-1944 original. Perhaps the original *Pietà* is the one de Borchgrave d'Altena (1965) refers to as having been removed in 1942 and rediscovered in 1965 in Brussels.

Bibliography
A.C.L. 53731 A, Notes on file.
de Borchgrave d'Altena (1942-43), p. 267, fig. 9.
de Borchgrave d'Altena (1965), p. 18.

No. 20   *Pietà*

Dommelen / comm. Valkenswaard / prov. Noord-Brabant / Nl.
Parochiekerk
original polychromy
h. 96 cm

The parish belonged in 1444 to Westerhoven; it became an independent parish in 1565.

Bibliography
Kerkelijke Kunst uit het Dekenaat Valkenswaard: Inventaris van de Katholieke en Protestantse Kerken in Aalst, Bergeyk, Borkel en Schaft, Dommelen, Riethoven, Valkenswaard, Waalre en Westerhoven (exh. cat.) (Valkenswaard: Nikolaaskerk, 1973), p. 23, fig. on p. 63.

218

No. 21   *Pietà*   Plate 25

Duras / comm. Sint-Truiden / arr. Hasselt / prov. Limburg / B.
Kerk van Onze-Lieve-Vrouw Tenhemelopneming te Gorsem (no longer in place)
stone, with neo-Gothic polychromy (*Beeldsnijkunst*)

This *Pietà* was exhibited in 1930, 1936 (de Borchgrave d'Altena, fig. 11), and 1953
(*Honderd Limburgse Madonnas*). *Honderd Limburgse Madonnas* compares it to the
Pietà of Tongeren (which one is not stated) and characterizes this *Pietà* as "Dit
geschonden stuk...", to mean "damaged." It would therefore have been stolen or
lost after 1953 and before 1977 (*Fotorepertorium*). *Beeldsnijkunst* suggests a comparison with a *Pietà* from the pilgrimage chapel in Dieburg (Rhineland).

Bibliography
A.C.L. 78019 B, Notes on file.
Catalogue de l'exposition de l'art de l'ancien Pays de Liège et des anciens arts wallons
(Liège, 1930), cat. no. 404.
Joseph de Borchgrave d'Altena, *A propos de l'exposition 'Les Madones du Limbourg'*
(Brussels: Ballieu, 1936), p. 16, fig. 11.
de Borchgrave d'Altena (1942-43), p. 266.
Honderd Limburgse Madonnas (1953), p. 23, cat. no. 66.
de Borchgrave d'Altena (1965), p. 6.
Fotorepertorium, Sint-Truiden (1977), p. 29.
Laat-gotische beeldsnijkunst (1990), inv. no. 445.

No. 22   *Pietà*   Plate 26

Eksel / comm. Hechtel-Eksel / arr. Maaseik / prov. Limburg / B.
Kapel van Onze-Lieve-Vrouw-van-Zeven-Weeën te Hoksent (stolen)
wood, with new polychromy; left arm of Christ repaired
h. 70 cm

Van de Weerd (1921) proposes that the Chapel dates back to the eighth century and
was founded by the Frankish bishop and saint, Willibrord. According to the foundation
story, Hoksent was donated in 710 by Bertilindis, a nun from the Abbey of Celles, to
Willibrord. It was part of her inheritance left by her parents, Wigibald and Odrada.
On his death Willibrord donated all his possessions to the Abbey of Echternach, and
the Chapel remained the property of that Abbey (Ooms 1959). Legend holds that it
was the first chapel in the region, where people from a wide area went to Mass (Van

de Weerd, 1934). Until 1840 it was independent of the Eksel parish and was administered by a special official chosen by the Hoksent locals.

The *Pietà* was situated in the present chapel, built in the seventeenth century and dedicated to the Virgin of the Seven Sorrows, on a Baroque altar behind the main altar (Bussels, illus. p. 25), until 1979 when it was stolen (Bussels, p. 35, n. 20). *Beeldsnijkunst* makes no mention of its disappearance.

Bibliography

Oudheidkundige Inventaris, vol. 6: *Kanton Peer* (Hasselt, 1928), p. 9.
Joseph de Borchgrave d'Altena, *A propos de l'exposition 'Les Madones du Limbourg'* (Brussels: Ballieu, 1936), p. 16, cat. nos. 2 and 3, fig. 45.
Ooms (1959), pp. 52-53.
Fotorepertorium, Neerpelt (1977), p. 15.
J. Bussels, *De O.L.Vrouw- en Sint-Antonius-kapel van Hoksent* (N.p., 1988), p. 35, with illus. on pp. 15 and 25.
Laat-gotische beeldsnijkunst (1990), inv. no. 236.

References

H. Van de Weerd, "De Kapel van Hoxent. Een bladzijde uit de bekeering der Kempen," *Limburg* 3 (1921-22), pp. 41-49, 87-89.
H. Van de Weerd, "Limburg in het testament van den H. Willibrord," *Limburg* 15 (1934-35), pp. 63-70, 105-09, 125-29.

No. 23   *Pietà*   Plate 27

Ellignies Sainte-Anne / comm. Beloeil / arr. Ath / prov. Hainaut / B.
Eglise de la Sainte-Vierge
stone, with polychromy
h. 105 cm

De Borchgrave d'Altena suggests comparison with the *Pietà* from Saint-Ghislain. See Inv. no. 71.

Bibliography

E.J. Soil de Moriamé, *Inventaire des Objects d'Art et d'Antiquité existant dans les Edifices publics des communes de l'arrondissement judiciaire de Tournai*, vol. 4 (Charleroi: Imprimerie Provinciale, 1926), cat. no. 749.
de Borchgrave d'Altena and Mambour (1974), pp. 6 and 11.

No. 11   *Pietà*   Plate 12

Bombaye / comm. Dahlem / arr. Liège / prov. Liège / B.
Chapelle de la Sainte-Croix
wood
h. 44.5 cm

Bibliography
Exposition Abbaye de Val-Dieu (exh. cat.) (Charneaux, 1966), cat. no. 265.

No. 12   *Pietà*   Plates 13-15

Borgloon / comm. Borgloon / arr. Tongeren / prov. Limburg / B.
Kapel van Onze-Lieve-Vrouw van Smarten
wood, with overpainting
h. 102 cm

Comparison with *Pietà* of Eglise Saint-Pierre in Waremme suggested (*Beeldsnijkunst*).
See Inv. no. 101.

Bibliography
de Borchgrave d'Altena (1942-43), pp. 268-69, plate 17.
Honderd Limburgse Madonnas (1953), p. 24, cat. no. 71.
Laat-gotische beeldsnijkunst (1990), inv. no. 66.

No. 13   *Pietà*   Plate 16

Bovigny / comm. Gouvy / arr. Bastogne / prov. Luxembourg / B.
Eglise Saint-Martin
oak with overpainting (two vertical blocks, feet of Christ have been restored)
h. 62 cm

Bibliography
A.C.L. 1275 N, Notes on file.

No. 14   *Pietà*

Brasschaat / comm, arr., and prov. Antwerpen / B.
Instituut Maria-ter-Heide

stone
h. 75 cm

R. Op de Beeck discusses the stylistic origin, provenance, and restorations of this *Pietà*, in the collection of the Marist Sisters Institute (Maria-ter-Heide) since their foundation in 1924. He suggests influences from southern Champagne or the Franche-Comté.

Bibliography
Roland Op de Beeck, *Une sculpture champenoise inédite du XVI siècle: La 'Piétà' de N.D. des Bruyères à Brasschaat-lez-Anvers* (N.p., n.d. [1974]).

No. 15   *Pietà*   Plate 17

Bree / comm. Bree / arr. Maaseik / prov. Limburg / B.
Sint-Michielskerk, on the altar of the chapel on the northeastern end of the nave
polychromed wood, clothed
h. 105 cm

This *Pietà* is considered one of the oldest in the southern Low Countries of a type marked by Rhenish and German influences. Baum described it as a *Gnadenbild*, comparable in type to the Bellaire *Pietà* (Inv. no. 4), and without any of the "fresh air of Burgundian art."
Ziegler (1990) discusses this *Pietà* at length, especially its miraculous transfer by oxen to Bree and the history of its devotions (confraternities, clothes, and gifts), which have been remarkably continuous until the present day. The rituals and legends are comparatively well-documented.

Bibliography
Julius Baum, "Die Lütticher Bildnerkunst im 14. Jahrhundert," in *Belgischer Kunstdenkmäler*, vol. 1, edited by Paul Clemen (Munich: Bruckmann, 1923), p. 177.
de Borchgrave d'Altena (1942-43), p. 266, fig. 3.
S.F. Maes and J. Dreesen, *De geschiedenis van Bree*, vol. 1: *De parochie-de oude kloosters* (Bree: "Ons Erf," Gewestelijke Kring voor Geschiedenis en Heemkunde te Bree, 1946), pp. 15-40.
Ooms (1959), pp. 37-40.
de Borchgrave d'Altena (1963), pp. 98-100.
de Borchgrave d'Altena (1965), pp. 6 and 7.
Fotorepertorium, Bree (1977), pp. 19-20.
Steyaert (1981), pp. 19-20.
Jozef Neyen, *Maria in de kerk van Bree* (Brussels: Carto, 1989), pp. 6-18.

No. 24   *Pietà*, capital   Plate 28

Ellignies Sainte-Anne / comm. Beloeil / arr. Ath / prov. Hainaut / B.
Eglise de la Sainte-Vierge
white stone with polychromy, filled in during the seventeenth century with painted
wood, integrated into a stone capital of 1811.

The column capital with reliefs of Saint Christopher and the *Pietà* is under the *jubé*.

Bibliography
A.C.L. 92736 M, Notes on file.

No. 25   *Pietà*

Geistingen / comm. Kinrooi / arr. Maaseik / prov. Limburg / B.
Sint-Lambertuskerk
wood, with polychromy

The Church is neo-Romanesque (circa 1850) and was enlarged in 1899-1900 by T.J.
Tonnaer of Delft. The *Pietà* was not included in *Beeldsnijkunst*.

Bibliography
Fotorepertorium, Maaseik (1975), pp. 21 and 22.

No. 26   *Pietà*

Genk / comm. Genk / arr. Hasselt / prov. Limburg / B.
Kapel Onze-Lieve-Vrouw van Zeven Smarten te Kaatsbeek
plaster; very damaged; right arm of Christ is broken off

Placed in the nave on a small wooden altar in a niche. Above it hangs a wooden
crucifix, the body of Christ is metal. Visited by farmers of the region. The Chapel was
decorated in May with offertory money. Nearly all the devotional imagery in the Chapel
is of popular saints that were purchased with the money from the offertory box. The
Chapel has been neglected since 1960 (*Heidebloemke Genk*, p. 203).

Bibliography
"O.-L.-V. van Smarten," *Heidebloemke Genk* 38 / 4-6 (1979), pp. 195-98; fig. 20 B.

No. 27   *Pietà*

Gennep / comm. Gennep / prov. Limburg / Nl.
Sint-Lambertuskerk
h. 77 cm

Bibliography
De Nederlandsche Monumenten van Geschiedenis en Kunst, vol. 5 / part 2: *De Provincie Limburg* (The Hague: Algemeene Landsdrukkerij, 1937), p. 60, fig. 97.
D.P.R.A. Bouvy, *Middeleeuwsche Beeldhouwkunst in de Noordelijke Nederlanden* (Amsterdam: A.A. Balkema, 1947), p. 186.

No. 28   *Pietà*   Plate 29

Ghent / comm. and arr. Gent / prov. Oost-Vlaanderen / B.
Kerk der H. Geboorte, on the northern side aisle
wood, with polychromy
h. 70.5 cm

Bibliography
A.C.L. 76310 B, Notes on file.

No. 29   *Pietà*   Plate 30
Ghent / comm. and arr. Gent / prov. Oost-Vlaanderen / B.
Onze-Lieve-Vrouw-ter-Hooie (Klein Begijnhof)
oak, with modern polychromy
h. 81.5 cm

This *Pietà*, currently in the entrance hall of the Head Mistress's residence, was originally in the Convent of Saint Begga. The tree behind the Virgin's head is unusual and in addition to making references to the crucifix and Golgotha may possibly have something to do with the special cult of Seven Sorrows of the Virgin in Ghent, the *Schreyboom*. Speelman (p. 47) notes that on 7 March 1313 a privilege accorded indulgences to the faithful of Ghent who visited the oratory of the Seven Sorrows or the *Schreyboom*. Speelman claims that there was a chapel built in 1771 and the image of the miraculous Mother of Sorrows was placed on the altar.

References
Ed. Speelman, *Belgium Marianum. Histoire du Culte de Marie en Belgique* (Paris and Tournai: Casterman, 1859).

No. 30   *Pietà*   Plate 31

Gistoux / comm. Chaumont-Gistoux / arr. Nivelles / prov. Brabant / B.
Eglise Saint-Jean-Baptiste, Chapelle Notre-Dame des Affligés
stone, with traces of polychromy
h. 55 cm

Bibliography
A.C.L. 10341 M, Notes on file.

No. 31   *Pietà*   Plate 32

Givry / comm. Quévy / arr. Mons / prov. Hainaut / B.
Chapelle Notre-Dame de Pitié
wood, with modern polychromy
h. circa 78 cm

Bibliography
A.C.L. 92117 A, Notes on file.

No. 32   *Pietà*   Plates 33-34

Groot-Gelmen / comm. Borgloon / arr. Tongeren / prov. Limburg / B.
Kapel van Onze-Lieve-Vrouw-van-Blijde-Vrede te Helshoven
oak, with some traces of polychromy (Kunst en Oudheden); with polychromy removed
(*Beeldsnijkunst*)
h. 74.5 cm

Tradition holds that the Chapel, first built in 1254 by the Knights of Saint John, is
a pilgrimage site and former hermitage with old and continuous devotions to Mary.
Miracles happened at the site having to do with the Baptism of stillborn babies (cf.
Vreren *Pietà*, Inv. no. 99). See chapter 6 above, pp.xx-xx for a full discussion of the
site, cult, and *Pietà*.
The *Pietà* that de Borchgrave d'Altena illustrates is highly polychromed. The *Pietà* in
situ has no polychromy visible to the naked eye.

Bibliography
Joseph de Borchgrave d'Altena, ''Notes au sujet de sculptures conservées à Wellen,''
Leodium 25 / 1 (1933), p. 12, fig. 11.

de Borchgrave d'Altena (1942-43), p. 268.
Honderd Limburgse Madonnas (1953), p. 23, cat. no. 67.
Fotorepertorium, Sint-Truiden (1977), p. 35.
Een keuze uit het kerkelijk kunstbezit van de parochies van Groot-Sint-Truiden, Kunst en Oudheden in Limburg, no. 19 (1977), p. 25, cat. no. 4.
Laat-gotische beeldsnijkunst (1990), cat. no. 30 (Catalogus II. 22), inv. no. 449.

References
Fons Appermans, *Genadeoord van Maria van de Blijde Vrede* (N.p., n.d.). Photocopy.
C. Wijnen, "De kapel van Helshoven," *Grepen uit het verleden van Hoepertingen* 13 (1988), pp. 751-58.

No. 33   *Pietà*   Plate 35

Gruitrode / comm. Meeuwen-Gruitrode / arr. Maaseik / prov. Limburg / B.
Sint-Gertrudiskerk, nave wall
wood, with neo-Gothic polychromy
h. 75 cm

The *Pietà* is situated on the upper section of the nave wall of a Late Gothic church built circa 1415; after a fire of 1909, the nave was restored by Martens and Lenaerts (*Fotorepertorium*). Perhaps this was when the sculpture received its polychromy.

Bibliography
Fotorepertorium, Bree (1977), pp. 23-25.
Laat-gotische beeldsnijkunst (1990), inv. no. 389.

Guvelingen / B.
See Sint-Jacobskerk in Schuurhoven, Inv. no. 79.

No. 34   *Pietà*   Plate 36

Hamont / comm. Hamont-Achel / arr. Maaseik / prov. Limburg / B.
Sint-Laurentiuskerk

wood, with neo-Gothic polychromy (*Beeldsnijkunst*)
h. 91 cm

This *Pietà* originally must have been situated elsewhere. The church was built in the neo-Gothic style in 1904 from a plan by Cuypers of Roermond (*Fotorepertorium*). When I visited the church in 1988 there was no *Pietà*.

Bibliography
de Borchgrave d'Altena (1942-43), p. 268.
Honderd Limburgse Madonnas (1953), cat. no. 103.
de Borchgrave d'Altena (1965), p. 15.
Gewijde Kunst in Limburgs bezit (exh. cat.) (Hasselt: Provinciaal Begijnhof, 1966), p. 29, cat. no. 23.
Fotorepertorium, Neerpelt (1977), p. 22.
Laat-gotische beeldsnijkunst (1990), inv. no. 170.

No. 35   *Pietà*, funerary relief with donors   Plate 37

Harchies / comm. Bernissart / arr. Ath / prov. Hainaut / B.
Eglise de la Sainte-Vierge
stone, with polychromy
h. 70 cm

Saints Peter and Andrew present the two deceased on both sides of the *Pietà*; inscribed is "Mater Dei Memento mei." The *Pietà* is placed under a canopy, a composition found in painting (cf. *Pietà* with the Duchess of Brittany, Paris, Bibliothèque Nationale, manuscrit français, 958, fol. Fv. in Simons 1991).

Bibliography
A.C.L. 93392 A, Notes on file.

References
Walter Simons, "De Dominicanen: Een orde van predikers," in *Het Pand: Acht eeuwen geschiedenis van het Oud Dominicanenklooster te Gent* (Tielt: Lannoo, 1991), p. 30.

No. 36   *Pietà*   Plate 38

Hasselt / comm. and arr. Hasselt / prov. Limburg / B.
Minderbroederskerk
wood, with new polychromy
h. 47 cm

This *Pietà* is believed to have come originally from the Minderbroedersklooster in 's-Hertogenbosch (Ooms, p. 73; *Beeldsnijkunst*). Ooms believes that the Friars took the *Pietà* away with them in 1629 when they fled 's-Hertogenbosch, perhaps bringing it then to Hasselt. A confraternity to Our Lady of the Seven Sorrows was founded in 1650 (Ooms, p. 75), just as the Hasselt friars were completing the church. A miracle was reported in 1647 of a child cured of a fracture by the statue (Ooms, p. 75). In 1797, during the suppression, the friars brought their statue to the Theunis family for safe-keeping (Ooms, p. 74). The statue was moved to different locations in the church several times during the late nineteenth century. In 1990 the *Pietà* was vandalized. Compare to the *Pietà* from Landelies and Private Collection (l'Abbé Maffei). (See Inv. nos. 44 and 138).

Bibliography
Devigne (1932), fig. 208.
Ooms (1959), pp. 73-75.
Laat-gotische beeldsnijkunst (1990), inv. no. 205.

No. 37   *Pietà*   Plate 39

Hasselt / comm. and arr. Hasselt / prov. Limburg / B.
Sint-Quintinus en Onze-Lieve-Vrouwekathedraal
wood, with neo-Gothic polychromy (*Beeldsnijkunst*)
h. 103 cm

De Borchgrave d'Altena places this *Pietà* with an iconographic type of the Virgin grasping the loin cloth. See *Pietà* from Saint-Ghislain, Inv. no. 71. Didier compares to the *Pietà* of Saint-Jacques in Liège, Inv. no. 52.

Bibliography
de Borchgrave d'Altena (1963), p. 10.
de Borchgrave d'Altena and Mambour (1974), p. 6.
Robert Didier, ''Sculptures mosanes des années 1400-1450,'' in *Clio et son regard: mélanges d'histoire, d'histoire de l'art et d'archéologie offerts à Jacques Stiennon à l'occasion de ses vingt-cinq ans d'enseignement à l'Université de Liège*, edited by Rita Lejeune and Joseph Deckers (Liège: Pierre Mardaga, 1982), p. 155.
Fotorepertorium, Hasselt, vol. 1 (1977), p. 23.
J.J.M. Timmers, *De kunst van het Maasland*, vol. 2: *De gotiek en de renaissance* (Assen: Van Gorcum, 1980), p. 159.
Laat-gotische beeldsnijkunst (1990), inv. no. 187.

No. 38   *Pietà*

's-Hertogenbosch / prov. Noord-Brabant / Nl.
Sint-Janskathedraal
oak
h. 91 cm

Purchased in 1950 by the church administration.

Bibliography
C. Peeters, *De Sint Janskathedraal te 's-Hertogenbosch* (The Hague: Staatsuitgeverij, 1985), p. 366, fig. 394 (on p. 382).

No. 39   *Pietà*   Plate 40

Hoevezavel / comm. Genk / arr. Hasselt / prov. Limburg / B.
Onze-Lieve-Vrouwekapel
oak, overpainted

Beeldsnijkunst states that the *Pietà* came from the castle of Booischot (prov. Antwerp, circa 1953) and that its original provenance is not known. Ooms claims that it stood for centuries in a corner of the same castle and that when father Anicetus Cool, a Fransciscan, began to build his new church, finished in 1953, the lord of Booischot gave him the statue. Mary wears a widow's veil.

Bibliography
Ooms (1959), pp. 62 and 63.
Laat-gotische beeldsnijkunst (1990), inv. no. 129.

No. 40   *Pietà*   Plate 41

Hondelange / comm. Messancy / arr. Arlon / prov. Luxembourg / B.
Chapelle du cimetière
wood, with polychromy
h. 82 cm

Bibliography
A.C.L. 43096 A, Notes on file.

No. 41   *Pietà*   Station with the Seventh Sorrow of the Virgin   Plate 42

Hondelange / comm. Messancy / arr. Arlon / prov. Luxembourg / B.
Cimetière
sandstone
h. 225 cm

Inscription: "PASSIO CHRISTI / COMPASSIO DEI PARENTI SEPTIES
VENERATUR."

Bibliography
A.C.L. 20799 B (Cl. All. 1914-18), Notes on file.

No. 42   *Pietà*

Horst / prov. Limburg / Nl.
Sint-Lambertuskerk
oak, with modern polychromy
h. 103 cm

Timmers (1949) identifies the sculptor as the Master of Beek. He relates this *Pietà* to
ones from Birgden (Germany), Hunsel (Netherlands), and Venray (Netherlands; see
Inv. no. 94) (Timmers 1980, p. 166).

Bibliography
De Nederlandsche Monumenten van Geschiedenis en Kunst, vol. 5 / Part 2: *De Provincie Limburg* (The Hague: Algemeene Landsdrukkerij, 1937), pp. 91, fig. 186.
Maria in de Kunst: Kloostergang der Basiliek van Onze Lieve Vrouwe (exh. cat.), Internationaal Maria Congres 1947 (Maastricht: N.p., n.d. [1947]), cat. no. 50.
J.J.M. Timmers, *Houten Beelden. De houtsculptuur in de noordelijke Nederlanden
tijdens de late middeleeuwen* (Amsterdam and Antwerp: Contact, 1949), pp. 41 and
77, fig. 71.
1000 Jaar kerkelijke kunst in Limburg (exh. cat.) (Hasselt: Provinciaal Begijnhof,
1961), cat. no. 88.
J.J.M. Timmers, *De kunst van het Maasland*, vol. 2: *De gotiek en de renaissance*
(Assen: Van Gorcum, 1980), pp. 166 and 167, plate 298.
J.J.M. Timmers, *Oude Schoonheid in Limburg* (Maasbree: Corrie Zelen, n.d. [ca.
1980]), p. 126, plate 127.

No. 43   *Pietà*, funerary with donor   Plate 43

Huy / comm. and arr. Huy / prov. Liège / B.
Collège Saint-Quirin
Funerary relief placed in the exterior wall

Bibliography
A.C.L. 66763 A, Notes on file.

No. 44   *Pietà*

Landelies / comm. Montigny-le-Tilleul / arr. Charleroi / prov. Hainaut / B.
Eglise Saint-Martin
with recent polychromy
h. 35 cm

See also Inv. nos. 36 and 138 for comparison.

Bibliography
Trésors d'art du Hainaut (exh. cat.) (Mons, 1953), p. 78, cat. no. 106.
de Borchgrave d'Altena and Mambour (1974), p. 14.
Steyaert (1981), p. 25, fig. 4.

No. 45   *Pietà*   Plate 44

Lessines / comm. Lessines / arr. Soignies / prov. Hainaut / B.
Hôpital Notre-Dame à la Rose
wood, with modern polychromy (Soil de Moriamé)
h. 58 cm

De Borchgrave d'Altena, in his entry for *La Madone dans l'Art*, said the prototype is
the Virgin of Merchtem (Inv. no. 64) and that this *Pietà* is the ''sister'' of the *Pietàs*
in Liège (Saint-Denis and Saint-Jacques) and Lummen (see Inv. nos. 51, 52, and 54).
In 1962 he compared this sculpture with the Monument de Mais in Virton (Inv. no.
98); Didier compares it with a sculpture from Arc-Ainières.

Bibliography
E.J. Soil de Moriamé, *Inventaire des Objets d'Art et d'Antiquité existant dans les
Edifices publics des communes de l'arrondissement judiciaire de Tournai*, vol. 4
(Charleroi: Imprimerie Provinciale, 1926), p. 28, cat. no. 123.

Exposition d'Arts Belgicum (exh. cat.) (Tournai: N.p., n.d. [1949]), p. 25, cat. no. 33.

La Madone dans l'Art en Hainaut (exh. cat.) (Tournai: Cathédrale de Tournai, 1960), 2nd ed., p. 26, cat. no. 51; (1st ed., cat. no. 50).

Joseph de Borchgrave d'Altena, ''La sculpture aux époques romane et gothique,'' in *Hainaut d'hier et d'aujourd'hui* (Brussels: Les Editions Labor, 1962), p. 279.

de Borchgrave d'Altena (1965), p. 14, fig. 8.

Robert Didier, ''La mise au tombeau d'Arc,'' *Revue des Archéologues et Historiens d'Art de Louvain* 3 (1970), pp. 87-89.

de Borchgrave d'Altena and Mambour (1974), pp. 12 and 13.

References
G. Raulier, *L'Hôpital Notre-Dame à la Rose et ses musées à Lessines* (Mons, 1986).

No. 46a / b   *Pietà* and Copy   Plates 45-46

Leuven / comm. and arr. Leuven / prov. Brabant / B.
Minderbroedersklooster, Kapel Onze-Lieve-Vrouw-ten-Troost of van Smarten
46a) Miraculous Image of Onze-Lieve-Vrouw-ten-Troost of van Smarten (of ter-Koorts) wood, with polychromy
h. 63 cm

De Maesschalck and van Uytven report that the renowned chapel in the Vlamingenstraat exists due to a woman, who daily venerated an image of the Virgin of the Seven Sorrows, which had been placed against a tree circa 1535; on all feast days of Mary the woman placed the statue in a beautifully decorated altar in front of her house. One day students wanted to harrass her and steal the statue but suddenly it became too heavy to lift. The miracle caused a stir that led to the building in 1540 of a little prayer place, replaced in 1601 by a true chapel, Onze-Lieve-Vrouw-ter-Koorts.

Bibliography
E. van Berlo, *Geschiedenis van het vermaard miraculeus beeld van O.L.V. ter Koorts (1535-1906)* (Leuven, 1906).
E. De Maesschalck and R. van Uytven, ''Het religieuze en zedelijke leven van de leken,'' in *Leuven, 'De beste stad van Brabant,'* vol. 1: *De geschiedenis van het stadsgewest Leuven tot omstreeks 1600,* edited by R. Van Uytven (Leuven: Vrienden Stedelijke Musea, 1980), p. 254.

46b) Copy of the Miraculous Image of Onze-Lieve-Vrouw-ten Troost of van Smarten (of ter-Koorts)

wood, with polychromy
h. 46 cm

A.C.L. has photograph (1958?) of an "old copy after the miraculous image," of smaller dimensions.

Bibliography
A.C.L. 171428 B, Notes on file (1958?).

No. 47   *Pietà*   Plate 47

Leuven / comm. and arr. Leuven / prov. Brabant / B.
Sint-Gertrudiskerk
wood, with polychromy
h. 130 cm

Bibliography
Joseph de Borchgrave d'Altena, *Notes pour servir à l'inventaire des oeuvres d'art du Brabant: Arrondissement de Louvain* (Brussels: Ballieu, 1941), pp. 165, 178, 290, and 294, plates 88 and 109.
de Borchgrave d'Altena (1942-43), p. 268, n. 2.

No. 48   *Pietà*   Plate 48

Leuven / comm. and arr. Leuven / prov. Brabant / B.
Sint-Michielskerk
oak, with polychromy
h. 92 cm

A.C.L. 32362 A records that this *Pietà* is in situ with a cloak on the Virgin (1942?); there is no longer a cloak on the Virgin in A.C.L. 166424 B (1957?).

Bibliography
A.C.L. 32362 A and 166424 B, Notes on file.
de Borchgrave d'Altena (1942-43), p. 268, n. 2.

No. 49   *Pietà*   Plate 49

Leuven / comm. and arr. Leuven / prov. Brabant / B.
Sint-Pietershospitaal
wood, with polychromy
h. 50 cm with crown

Bibliography
A.C.L. 158942 B, Notes on file.

No. 50   *Pietà*   Plate 50

Liège / comm., arr., and prov. Liège / B.
Chapelle Sainte-Agathe / Ancien couvent des Sépulchrines
wood, restored? (A.C.L.)
h. 60 cm

De Borchgrave d'Altena (1942-43) also illustrates another *Pietà* from Sainte-Agathe,
fig. 23.

Bibliography
A.C.L. 168576 B, Notes on file.
de Borchgrave d'Altena (1942-43), pp. 263 and 70, fig. 24.

No. 51   *Pietà*   Plates 51-52

Liège / comm, arr., and prov. Liège / B.
Eglise Saint-Denis, in chapel of side aisle
wood, with modern polychromy
h. 70 cm (A.C.L. 36051 A); h. 66 cm (*Lambert Lombard*)

The photographic documentation constitutes curious evidence of ritual additions and
subtractions. This has not been discussed in the scholarly literature. A.C.L. 19254 B
(Cl. All. 1914-18) shows the *Pietà* crowned with seven swords piercing her heart; de
Borchgrave d'Altena (1926) and Devigne (1932) illustrate the sculpture with the same
photograph in which the Virgin shows neither of those cultic additions of crown or
swords; A.C.L. 36051 A shows the Virgin with the crown only.

Bibliography

A.C.L. 19254 B, 36051 A, Notes on file.

Joseph de Borchgrave d'Altena, *Notes et Documents pour servir à l'histoire de l'art et de l'iconographie en Belgique, 1re série: Sculptures conservées au Pays Mosan* (Verviers: G. Leens, 1926), pp. 130 and 31; fig. 78.

Devigne (1932), pp. 142, 248; plate XLIII, fig. 207.

de Borchgrave d'Altena (1942-43), pp. 263 and 70, fig. 11.

Emile Mâle, *L'Art religieux de la fin du moyen âge* (Paris: Armand Colin, 1949), p. 122.

de Borchgrave d'Altena (1965), p. 11.

Lambert Lombard et Son Temps (exh. cat.) (Liège: Musée de l'Art Wallon, 1966), p. 12, cat. no. 19, plate V.

No. 52   *Pietà*   Plate 53

Liège / comm., arr., and prov. Liège / B.

Eglise Saint-Jacques (originally from the lost church of Saint-Remy in Liège)

Mosan sable stone, with original polychromy (?); back side hollowed out (Stiennon)

h. 68 cm

This famous *Pietà* is known as the Mère de Consolation, Notre-Dame Consolatrice des Affligés, or Notre-Dame de Saint-Remy (Didier, p. 154). It was transferred on 4 December 1803 to the church of Saint-Jacques (Coenen, p. 23), where it is integrated into a neo-Gothic retable of 1885 (Didier, p. 171); it is venerated as the *Consolatrice des Affligés*.

Coenen discusses three notices attesting to the devotion to this *Pietà*. Part one of the first, dating from 1657, describes the numerous cures obtained from 1643 to 1657 in front of the statue, then placed on the main altar of the church of Saint-Remy, and part two is a pilgrim's manual. The second notice lists the main cures and miracles, especially of two children of Liège (Coenen, pp. 23 and 24). Hendrix has earlier references, however, in a testament of 1624 in which Marie Mahoun asks that her body be buried "à l'opposite de ntre [sic] dame de pitié" and the foundation in 1635 of a *rente* for masses in honor of the Holy Virgin (p. 19). In 1799 during the French Revolution the property of Saint-Remy was demolished but the statue was deposited with Barale, a canon from Saint-Jacques, and transferred to that church on 4 December 1803 during the reorganization of the parishes in that city (Coenen).

Forgeur discusses a sculpted wood, polychromed *Pietà* in the collection of the Commission publique d'assistance sociale de Liège, which bears on the face of the sockel the following inscription: "Mère de consolation. Vray pourtraict de l'image miraculeuse de Nostre Damme de S. Remy en Liège. 1657." He analyzes the heraldry, suggests the arms belong to the Netherlandish family of Enkevoort, relates them to the daughter Hélène d'Enckevoort, and concludes that the copy was made for the convent of canonesses, dedicated to Saint Agatha, that she built after taking refuge in Liège from the soldiers of the United Provinces. The copy is mentioned by de Borchgrave d'Altena (1942-43, p. 268, n. 1) who says that there is more than one copy, another of which, from 1645, was exhibited in Liège in 1926 from the Medard collection.

Bibliography
Jules Helbig, *La sculpture et les arts plastiques au pays de Liège et sur les bords de la Meuse* (Bruges: Desclée, De Brouwer et Cie, 1890) p. 21.
Joseph de Borchgrave d'Altena, *Notes et Documents pour servir à l'histoire de l'art et de l'iconographie en Belgique, 1re série: Sculptures conservées au Pays Mosan* (Verviers: G. Leens, 1926), p. 131.
J. Coenen, *Les Madones de Liège et de Chèvremont* (Liège: Demarteau, 1923), pp. 20-24.
Abbé L. Hendrix, *Notre-Dame de Saint-Rémy, Consolatrice des Affligés: Son Histoire et son Culte* (Liège: Ecole professionnelle Saint-Jean Berchmans, 1925), esp. pp. 17-19.
Devigne (1932), p. 141, fig. 204.
de Borchgrave d'Altena (1942-43), p. 268, n. 1.
de Borchgrave d'Altena (1965), pp. 11-12.
Robert Didier, "Sculptures mosanes des années 1400-1450," in *Clio et Son Regard: Mélanges offerts à Jacques Stiennon à l'occasion de ses vingt-cinq ans d'enseignement à l'Université de Liège*, edited by Rita Lejeune and Joseph Deckers (Liège: Pierre Mardaga, 1982), p. 154, n. 23 and fig. 11 with full bibliography on p. 171, n. 23.
J.J.M Timmers, *De Kunst van het Maasland*, vol. 2: *De gotiek en de renaissance* (Assen: Van Gorcum, 1980), p. 159, plate 280.
Richard Forgeur, "Une réplique de la pieta de l'église de Saint-Remy à Liège," *Leodium* 74 / 1-6 (1989), pp. 5-8.

No. 53   *Pietà*

Lier / comm. Lier / arr. Mechelen / prov. Antwerpen / B.
Sint-Gummaruskerk, ambulatory of the choir behind the high altar

Leemans attributes the sculpture to Thomas Haesaert (circa 1600).

Bibliography
H. Bierens de Haan, *Het houtsnijwerk in Nederland tijdens de gotiek en de renaissance* (The Hague, 1921), pp. 24 and 25.
de Borchgrave d'Altena (1942-43), p. 268.

234

Hertha Leemans, *Tentoonstelling Sint-Gummarus te Lier* (exh. cat.) (Lier: Sint-Gummarus, 1965), cat. no. 198.

No. 54   *Pietà*   Plate 54

Lummen / comm. Lummen / arr. Hasselt / prov. Limburg / B.
Onze-Lieve-Vrouwekerk
wood, with neo-Gothic polychromy
h. 58 cm (*Fotorepertorium*); h. 76 cm. (*Beeldsnijkunst*)

There is some confusion surrounding this *Pietà*. I have visited the church, built in 1870-72 in a neo-Romanesque style (*Fotorepertorium*, p. 43), several times and found no *Pietà* there. The *Beeldsnijkunst* entry writes that this is an "interpretation of a model from around 1400." When de Borchgrave d'Altena (1942-43) illustrated the sculpture he suggested a comparison with the *Pietà* of Saint-Remy (Inv. no. 52) but the photograph he uses is the *Pietà* of Saint-Denis (Inv. no. 51). The A.C.L. notes that its model is the art of Rogier van der Weyden.

Bibliography
A.C.L. 89947 A, Notes on file.
"Het Kerkelijk Meubelair," *De Limburgse Kempen* (1936), fig. 10.
de Borchgrave d'Altena (1942-43), pp. 263-70, fig. 16.
Honderd Limburgse Madonnas (1953), p. 24, cat. no. 63.
de Borchgrave d'Altena (1965), p. 12.
Gewijde kunst in Limburgs bezit (exh. cat.) (Hasselt: Provinciaal Begijnhof, 1966), cat. no. 22.
Fotorepertorium, Hasselt, vol. 2 (1978), no. 44.
Laat-gotische beeldsnijkunst (1990), inv. no. 334.

No. 55   *Pietà*

Luyksgestel / prov. Noord-Brabant / Nl.
Sint-Martinuskerk
lindenwood, with polychromy
h. 93 cm

Bibliography
Kerkelijke Kunst uit het Dekenaat Valkenswaard: Inventaris van de Katholieke en Protestantse Kerken in Aalst, Bergeyk, Borkel en Schoft, Dommelen, Riethoven,

Valkenswaard, Waalre en Westerhoven, (exh. cat.) (Valkenswaard: Nikolaaskerk, 1973), p. 68, illus. on cat. no. 28.

No. 56   *Pietà*

Maaseik / comm. and arr. Maaseik / prov. Limburg / B.
Ursulinenklooster (originally from the Minderbroederskloosters Maaseik?)
stone, overpainted

Bibliography
Laat-gotische beeldsnijkunst (1990), inv. no. 351.

No. 57   *Pietà*

Maastricht / prov. Limburg / Nl.
Onze-Lieve-Vrouwekerk
stone, with modern polychromy
h. 81.5 cm

Bibliography
Wilhelm Pinder, *Die deutsche Plastik von ausgehenden Mittelalter bis zum Ende der Renaissance* (Potsdam: Akademische Verlagsgesellschaft Athenaion 1924), p. 171.
Devigne (1932), pp. 140-42, fig. 55, plate XII.
De Monumenten van Geschiedenis en Kunst in de Provincie Limburg, vol. 1: *De Monumenten in de Gemeente Maastricht* (The Hague: Algemeene Landsdrukkerij, 1926), pp. 532-34, fig. 507.
Die Parler und der Schöne Stil 1350-1400: Europäische Kunst unter den Luxemburgen (exh. cat.), vol. 1 (Cologne: Museen der Stadt Köln, 1978) p. 117, illus. with bibliography.

No. 58   *Pietà*

Maastricht / prov. Limburg / Nl.
Sint-Matthiaskerk
wood
h. 69 cm

Bibliography
Devigne (1932), p. 141, fig. 206.
De Monumenten van Geschiedenis en Kunst in de Provincie Limburg, vol. 1: *De Monumenten in de Gemeente Maastricht* (The Hague: Algemeene Landsdrukkerij, 1926), pp. 269-70, fig. no. 224.

No. 59   *Pietà*

Maastricht / prov. Limburg / Nl.
Sint-Servaaskerk
lindenwood, restored by Cuypers
h. 1.27 m

De Monumenten (p. 381) notes that it was "clothed in the mode of 1570, Christ's head set straight up, bones and feet damaged and mutilated (recorded by Jhr. Mr. V. de Stuers)."

Bibliography
De Monumenten van Geschiedenis en Kunst in de Provincie Limburg, vol. 1: *De Monumenten in de Gemeente Maastricht* (The Hague: Algemeene Landsdrukkerij, 1926), pp. 380-81.
de Borchgrave d'Altena (1965), p. 6.

No. 60   *Pietà*

Marches-les-Dames / comm., arr. and prov. Namur / B.
Couvent des Carmélites
stone

Bibliography
Devigne (1932), p. 249, fig. 213.

No. 61   *Pietà*   Plate 55

Mechelen / arr. and comm. Mechelen / prov. Antwerpen / B.
Onze-Lieve-Vrouwgasthuis, Inv. no. B8
oak, with neo-Gothic polychromy; sockel restored; no mark
h. 86 cm

Bibliography
A.C.L. 153637 M, Notes on file.

No. 62   *Pietà*   Plate 56

Meeuwen / comm. Meeuwen-Gruitrode / arr. Maaseik / prov. Limburg / B.
Kerk van Onze-Lieve-Vrouw Tenhemelopneming te Wijshagen

wood, with neo-Gothic polychromy; base restored
h. 90 cm

Bibliography
de Borchgrave d'Altena (1942-43), p. 268.
Fotorepertorium, Bree (1977), pp. 29 and 30.
Laat-gotische beeldsnijkunst (1990), inv. no. 396.

No. 63   *Pietà*   Plate 57

Meldert / comm. Lummen / arr. Hasselt / prov. Limburg / B.
Sint-Willibrorduskerk (no longer in place)
wood, with polychromy
h. 62 cm

Bibliography
A.C.L. 146610 B, Notes on file.
Fotorepertorium, Hasselt, vol. 2 (1978), pp. 49-50.
Honderd Limburgse Madonnas (1953), p. 25, cat. no. 74.

No. 64   *Pietà*

Merchtem / comm. Merchtem / arr. Halle-Vilvoorde / prov. Brabant / B.
Onze-Lieve-Vrouwekerk
oak

Bibliography
de Borchgrave d'Altena (1942-43), pp. 267 and 269, fig. 5.

Joseph de Borchgrave d'Altena, *Oeuvres de nos imagiers romans et gothiques. Sculpteurs, ivoiriers, orfèvres, fondeurs: 1025 à 1550* (Brussels: Raymond Dupriez, 1944), plate LXII.
de Borchgrave d'Altena (1965), p. 11, fig. 15.
Theodor Müller, *Sculpture in the Netherlands, Germany, France, and Spain 1400 to 1500* (Harmondsworth, Middlesex: Penguin Books Ltd, 1966), p. 97.

No. 65   *Pietà*   Plate 58

Noville / comm. and arr. Bastogne / prov. Luxembourg / B.
Chapelle Saint-Hubert à Wicourt
wood, with polychromy
h. 57 cm

Bibliography
Exposition de l'Art religieux d'Ardenne (exh. cat.) (Nivelles: Quinot, 1952), p. 19, cat. no. 28.
Exposition d'art et de Folklore religieuse du Luxembourg à Saint-Hubert (exh. cat.) (Saint-Hubert, 1958), cat. no. 91.

No. 66   *Pietà*   Plate 59

Opitter / comm. Bree / arr. Maaseik / prov. Limburg / B.
Sint-Pieterskerk te Tongerlo
wood, with neo-Gothic polychromy
h. 120 cm

Bibliography
de Borchgrave d'Altena (1963), p. 173.
de Borchgrave d'Altena (1965), p. 17.
R. Didier and R. Krohm, *Duitse middeleeuwse beeldhouwwerken in Belgische verzamelingen. Les sculptures médiévales allemandes dans les collections belges* (exh. cat.), Europalia 77 Bundesrepublik Deutschland (Brussels: Generale Bankmaatschappij; Société Générale de Banque, 1977), pp. 67-68.
Laat-gotische beeldsnijkunst (1990), inv. no. 101.

No. 67   *Pietà*   Plate 60

Opitter / comm. Bree / arr. Maaseik / prov. Limburg / B.
Sint-Trudokerk (stolen)
wood, with neo-Gothic polychromy (*Beeldsnijkunst*)
h. 86 cm

De Borchgrave d'Altena placed this work within the circle of the *atelier* of the Master
of Beek. See *Pietà* from Horst (Inv. no. 42).

Bibliography
G. Terme, *L'art ancien au pays de Liège. Mobiliers et sculptures. Album de l'exposition
universelle de Liège 1905*, vol. 2: *Mémorial de l'exposition de Saint-Trond 1907* (N.p.,
n.d. [1907]), cat. no. 218.
de Borchgrave d'Altena (1942-43), p. 267, fig. 19.
Gewijde kunst in Limburgs bezit (exh. cat.) (Hasselt: Provinciaal Begijnhof, 1966),
cat. no. 80.
De glans van Prémontré. Oude kunst uit Witherenabdijen der Lage Landen (exh. cat.)
(Heverlee: Abdij van Park, 1973), cat. no. 269.
A.M.J. Stoffels, *Het kerkelijk kunstbezit van de Sint-Trudoparochie te Opitter* (exh.
cat.), Kunst en Oudheden in Limburg, no. 6 (Sint-Truiden: Provinciaal Museum,
1975), cat. no. 8.
Laat-gotische beeldsnijkunst (1990), inv. no. 104.

No. 68   *Pietà*   Plate 61

Opoeteren / comm. and arr. Maaseik / prov. Limburg / B.
Sint-Denijskerk
wood, with neo-Gothic polychromy; Christ's foot damaged
h. 90 cm

Bibliography
de Borchgrave d'Altena (1942-43), p. 268.
Honderd Limburgse Madonnas (1953), cat. no. 72.
de Borchgrave d'Altena (1965), p. 15.
Fotorepertorium, Maaseik (1977), p. 37.
Laat-gotische beeldsnijkunst (1990), inv. no. 370.

No. 69   *Pietà* in mandorla   Plate 62

Oudegem / arr. and comm. Dendermonde / prov. Oost-Vlaanderen / B.
Onze-Lieve-Vrouwekerk
wood, with polychromy
h. 74 cm; h. 103 cm with mandorla

Bibliography
A.C.L. 96659 B, Notes on file.

No. 70   *Pietà*

Rukkelingen-Loon / comm. Heers / arr. Tongeren / prov. Limburg / B.
Sint-Quirinuskerk
wood, with modern polychromy (after 1946)
h. 75 cm

The old polychromy is illustrated by de Borchgrave d'Altena (1942-43 and 1946), the new in *Beeldsnijkunst*. The *Pietà* seems to have been absent from the church when the inventory of the church furnishings was done in 1960 (*Bondige inventaris*). Recently it has been attributed to the Master of the Calvary of Fize-le-Marsal, and located in Sint-Quirinuskerk (*Beeldsnijkunst*).

Bibliography
de Borchgrave d'Altena (1942-43), p. 268, fig. 15 ("Roclenge-Looz").
Joseph de Borchgrave d'Altena, *La Passion du Christ dans la Sculpture en Belgique du XI au XVIe S* (Paris and Brussels: Editions du Cercle d'Art, 1946), p. 99, fig. 45.
de Borchgrave d'Altena (1965), p. 11.
Art mariale au pays de Waremme (Waremme, 1981), cat. no. 17.
Laat-gotische beeldsnijkunst (1990), inv. no. 244.

References
"Bondige inventaris der kunstvoorwerpen van het arrondissement Tongeren," *Bulletin de la Commission royale des Monuments and des Sites / Bulletin van de Koninklijke Commissie voor Monumenten en Landschappen* 11 (1960), p. 268.

No. 71   *Pietà*   Plate 63

Saint-Ghislain / comm. Saint-Ghislain / arr. Mons / prov. Hainaut / B.
Eglise Saint-Ghislain

stone, with polychromy
h. 123 cm

De Borchgrave d'Altena says that this "remarkable statue could have come from the abbey of Saint-Ghislain," which records a chapel of "Notre-Dame de pitié" there in 1586. Or, it may have come from a city edifice, "La porte à le [sic] Mère Dieu." Until 1951 the *Pietà* had been placed in a chapel of the rue du Moulin; it has been in the church of Saint-Ghislain since 1963. Steyaert (1981) discusses this sculpture as an iconographic type (related to the Tournai Book of Hours of circa 1400, Steyaert, n. 36 for references) where Mary grasps the loincloth.

Bibliography
de Borchgrave d'Altena and Mambour (1974), p. 6, p. 10 (with bibliography), no. 20, illus. p. 11.
Steyaert (1981), p. 26.

No. 72   *Pietà*

Saint-Symphorien / comm. and arr. Mons / prov. Hainaut / B.
Eglise Saint-Symphorien
wood, with polychromy
h. circa 35 cm

De Borchgrave d'Altena alerts us to look for this *Pietà* which is "posée sur le dais à lambrequin" on the Marian altar in the church.

Bibliography
La Madone dans l'Art du Hainaut (exh. cat.) (Tournai: Cathédrale de Tournai, 1960), p. 30, cat. no. 69.
de Borchgrave d'Altena and Mambour (1974), p. 16, illus.

No. 73   *Pietà*   Plates 64-65

Schönberg / comm. Sankt-Vith / arr. Verviers / prov. Liège / B.
Eglise Saint-Georges, Inv. no. Sankt-Vith, 235
oak, with polychromy
h. 90 cm

The polychromy of this *Pietà* has been treated but there is no record on file (compare plates 64, 65). Note nail holes in Christ's hand on A.C.L. 7359 A.

Bibliography
A.C.L. 7359 A, Notes on file.

No. 74   *Pietà*   Plate 66

Silenrieux / comm. Cerfontaine / arr. Philippeville / prov. Namur / B.
Eglise Sainte-Anne
alabaster
h. 67 cm

Bibliography
A.C.L. 91674 B, Notes on file.

No. 75   *Pietà*   Plate 67

Sint-Amandsberg / comm. and arr. Gent / prov. Oost-Vlaanderen / B.
Begijnhof Sint-Amandsberg
oak, with modern polychromy; sockel dates from last quarter of the nineteenth century (*Werken en Kerken*)
h. 89.5 cm

The group is set on a polygonal sockel bearing a shield painted with Saint Michael slaying the dragon.

Bibliography
Werken en Kerken: 750 jaar begijnhofleven te Gent. (exh. cat.) (Ghent: Stad Gent, 1984), p. 235, cat. no. 377.

No. 76   *Pietà*   Plate 68

Sint-Pieters-Kapelle / comm. Herne / arr. Nivelles / prov. Brabant / B.
Sint-Pieterskerk, north side aisle
oak, with polychromy
h. 87 cm (*Ars Sacra*); h. 108 cm (*La Madone*)

Bibliography
E.J. Soil de Moriamé, *Inventaire des Objects d'Art et d'Antiquité existant dans les Edifices publics des communes de l'arrondissement judiciaire de Tournai*, vol. 6 (Charleroi: Imprimerie Provinciale, 1926), p. 158, no. 1215.
Trésors d'art du Hainaut (exh. cat.) (Mons, 1953), p. 74, cat. no. 94.
Catalogue d'exposition d'arts religieux (exh. cat.) (Tournai, 1958), pp. 20-21.
La Madone dans l'Art en Hainaut (exh. cat.) (Tournai: Cathédrale de Tournai, 1960), 2nd ed., cat. no. 11; 1st ed. cat. no. 13.
de Borchgrave d'Altena (1965), p. 14.
de Borchgrave d'Altena and Mambour (1974), pp. 9-10, illus.
Ars Sacra: Inventaris en beschrijving van kerkelijke kunstschatten in het Pajottenland (exh. cat.) (Sint-Kwintens-Lennik: Kulturele Kring 'Andreas Masius,' 1975), pp. 63 and 64, plate 38.
B. Roobaert, ''De Sint-Pieterskerk van Herne (1580-1628),'' *Het oude land van Edingen en omliggende* 15 (1987), pp. 57-66.

No. 77   *Pietà*   Plate 69

Sint-Truiden / comm. Sint-Truiden / arr. Hasselt / prov. Limburg / B.
Minderbroederskerk
wood, with polychromy

Bibliography
1000 Jaar kerkelijke kunst in Limburg (exh. cat.) (Hasselt: Provinciaal Begijnhof, 1961), p. 25, cat. no. 75.

No. 78   *Pietà* with sword and seven medallions   Plate 70

Sint-Truiden / comm. Sint-Truiden / arr. Hasselt / prov. Limburg / B.
Minderbroedersklooster
wood, with new polychromy
h. circa 127 cm (including medallions)

Bibliography
Devigne (1932) plate XLVI, fig. 217.
Honderd Limburgse Madonnas (1953), p. 25, cat. no. 77.
1000 Jaar kerkelijke kunst in Limburg (exh. cat.) (Hasselt: Provinciaal Begijnhof, 1961), cat. no. 131.

Gewijde kunst in Limburgs bezit (exh. cat.) (Hasselt: Provinciaal Begijnhof, 1966), p. 29, cat. no. 24.
Laat-gotische beeldsnijkunst (1990), inv. no. 490.

No. 79   *Pietà*   Plate 71

Sint-Truiden / comm. Sint-Truiden / arr. Hasselt / prov. Limburg / B.
Sint-Jacobskerk te Schuurhoven (originally in the parish church of Guvelingen)
wood, with new polychromy
h. 59 cm (*Beeldsnijkunst*); h. 94 cm (*Fotorepertorium*)

There is some confusion surrounding the precise date that this *Pietà* was moved to Sint-Jacobskerk after the church in Guvelingen burned. It was already in Sint-Jacobs in 1966 (*Gewijde Kunst in Limburgs bezit*) and perhaps as early as 1942-43.

Bibliography
de Borchgrave d'Altena (1942-43),p. 270, fig. 22.
G. Boes, "L'Eglise de Guvelingen près de St-Trond," *Revue belge d'Archéologie et d'Histoire de l'art* 17 (1947 / 48), pp. 107-18,. esp. p. 118 and fig. 11.
Honderd Limburgse Madonnas (1953), p. 24, cat. no. 70.
de Borchgrave d'Altena (1963), pp. 165-66.
Gewijde kunst in Limburgs bezit (exh. cat.) (Hasselt: Provinciaal Begijnhof, 1966), p. 29, cat. no. 25.
Dusar (1970), illus. p. 179; plate 162.
Sint-Trudo's Erf (exh. cat.) (Sint-Truiden: Klein-Seminarie, 1970), pp. 89-90, cat. no. 14.
Fotorepertorium, Sint-Truiden (1977), p. 64.
Kerkelijke kunst in Sint-Truiden (exh. cat.) (Sint-Truiden, 1984), pp. 178-79.
Laat-gotische beeldsnijkunst (1990), inv. no. 478.

No. 80   *Pietà*   Plate 72

Sint-Truiden / comm. Sint-Truiden / arr. Hasselt / prov. Limburg / B.
Sint-Martinuskerk, south nave wall eastern bay
wood, with polychromy

Bibliography
Fotorepertorium, Sint-Truiden (1977), p. 66.

No. 81   *Pietà*   Plates 73-74

Sittard / prov. Limburg / Nl.
Dominicanessenklooster Sint-Agnetenberg
oak, polychromy missing
h. 80 cm

This *Pietà* is discussed above in chapter 6, pp.xx-xx. Bouvy compared it to the *Pietà* from the church in Roermond (cf. Bouvy, fig. 298).

Bibliography
Devigne (1932), fig. 205, plate XLIII.
Maria in de Kunst: Kloostergang der Basiliek van Onze Lieve Vrouwe (exh. cat.), Internationaal Maria Congres 1947 (Maastricht: N.p., n.d. [1947]), cat. no. 48.
D.P.R.A. Bouvy, *Middeleeuwsche Beeldhouwkunst in de Noordelijke Nederlanden* (Amsterdam: A.A. Balkema, 1947), p. 187.
De Nederlandsche Monumenten van Geschiedenis en Kunst. vol. 4 / Part 2: *De Provincie Limburg* (The Hague: Algemeene Landsdrukkerij, 1937), p. 220, fig. 458.
1000 Jaar kerkelijke kunst in Limburg (exh. cat.) (Hasselt: Provinciaal Begijnhof, 1961), cat. no. 62, illus.
Rosa mystica (exh. cat.) (Sittard: Alberts' Drukkerijen, 1975), p. 21, cat. no. 29.
J.J.M. Timmers, *De kunst van het Maasland*, vol. 2: *De gotiek en de renaissance* (Assen: Van Gorcum, 1980), p. 159.

No. 82   *Pietà*   ex voto funerary relief with Virgin of Sorrows,   Plate 75
Saint Nicholas, and a kneeling donor

Soignies / comm. and arr. Soignies / prov. Hainaut / B.
Eglise Saint-Vincent
marble or alabaster (?)
h. 240 cm

The figure is Nicholas de Hosnont, deceased circa 1633.

Bibliography
A.C.L. 56269 A, Notes on file.

No. 83   *Pietà*   Plate 76

Tienen / comm. Tienen / arr. Leuven / prov. Brabant / B.
Kerk van Onze-Lieve-Vrouw-ten-Poel (stolen in 1970)
wood, with polychromy

Bibliography
A.C.L. 76026 B, Notes on file.

No. 84   *Pietà*   Plate 77

Tongeren / comm. and arr. Tongeren / prov. Limburg / B.
Minderbroedersklooster (formerly on a house in the beguinage of Saint Catherine in Tongeren)
wood, with neo-Gothic polychromy; crown not original (*Beeldsnijkunst*)
h. 41 cm

This *Pietà* is discussed above in chapter 6, pp.xx-xx. Paquay first noted that this statue came from a niche of a house of an adjacent street, Bredestraat. It was transferred before 1913 to the Minderbroedersklooster (*Het Catharinabegijnhof*). See also the Vreren *Pietà*, Inv. no. 99, which was reportedly brought to the beguinage at the end of the seventeenth century for a period.

Bibliography
J. Paquay, ''Tongres. Monographie illustrée,'' *Bulletin de la Société Scientifique et Littéraire du Limbourg* 30 (1912), p. 36.
Honderd Limburgse Madonnas (1953), as unnumbered image after cat. no. 77.
Het Catharinabegijnhof te Tongeren (exh. cat.), Kunst en Oudheden in Limburg, no. 11 (Sint-Truiden: Provinciaal Museum, 1975), p. 21, cat. no. 17, illus. 6.
Laat-gotische beeldsnijkunst (1990), inv. no. 546.

No. 85   *Pietà*   Plates 78-80

Tongeren / comm. and arr. Tongeren / prov. Limburg / B.
Onze-Lieve-Vrouw-Geboortekerk, north nave aisle
wood, recent neo-Gothic polychromy (red garments with small golden border and blue mantel); restored in 1953 by E.H. Claesen
h. 109 cm

This *Pietà* has long been considered one of the oldest in Belgium and most discussion has therefore centered on comparison with German prototypes (cf. de Borchgrave d'Altena and Steyaert). For pre-restoration photographs see Devigne and A.C.L. 60456 B. Ooms cites Van Mierlo's transcription of the text along the border of the Virgin's garment: "O ghi allen die bi den weghe lijdt, merct ende ansiet oft daer es rouwe di gelickt minen rouwen."

It had been placed in the Romanesque cloister and is now situated in a chapel on the north side aisle of the nave. The church burned in 1677.

Bibliography

Jean Paquay, *Monographie illustrée de la Collégiale Notre-Dame à Tongres* (Tongeren: Imprimerie Collée, 1911), pp. 48-52.

Julius Baum, "Die Lütticher Bildnerkunst im 14. Jahrhundert," in *Belgische Kunstdenkmäler*, vol. 1, edited by Paul Clemen (Munich: Bruckmann, 1923), p. 177.

Joseph de Borchgrave d'Altena, *Notes et Documents pour servir à l'histoire de l'art et de l'iconographie en Belgique. 1re série. Sculptures conservées au Pays Mosan* (Verviers: G. Leens, 1926), pp. 89-95, fig. 52.

Devigne (1932), p. 141, 248, fig. 200.

de Borchgrave d'Altena (1942-43), pp. 265, fig. 2.

Maria in de Kunst: Kloostergang der Basiliek van Onze Lieve Vrouwe (exh. cat.), Internationaal Maria Congres 1947 (Maastricht: N.p., n.d. [1947]), cat. no. 47.

J.J.M. Timmers, *Houten Beelden. De houtsculptuur in de noordelijke Nederlanden tijdens de late middeleeuwen* (Amsterdam and Antwerp: Contact, 1949), pp. 14 and 71, figs. 6 and 7

Ooms (1959), pp. 184-85, illus.

Wolfgang Krönig, "Rheinische Vesperbilder aus Leder und ihr Umkreis," *Westdeutscher Jahrbuch für Kunstgeschichte* 24 (1962), pp. 133-34, fig. 70.

de Borchgrave d'Altena (1965), pp. 4-5, fig. 3.

Dusar (1970), p. 170.

Fotorepertorium, Tongeren (1976).

Steyaert (1981), pp. 19-20.

J.E. Ziegler, "The Medieval Virgin as Object: Art or Anthropology?" *Historical Reflections / Réflexions Historiques* 16 / 2-3 (1989), pp. 251-64.

Laat-gotische beeldsnijkunst (1990), inv. no. 561.

No. 86   *Pietà*, epitaph in relief   Plate 81

Tongeren / comm. and arr. Tongeren / prov. Limburg / B.
Onze-Lieve-Vrouw-Geboortekerk, in cloister

Funerary monument for Houbrecht van de Liebaert (1528) with, as identified by *Beeldsnijkunst*, Saint Hubert in the upper register and a *Pietà* in the lower. To the right of the Virgin is the deceased in prayer with Saint Hubert and to her left a nobleman (Sebastian?) with a cross-bow.

Bibliography
Devigne (1932), fig. 198.
Dusar (1970), p. 170.
Sint-Hubertus in Limburgse bedehuizen. Tentoonstelling te As in de Sint-Aldegondiskerk (exh. cat.), Kunst en Oudheden in Limburg, no. 1 (Hasselt: Provinciaal Begijnhof, 1972), cat. no. 3.
Laat-gotische beeldsnijkunst (1990), inv. no. 573.

No. 87   *Pietà*

Tongeren / comm. and arr. Tongeren / prov. Limburg / B.
Onze-Lieve-Vrouw-Geboortekerk, Treasury
alabaster
h. 65 cm

Bibliography
Mechelen 4 eeuwen aartsbisschoppelijke stad (exh. cat.) (Mechelen: De Eendract, 1961), p. 192, cat. no. 940.
Gids voor de Schatkamer (N.p., n.d.), cat. no. 49, typescript.

No. 88   *Pietà*   Plate 82

Tongeren / comm. and arr. Tongeren / prov. Limburg / B.
Sint-Jan Baptistkerk
wood, with polychromy
h. 70 cm

Paquay says the statue, a "miraculous statue", came from the convent of the regular canons of Ter-Nood-Gods at Tongeren and that a confraternity of the Seven Sorrows of the Virgin was established on 3 April 1500 (cf. Persoons); during the French occupation, when the Augustinian convent was sold, the statue was brought to safety and hidden in "De Kat," a brewery (Ooms). Pope Pius VII authorized the transfer of the statue to Sint-Jan on 26 April 1804.

Bibliography
Jean Paquay, "Tongres: Monographie Illustrée," *Bulletin de la Société Scientifique et Littéraire du Limbourg* 31 (1913), pp. 58-63.
Ooms (1959), pp. 185-86, illus. p. 184.
Fotorepertorium, Tongeren (1976), pp. 65-67.

References
E. Persoons, "Prieuré de Ter-Nood-Gods à Tongres," *Monasticon Belge*, vol. 6: *Province de Limbourg* (Liège: Centre national de Recherches d'histoire religieuse, 1976), pp. 267-76.

No. 89   *Pietà*   Plate 83

Tournai / comm. and arr. Tournai / prov. Hainaut / B.
Couvent des Soeurs Noires
wood, with modern polychromy
h. 26.5 cm (A.C.L.); h. 28 cm (*Trésors Sacrés*)

This *Pietà* would have to be cleaned with care due to its exceptionally heavy modelling and many layers of pigment.

Bibliography
A.C.L. 108883 M, Notes on file.
La Madone dans l'Art en Hainaut (exh. cat.) (Tournai: Cathédrale de Tournai, 1960), p. 27, cat. no. 52.
Trésors Sacrés des églises et couvents de Tournai (exh. cat.) (Tournai: Trésor et Archives de la Cathédrale, 1973), p. 92, cat. no. 203.
de Borchgrave d'Altena and Mambour (1974), p. 16, illus.

No. 90   *Pietà*   Plate 84

Veltem-Beisem / comm. Herent / arr. Leuven / prov. Brabant / B.
Sint-Laurentiuskerk
oak, with recent polychromy
h. 132 cm

Bibliography
A.C.L. 83994 A, Notes on file.
de Borchgrave d'Altena (1942-43), p. 270.

No. 91   *Pietà*

Venlo / prov. Limburg / Nl.
Sint-Martinuskerk
stone
h. 74 cm

Bibliography
De Nederlandsche Monumenten van Geschiedenis en Kunst, vol. 5 / part 2: *De Provincie Limburg* (The Hague: Algemeene Landsdrukkerij, 1937), p. 178 and plate 326.

No. 92   *Pietà*

Venlo / prov. Limburg / Nl.
Sint-Martinuskerk
wood
h. 74 cm

Bibliography
De Nederlandsche Monumenten van Geschiedenis en Kunst, vol. 5 / part 2: *De Provincie Limburg* (The Hague: Algemeene Landsdrukkerij, 1937), p. 179 and plate 328.

No. 93   *Pietà*

Venlo / prov. Limburg / Nl.
Sint-Nicholaaskerk
wood
h. 103 cm

Bibliography
De Nederlandsche Monumenten van Geschiedenis en Kunst, vol. 5 / part 2: *De Provincie Limburg* (The Hague: Algemeene Landsdrukkerij, 1937), p. 184 and fig. 348.

No. 94   *Pietà*

Venray / prov. Limburg / Nl.
St.-Pietersbandenkerk
h. 70.5 cm

Bibliography
De Nederlandsche Monumenten van Geschiedenis en Kunst, vol. 5 / part 2: *De Provincie Limburg* (The Hague: Algemeene Landsdrukkerij, 1937), p. 220, fig. 458.

No. 95   *Pietà*

Venray / prov. Limburg / Nl.
Ursulinenklooster ''Jerusalem''
wood
h. 69 cm; damaged

Bibliography
De Nederlandsche Monumenten van Geschiedenis en Kunst, vol. 5 / part 2: *De Provincie Limburg* (The Hague: Algemeene Landsdrukkerij, 1937), p. 228.

No. 96   *Pietà*

Venray / prov. Limburg / Nl.
Ursulinenklooster ''Jerusalem''
wood
h. 50 cm

Bibliography
De Nederlandsche Monumenten van Geschiedenis en Kunst, vol. 5 / part 2: *De Provincie Limburg* (The Hague: Algemeene Landsdrukkerij, 1937), p. 228, plate 486.

No. 97   *Pietà*

Vinalmont / comm. Wanze / arr. Huy / prov. Liège / B.
Eglise Saint-Pierre

Comenne compares this *Pietà* to the *Pietà* from the Musée d'Art religieux et d'Art mosan, originally from the Chapel of Saint-Maur in Liège (see Inv. no. 127).

Bibliography
Trésors d'art de la Hesbaye liégeoise et ses abords (exh. cat.) (Lexhy: Château de Lexhy, 1972).
La Vierge dans l'art hutois (exh. cat.) (Huy: Chapelle de Saint-Pierre, 1977).

Jacques Comenne, "Réflexions sur deux Pietàs au Pays mosan," *Leodium* 64 (1979), pp. 51-60, fig. 2.

No. 98   *Pietà*, tombstone Mais   Plate 85

Virton / comm. and arr. Virton / prov. Luxembourg / B.
Local cemetery
stone (from Grandcourt)
h. 140 cm

On the relief it is written that Jehanne, wife of Jehan Guillaume de Mais, of Virton, died 23 February 1500; her husband died in 1507. Below the *Pietà* is a scene of the carrying of the cross. The frame of the *Pietà* contains four colonnettes, two tuscan and two ionic.

Bibliography
de Borchgrave d'Altena (1965), pp. 1-19; fig. 1.

No. 99   *Pietà*   Plate 86

Vreren / comm. and arr. Tongeren / prov. Limburg / B.
Kapel van Onze-Lieve-Vrouw der Zeven Weeën of Vordkapel
terra-cotta, with polychromy (Ooms); inscription on base is "AVE MATER DOLOROSA"
h. 25 cm

Schoutens (p. 3) reports that for centuries the village of Vreren [Freeren] had a miraculous image of the Virgin, venerated as The Virgin of the Seven Sorrows. Originally it is held (no source indicated) that it stood in a wall of a building near-by a house of ill-repute. It was then found at a site where in 1669 a chapel was built in its honor, called the *capella B.M.V. in Vorda*, a short distance from the parish church of Vreren (Schoutens, p. 4). The chapel became a pilgrimage site with a cult, mostly to revive stillborn children (cf. Helshoven *Pietà*, Inv. no. 32), with examples of miracles reported in 1730-1750 (Schoutens, p. 4-14). The cult was still active at the time of publication (i.e., 1878).
Ooms elaborates on Schoutens' information by saying that the miraculous transfer of the statue took place during the night and it was found in a tree on the site of the future chapel. The new chapel was built through the Lord of Vreren. Ooms also reports (p. 191) more occurances around and movements of the sculpture — that the

miraculous image was brought to safety in the beguinage in Tongeren (cf. Tongeren, Saint Catherine Beguinage *Pietà*, Inv. no. 84) during the period of fighting between the German Empire and the French in 1688 and that two Beguines from Tongeren brought the statue to the gate to Liège where two girls from Vreren brought it back to the chapel. Ooms claims that the statue was repaired during World War I to celebrate its 250th anniversary and again in 1945. At this time it was transferred inside from the gable of the outside of the chapel. At the time Ooms writes there is a replica in the niche.

On 12 November 1816 Pope Paul VII accorded a full indulgence to the faithful who on certain days made the pilgrimage; for the surrounding villages this happens during the month of May (Ooms, 192).

Bibliography
Ooms (1959), pp. 190-92.
Stephanus Schoutens, *Onze-Lieve-Vrouw der Zeven Weeën of van Vordkapel te Freeren* (Sint-Truiden, 1878), pp. 3-14.

No. 100   *Pietà*   Plate 87

Vreren / comm. and arr. Tongeren / prov. Limburg / B.
Sint-Medarduskerk
oak
h. 90 cm

Fotorepertorium records that this *Pietà* came originally from the Onze-Lieve-Vrouw van Zeven Smarten kapel.

Bibliography
Honderd Limburgse Madonnas (1953), n. 119.
Fotorepertorium, Tongeren (1976), pp. 80-81.

No. 101   *Pietà*   Plates 88-89

Waremme / comm. and arr. Waremme / prov. Liège / B.
Eglise Saint-Pierre
oak, with neo-Gothic polychromy
h. 86 cm

The polychromy of this *Pietà* has been altered, although there exists no published record of it. Compare plates 88, 89.

Bibliography
Catalogue de l'exposition de l'art de l'ancien Pays de Liège et des anciens arts wallons (exh. cat.) (Liège, 1930), p. 102, fig. 18.
de Borchgrave d'Altena (1942-43), p. 268.
Trésors d'art de la Hesbaye liégeoise et ses abords (exh. cat.) (Lexhy: Château de Lexhy, 1972), p. 129.
Trésors d'Art et d'Histoire de Waremme et de sa région (exh. cat.) (Liège: Soledi, 1979), pp. 137-38, cat. no. 163, fig. 82.

No. 102   *Pietà*

Wellen / comm. Wellen / arr. Tongeren / prov. Limburg / B.
Sint-Jan Baptistkerk
h. 110 cm

De Borchgrave d'Altena compared this *Pietà* to a sculpted group of the *Trinity* from the private collection Henrijean (see References).

Bibliography
Catalogue de l'exposition de l'art de l'ancien Pays de Liège et des anciens arts wallons (exh. cat.) (Liège, 1930), fig. 22.
Joseph de Borchgrave d'Altena, ''Notes au sujet de sculptures conservées à Wellen,'' *Leodium* 26 / 1 (1933), p. 12, fig. 9.
de Borchgrave d'Altena (1942-43), p. 268.

References
G. Terme, *Exposition de l'art ancien au pays de Liège: Catalogue général*, vol. 1 (exh. cat.) (Liège: Aug. Bénard, 1905), cat. no. 1362; vol. 2, Plate 5.

No. 103   *Pietà* in retable altar   Plate 90

Winamplanche / comm. Spa / arr. Verviers / prov. Liège / B.
Eglise Saint-André
wood, with polychromy
h. 135 cm (to crown of thorns)

The *Pietà* is placed in a large retable altar probably dedicated to *Notre-Dame du Rosaire*. The altar dates from around 1640 and originally comes from the chapel of Saint-Géréon in Malmédy (*Trésors*, p. 120). The Virgin is accompanied by four putti heads and a series of reliefs of the fifteen mysteries (A.C.L.). When the furniture from the old chapel was moved in 1859 to the new church, the tabernacle was purchased from the church of Sart and the *Pietà* was purchased, although the place from which it was acquired is not known (*Trésors*, p. 120).

Bibliography
A.C.L., Notes on file.
Trésors d'art religieux au marquisat de Franchimont (exh. cat.) (Liège: Soledi, 1971), p. 118, cat. no. 56, p. 120, cat. no. 59.

References
J. Bastin, "L'ancienne église de Saint-Géréon à Malmédy," *Cahiers Ardennais* (1938), pp. 161-62.

No. 104   *Pietà*   Plates 91-93

Winterslag / comm. Genk / arr. Hasselt / prov. Limburg / B.
Kapel van Onze-Lieve-Vrouw (formerly in the now lost Kapel Onze-Lieve-Vrouw-van-Rust)
oak, with lost polychromy; hollow in the back covered before 1933; restored in 1949 by R. Mailleux of Genk; with additions of other kinds of wood (*Heidebloemke*)
h. 74 cm

Older studies stress the cult situation of this *Pietà*. Ooms, for example, says that earlier there were two cross-bowmen guilds [*schuttersgilden*] and that each built its own chapel (cf. the *Pietà* of Ginderbuiten, Leuven, Stadmuseum, Inv. no. 123). The guild in the Benedenstraat built the chapel, probably in the early nineteenth century, dedicated to Onze-Lieve-Vrouw-van-Rust (*Heidebloemke*, p. 276), where the statue stood above the altar in a niche. However, the statue is certainly older than the chapel. The *Pietà* was transferred to its present location in 1948 (*Heidebloemke*, p. 276). The *Pietà* was venerated, Ooms claims, by the sick, destitute, mothers in fear for the lives of their children, and above all by epileptics and victims of mental disorders; there is a cure of a mentally ill child associated with the *Pietà*.
Originally there would have been a sword through Mary's breast and traces of the sword in her left hand, which was removed during the restoration of 1948 (*Heidebloemke*, p. 277). The article of 1980 also reveals that the oldest inhabitants recall the statue named as the Moeder der Smarten and that the name Onze-Lieve-Vrouw-van-Rust is accidental, and probably happened under the influence of the devotional statue of Onze-Lieve-Vrouw-van-Rust in Heppeneert (*Heidebloemke*, p. 277).

The article published in *Heidebloemke Genk* gives a comprehensive description of the present condition of the statue and repairs and alterations to it. The original chapel disappeared in 1950 but people still surround the *Pietà* with flowers in May.

Recent publication (*Beeldsnijkunst*) stresses the stylistic affiliation of this *Pietà* with the *Schöne* style of Bohemia and compares this sculpture with others in the southern Low Countries based on the same models (Diest Stedelijk Museum, Maastricht Onze-Lieve-Vrouwekerk, and Leuven Stadsmuseum, Inv. nos. 116, 57, and 123).

Bibliography

P. Roomen, "De kapel van O.-L.-V. ter Rust Winterslag (Genk)," *Limburg* 15 (1933-34), pp. 73-75.
Ooms (1959), pp. 58-59.
Fotorepertorium, Genk (1979), pp. 19-20.
"Kapel O.-L.-V. Van Rust," *Heidebloemke Genk* 39 / 3&4 (1980), pp. 265-80.
Laat-gotische beeldsnijkunst (1990), cat. no. 6, inv. no. 131.

No. 105   *Pietà*

Zammelen / comm. Kortessem / arr. Tongeren / prov. Limburg / B.
Kapel van Onze-Lieve-Vrouw van Bijstand
modern polychromy, with inscription on the base which reads, "VERTROOSTERSSE DER VERDRUCKTEN BIDT VOOR ONS."

Ooms reports that the rural chapel was built in 1801 and that on the altar stood this old *Pietà*. He says the statue may be related to the convent of the Sepulcrines or Bonnefanten in Tongeren; that when the convent was suppressed by the French in 1798, perhaps one of the sisters, Mother Isabella Mellemans, fled with the statue and on her way home to Ulbeek left it behind with one or another of the farmers who lived on her property in Jesseren. The cult venerating the statue was still active when Ooms published his study in 1959.

Bibliography
Ooms (1959), pp. 193-94.

No. 106   *Pietà*   Plate 94

Zepperen / comm. Sint-Truiden / arr. Hasselt / prov. Limburg / B.
Sint-Genovevakerk, east wall of north transept
wood, with modern polychromy
h. 118 cm

Bibliography

G. Terme, *Exposition de l'art ancien au pays de Liège: Catalogue général*, vol. 1 (exh. cat.) (Liège: Aug. Bénard, 1905), cat. no. 169.

Catalogue de l'exposition de l'art de l'ancien Pays de Liège et des anciens arts wallons (exh. cat.) (Liège, 1930), cat. no. 412.

Joseph de Borchgrave d'Altena, *A propos de l'Exposition 'Les Madones du Limbourg'* (Brussels: Ballieu, 1936), p. 16, fig. 46.

Honderd Limburgse Madonnas (1953), p. 24, cat. no. 68.

Fotorepertorium, Sint-Truiden (1977), p. 77.

Laat-gotische beeldsnijkunst (1990), inv. no. 520.

No. 107　　*Pietà*　　Plate 95

Zichem / comm. Scherpenheuvel-Zichem / arr. Leuven / prov. Brabant / B.
Sint-Eustachiuskerk
wood
h. 64 cm

Bibliography

Joseph de Borchgrave d'Altena, *Notes pour servir à l'inventaire des oeuvres d'art du Brabant: arrondissement de Bruxelles* (Brussels: Lesigne, 1947), p. 223.

No. 108　　*Pietà*

Zonhoven / comm. Zonhoven / arr. Hasselt / prov. Limburg / B.
Kapel Ter Donk
lindenwood, with polychromy removed
h. 49 cm

Bibliography

Het hart van Zonhoven. Album met commentaar, samengesteld naar aanleiding van 200 jaar Sint-Quintinuskerk en Gemeentehuis (1788) (Zonhoven: Gemeentebestuur, 1988), pp. 176-77.

Laat-gotische beeldsnijkunst (1990), inv. no. 642.

No. 109　　*Pietà*　　Plate 96

Zoutleeuw / comm. Zoutleeuw / arr. Leuven / prov. Brabant / B.
Sint-Leonarduskerk

wood, with polychromy; restored in 1917
h. 112.5 cm (A.C.L.); h. 115 cm (Vandeput)

Bibliography
A.C.L.35093 E, 70104 B, and 18847 B, Notes on file.
de Borchgrave d'Altena (1942-43), pp. 267 and 269, fig. 6.
de Borchgrave d'Altena (1965), p. 11.
E. Vandeput, *De Sint-Leonarduskerk. Hart van Zoutleeuw* (Zoutleeuw, 1978), 2nd ed.
(Zoutleeuw, 1986), p. 39, illus.

No. 110   *Pietà*   Plate 97

Zoutleeuw / comm. Zoutleeuw / arr. Leuven / prov. Brabant / B.
Sint-Leonarduskerk
wood, with polychromy
h. 92 cm

Bibliography
A.C.L. 34388 B, Notes on file.
de Borchgrave d'Altena (1942-43), p. 268, fig. 14.
E. Vandeput, *De Sint-Leonarduskerk. Hart van Zoutleeuw* (Zoutleeuw, 1978), 2nd ed.
(Zoutleeuw, 1986), p. 75, illus. p. 76.

No. 111   *Pietà*, double sided medallion with Holy Face

Antwerp / B.
Museum Mayer van den Bergh
metal
d. 6.2 cm

Used for the manufacture of metal devotional objects or pilgrims' badges (de Coo, p. 272).

Bibliography
J. De Coo, *Museum Mayer van den Bergh*, vol. 2: *Beeldhouwkunst, Plaketten, Antiek* (Antwerp: Museum Mayer van den Bergh, 1969), p. 272, cat. no. 272.

No. 112   *Pietà*

Antwerp / B.
Museum Vleeshuis
alabaster
h. 12 cm

Bibliography
Musea van Oudheden en Toegepaste Kunst, vol. 2: *Glasschildering, Beeldhouwwerk* (Deurne and Antwerp: C. Govaerts, 1948), p. 24, cat. no. 25, B 15.
Oude Mechelse Kunstnijverheden (exh. cat.) (Brussels and Mechelen: Koninklijke Musea voor Kunst en Geschiedenis, 1954), cat. no. 177.

No. 113   *Pietà*   Plate 98

Bruges / B.
Gruuthusemuseum
polychromed wood
h. 38 cm

Bibliography
de Borchgrave d'Altena (1942-43), p. 268.
Aanwijzende fotografische inventaris van de drie rechterlijke kantons Brugge, edited by Koninklijk Instituut voor het Kunstpatrimonium Brussel (Antwerp: De Sikkel, 1965), p. 275.
Valentin Vermeersch, *Gids Gruuthuse museum: Stedelijk Museum voor Oudheidkunde en Toegepaste kunsten* (Bruges: Gruuthuse Museum, 1979), p. 120, cat. no. 102.

No. 114   *Pietà*   Plate 99

Bruges / B.
Sint-Janshospitaal
oak
h. 67 cm, the left arm of Christ and part of forearm of Mary broken

It is not unlikely that this *Pietà* originally came from one of Bruges' hospitals or the beguinage, the possessions of which were passed on to the Burgelijke Godshuizen ("O.C.M.W.", the present owner) after the French Revolution.

Bibliography
De Madonna in de Kunst (Antwerp: Koninklijk Museum voor Schone Kunsten, 1965),
cat. no. 236.
Sint-Janshospitaal Brugges 1188/1976 (exh. cat.), vol. 2 (Bruges: Sint-Janshospitaal,
1976), pp. 461-62, cat. no. B. 13.

No. 115   *Pietà*   Plate 100

Brussels / B.
Musée Royal des Beaux-Arts / Koninklijk Museum voor Schone Kunsten, Inv. no. 3705
marble
h. 25 cm

Bibliography
A.C.L. 186174 B, Notes on file.

No. 116   *Pietà*   Plate 101

Diest / B.
Stedelijk Museum (formerly in the Beguinage Church)
wood, modern polychromy removed during 1956 restoration (*Kunstschatten*, p. 73)
h. 82 cm

This *Pietà* is discussed above in chapter 6, pp.xx-xx.

Bibliography
de Borchgrave d'Altena (1942-43), p. 266.
Joseph de Borchgrave d'Altena, *Notes pour servir à l'Inventaire des Oeuvres d'Art du
Brabant: Arrondissement de Bruxelles* (Brussels: Lesigne, 1947) p. 209.
de Borchgrave d'Altena (1963), p. 93.
Bondige inventaris der kunstvoorwerpen van het arrondissement Leuven (Leuven:
Koninklijke Commissie voor Monumenten en Landschappen, 1961), p. 36.
Schatten der Begijnhoven (exh. cat.) (Ghent: Snoeck-Ducaju & Zoon, 1961), p. 68,
cat. no. 81.
de Borchgrave d'Altena (1965), p. 6.
Kunstschatten uit het Diestse Begijnhof (exh. cat.) (Diest: Stedelijk Museum, 1988),
pp. 73-75, cat. no. 45.

N.B. All references cited in the above bibliography to H. Kunze, *Die gotische Skulptur
in Mitteldeutschland* (Bonn: Friedrich Cohen, 1925) p. 266 should be ignored. There
is no reference to this *Pietà* in his study.

No. 117   *Pietà*   Plate 102

Ghent / B.
Museum voor Schone Kunsten
alabaster
h. 26 cm

Bibliography
A.C.L. 77437 B, Notes on file (with no. 1914 G.W.).
G. Chabot, *Gids van het Museum voor Schone Kunsten Gent* (Ghent: N.p., 1956),
typescript.

No. 118   *Pietà*, with donors   Plate 103

Ghent / B.
Museum voor Schone Kunsten
Tournai stone, with original polychromy; the inside of Mary's mantel was blue-green
(Konrad, p. XIII)
h. 64.5 cm

Purchased from 1989 Velghe auction in Paris and offered to the Museum by the Friends
of the Museum (*Ville de Gand*).

Bibliography
Ville de Gand. Catalogue du Musée des Beaux-Arts (Ghent: Annoot-Braeckman, Ad.
Hoste, 1909), p. 96.
Martin Konrad, *Meisterwerke der Skulptur in Flandern und Brabant*, vol. 1 (Berlin:
Imago, 1928), pp. XIII and 6, plate 47.
De vrienden van het museum van Gent. 65 jaar op de bres (exh. cat.) (Ghent: N.p.,
n.d. [1964]), p. 36, cat. no. 113, plate CXIV.

No. 119   *Pietà*

's-Hertogenbosch / Nl.
Noordbrabants Museum (formerly in Sint-Janskathedraal)
wood, with polychromy
h. 89 cm

Bibliography
Maria in ons bisdom ('s-Hertogenbosch: Provinciaal Genootschap, 1953), cat. no. 5.
Beelden uit Brabant. Laatgotische kunst uit het oude hertogbom, 1400-1520 (exh. cat.)
('s-Hertogenbosch: Noordbrabants Museum, 1971), pp. 56 and 57, fig. 45.
C. Peeters, *De Sint Janskathedraal te 's-Hertogenbosch* (The Hague: Staatsuitgeverij, 1985), p. 366.

No. 120   *Pietà*   Plate 104

Huy / comm. and arr. Huy / prov. Liège / B.
Musée Communal (originally in the Franciscan Convent)
oak

Bibliography
A.C.L. 62765 A, Notes on file.

No. 121   *Pietà*   Plate 105

Lawrence, Kansas / U.S.A.
Helen Foresman Spencer Museum of Art, University of Kansas, Lawrence, Kansas
oak
h. 92.7 cm
Gift of Allan Gerdau, no. 58.22

John Steyaert (1979) compared this *Pietà* to what he considered an early example of the type in the Sint-Janshospitaal in Bruges (Inv. no. 114) and found that it does not show the "typical stylization found in Brussels or Antwerp during the late Gothic." Closer comparisons are with *Pietàs* from Helshoven (Inv. no. 32) and Hoevezavel (Inv. no. 39).

Bibliography
Donald G. Humphrey, *Medieval Art* (exh. cat.) (Tulsa, Oklahoma: Philbrook Art Center, 1965), cat. no. 88.
Handbook of the Collection (Lawrence, Kansas: Helen Foresman Spencer Museum of Art, 1978), p. 27, illus.
John Steyaert, University of Minnesota, Minneapolis, letter to Diane Cearfoss, Spencer Museum files, 1979.
Douglas Hyland and Marilyn Stokstad, eds., *Catalogue of the Sculpture Collection* (Lawrence, Kansas: Helen Foresman Spencer Museum of Art, 1981), p. 41, cat. no. 43.

Helen Foresman Spencer Museum of Art Curatorial Files, notes by John Steyaert, 23 February 1990.

No. 122   *Pietà*   Plate 106

Leuven / B.
Stedelijk Museum, Inv. no. B 673
oak, with polychromy
h. 57 cm

Purchased by the Stedelijk Museum in 1964 through the financial intermediary of the "Vereniging voor de Verrijking van het Kunstpatrimonium" (*Aanwinsten*). There is no additional information published in the catalogue or inventories.

Bibliography
Aanwinsten der Provinciale en Gemeentelijke Musea 1945-1967 (exh. cat.) (Ghent: Snoeck-Ducaju & Zoon, 1967), p. 80, cat. no. 78. For an exhibition held in Brussels at the Paleis voor Schone Kunsten, 13 January - 25 February 1968 [sic].

No. 123   *Pietà*   Plates 107-108

Leuven / B.
Stedelijk Museum, Inv. no. C / 6 (originally in the Kapel van Onze-Lieve-Vrouw van Ginderbuiten te Leuven)
oak, restored at the museum in Leuven in 1969 when neo-Gothic paint layers were removed; old polychromy discovered underneath; Christ's left arm and part of rock restored in the nineteenth century (Steyaert, n. 2); wood block hollowed out on the back side (*Erasmus en Leuven*)
h. 132.5 cm

This *Pietà* received unusually comprehensive scholarly treatment, compared to others in the southern Low Countries, by John Steyaert in 1981. He rightly argued there that this "*Pietà* holds a particularly important place among Netherlandish examples, firstly, because it can be precisely dated. Its provenance and original function are fully established for, until the time of the French Revolution, it served as central cult image in the Crossbowmens' Guild chapel of Onze-Lieve-Vrouw-van-Ginderbuiten in Leuven" (p. 16; and Smeyers). Steyaert dated the sculpture to circa 1365, established it as Calvary *Pietà* type with roots in mid-Trecento painting in Italy (p. 21), and discussed its influence on regional types (p. 24). He noted the cult of the Seven Sorrows of Mary, instituted in the chapel in 1494, as among the earliest appearance of the cult in Europe (p. 22) and related the sculpture as narrative to Rogier van der Weyden's *Deposition* (now in Prado, Madrid *Het Laatgotische beeldsnijcentrum Leuven*, p. 58) (painted around 1435 for the Chapel and once sited on one its altars) (p. 23). Steyaert says that it was probably at this time that the swords were added to the statue; "a small aperture at her right side testifies to the original location of this adjunct, which has since been removed" (n. 25).

During the French Revolution the *Pietà* was confiscated and placed on deposit in Leuven; since 1802 it was placed by the city in Sint-Pieterskerk; and from 1965 in the museum (*Erasmus en Leuven*, p. 56). Van Even (p. 365) says that it was placed in a chapel of the church dedicated to the Seven Sorrows.

Compare plates 107 and 108 for various stages of additions and subtractions of cult items.

Bibliography
E. Van Even, *Louvain monumental ou description historique et artistique de tous les édifices civils et religieux de la dite ville* (Leuven, 1860), p. 237.

E. Van Even, *Louvain dans le passé et dans le présent* (Leuven: Auguste Fonteyn, 1895), pp. 365, 440.

Kunstwerken van de geteisterde kerken van Leuven (Leuven, 1945), p. 12, cat. no. 24.

Bondige inventaris der kunstvoorwerpen van het Arrondissement Leuven (Brussels, 1961), p. 101.

Ars Sacra Antiqua (exh. cat.) (Leuven: Stedelijk Museum, 1962), p. 47, cat. no. B/28.

J.-B. Hous, *Leuvense Kroniek (1780-1829)*, edited by J. De Kempeneer (Heverlee, 1964), p. 104.

Het werk van Rogier de la Pasture Van der Weyden (exh. cat.) (Leuven: Stedelijk Museum, 1964), Bijlage, p. 19, no. 23.

Erasmus en Leuven (exh. cat.) (Leuven: Orientaliste, 1969), pp. 55 and 56, cat. no. 38.

Het Laatgotische beeldsnijcentrum Leuven (exh. cat.) (Leuven: Stedelijk Museum, 1979) pp. 57 and 58, cat. nos. I.16 and I.17.

Steyaert (1981), pp. 15-28.

References
M. Smeyers, "De Kapel van de H. Drievuldigheid in de Sint-Pieterskerk te Leuven en het geslacht van Baussele," in *Dirk Bouts en zijn tijd* (exh. cat.) (Leuven: Stedelijk Museum, 1965), p. 503, pp. 503-08.

No. 124   *Pietà*   Plate 109

Liège / B.
Musée d'Art religieux et d'Art mosan, Inv. no. C 32 / 12 (originally from the Dominican Convent in Liège)
oak, with polychromy
h. 90 cm (Lemeunier); h. 97 cm (*Oeuvres maîtresses*)

A.C.L. notes it came from Collection Becker, Brussels (60506 B); it was assigned Cat. no. 110 in the Musée Diocésain and Inv. no. I / 48 when on deposit with the Musée Curtius.

Bibliography
A.C.L. 60506 B, 35067 A, and 4320, Notes on file.
Devigne (1932), p. 141, fig. 202.
Oeuvres maîtresses du Musée d'Art religieux et d'Art mosan (exh. cat.) (Liège, 1980), p. 54, cat. no. B 87, illus. pp. 54 and 55.
A. Lemeunier, Musée d'Art religieux et d'Art mosan de Liège, letter to author, 1988.

No. 125   *Pietà*

Liège / B.
Musée d'Art religieux et d'Art mosan, Inv. no. C 40
oak, with traces of polychromy
h. 35 cm

Bibliography
Oeuvres maîtresses du Musée d'Art religieux et d'Art mosan (exh. cat.) (Liège, 1980), B. 65.
A. Lemeunier, Musée d'Art religieux et d'Art mosan de Liège, letter to author, 1988.

No. 126   *Pietà*   Plate 110

Liège / B.
Musée d'Art religieux et d'Art mosan, Inv. no. C 106-39 (formerly Musée Diocésain, cat. no. 673)
wood, with traces of blue and gold pigment
h. 31.5 cm

Bibliography
A.C.L. 162718 B, Notes on file.
A. Lemeunier, Musée d'Art religieux et d'Art mosan de Liège, letter to author, 1988.

No. 127   *Pietà*

Liège / B.
Musée d'Art religieux et d'Art mosan, Inv. no. C 141 / 78 (from the Chapelle Saint-Maur of Liège)
h. 72 cm

Comenne compares to the *Pietà* from Vinalmont (see Inv. no. 97).

Bibliography
Jacques Comenne, "La Chapelle Saint-Maur à Liège," *Bulletin de la Commission royale des Monuments and des Sites / Bulletin van de Koninklijke Commissie voor Monumenten en Landschappen* (1979), pp. 165-83.
Jacques Comenne, "Refléxions sur deux Pietàs du Pays mosan," *Leodium* 64 (1979), pp. 7-12, 51-92, 52, fig. I.
A. Lemeunier, Musée d'Art religieux et d'Art mosan de Liège, letter to author, 1988.

No. 128   *Pietà*   Plate 111

Liège / B.
Musée Curtius, Inv. no. 54 / 6 (originally from the church of Eben-Emael)
wood, with traces of red polychromy on Christ's throat, right side, hands and feet; the Virgin wears a red gown and a blue mantel (*Aanwinsten*); left forearm and right hand of Christ restored (Didier and Krohm)
h. 38 cm

Bibliography
H. Appel, "Die Vesperbilder von Heimbach und Drove," *Jahrbuch der rheinischen Denkmalpflege* 24 (1962), pp. 187-88.
Aanwinsten der Provinciale en Gemeentelijke Musea 1945-1967 (exh. cat.) (Ghent: Snoeck-Ducaju & Zoon, 1967), cat. no. 94. For an exhibition held in Brussels at the Paleis voor Schone Kunsten, 13 January - 25 February 1968 [sic], cat. no. 94.
W. Schulten, "Die Marienklage aus Asbach," *Beiträge zur rheinische Kunstgeschichte und Denkmalpflege*, vol. 2: *Die Kunstdenkmäler des Rheinlandes* 20 (1974), p. 172.

R. Didier and R. Krohm, *Duitse middeleeuwse beeldhouwwerken in Belgische ver-zamelingen. Les sculptures médiévales allemandes dans les collections belges* (exh. cat.), Europalia 77 Bundesrepublik Deutschland (Brussels: Generale Bankmaatschappij; Société Générale de Banque, 1977), pp. 67-69, cat. no. 28.

No. 129   *Pietà*

Louvain-la-Neuve / B.
Musée de Louvain-la-Neuve, No. VH 407
wood (lindenwood?), with polychromy
h. 61 cm

Duyckaerts reports on the technical analysis of this *Pietà*. It has received radiographic and other modes of conservation investigation, such as a stratigraphic analysis of the four or five successive layers of polychromy. Duyckaerts claims that there are alterations to the figures that have "profoundly modified" the physiognomy of the original work, especially the head of the Virgin.

Bibliography
Etienne Duyckaerts, "Note sur une Pietà remaniée du musée de Louvain-la-Neuve," *Revue des Archéologues et Historiens d'art de Louvain* 20 (1987), pp. 113-18.

No. 130   *Pietà*

Maastricht / Nl.
Bonnefanten Museum, Inv. no. 308 BM
lindenwood, with traces of original polychromy
h. 108 cm

The Museum label states that the *Pietà* is on loan from the Bischoppelijk Museum Roermond and that it comes from the Franciscan Convent in Heythuizen. The *Pietà* must have been in another setting earlier, as Heythuizen was founded only in the nineteenth century (*Dictionnaire*). Close comparison has been made with the *Pietà* in Tongeren, Stedelijk Museum (Inv. no. 136).

Bibliography
Devigne (1932).
1000 Jaar kerkelijke kunst in Limburg (exh. cat.) (Hasselt: Provinciaal Begijnhof, 1961), cat. no. 90.

268

Liège et Bourgogne (exh. cat.) (Liège: Musée de l'art Wallon, 1968), p. 120, cat. no. 56.

J.J.M. Timmers, *De kunst van het Maasland*, vol. 2: *De gotiek en de renaissance* (Assen: Van Gorcum, 1980), p. 157, fig. 275.

Steyaert (1981), p. 20, no. 17.

Geloof in beelden 1984. Middeleeuwse beeldhouwwerken in het Maasland (exh. cat.) (Maastricht: Bonnefanten Museum, 1984), cat. no. 16.

Laat-gotische beeldsnijkunst (1990), cat. no. 5, inv. no. 614.

References

"Franciscaines de la Pénitence et de la Charité chrétienne de Heythuizen," in *Dictionnaire d'histoire et de géographie ecclésiastiques*, vol. 18 (Paris: Letouzey et Ané, 1977), cols. 642-44.

No. 131   *Pietà*   Plate 112

Mechelen / B.
Stadsmuseum, Inv. no. B2
wood, with modern polychromy; mark of Mechelen on the back
h. 63 cm (A.C.L.); h. 30 cm (*Kunstnijverheden*)

Formerly in the niche of a house dedicated to "de Noet Gods" on the corner of the Tuinstraatje, adjacent to the beguinage, this *Pietà* is in very bad condition. It was removed from its outdoor site by the former director of the Museum, who left no record on file (conservator). It is discussed above in chapter 6, pp.xx-xx.

Bibliography
A.C.L. 149187 B, Notes on file.
Oude Mechelse Kunstnijverheden (exh. cat.) (Brussels and Mechelen: Koninklijke Musea voor Kunst en Geschiedenis, 1954), cat. no. 67.
Steyaert (1981), p. 20.
Conservator of Museum, conversation with author, 12 November 1990.

No. 132   *Pietà*   Plate 113

Namur / B.
Musée Diocésain, Inv. no. 274 (formerly Fosses-la-Ville)
wood
h. 94 cm

Bibliography
A.C.L. 60841 B, Notes on file.
Devigne (1932), p. 249.
A. Lanotte, ''Musée diocésain et trésor de la cathédrale. Trésor d'Oignies,'' *Musées de Namur*, Musea Nostra, no. 10 (N.p, n.d.), p. 41.

No. 133   *Pietà*   Plate 114

Nivelles / B.
Museé Archéologique, Cat. no. 21
oak, with polychromy; restored
h. 120 cm

Bibliography
de Borchgrave d'Altena (1942-43), fig. 7.
Joseph de Borchgrave d'Altena, *La Passion du Christ dans la Sculpture en Belgique du XI au XVIe S* (Paris and Brussels: Editions du Cercle d'Art, 1946), pp. 54-55, fig. 24.
Kunstschatten van Brabant (exh. cat.) (Brussels: C. Van Cortenbergh, 1954), p. 65, cat. no. 139.
Gloires des Communes belges (exh. cat.) (Brussels: Jean Malvaux, 1960), p. 97, cat. no. 147.
de Borchgrave d'Altena (1965), p. 11, fig. 6.
Hommage à Roger de la Pasture-Van der Weyden 1464-1964 (exh. cat.) (Brussels: Dereume, 1964,) p. 52, illus. 55.

No. 134   *Pietà*   Plate 115

Nivelles / B.
Museé Archéologique, Cat. no. 75
oak, with traces of polychromy
h. 99 cm

See *Laatgotiek* and Didier for stylistic discussion and relation of this *Pietà* type to retables. Acquired by the Museum before 1895 (*De eeuw van Bruegel*).

Bibliography
de Borchgrave d'Altena (1942-43), p. 267, fig. 10.
Kunstschatten van Brabant (exh. cat.) (Brussels: C. Van Cortenbergh, 1954), p. 65, cat. no. 143.

R. Didier, "Christ attendant la mort au calvaire et Piëta, deux sculptures anversoises conservées à Binche," *Bulletin de la Commission des Monuments et des Sites / Bulletin van de Koninklijke Commissie voor Monumenten en Landschappen* 14 (1963), p. 74.
De eeuw van Bruegel. De schilderkunst in België in de 16de eeuw (exh. cat.) (Brussels: S.L. Laconti N.V., 1963), pp. 249-50, cat. no. 448, illus. no. 303.
Aspekten van de Laatgotiek in Brabant (exh. cat.) (Leuven: Stedelijk Museum, 1971), pp. 496-97, cat. no. NB / 9, plate NB / IX.

No. 135   *Pietà*

Sint-Truiden / B.
Museum Vrienden van de Minderbroeders
wood
h. 37 cm (?)

Bibliography
Laat-gotische beeldsnijkunst (1990), inv. no. 510.

No. 136   *Pietà*   Plates 116-117

Tongeren / B.
Stedelijk Museum (originally from the Agnetenklooster for Franciscan nuns in Tongeren)
wood, lindenwood; badly damaged
h. 108 cm

This *Pietà* is discussed above in chapter 6, pp.XX-XX.
The Agnetenklooster was founded only in 1438 and when it acquired the *Pietà* remains a mystery. The *Pietà* stood in the church of the Agnetenklooster until 1796; it was conserved in 1962 by the Nationaal Instituut voor het Kunstpatrimonium in Brussels (Stadsmuseum *Handout*). This *Pietà* has been related as a type to the *Pietà* from the Bonnefanten Museum in Maastricht. See Inv. no. 130.

Bibliography
Catalogue de l'exposition de l'art de l'ancien Pays de Liège et des anciens arts wallons (exh. cat.) (Liège, 1930).
Devigne (1932), p. 249, fig. 206, plate XLIV.
J. Paquay, "Tongres. Monographie illustrée," *Bulletin de la Société Scientifique et Littéraire du Limbourg* 31 (1913), p. 53.

Joseph de Borchgrave d'Altena, *Notes et documents pour servir à l'histoire de l'art et de l'iconographie en Belgique, 1ère Série: Sculptures conservées au Pays Mosan* (Verviers: G. Leens, 1926), pp. 89-95, fig. 53.
Oudheidkundig Inventaris der Monumenten en Kunstvoorwerpen, vol. 9 / no. 7 (Hasselt: Museum der Commissie van Openbaren Onderstand, 1935), no. 76, fig. 63.
de Borchgrave d'Altena (1942-43), pp. 265-66, fig. 1.
Wolfgang Krönig, "Rheinische Vesperbilder aus Leder und ihr Umkreis," *Westdeutches Jahrbuch für Kunstgeschichte* 24 (1962), n. 74.
de Borchgrave d'Altena (1965), pp. 6-7.
Dusar (1970), plate 163.
Steyaert (1981), p. 20.
Stadsmuseum Tongeren, Handout, Cat. no. 45, typescript.

No. 137   *Pietà*, with donor   Plate 118

Tongeren / B.
Stedelijk Museum
wood, with new polychromy; restored base (*Beeldsnijkunst*)
h. 118 cm

Beeldsnijkunst suggests that the donor may be a regular canon from the priory of Ter-Nood-Gods, which on 13 April 1500 instituted a confraternity to Our Lady of the Seven Sorrows (cf. Persoons).

Bibliography
Joseph de Borchgrave d'Altena, *Notes et documents pour servir à l'histoire de l'art et de l'iconographie en Belgique, 1ère Série: Sculptures conservées au Pays Mosan* (Verviers: G. Leens, 1926), p. 95, fig. 55.
Catalogue de l'exposition de l'art de l'ancien Pays de Liège et des anciens arts wallons (Liège, 1930), cat. no. 415.
Devigne (1932), p. 249, fig. 210.
de Borchgrave d'Altena (1942-43), fig. 12, n. 10 on p. 268.
De Madonna in de kunst (exh. cat.) (Antwerp: Koninklijk Museum voor Schone Kunsten, 1954), cat. no. 184.
de Borchgrave d'Altena (1965), p. 17.
Laat-gotische beeldsnijkunst (1990), inv. no. 615.

References
E. Persoons, "Prieuré de Ter-Nood-Gods à Tongres," *Monasticon Belge*, vol. 6: *Province de Limbourg* (Liège: Centre national de Recherches d'histoire religieuse, 1976), pp. 267-76.

272

No. 138   *Pietà*

Private Collection (l'Abbé Maffei)
See Inv. nos. 36 and 44 for comparison.

Bibliography
Joseph de Borchgrave d'Altena, *'Un Cabinet d'Amateur': A Propos des Sculptures*
(Brussels: Alphonse Ballieu, 1937), p. 71, fig. 21, no. 37.
de Borchgrave d'Altena (1942-43), p. 268.

No. 139   *Pietà*

Private Collection (Antwerp)
wood
h. 21.5 cm

Bibliography
Martin Konrad, *Meisterwerke der Skulptur in Flandern und Brabant* (Berlin: Imago
Verlagsgesellschaft M.B.H., 1928), p. XIII, plate 47 b.

No. 140   *Pietà*

Private Collection (Antwerp)
wood, with traces of polychromy
h. 47.5 cm

Bibliography
Gotische groepen uit Antwerps privé-bezit (exh. cat.), edited by Bernard Blondeel
(Antwerp: Bank Brussel Lambert, n.d.), cat. no. 30.

No. 141   *Pietà*

Private Collection (Antwerp)
h. 79 cm with original polychromy

Bibliography
Gotische groepen uit Antwerps privé-bezit (exh. cat.), edited by Bernard Blondeel
(Antwerp: Bank Brussel Lambert, n.d.), cat. no. 31.

No. 142   *Pietà*

Private Collection (Antwerp)
oak, with original polychromy
h. 96 cm

Bibliography
Gotische groepen uit Antwerps privé-bezit (exh. cat.), edited by Bernard Blondeel
(Antwerp: Bank Brussel Lambert, n.d.), cat. no. 51.

No. 143   *Pietà*   Plate 119

Liège / B.
Private Collection J.B. [J. Baijot?] (formerly located on a street corner, Thier-à-Liège)
oak, with polychromy
h. 100 cm

L'Art ancien says this object's origin is well established, that it was found at the beginning of the nineteenth century in a little aedicule at the foot of Thier-à-Liège and that
it would have come from the Benedictine priory of Saint-Léonard. A.C.L. photograph
shows the *Pietà* still on the street corner, and with an inscription on the base that says,
"NOTRE DAME DE PITIE P.P.N."

Bibliography
A.C.L. 159103 B, Notes on file.
Exposition de l'art ancien au pays de Liège (exh. cat.) (Liège: Aug. Bénard, 1905),
p. 29, cat. no. 17 with illustration.
Art ancien dans le Patrimoine Privé Liégeois (exh. cat.) (Liège: Institut Saint-Joseph,
1973), pp. 29 and 30, cat. no. 17.
J.J.M. Timmers, *De kunst van het Maasland*, vol. 2: *De gotiek en de renaissance*
(Assen: Van Gorcum, 1980), p. 159.

No. 144   *Pietà*

Private Collection (Paris, Charles Ratton)
h. 37 cm
oak, with original polychromy; Mechelen *atelier* stamp on the back

Bibliography
Willy Godenne, ''Préliminaires à l'inventaire général des statuettes d'origine malinoise, présumées des XVe et XVIe siècles,'' *Handelingen van de Koninklijke Kring voor Oudheidkunde, Letteren en Kunst van Mechelen* 73 (1969), pp. 65-66.

No. 145   *Pietà* by Conrat Meijt

Lost but mentioned in the documents

Duverger, p. 73, No. XIII: Margaret of Austria pays C. Meijt 50 philippus to make a wood *Pietà* for the Annunciatenklooster in Bruges on 7 May 1519. Duverger (p. 46) says this work remains unknown but perhaps this is the *Pietà* that was polychromed by Bernard van Orley. For the latter see Duverger, p. 74, No. XVI: Margaret pays 50 philippus of gold to Bernard van Orley a.o. to polychrome an image in wood ''de nostre Dame de pitié tenant le crucifix devant elle.''

Bibliography
Jos. Duverger, *Conrat Meijt (ca. 1480-1551)*, Académie royale de Belgique, Classe des Beaux-Arts, Mémoires in -4, no. 5 (Brussels, 1934), pp. 19, 46, 73, 110.

No. 146   *Pietà* by Walter Pompe after Andries de Nole

Antwerpen / B.
Museum Vleeshuis, Inv. no. 25A87
terra-cotta; 1725 as dated on Christ's foot
h. 54 cm

This work is believed to be based on an alabaster *Pietà*, now lost, attributed to Andries de Nole, who died in 1638. De Nole's *Pietà* was originally set against a pillar in the Houtbrekerskapel of the Onze-Lieve-Vrouwekerk in Antwerp. Casteels (p. 90) claims that the *Pietà* was destined to decorate Andries' own tomb monument. The history of Walter Pompe's sculpture is complex. Casteels (p. 92) says that the only certain thing is that a *Pietà* had been executed in the *atelier* of Robrecht-Andries and that Pompe was clearly inspired by it. She questions whether it was a replica, as some scholars have presumed, and if so, to what scale. De Borchgrave d'Altena believes that both these works were inspired by the type of *Pietà* from Saint-Jacques in Liège (Inv. no. 52).

Bibliography
A.C.L. 185873 B, Notes on file.

de Borchgrave d'Altena (1942-43), p. 268, n. 1.

Marguerite Casteels, *De Beeldhouwers de Nole te Kamerijk, te Utrecht en te Antwerpen*, Verhandelingen van de Koninklijke Vlaamse Academie voor Wetenschappen, Letteren en Schone Kunsten van België, Klasse der Schone Kunsten 16 (Brussels: Paleis der Academiën, 1961), pp. 89-92, figs. 113-14.

Léon van Liebergen, ed., *Walter Pompe beeldhouwer, 1703-1777* (exh. cat.) (Uden: Museum voor Religieuze Kunst, 1979), p. 77, cat. no. 3, plate 43.

References

Martin Konrad, *Meisterwerke der Skulptur in Flandern und Brabant* (Berlin: Imago, 1928), pp. 7-8 and plate 48.

No. 147 *Pietà* by Claus Sluter (1388-90)

Now lost, Sluter's *Pietà* has been the focus of some debate, in terms of its intended setting for the chapter room of the Carthusians of Champmol in Dijon and whether the *Pietà* in the Liebieghaus in Frankfurt am Main is a copy or a replica (*Gotische Bildwerke*).

Bibliography

J. Duverger, *Brussel als kunstcentrum in de XIVe en de XVe eeuw. Bouwstoffen tot de Nederlandsche Kunstgeschiedenis* (Antwerp: De Sikkel, 1935,) pp. 26-27.

J.S. Witsen Elias, "De Pietà's te Blaricum en te Emnes," *Mededeelingen van het museum voor het Gooi en Omstreken* (1942), n. 6.

de Borchgrave d'Altena (1942-43), p. 266.

Wolfgang Krönig, "Rheinische Vesperbilder aus Leder und ihr Umkreis," *Westdeutscher Jahrbuch für Kunstgeschichte* 24 (1962), p. 108.

Gotische Bildwerke aus dem Liebieghaus (Frankfurt am Main: Liebieghaus, 1966), inv. no. 35, cat. no. 8, illus. no. 8.

Steyaert (1981), p. 19 (n. 12), p. 21 (n. 21).

LIST OF FIGURES

LIST OF PLATES

1. Aldeneik, Sint-Annakerk (Inv. no. 1)
   copyright A.C.L. 87898 A
2. Antwerp, Klooster Gasthuiszusters Augustinessen (Inv. no. 2)
   copyright A.C.L. 180449 B
3. Bellaire, Eglise de la Visitation (Inv. no. 4), in situ, with Virgin clothed
   copyright A.C.L. 9571 A
4. Bellaire, Eglise de la Visitation (Inv. no. 4), Virgin unclothed
   copyright A.C.L. 218605 B
5. Beringen, Kerk van Sint-Pieters-Banden (Inv. no. 5), view to altar [orig.: Smeedskapel]
   copyright A.C.L. 49770 M
6. Beringen, Kerk van Sint-Pieters-Banden (Inv. no. 5) [orig.: Smeedskapel]
   copyright A.C.L. 49771 M
7. Berlingen, Kluiskapel Onze-Lieve-Vrouw van Zeven Smarten te Oetsloven, (Inv. no. 6), view to altar
   copyright A.C.L. 200552 M
8. Berlingen, Kluiskapel Onze-Lieve-Vrouw van Zeven Smarten te Oetsloven, (Inv. no. 6), Virgin clothed
   copyright A.C.L. 131897 A
9. Berlingen, Kluiskapel Onze-Lieve-Vrouw van Zeven Smarten te Oetsloven, (Inv. no. 6), detail
   copyright A.C.L. 200556 M
10. Binche, Eglise Saint-Ursmer (Inv. no. 9)
    copyright A.C.L. 153994 B
11. Bocholt, Sint-Laurentiuskerk (Inv. no. 10)
    copyright A.C.L. 35549 B
12. Bombaye, Chapelle de la Sainte-Croix (Inv. no. 11)
    copyright A.C.L. 199249 B
13. Borgloon, Kapel van Onze-Lieve-Vrouw van Smarten (Inv. no. 12), exterior
    copyright A.C.L. 200583 M
14. Borgloon, Kapel van Onze-Lieve-Vrouw van Smarten (Inv. no. 12)
    copyright A.C.L. 200582 M
15. Borgloon, Kapel van Onze-Lieve-Vrouw van Smarten (Inv. no. 12)
    copyright A.C.L. 146608 B
16. Bovigny, Eglise Saint-Martin (Inv. no. 13)
    copyright A.C.L. 17693 M
17. Bree, Sint-Michielskerk (Inv. no. 15)
18. Bruyelle, Notre-Dame d'Espoir (Inv. no. 16)
    copyright A.C.L. 71888 M

19. Bütgenbach, Eglise Saint-Etienne (Inv. no. 17)
    copyright A.C.L. 7319 A
20. Dendermonde, Onze-Lieve-Vrouwekerk (Inv. no. 18)
    copyright A.C.L. 17667 A
21. Diest, Onze-Lieve-Vrouwekerk (Inv. no. 19), general view of original in situ, Virgin clothed
    copyright A.C.L. 131889 A
22. Diest, Onze-Lieve-Vrouwekerk (Inv. no. 19), original, with polychromy, without clothes
    copyright A.C.L. 53731 A
23. Diest, Onze-Lieve-Vrouwekerk (Inv. no. 19), original (?), without polychromy
    copyright A.C.L. 259751 M
24. Diest, Onze-Lieve-Vrouwekerk (Inv. no. 19), copy
    copyright A.C.L. 173283 M
25. Duras, Kerk van Onze-Lieve-Vrouw Tenhemelopneming te Gorsem (Inv. no. 21)
    copyright A.C.L. 78019 B
26. Eksel, Kapel van Onze-Lieve-Vrouw-van-Zeven-Weeën te Hoksent (Inv. no. 22)
    copyright A.C.L. 57977
27. Ellignies, Eglise de la Sainte-Vierge (Inv. no. 23)
    copyright A.C.L. 92747 M
28. Ellignies, Eglise de la Sainte-Vierge (Inv. no. 24)
    copyright A.C.L. 92736 M
29. Ghent, Kerk der H. Geboorte (Inv. no. 28)
    copyright A.C.L. 76310 B
30. Ghent, Onze-Lieve-Vrouw-ter-Hooie (Klein Begijnhof) (Inv. no. 29)
    copyright A.C.L. 34641 B
31. Gistoux, Eglise Saint-Jean-Baptiste, Chapelle Notre-Dame des Affligés (Inv. no. 30)
    copyright A.C.L. 10341 M
32. Givry, Chapelle Notre-Dame de Pitié (Inv. no. 31)
    copyright A.C.L. 92117 A
33. Groot-Gelmen, Kapel van Onze-Lieve-Vrouw-van-Blijde-Vrede te Helshoven (Inv. no. 32), chapel exterior
34. Groot-Gelmen, Kapel van Onze-Lieve-Vrouw-van-Blijde-Vrede te Helshoven (Inv. no. 32)
35. Gruitrode, Sint-Gertrudiskerk (Inv. no. 33)
    copyright A.C.L. 45955 B
36. Hamont, Sint-Laurentiuskerk (Inv. no. 34)
    copyright A.C.L. 25579 B
37. Harchies, Eglise de la Sainte-Vierge (Inv. no. 35)
    copyright A.C.L. 92701 M
38. Hasselt, Minderbroederskerk (Inv. no. 36)
    copyright A.C.L. 72310 A
39. Hasselt, Sint-Quintinus en Onze-Lieve-Vrouwekathedraal (Inv. no. 37)
    copyright A.C.L. 70193 B
40. Hoevezavel, Onze-Lieve-Vrouwekapel (Inv. no. 39)
41. Hondelange, Chapelle du cimetière (Inv. no. 40)
    copyright A.C.L. 43096 A

42. Hondelange, Chapelle du cimetière (Inv. no. 41)
copyright A.C.L. 20799 B

43. Huy, Collège Saint-Quirin (Inv. no. 43)
copyright A.C.L. 66763 A

44. Lessines, Hôpital Notre-Dame à la Rose (Inv. no. 45)
copyright A.C.L. 10225 B

45. Leuven, Minderbroedersklooster, Kapel Onze-Lieve-Vrouw-ten-Troost of van Smarten (Inv. no. 46a), original
copyright A.C.L. 171427 B

46. Leuven, Minderbroedersklooster, Kapel Onze-Lieve-Vrouw-ten-Troost of van Smarten (Inv. no. 46b), copy
copyright A.C.L. 171428 B

47. Leuven, Sint-Gertrudiskerk (Inv. no. 47)
copyright A.C.L. 169382 B

48. Leuven, Sint-Michielskerk (Inv. no. 48)
copyright A.C.L. 166424 B

49. Leuven, Sint-Pietershopitaal (Inv. no. 49)
copyright A.C.L. 158942 B

50. Liège, Chapelle Saint-Agathe (Inv. no. 50)
copyright A.C.L. 168576 B

51. Liège, Eglise Saint-Denis (Inv. no. 51), Virgin with crown and swords
copyright A.C.L. 19254 B

52. Liège, Eglise Saint-Denis (Inv. no. 51), without crown and swords
copyright A.C.L. 153746

53. Liège, Eglise Saint-Jacques (Inv. no. 52)
copyright A.C.L. 26663 B

54. Lummen, Onze-Lieve-Vrouwekerk (Inv. no. 54)
copyright A.C.L. 89947 A

55. Mechelen, Onze-Lieve-Vrouwgasthuis (Inv. no. 61)
copyright A.C.L. 153637 M

56. Meeuwen, Kerk van Onze-Lieve-Vrouw Tenhemelopneming te Wijshagen (Inv. no. 62)
copyright A.C.L. 90863 M

57. Meldert, Sint-Willibrorduskerk (Inv. no. 63)
copyright A.C.L. 146610 B

58. Noville, Chapelle Saint-Hubert à Wicourt (Inv. no. 65)
copyright A.C.L. 78734 B

59. Opitter, Sint-Pieterskerk te Tongerlo (Inv. no. 66)
copyright A.C.L. 35596 B

60. Opitter, Sint-Trudokerk (Inv. no. 67)
copyright A.C.L. 20164 B

61. Opoeteren, Sint-Denijskerk (Inv. no. 68)
copyright A.C.L. 156826 B

62. Oudegem, Onze-Lieve-Vrouwekerk (Inv. no. 69)
copyright A.C.L. 96659 B

87. Vreren, Sint-Medarduskerk (Inv. no. 100)
copyright A.C.L. 153056 B

88. Waremme, Eglise Saint-Pierre (Inv. no. 101), with neo-Gothic polychromy
copyright A.C.L. 69989 A

89. Waremme, Eglise Saint-Pierre (Inv. no. 101), with some polychromy absent
copyright A.C.L. 144534 M

90. Winamplanche, Eglise Saint-André (Inv. no. 103)
copyright A.C.L. 66729 M

91. Winterslag, Kapel van Onze-Lieve-Vrouw (Inv. no. 104), Procession of Onze-Lieve-Vrouw-van-Rust
collection Heidebloemke

92. Winterslag, Kapel van Onze-Lieve-Vrouw (Inv. no. 104), Onze-Lieve-Vrouw-van-Rust
collection Heidebloemke

93. Winterslag, Kapel van Onze-Lieve-Vrouw (Inv. no. 104), Onze-Lieve-Vrouw-van-Rust, detail
collection Heidebloemke

94. Zepperen, Sint-Genovevakerk (Inv. no. 106)
copyright A.C.L. 73876 A

95. Zichem, Sint-Eustachiuskerk (Inv. no. 107)
copyright A.C.L. 34508 A

96. Zoutleeuw, Sint-Leonarduskerk (Inv. no. 109)
copyright A.C.L. 35093 E

97. Zoutleeuw, Sint-Leonarduskerk (Inv. no. 110)
copyright A.C.L. 34388 E

98. Bruges, Gruuthusemuseum (Inv. no. 113)
copyright A.C.L. 133754 B

99. Bruges, Sint-Janshospitaal (Inv. no. 114)
copyright A.C.L. 143137 B

100. Brussels, Musée Royal des Beaux-Arts / Koninklijk Museum voor Schone Kunsten (Inv. no. 115)
copyright A.C.L. 186174 B

101. Diest, Stedelijk Museum (Beguinage Church) (Inv. no. 116)

102. Ghent, Museum voor Schone Kunsten (Inv. no. 117)
copyright A.C.L. 77437 B

103. Ghent, Museum voor Schone Kunsten (Inv. no. 118)
copyright A.C.L. 77421 B

104. Huy, Musée Communal (Inv. no. 120)
copyright A.C.L. 62765 A

105. Lawrence, Kansas (Inv. no. 121)
Spencer Museum of Art, University of Kansas, Gift of Allan Gerdau

106. Leuven, Stedelijk Museum (Inv. no. 122)
copyright A.C.L. 205753 B

107. Leuven, Stedelijk Museum (Inv. no. 123)
copyright A.C.L. 2884 M

108. Leuven, Stedelijk Museum, Engraving circa 1552 illustrating a lottery held for the crossbowmen's guild of Leuven with *Pietà* on the high altar
copyright A.C.L. 2883 M
109. Liège, Musée d'Art religieux et d'Art mosan (Inv. no. 124)
copyright A.C.L. 43200 N
110. Liège, Musée d'Art religieux et d'Art mosan (Inv. no. 126)
copyright A.C.L. 162718 B
111. Liège, Musée Curtius (Inv. no. 128)
copyright A.C.L. 178604 B
112. Mechelen, Stadsmuseum (Inv. no. 131)
113. Namur, Musée Diocésain (Inv. no. 132)
copyright A.C.L. 106428 B
114. Nivelles, Musée Archéologique (Inv. no. 133)
copyright A.C.L. 7897 B
115. Nivelles, Musée Archéologique (Inv. no. 134)
copyright A.C.L. 7896 B
116. Tongeren, Stedelijk Museum (Inv. no. 136)
117. Tongeren, Stedelijk Museum (Inv. no. 136), detail
118. Tongeren, Stedelijk Museum (Inv. no. 137), *Pietà* with donor
119. Liège, Private Collection (Inv. no. 143)
copyright A.C.L. 159103 B

Fig. 1. Exhibition, *Les Madones du Limbourg*, Sint-Truiden, Begijnhofkerk, 1935. *Pietàs* from left to right: Opoeteren, Schuurhoven in Sint-Truiden, and Zepperen

Photo: Provinciaal Museum voor Religieuze Kunst, Begijnhof, Sint-Truiden

Fig. 2. Exhibition, *Les Madones du Limbourg*, Sint-Truiden, Begijnhofkerk, 1935. *Pietàs* from left to right: Opoeteren, Schuurhoven in Sint-Truiden

Photo: Provinciaal Museum voor Religieuze Kunst, Begijnhof, Sint-Truiden

Poort-Acker-Godshuys te Gend.
Gesticht ten jaere 1278, door de Graevin van Vlaenderen Margareta van Constantinopel.

Fig. 3. View of the Beguinage church of Poortakker in Ghent with calvary and *Pietà*,
first half of the nineteenth century, oil on paper
Ghent, Archives de la ville / Stadsarchief, Atlas Goetghebuer D 37 / F 67

Fig. 4. Lier, Beguinage, Calvary with *Pietà*, 1840
copyright A.C.L. 129483 A

1. Aldeneik, Sint-Annakerk (Inv. no. 1)
copyright A.C.L. 87898 A

2. Antwerp, Klooster Gasthuiszusters Augustinessen (Inv. no. 2)
copyright A.C.L. 180449 B

3. Bellaire, Eglise de la Visitation (Inv. no. 4), in situ, with Virgin clothed
copyright A.C.L. 9571 A

4. Bellaire, Eglise de la Visitation (Inv. no. 4), Virgin unclothed
copyright A.C.L. 218605 B

5. Beringen, Kerk van Sint-Pieters-Banden (Inv. no. 5), view to altar [orig.: Smeedskapel]
copyright A.C.L. 49770 M

6. Beringen, Kerk van Sint-Pieters-Banden (Inv. no. 5) [orig.: Smeedskapel]
copyright A.C.L. 49771 M

7. Berlingen, Kluiskapel Onze-Lieve-Vrouw van Zeven Smarten te Oetsloven,
   (Inv. no. 6), view to altar

copyright A.C.L. 200552 M

8. Berlingen, Kluiskapel Onze-Lieve-Vrouw van Zeven Smarten te Oetsloven,
   (Inv. no. 6), Virgin clothed

copyright A.C.L. 131897 A

9. Berlingen, Kluiskapel Onze-Lieve-Vrouw van Zeven Smarten te Oetsloven,
   (Inv. no. 6), detail
   copyright A.C.L. 200556 M

10. Binche, Eglise Saint-Ursmer (Inv. no. 9)
   copyright A.C.L. 153994 B

11. Bocholt, Sint-Laurentiuskerk (Inv. no. 10)
    copyright A.C.L. 35549 B

12. Bombaye, Chapelle de la Sainte-Croix (Inv. no. 11)
copyright A.C.L. 199249 B

13. Borgloon, Kapel van Onze-Lieve-Vrouw van Smarten (Inv. no. 12), exterior
copyright A.C.L. 200583 M

14. Borgloon, Kapel van Onze-Lieve-Vrouw van Smarten (Inv. no. 12)
copyright A.C.L. 200582 M

15. Borgloon, Kapel van Onze-Lieve-Vrouw van Smarten (Inv. no. 12)
copyright A.C.L. 146608 B

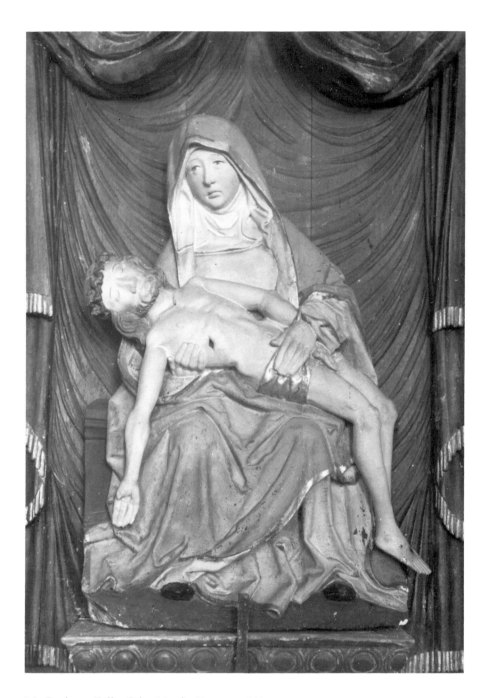

16. Bovigny, Eglise Saint-Martin (Inv. no. 13)
    copyright A.C.L. 17693 M

17. Bree, Sint-Michielskerk (Inv. no. 15)

18. Bruyelle, Notre-Dame d'Espoir (Inv. no. 16)
copyright A.C.L. 71888 M

19. Bütgenbach, Eglise Saint-Etienne (Inv. no. 17)
    copyright A.C.L. 7319 A

20. Dendermonde, Onze-Lieve-Vrouwekerk (Inv. no. 18)
copyright A.C.L. 17667 A

21. Diest, Onze-Lieve-Vrouwekerk (Inv. no. 19), general view of original in situ,
Virgin clothed

copyright A.C.L. 131889 A

22. Diest, Onze-Lieve-Vrouwekerk (Inv. no. 19), original, with polychromy,
without clothes

23. Diest, Onze-Lieve-Vrouwekerk (Inv. no. 19), original (?), without polychromy

24. Diest, Onze-Lieve-Vrouwekerk (Inv. no. 19), copy
copyright A.C.L. 173283 M

25. Duras, Kerk van Onze-Lieve-Vrouw Tenhemelopneming te Gorsem (Inv. no. 21)
copyright A.C.L. 78019 B

26. Eksel, Kapel van Onze-Lieve-Vrouw-van-Zeven-Weeën te Hoksent (Inv. no. 22)

27. Ellignies, Eglise de la Sainte-Vierge (Inv. no. 23)
copyright A.C.L. 92747 M

28. Ellignies, Eglise de la Sainte-Vierge (Inv. no. 24)
   copyright A.C.L. 92736 M

29. Ghent, Kerk der H. Geboorte (Inv. no. 28)
copyright A.C.L. 76310 B

30. Ghent, Onze-Lieve-Vrouw-ter-Hooie (Klein Begijnhof) (Inv. no. 29)
copyright A.C.L. 34641 B

31. Gistoux, Eglise Saint-Jean-Baptiste, Chapelle Notre-Dame des Affligés
(Inv. no. 30)

copyright A.C.L. 10341 M

32. Givry, Chapelle Notre-Dame de Pitié (Inv. no. 31)
copyright A.C.L. 92117 A

33. Groot-Gelmen, Kapel van Onze-Lieve-Vrouw-van-Blijde-Vrede te Helshoven
(Inv. no. 32), chapel exterior

34. Groot-Gelmen, Kapel van Onze-Lieve-Vrouw-van-Blijde-Vrede te Helshoven
(Inv. no. 32)

35. Gruitrode, Sint-Gertrudiskerk (Inv. no. 33)
copyright A.C.L. 45955 B

36. Hamont, Sint-Laurentiuskerk (Inv. no. 34)
copyright A.C.L. 25579 B

37. Harchies, Eglise de la Sainte-Vierge (Inv. no. 35)

38. Hasselt, Minderbroederskerk (Inv. no. 36)
copyright A.C.L. 72310 A

39. Hasselt, Sint-Quintinus en Onze-Lieve-Vrouwekathedraal (Inv. no. 37)
copyright A.C.L. 70193 B

40. Hoevezavel, Onze-Lieve-Vrouwekapel (Inv. no. 39)

41. Hondelange, Chapelle du cimetière (Inv. no. 40)
   copyright A.C.L. 43096 A

42. Hondelange, Chapelle du cimetière (Inv. no. 41)
copyright A.C.L. 20799 B

43. Huy, Collège Saint-Quirin (Inv. no. 43)

44. Lessines, Hôpital Notre-Dame à la Rose (Inv. no. 45)
copyright A.C.L. 10225 B

45. Leuven, Minderbroedersklooster, Kapel Onze-Lieve-Vrouw-ten-Troost of van
Smarten (Inv. no. 46a), original

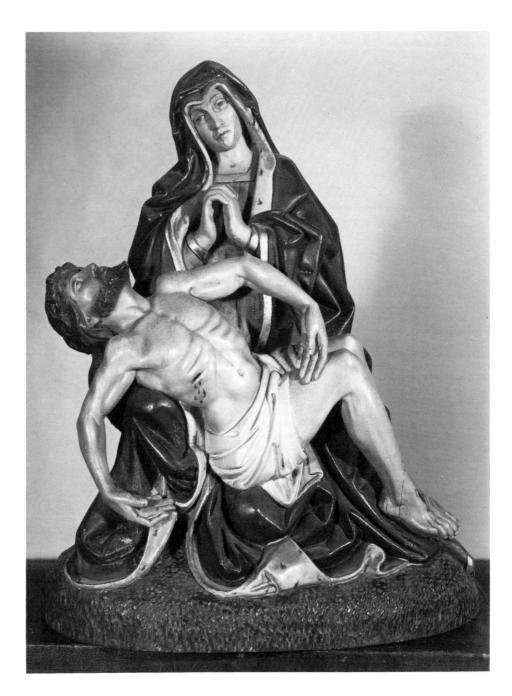

46. Leuven, Minderbroedersklooster, Kapel Onze-Lieve-Vrouw-ten-Troost of van Smarten (Inv. no. 46b), copy

copyright A.C.L. 171428 B

47. Leuven, Sint-Gertrudiskerk (Inv. no. 47)

48. Leuven, Sint-Michielskerk (Inv. no. 48)

49. Leuven, Sint-Pietershopitaal (Inv. no. 49)
   copyright A.C.L. 158942 B

50. Liège, Chapelle Saint-Agathe (Inv. no. 50)

51. Liège, Eglise Saint-Denis (Inv. no. 51), Virgin with crown and swords
copyright A.C.L. 19254 B

52. Liège, Eglise Saint-Denis (Inv. no. 51), without crown and swords
copyright A.C.L. 153746

53. Liège, Eglise Saint-Jacques (Inv. no. 52)
   copyright A.C.L. 26663 B

54. Lummen, Onze-Lieve-Vrouwekerk (Inv. no. 54)
copyright A.C.L. 89947 A

55. Mechelen, Onze-Lieve-Vrouwgasthuis (Inv. no. 61)
copyright A.C.L. 153637 M

56. Meeuwen, Kerk van Onze-Lieve-Vrouw Tenhemelopneming te Wijshagen
    (Inv. no. 62)

57. Meldert, Sint-Willibrorduskerk (Inv. no. 63)
copyright A.C.L. 146610 B

58. Noville, Chapelle Saint-Hubert à Wicourt (Inv. no. 65)
copyright A.C.L. 78734 B

59. Opitter, Sint-Pieterskerk te Tongerlo (Inv. no. 66)
copyright A.C.L. 35596 B

60. Opitter, Sint-Trudokerk (Inv. no. 67)

61. Opoeteren, Sint-Denijskerk (Inv. no. 68)
copyright A.C.L. 156826 B

62. Oudegem, Onze-Lieve-Vrouwekerk (Inv. no. 69)
copyright A.C.L. 96659 B

63. Saint-Ghislain, Eglise Saint-Ghislain (Inv. no. 71)

64. Schönberg, Eglise Saint-Georges (Inv. no. 73)

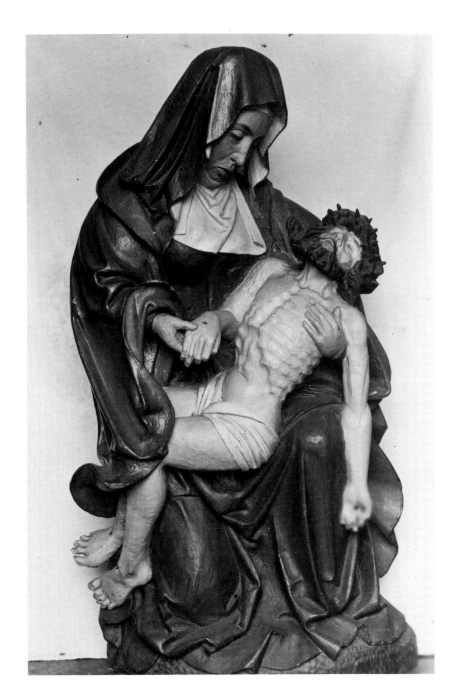

65. Schönberg, Eglise Saint-Georges (Inv. no. 73)
   copyright A.C.L. 7359 A

66. Silenrieux, Eglise Sainte-Anne (Inv. no. 74)
copyright A.C.L. 91674 B

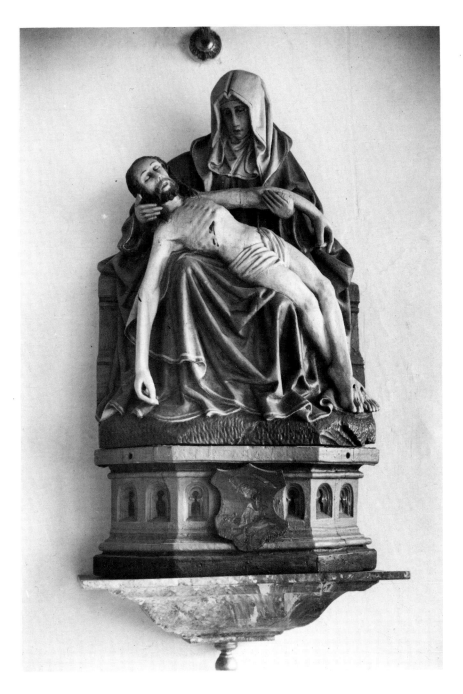

67. Sint-Amandsberg, Begijnhof (Inv. no. 75)
copyright A.C.L. 39411 B

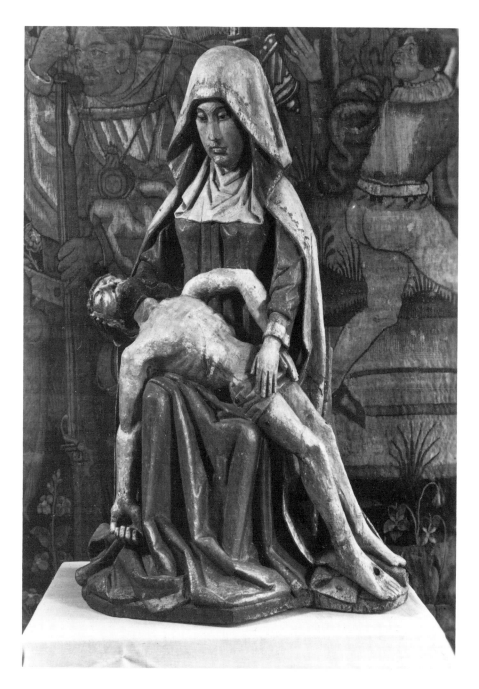

68. Sint-Pieters-Kapelle, Sint-Pieterskerk (Inv. no. 76)
   copyright A.C.L. 144786 B)

69. Sint-Truiden, Minderbroederskerk (Inv. no. 77)

70. Sint-Truiden, Minderbroedersklooster (Inv. no. 78)
copyright A.C.L. 70636 B

71. Sint-Truiden, Sint-Jacobskerk te Schuurhoven (Inv. no. 79)
copyright A.C.L. 39825 A

72. Sint-Truiden, Sint-Martinuskerk (Inv. no. 80)
   copyright A.C.L. 39830 A

73. Sittard, Dominicanessenklooster Sint-Agnetenberg (Inv. no. 81)
copyright Sittard, Gemeentearchief

74. Sittard, Dominicanessenklooster Sint-Agnetenberg (Inv. no. 81), detail
copyright Sittard, Gemeentearchief

75. Soignies, Eglise Saint-Vincent (Inv. no. 82)
copyright A.C.L. 79192 A

76. Tienen, Onze-Lieve-Vrouw-ten-Poel (Inv. no. 83)

77. Tongeren, Minderbroedersklooster (Saint Catherine Beguinage) (Inv. no. 84)

78. Tongeren, Onze-Lieve-Vrouw-Geboortekerk (Inv. no. 85), view to chapel

79. Tongeren, Onze-Lieve-Vrouw-Geboortekerk (Inv. no. 85), pre-restoration
copyright A.C.L. 7940 B

80. Tongeren, Onze-Lieve-Vrouw-Geboortekerk (Inv. no. 85), after 1953
restoration, clothed

81. Tongeren, Onze-Lieve-Vrouw-Geboortekerk (Inv. no. 86), epitaph in cloister

82. Tongeren, Sint-Jan Baptistkerk (Inv. no. 88)
copyright A.C.L. 38321 E

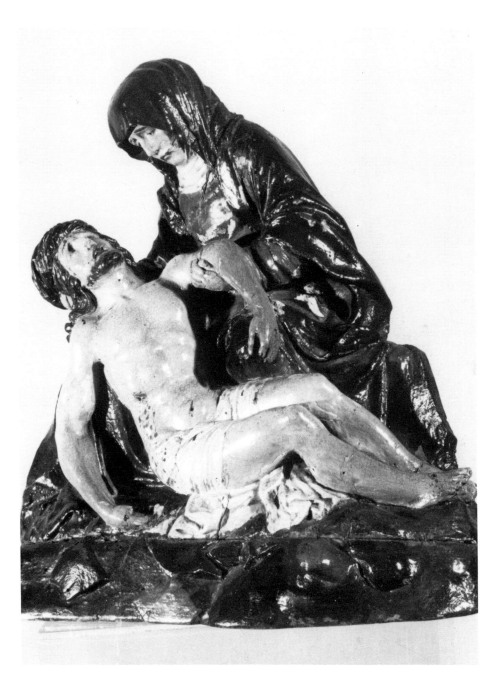

83. Tournai, Couvent des Soeurs Noires (Inv. no. 89)

copyright A.C.L. 108883 M

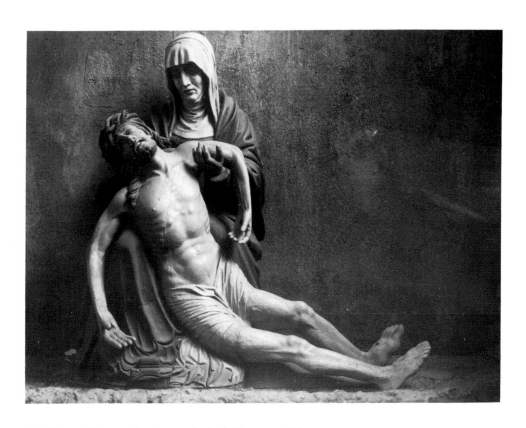

84. Veltem-Beisem, Sint-Laurentiuskerk (Inv. no. 90)

85. Virton, Local cemetery (Inv. no. 98)
    copyright A.C.L. 81309 A

86. Vreren, Kapel van Onze-Lieve-Vrouw der Zeven Weeën of Vordkapel
(Inv. no. 99)

copyright A.C.L. 65640 A

87. Vreren, Sint-Medarduskerk (Inv. no. 100)
copyright A.C.L. 153056 B

88. Waremme, Eglise Saint-Pierre (Inv. no. 101), with neo-Gothic polychromy
copyright A.C.L. 69989 A

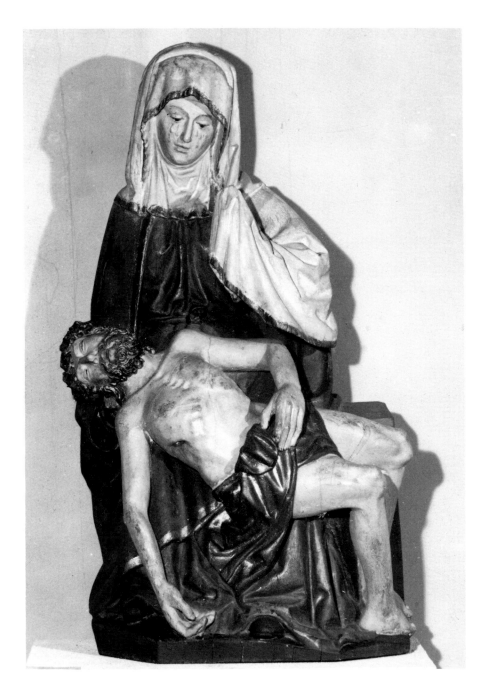

89. Waremme, Eglise Saint-Pierre (Inv. no. 101), with some polychromy absent
copyright A.C.L. 144534 M

90. Winamplanche, Eglise Saint-André (Inv. no. 103)
copyright A.C.L. 66729 M

91. Winterslag, Kapel van Onze-Lieve-Vrouw (Inv. no. 104),
Procession of Onze-Lieve-Vrouw-van-Rust

collection *Heidebloemke*

92. Winterslag, Kapel van Onze-Lieve-Vrouw (Inv. no. 104), Onze-Lieve-Vrouw-van-Rust
collection *Heidebloemke*

93. Winterslag, Kapel van Onze-Lieve-Vrouw (Inv. no. 104),
     Onze-Lieve-Vrouw-van-Rust, detail
collection *Heidebloemke*

94. Zepperen, Sint-Genovevakerk (Inv. no. 106)

95. Zichem, Sint-Eustachiuskerk (Inv. no. 107)
copyright A.C.L. 34508 A

96. Zoutleeuw, Sint-Leonarduskerk (Inv. no. 109)

97. Zoutleeuw, Sint-Leonarduskerk (Inv. no. 110)
    copyright A.C.L. 34388 E

98. Bruges, Gruuthusemuseum (Inv. no. 113)
   copyright A.C.L. 133754 B

99. Bruges, Sint-Janshospitaal (Inv. no. 114)
copyright A.C.L. 143137 B

100. Brussels, Musée Royal des Beaux-Arts / Koninklijk Museum voor Schone Kunsten
(Inv. no. 115)

101. Diest, Stedelijk Museum (Beguinage Church) (Inv. no. 116)

102. Ghent, Museum voor Schone Kunsten (Inv. no. 117)
copyright A.C.L. 77437 B

103. Ghent, Museum voor Schone Kunsten (Inv. no. 118)
    copyright A.C.L. 77421 B

104. Huy, Musée Communal (Inv. no. 120)
copyright A.C.L. 62765 A

105. Lawrence, Kansas (Inv. no. 121)
    Spencer Museum of Art, University of Kansas, Gift of Allan Gerdau

106. Leuven, Stedelijk Museum (Inv. no. 122)
copyright A.C.L. 205753 B

107. Leuven, Stedelijk Museum (Inv. no. 123)
copyright A.C.L. 2884 M

108. Leuven, Stedelijk Museum, Engraving circa 1552 illustrating a lottery held for the
crossbowmen's guild of Leuven with *Pietà* on the high altar

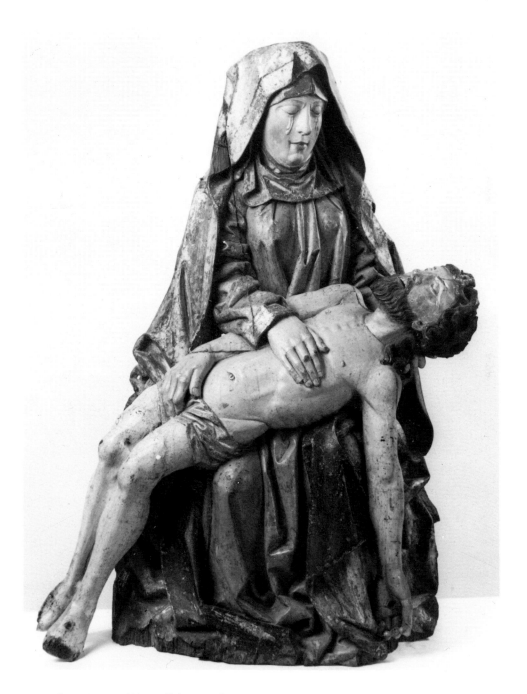

109. Liège, Musée d'Art religieux et d'Art mosan (Inv. no. 124)
copyright A.C.L. 43200 N

110. Liège, Musée d'Art religieux et d'Art mosan (Inv. no. 126)
copyright A.C.L. 162718 B

111. Liège, Musée Curtius (Inv. no. 128)

112. Mechelen, Stadsmuseum (Inv. no. 131)

113. Namur, Musée Diocésain (Inv. no. 132)
    copyright A.C.L. 106428 B

114. Nivelles, Musée Archéologique (Inv. no. 133)
copyright A.C.L. 7897 B

115. Nivelles, Musée Archéologique (Inv. no. 134)
copyright A.C.L. 7896 B

116. Tongeren, Stedelijk Museum (Inv. no. 136)

117. Tongeren, Stedelijk Museum (Inv. no. 136), detail

118. Tongeren, Stedelijk Museum (Inv. no. 137), *Pietà* with donor

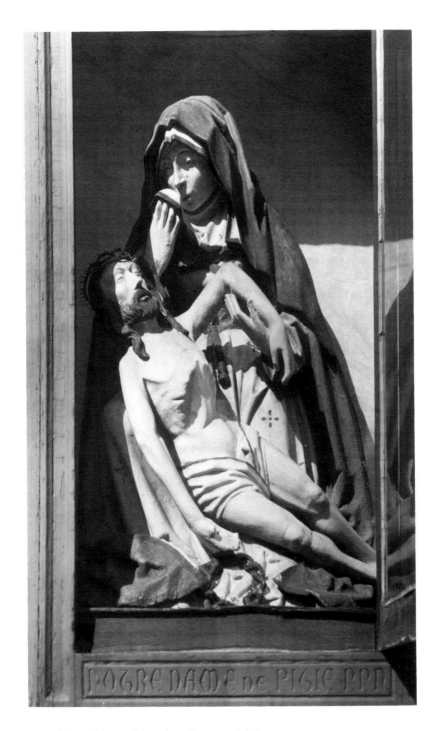

119. Liège, Private Collection (Inv. no. 143)
copyright A.C.L. 159103 B

Index of persons and places*

---

* The index does not include the footnotes.

MARGARETA ANTHONIS, *see* Anthonis, Margareta.
MARROW, James, 34-38.
MAUDE, Henri de, 129.
MECHELEN, 123, 124, 129, 164.
MECHTILD OF HACKEBORN, *see* Hackeborn, Mechtild of.
MICHELANGELO, 154, 157.
MILHAVEN, John Giles, 170, 171.
MÂLE, Emile, 33-36, 38.

NEEDHAM, Rodney, 17, 18, 155.
NETHERLANDS, the, *see* Low Countries.
NIETZSCHE, Frederich, 29-31.
NIVELLES, 73.

OLDENZAEL, 125.
OOSTEN, Gertrude of, 112.
OSIRIS, 154.

PAGLIA, Camille, 154.
PANOFSKY, Erwin, 25-27, 31-33, 36-38, 57.
PANTALEON, Jacques, 98.
PASSARGE, Walter, 122, 123.
PATER, Walter, 58-60.
PETRI, Petrus, 127.
PETRUS PETRI, *see* Petri, Petrus.
PHILIPPEN, L.J.M., 74.
PILATE, Bernard, 129.
PINDER, Wilhelm, 27-32, 36, 37, 39.
POCH, Maigne Au, 129.
PODRO, Michael, 26.
POE, Edgar Ellen, 155.
PREMONSTRATENSIANS, 69.
PSEUDO-BONAVENTURE, 35.

QUINTIJN, R.M., 98, 99.

RHINELAND, the, 20, 35, 39, 69, 71, 131.
ROBERT OF THOROTE, *see* Thorote, Robert of.
ROERMOND, 125.
ROGIER VAN DER WEYDEN, *see* Weyden, Rogier van der.

ROME, 157.
RUTEBEUF, 82.

SALZINNES, 145.
SAXONY, Ludolf of, 28, 35.
SIMMEL, Georg, 120, 121.
SIMONS, Walter, 73, 74, 126.
SIMSON, Otto Von, 37.
SINT-TRUIDEN, 83, 101, 126, 127.
    Church of Our Lady, 128.
SITTARD, 125, 126, 163-165, 169.
    Convent of St. Agnes, 125.
SMITH, John E., 17.
SPAIN, 21.
STEYAERT, John, 123.
SUMER, 154.
SUMMERS, David, 95.
SUSO, Henry, 28.

THOMAS AQUINAS, *see* Aquinas, Thomas.
THOMAS OF CANTIMPRÉ, *see* Cantimpré, Thomas of.
THOROTE, Robert of, Bishop of Liège, 82.
TIENEN, 126.
TIMMERS, J.J.M., 125.
TOLSTOY, 60.
TONGEREN, 122-126, 128.
    Beguinage of St. Catherine, 122, 124, 125, 129.
    City Museum, 124, 125.
    Convent of St. Agnes, 124, 125, 164, 165.
    Franciscan convent, 123, 124.
TOURNAI, 99, 129, 143.
    Church of the Madeleine, 129.
    Guillaume de Ventadour, Bishop of, 82.
TRISTAN, 31.
TURNER, Victor, 79, 87, 120.

VENTADOUR, Guillaume de, Bishop of Tournai, 82.
VILLERS, 145.

WAGNER, Richard, 31.
WAGNER, Marina, 154.

TABLE OF CONTENTS

414

DRUK N.V. VONKSTEEN
MARKTPLEIN   33
8920 LANGEMARK